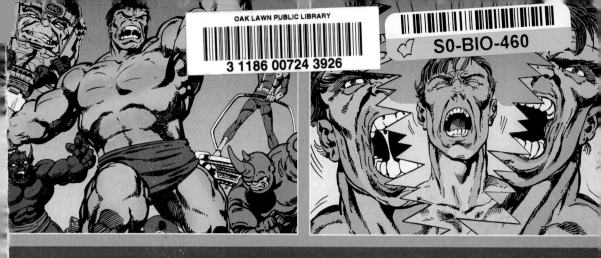

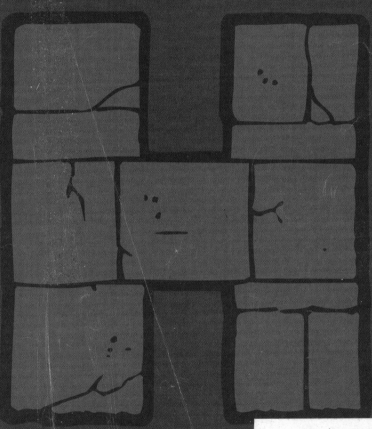

HULK VISIONARIES:
JOHN BYRNE
VOL. 1

HULK VISIONARIES:
JOHN BYRNE
VOL. 1

STORY & ART: JOHN BYRNE

WITH SAL BUSCEMA, ART, INCREDIBLE HULK ANNUAL #14

BOB WIACEK, INKS, INCREDIBLE HULK #314

KEITH WILLIAMS, ADDITIONAL INKS, INCREDIBLE HULK # 315-319

COLORS: ANDY YANCHUS
LETTERS: RICK PARKER & JIM NOVAK
EDITOR: DENNIS O'NEIL & AL MILGROM

COVER ART: JOHN BYRNE
COVER COLORS: AVALON'S ANDY TROY
COLOR RECONSTRUCTION: JERRON QUALITY COLOR

COLLECTION EDITOR: MARK D. BEAZLEY
SENIOR EDITOR, SPECIAL PROJECTS: JEFF YOUNGQUIST
EDITOR, SPECIAL PROJECTS: JENNIFER GRÜNWALD
ASSISTANT EDITORS: CORY LEVINE & JOHN DENNING
SENIOR VICE PRESIDENT OF SALES: DAVID GABRIEL
PRODUCTION: JOHN DAUGHERITY & JERRON QUALITY COLOR
RESEARCH: STUART VANDAL

EDITOR IN CHIEF: JOE QUESADA
PUBLISHER: DAN BUCKLEY

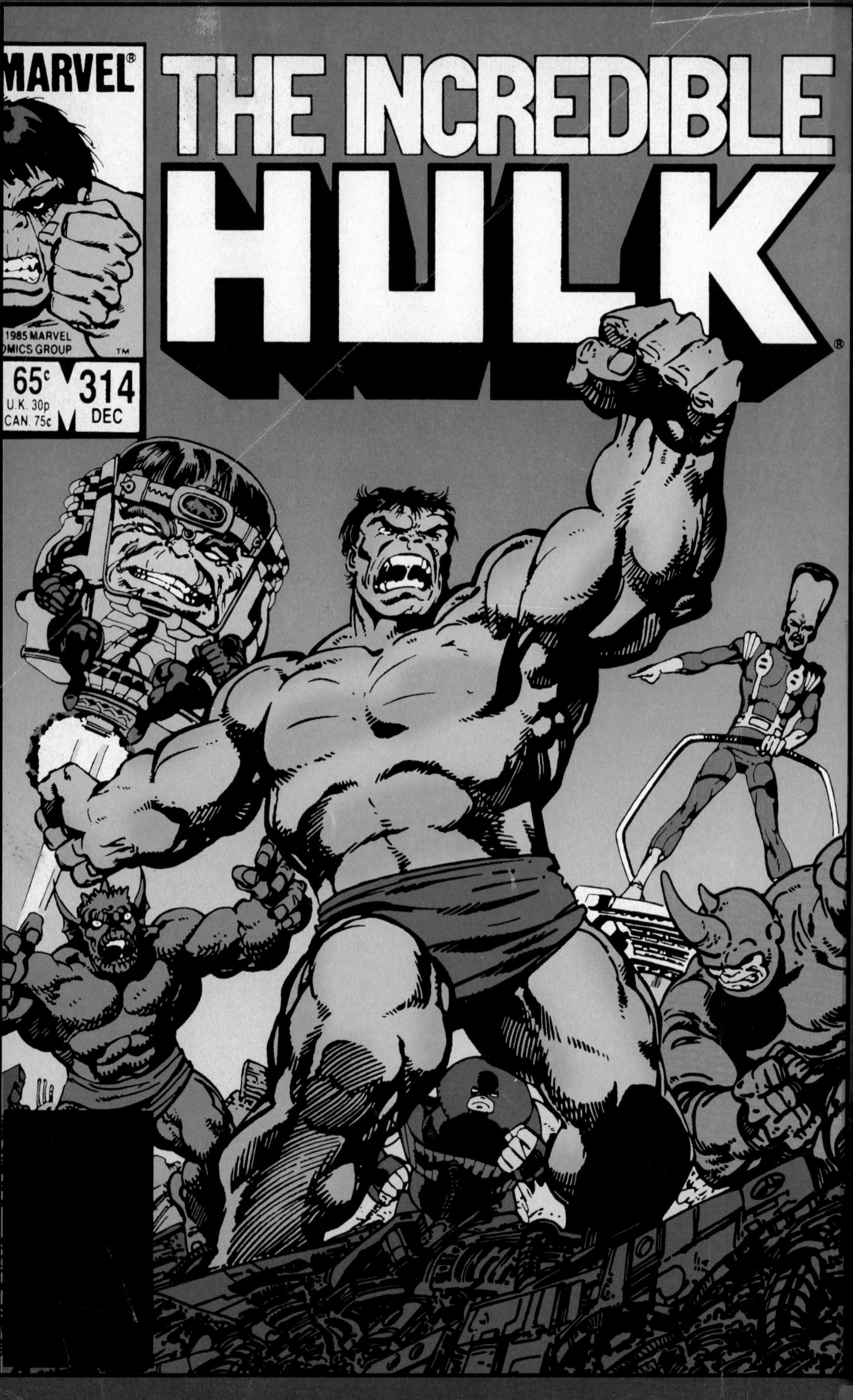

MARVEL®
THE INCREDIBLE
HULK®
1985 MARVEL
OMICS GROUP
TM
65¢
U.K. 30p
CAN. 75c
314
DEC

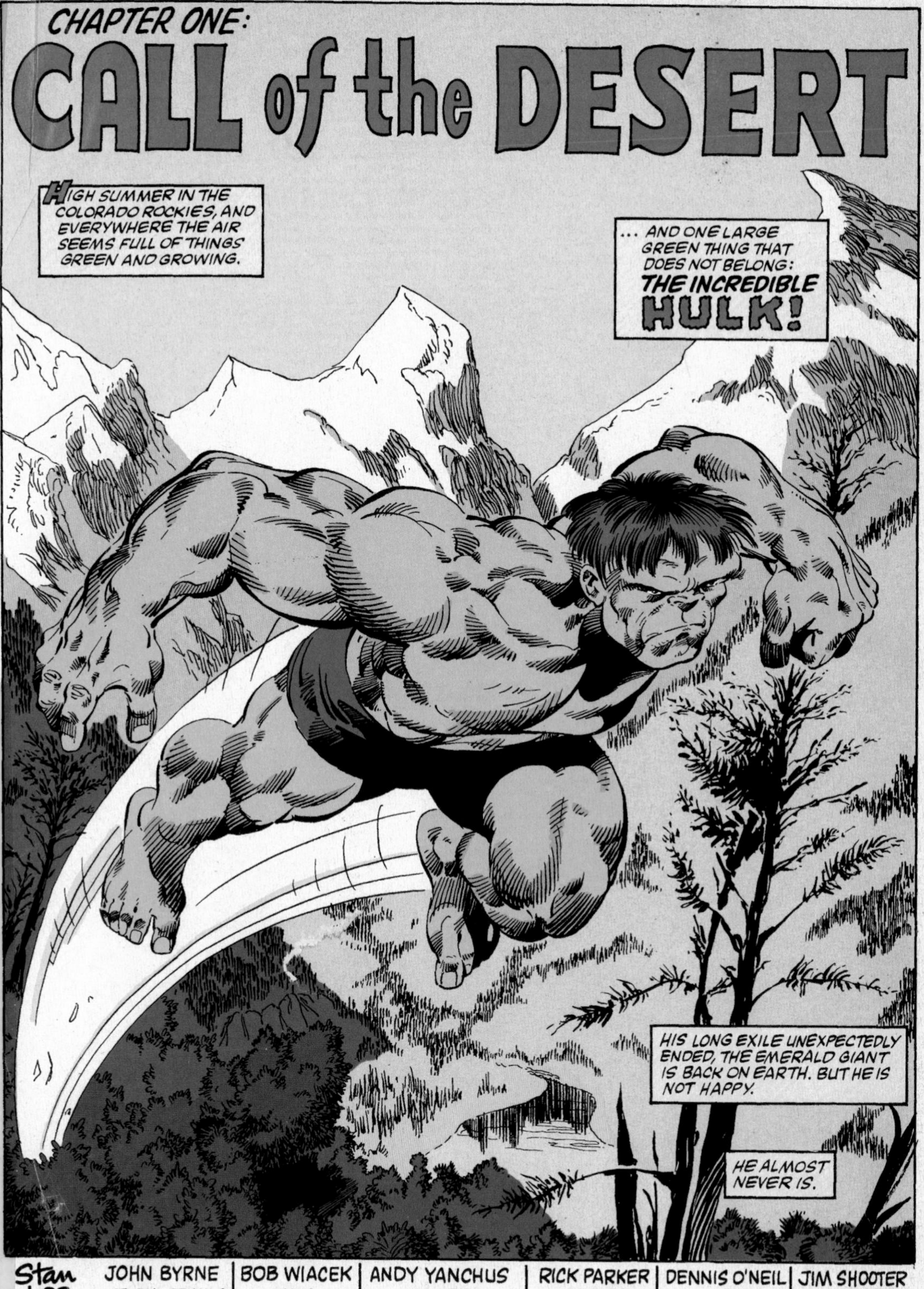
CHAPTER ONE:
CALL of the DESERT
HIGH SUMMER IN THE COLORADO ROCKIES, AND EVERYWHERE THE AIR SEEMS FULL OF THINGS GREEN AND GROWING.
... AND ONE LARGE GREEN THING THAT DOES NOT BELONG: THE INCREDIBLE HULK!
HIS LONG EXILE UNEXPECTEDLY ENDED, THE EMERALD GIANT IS BACK ON EARTH. BUT HE IS NOT HAPPY.
HE ALMOST NEVER IS.

Stan Lee PRESENTS: JOHN BYRNE STORY + PENCILS | BOB WIACEK INKS | ANDY YANCHUS COLORS | RICK PARKER LETTERS | DENNIS O'NEIL EDITOR | JIM SHOOTER ED. IN CHIEF

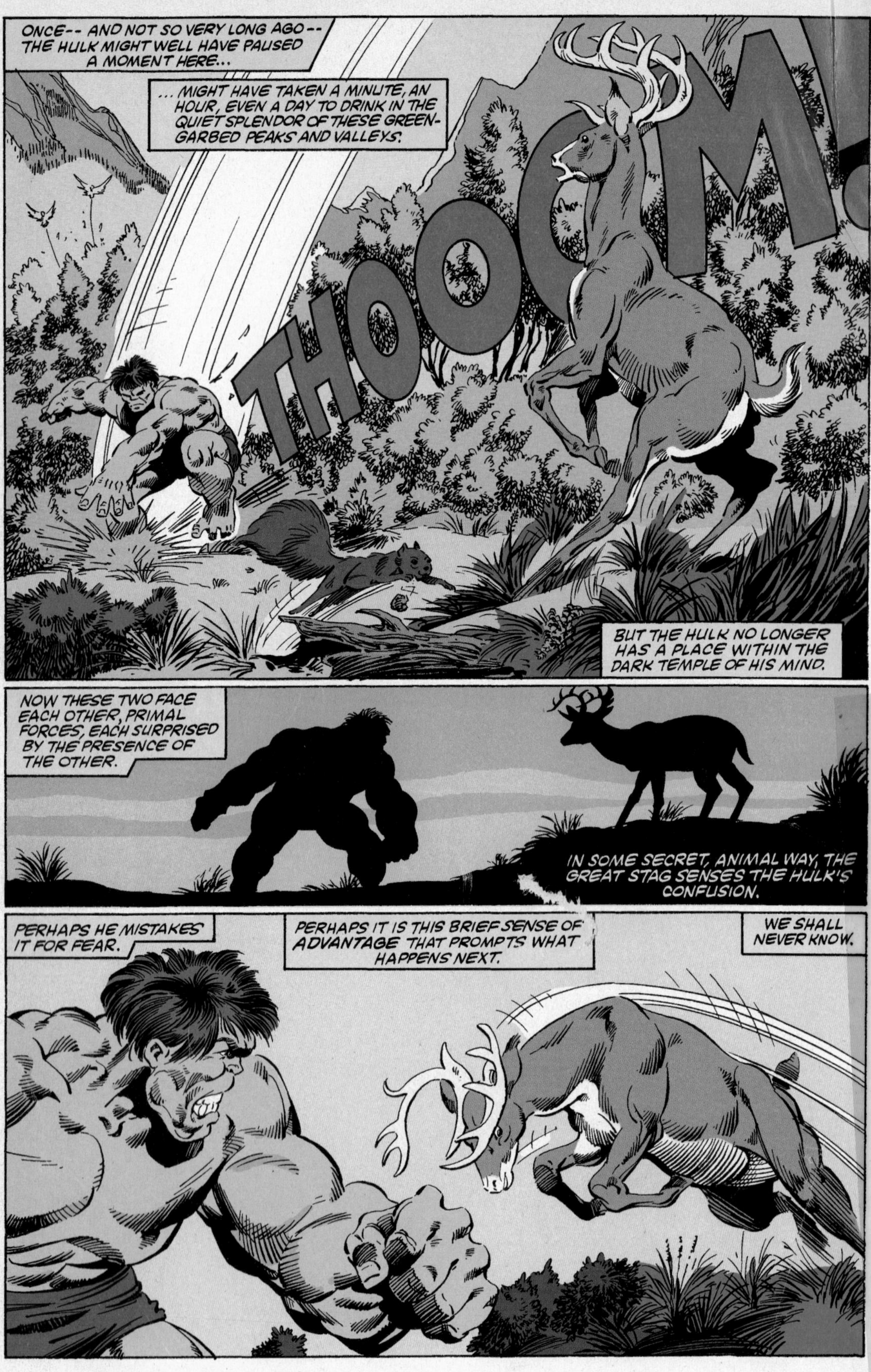
ONCE-- AND NOT SO VERY LONG AGO-- THE HULK MIGHT WELL HAVE PAUSED A MOMENT HERE...
...MIGHT HAVE TAKEN A MINUTE, AN HOUR, EVEN A DAY TO DRINK IN THE QUIET SPLENDOR OF THESE GREEN-GARBED PEAKS AND VALLEYS.
THOOOM!
BUT THE HULK NO LONGER HAS A PLACE WITHIN THE DARK TEMPLE OF HIS MIND.
NOW THESE TWO FACE EACH OTHER, PRIMAL FORCES, EACH SURPRISED BY THE PRESENCE OF THE OTHER.
IN SOME SECRET, ANIMAL WAY, THE GREAT STAG SENSES THE HULK'S CONFUSION.
PERHAPS HE MISTAKES IT FOR FEAR.
PERHAPS IT IS THIS BRIEF SENSE OF ADVANTAGE THAT PROMPTS WHAT HAPPENS NEXT.
WE SHALL NEVER KNOW.

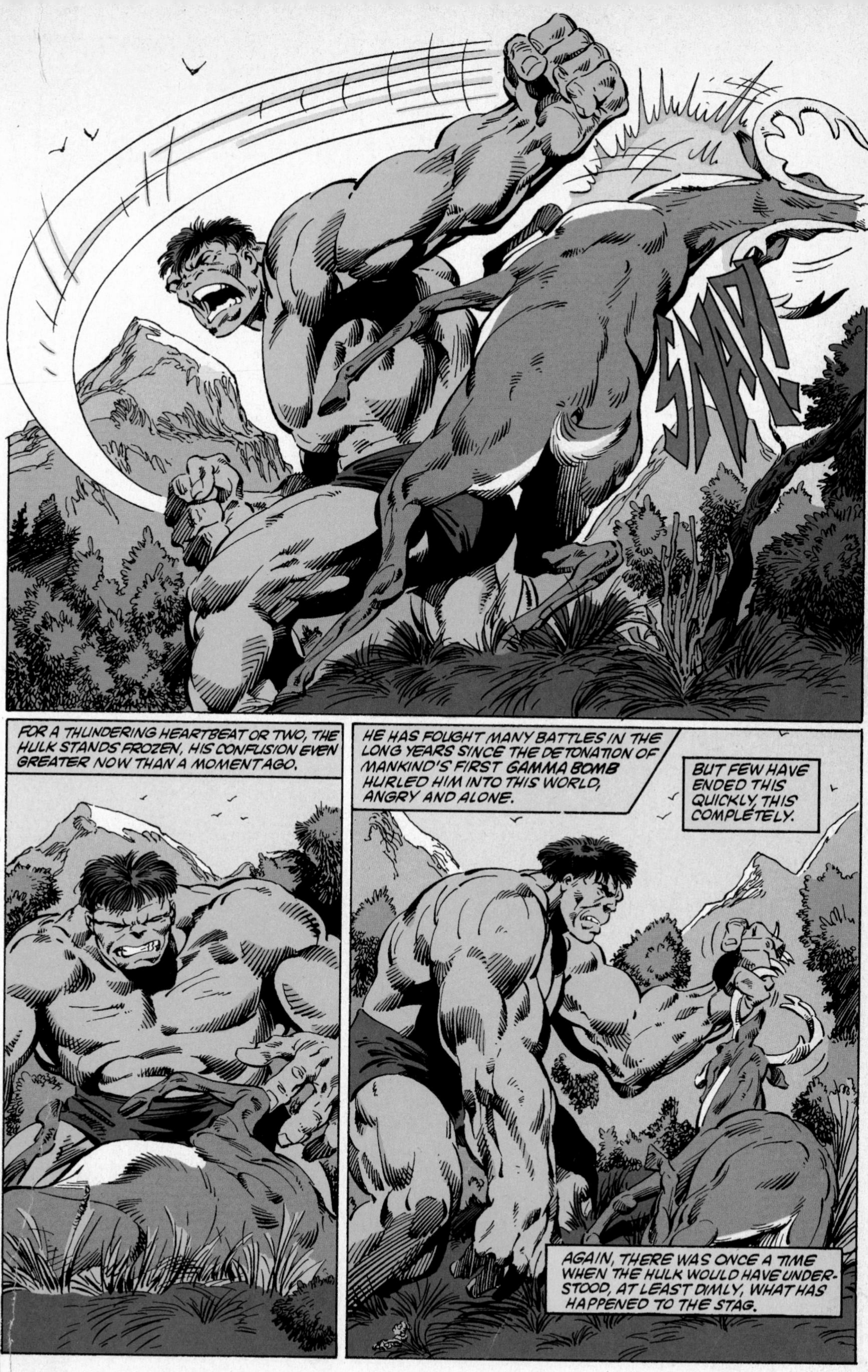
SNAP!
FOR A THUNDERING HEARTBEAT OR TWO, THE HULK STANDS FROZEN, HIS CONFUSION EVEN GREATER NOW THAN A MOMENT AGO.
HE HAS FOUGHT MANY BATTLES IN THE LONG YEARS SINCE THE DETONATION OF MANKIND'S FIRST GAMMA BOMB HURLED HIM INTO THIS WORLD, ANGRY AND ALONE.
BUT FEW HAVE ENDED THIS QUICKLY, THIS COMPLETELY.
AGAIN, THERE WAS ONCE A TIME WHEN THE HULK WOULD HAVE UNDERSTOOD, AT LEAST DIMLY, WHAT HAS HAPPENED TO THE STAG.

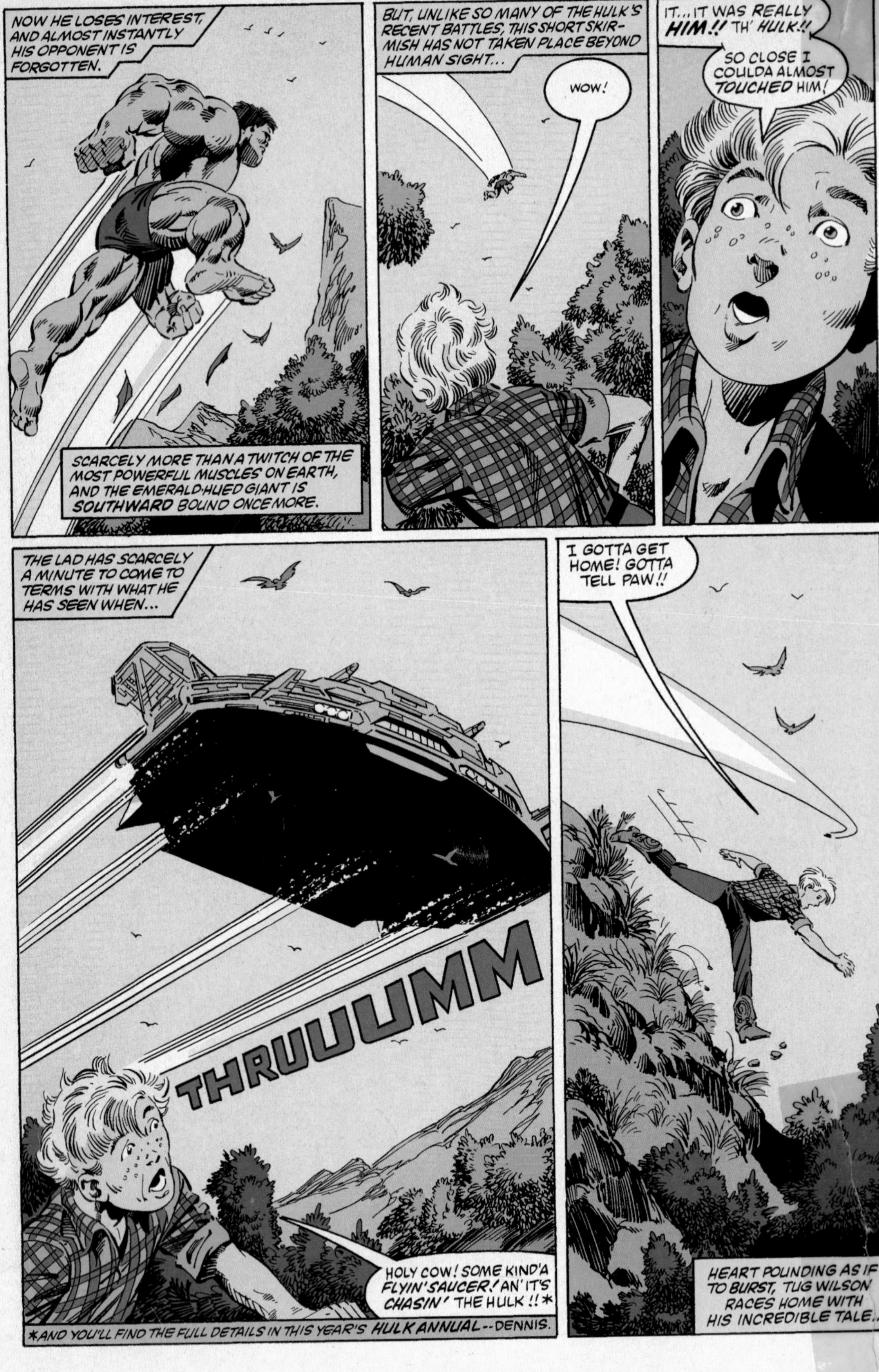

NOW HE LOSES INTEREST, AND ALMOST INSTANTLY HIS OPPONENT IS FORGOTTEN.
SCARCELY MORE THAN A TWITCH OF THE MOST POWERFUL MUSCLES ON EARTH, AND THE EMERALD-HUED GIANT IS SOUTHWARD BOUND ONCE MORE.
BUT, UNLIKE SO MANY OF THE HULK'S RECENT BATTLES, THIS SHORT SKIR-MISH HAS NOT TAKEN PLACE BEYOND HUMAN SIGHT...
WOW!
IT... IT WAS REALLY HIM!! TH' HULK!!
SO CLOSE I COULDA ALMOST TOUCHED HIM!
THE LAD HAS SCARCELY A MINUTE TO COME TO TERMS WITH WHAT HE HAS SEEN WHEN...
THRUUUMM
HOLY COW! SOME KIND'A FLYIN' SAUCER! AN' IT'S CHASIN' THE HULK!!*
*AND YOU'LL FIND THE FULL DETAILS IN THIS YEAR'S HULK ANNUAL -- DENNIS.
I GOTTA GET HOME! GOTTA TELL PAW!!
HEART POUNDING AS IF TO BURST, TUG WILSON RACES HOME WITH HIS INCREDIBLE TALE...

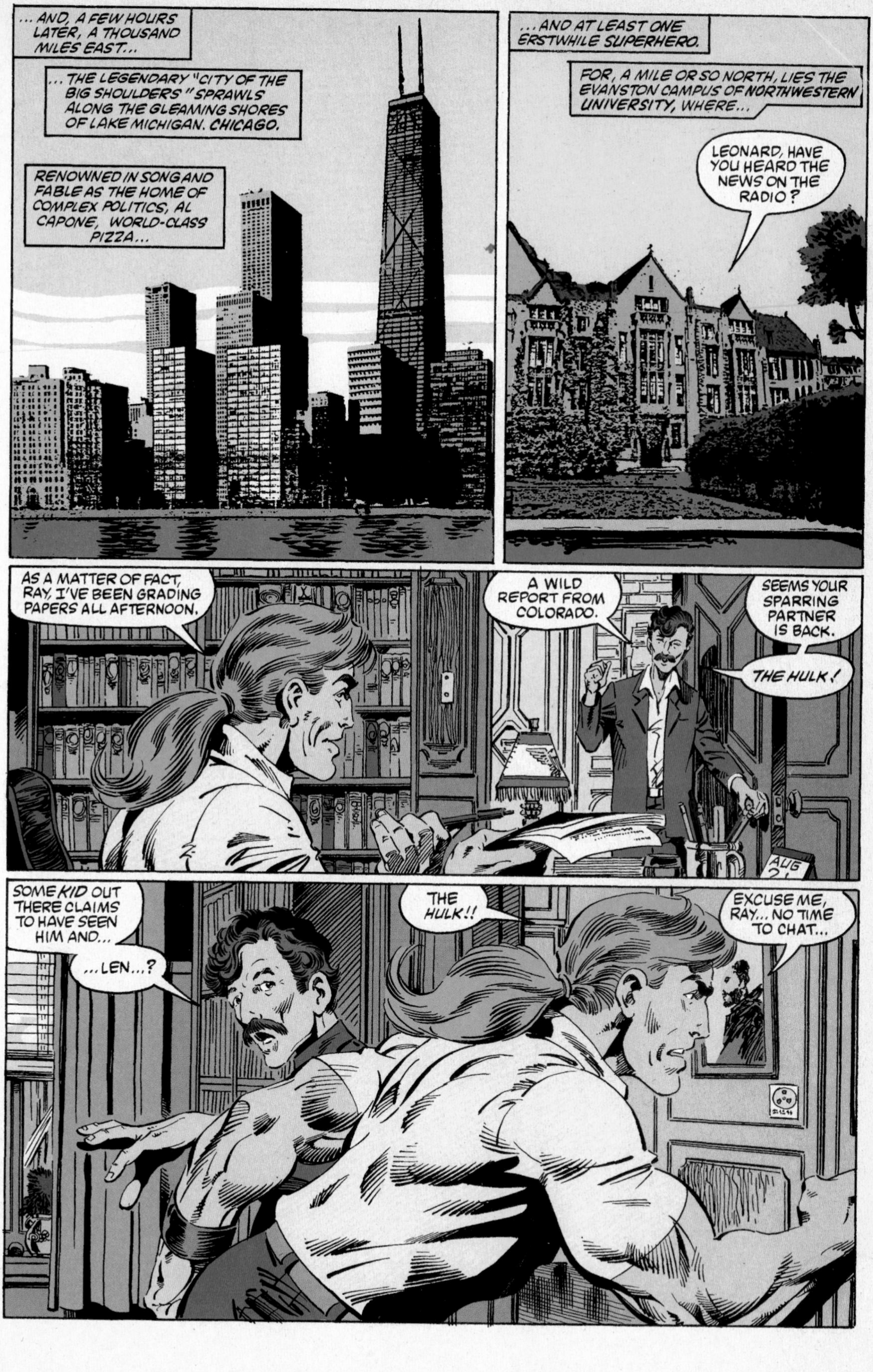
...AND, A FEW HOURS LATER, A THOUSAND MILES EAST...
...THE LEGENDARY "CITY OF THE BIG SHOULDERS" SPRAWLS ALONG THE GLEAMING SHORES OF LAKE MICHIGAN. CHICAGO.
RENOWNED IN SONG AND FABLE AS THE HOME OF COMPLEX POLITICS, AL CAPONE, WORLD-CLASS PIZZA...
...AND AT LEAST ONE ERSTWHILE SUPERHERO.
FOR, A MILE OR SO NORTH, LIES THE EVANSTON CAMPUS OF NORTHWESTERN UNIVERSITY, WHERE...
LEONARD, HAVE YOU HEARD THE NEWS ON THE RADIO?
AS A MATTER OF FACT, RAY, I'VE BEEN GRADING PAPERS ALL AFTERNOON.
A WILD REPORT FROM COLORADO.
SEEMS YOUR SPARRING PARTNER IS BACK.
THE HULK!
AUG 21
SOME KID OUT THERE CLAIMS TO HAVE SEEN HIM AND...
...LEN...?
THE HULK!!
EXCUSE ME, RAY... NO TIME TO CHAT...

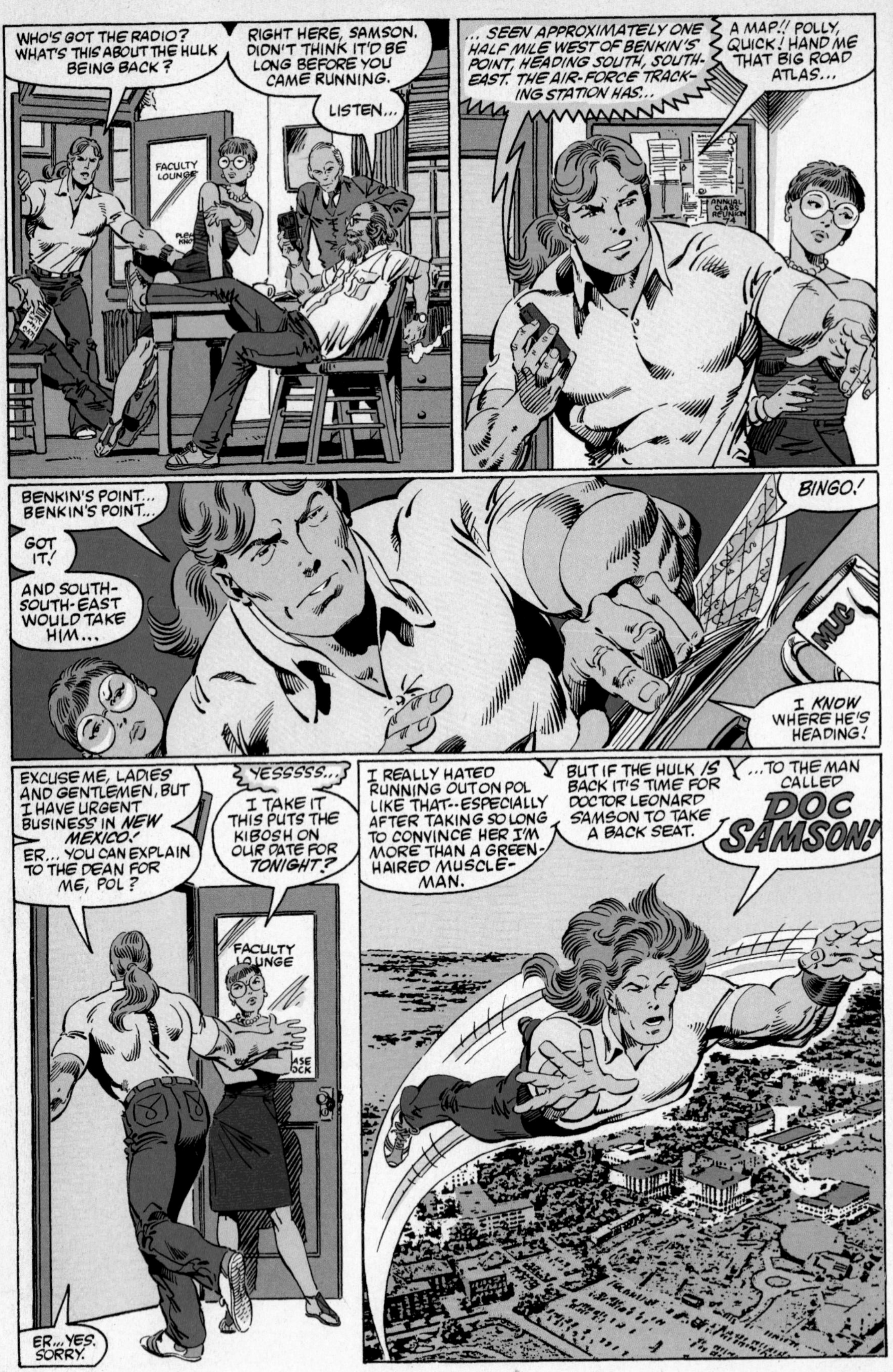
WHO'S GOT THE RADIO? WHAT'S THIS ABOUT THE HULK BEING BACK?
RIGHT HERE, SAMSON. DIDN'T THINK IT'D BE LONG BEFORE YOU CAME RUNNING.
LISTEN...
FACULTY LOUNGE
...SEEN APPROXIMATELY ONE HALF MILE WEST OF BENKIN'S POINT, HEADING SOUTH, SOUTH-EAST. THE AIR-FORCE TRACKING STATION HAS...
A MAP!! POLLY, QUICK! HAND ME THAT BIG ROAD ATLAS...
ANNUAL CLASS REUNION '74
BENKIN'S POINT... BENKIN'S POINT...
GOT IT!
AND SOUTH-SOUTH-EAST WOULD TAKE HIM...
BINGO!
MUG
I KNOW WHERE HE'S HEADING!
EXCUSE ME, LADIES AND GENTLEMEN, BUT I HAVE URGENT BUSINESS IN NEW MEXICO! ER... YOU CAN EXPLAIN TO THE DEAN FOR ME, POL?
YESSSSS...
I TAKE IT THIS PUTS THE KIBOSH ON OUR DATE FOR TONIGHT?
FACULTY LOUNGE
ER... YES. SORRY.
I REALLY HATED RUNNING OUT ON POL LIKE THAT--ESPECIALLY AFTER TAKING SO LONG TO CONVINCE HER I'M MORE THAN A GREEN-HAIRED MUSCLE-MAN.
BUT IF THE HULK IS BACK IT'S TIME FOR DOCTOR LEONARD SAMSON TO TAKE A BACK SEAT.
...TO THE MAN CALLED DOC SAMSON!

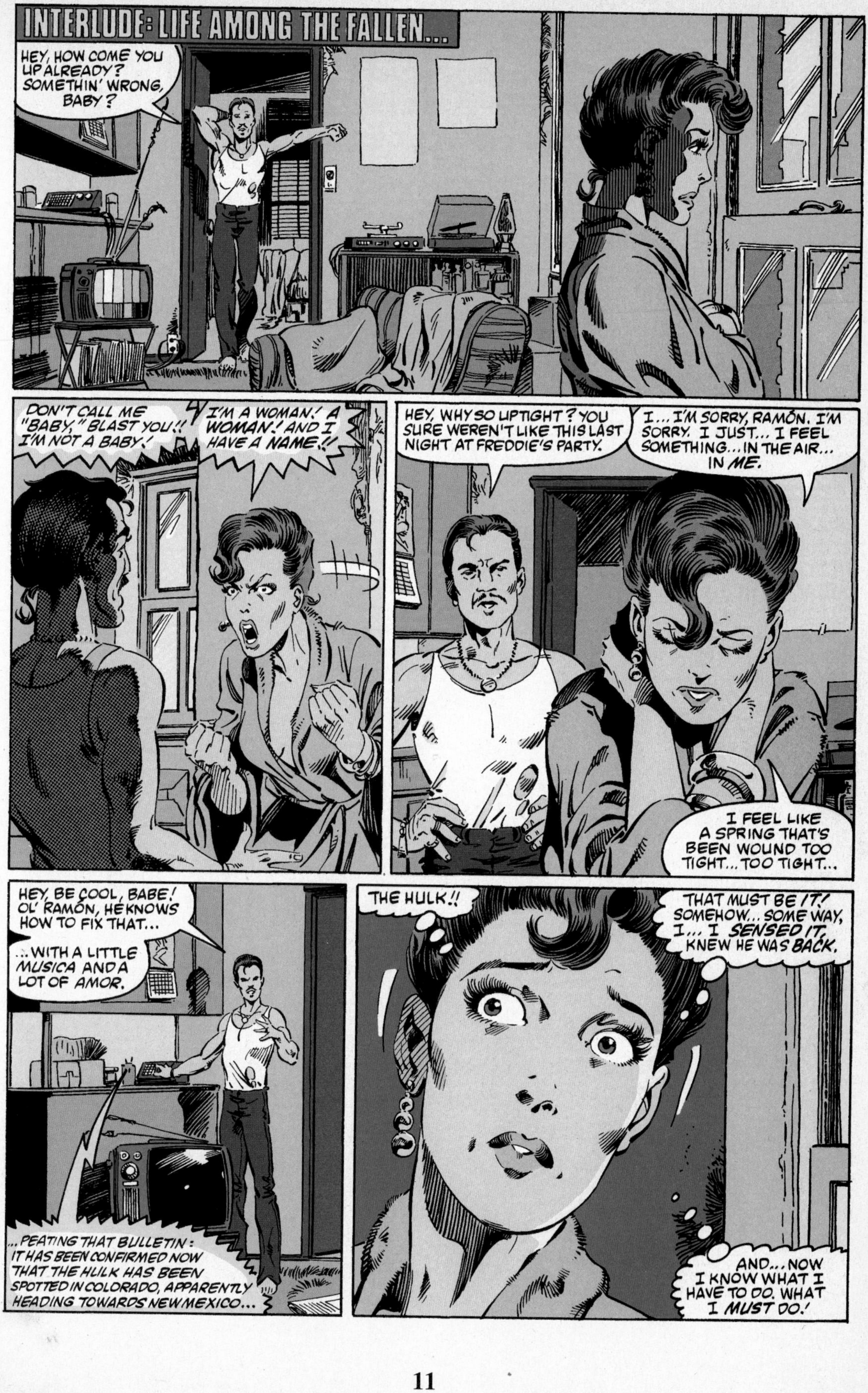
INTERLUDE: LIFE AMONG THE FALLEN...
HEY, HOW COME YOU UP ALREADY? SOMETHIN' WRONG, BABY?
DON'T CALL ME "BABY," BLAST YOU!! I'M NOT A BABY!
I'M A WOMAN! A WOMAN! AND I HAVE A NAME!!
HEY, WHY SO UPTIGHT? YOU SURE WEREN'T LIKE THIS LAST NIGHT AT FREDDIE'S PARTY.
I... I'M SORRY, RAMÓN. I'M SORRY. I JUST... I FEEL SOMETHING... IN THE AIR... IN ME.
I FEEL LIKE A SPRING THAT'S BEEN WOUND TOO TIGHT... TOO TIGHT...
HEY, BE COOL, BABE! OL' RAMÓN, HE KNOWS HOW TO FIX THAT...
...WITH A LITTLE MUSICA AND A LOT OF AMOR.
...PEATING THAT BULLETIN: IT HAS BEEN CONFIRMED NOW THAT THE HULK HAS BEEN SPOTTED IN COLORADO, APPARENTLY HEADING TOWARDS NEW MEXICO...
THE HULK!!
THAT MUST BE IT! SOMEHOW... SOME WAY, I... I SENSED IT, KNEW HE WAS BACK.
AND... NOW I KNOW WHAT I HAVE TO DO. WHAT I MUST DO!

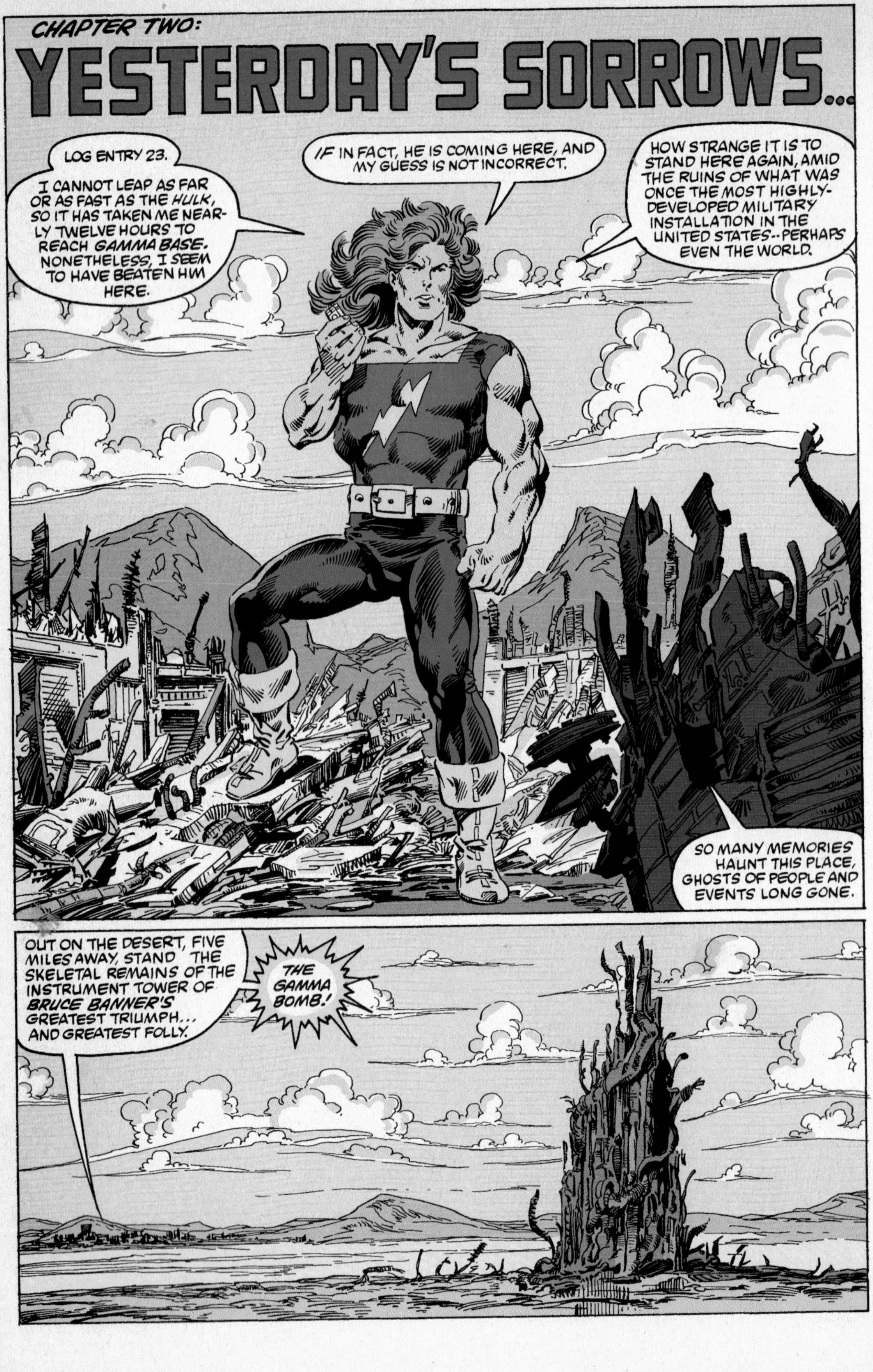
CHAPTER TWO:
YESTERDAY'S SORROWS...
LOG ENTRY 23.
I CANNOT LEAP AS FAR OR AS FAST AS THE HULK, SO IT HAS TAKEN ME NEARLY TWELVE HOURS TO REACH GAMMA BASE. NONETHELESS, I SEEM TO HAVE BEATEN HIM HERE.
IF IN FACT, HE IS COMING HERE, AND MY GUESS IS NOT INCORRECT.
HOW STRANGE IT IS TO STAND HERE AGAIN, AMID THE RUINS OF WHAT WAS ONCE THE MOST HIGHLY-DEVELOPED MILITARY INSTALLATION IN THE UNITED STATES--PERHAPS EVEN THE WORLD.
SO MANY MEMORIES HAUNT THIS PLACE, GHOSTS OF PEOPLE AND EVENTS LONG GONE.
OUT ON THE DESERT, FIVE MILES AWAY, STAND THE SKELETAL REMAINS OF THE INSTRUMENT TOWER OF BRUCE BANNER'S GREATEST TRIUMPH... AND GREATEST FOLLY.
THE GAMMA BOMB!

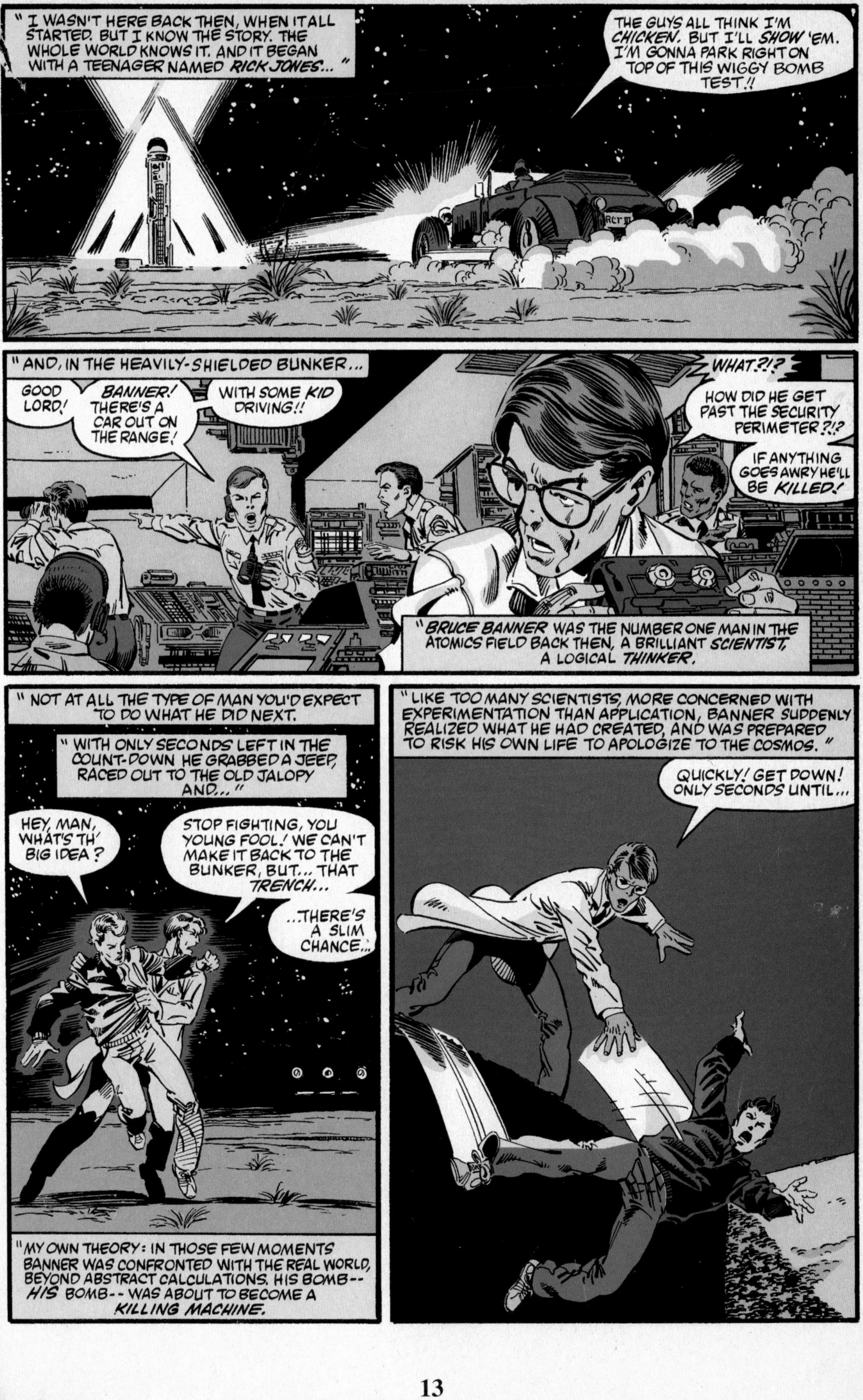

"I WASN'T HERE BACK THEN, WHEN IT ALL STARTED. BUT I KNOW THE STORY. THE WHOLE WORLD KNOWS IT. AND IT BEGAN WITH A TEENAGER NAMED RICK JONES..."
THE GUYS ALL THINK I'M CHICKEN. BUT I'LL SHOW 'EM. I'M GONNA PARK RIGHT ON TOP OF THIS WIGGY BOMB TEST!!
"AND, IN THE HEAVILY-SHIELDED BUNKER...
GOOD LORD!
BANNER! THERE'S A CAR OUT ON THE RANGE!
WITH SOME KID DRIVING!!
WHAT?!?
HOW DID HE GET PAST THE SECURITY PERIMETER?!?
IF ANYTHING GOES AWRY HE'LL BE KILLED!
"BRUCE BANNER WAS THE NUMBER ONE MAN IN THE ATOMICS FIELD BACK THEN, A BRILLIANT SCIENTIST, A LOGICAL THINKER.
"NOT AT ALL THE TYPE OF MAN YOU'D EXPECT TO DO WHAT HE DID NEXT.
"WITH ONLY SECONDS LEFT IN THE COUNT-DOWN HE GRABBED A JEEP, RACED OUT TO THE OLD JALOPY AND..."
HEY, MAN, WHAT'S TH' BIG IDEA?
STOP FIGHTING, YOU YOUNG FOOL! WE CAN'T MAKE IT BACK TO THE BUNKER, BUT... THAT TRENCH...
...THERE'S A SLIM CHANCE...
"MY OWN THEORY: IN THOSE FEW MOMENTS BANNER WAS CONFRONTED WITH THE REAL WORLD, BEYOND ABSTRACT CALCULATIONS. HIS BOMB-- HIS BOMB-- WAS ABOUT TO BECOME A KILLING MACHINE.
"LIKE TOO MANY SCIENTISTS, MORE CONCERNED WITH EXPERIMENTATION THAN APPLICATION, BANNER SUDDENLY REALIZED WHAT HE HAD CREATED, AND WAS PREPARED TO RISK HIS OWN LIFE TO APOLOGIZE TO THE COSMOS."
QUICKLY! GET DOWN! ONLY SECONDS UNTIL...

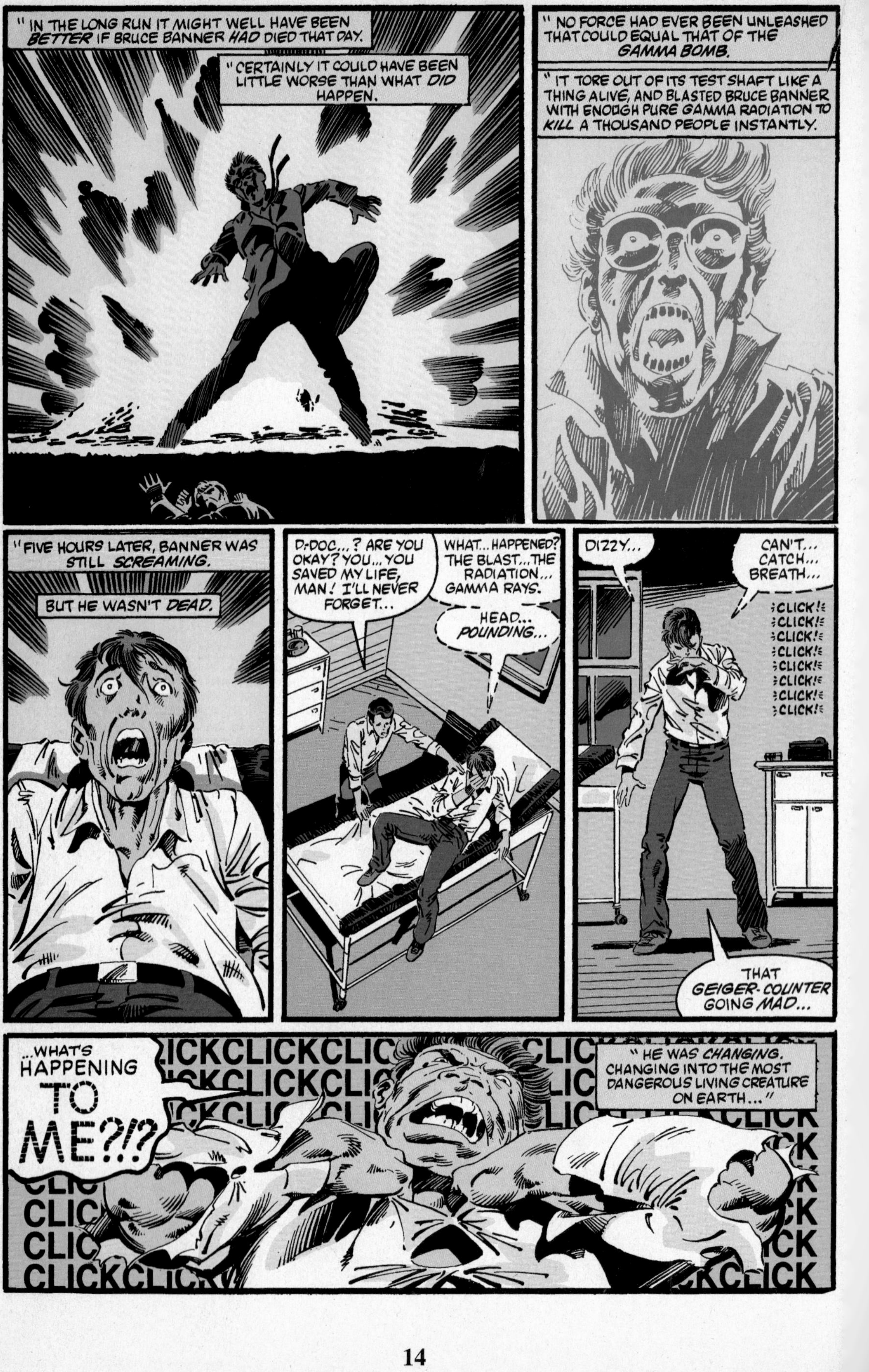
"IN THE LONG RUN IT MIGHT WELL HAVE BEEN BETTER IF BRUCE BANNER HAD DIED THAT DAY.
"CERTAINLY IT COULD HAVE BEEN LITTLE WORSE THAN WHAT DID HAPPEN.
"NO FORCE HAD EVER BEEN UNLEASHED THAT COULD EQUAL THAT OF THE GAMMA BOMB.
"IT TORE OUT OF ITS TEST SHAFT LIKE A THING ALIVE, AND BLASTED BRUCE BANNER WITH ENOUGH PURE GAMMA RADIATION TO KILL A THOUSAND PEOPLE INSTANTLY.
"FIVE HOURS LATER, BANNER WAS STILL SCREAMING.
BUT HE WASN'T DEAD.
D-DOC...? ARE YOU OKAY? YOU... YOU SAVED MY LIFE, MAN! I'LL NEVER FORGET...
WHAT... HAPPENED? THE BLAST... THE RADIATION... GAMMA RAYS.
HEAD... POUNDING...
DIZZY...
CAN'T... CATCH... BREATH...
CLICK! CLICK! CLICK! CLICK! CLICK! CLICK! CLICK!
THAT GEIGER-COUNTER GOING MAD...
...WHAT'S HAPPENING TO ME?!?
CLICKCLICKCLICK
"HE WAS CHANGING. CHANGING INTO THE MOST DANGEROUS LIVING CREATURE ON EARTH..."

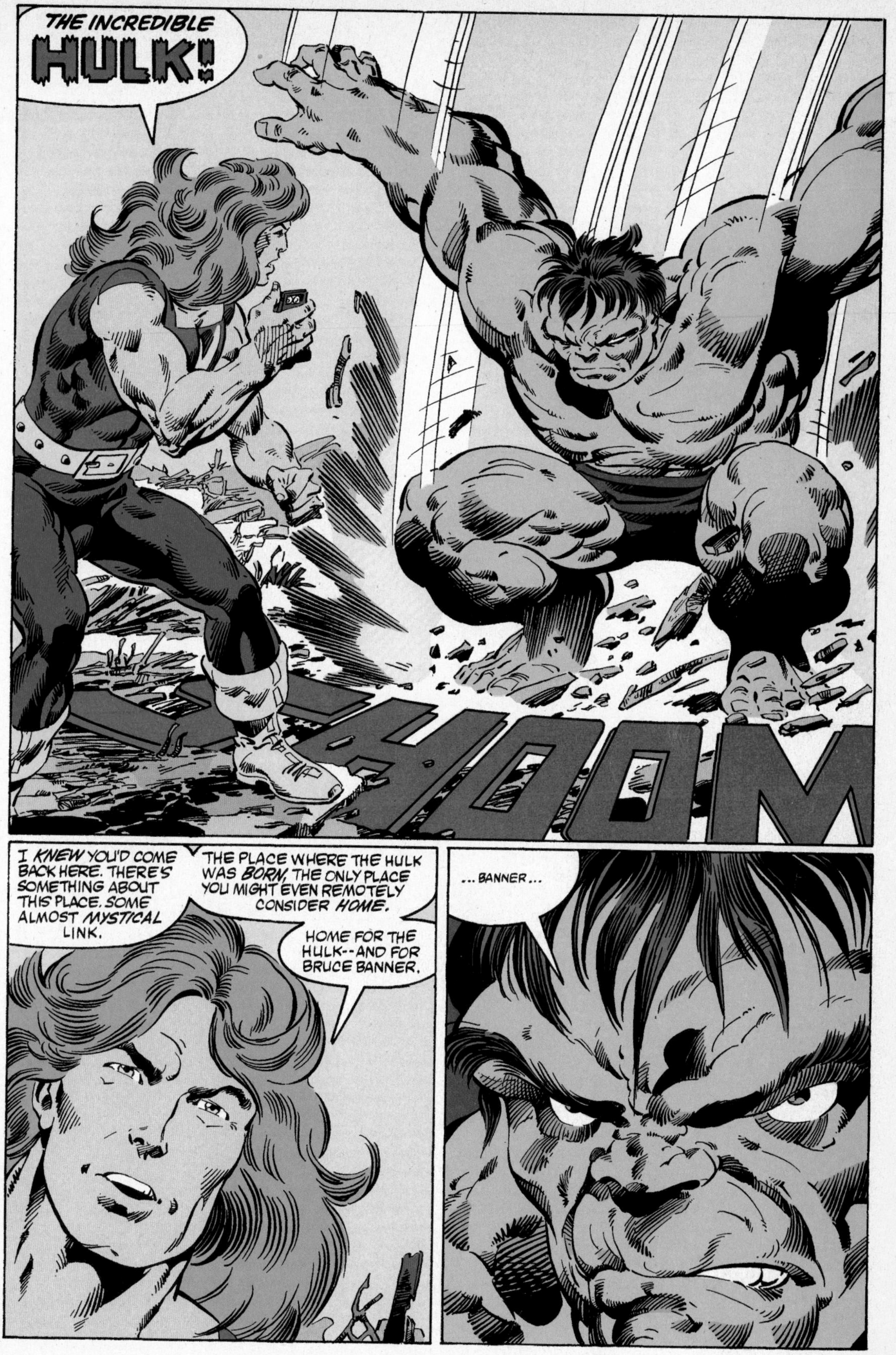
THE INCREDIBLE HULK!
HOOM
I KNEW YOU'D COME BACK HERE. THERE'S SOMETHING ABOUT THIS PLACE. SOME ALMOST MYSTICAL LINK.
THE PLACE WHERE THE HULK WAS BORN, THE ONLY PLACE YOU MIGHT EVEN REMOTELY CONSIDER HOME.
HOME FOR THE HULK--AND FOR BRUCE BANNER.
...BANNER...

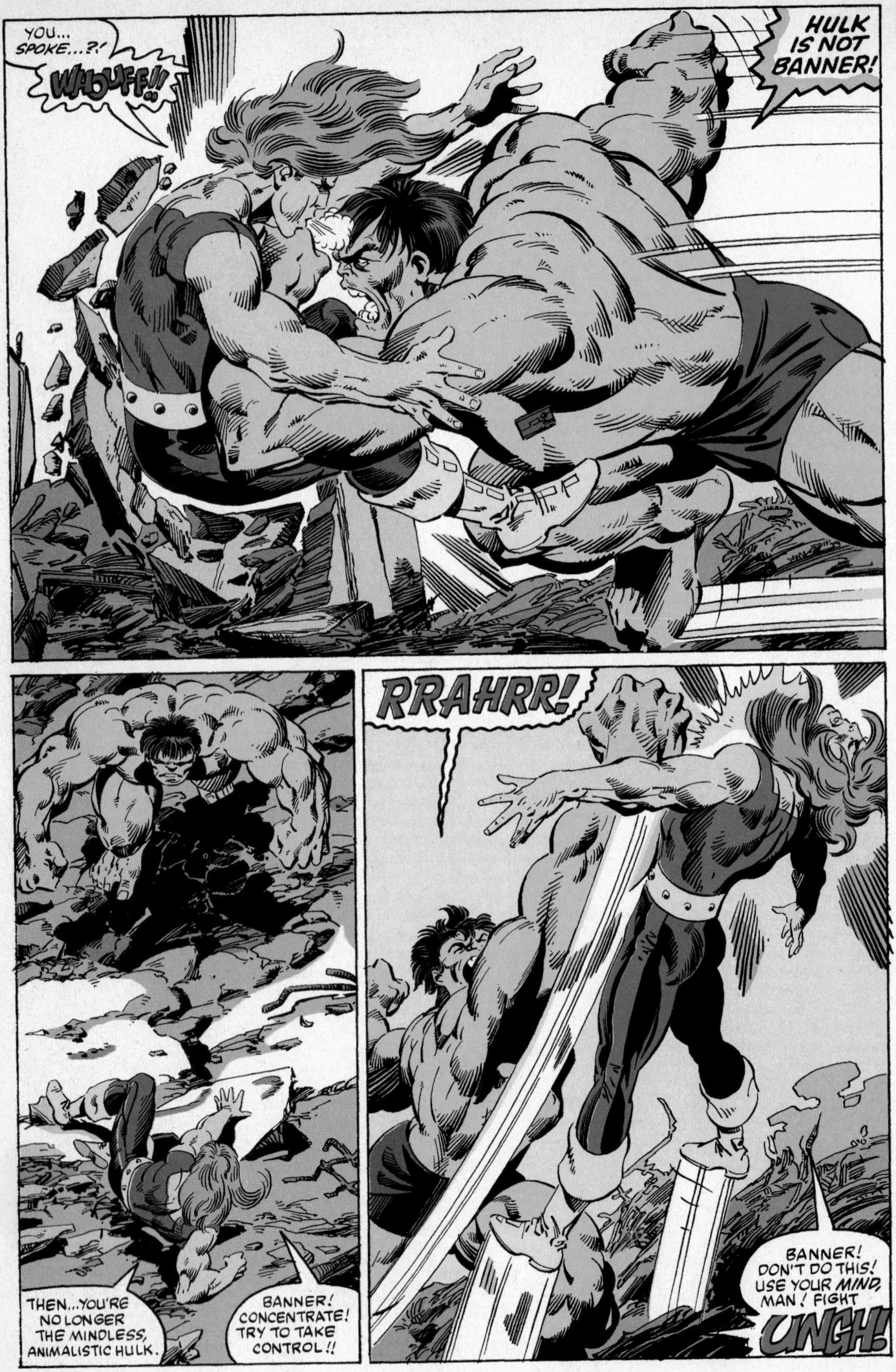
YOU... SPOKE...?!
WHOUFF!!
HULK IS NOT BANNER!
THEN...YOU'RE NO LONGER THE MINDLESS, ANIMALISTIC HULK.
BANNER! CONCENTRATE! TRY TO TAKE CONTROL!!
RRAHRR!
BANNER! DON'T DO THIS! USE YOUR MIND, MAN! FIGHT
UNGH!

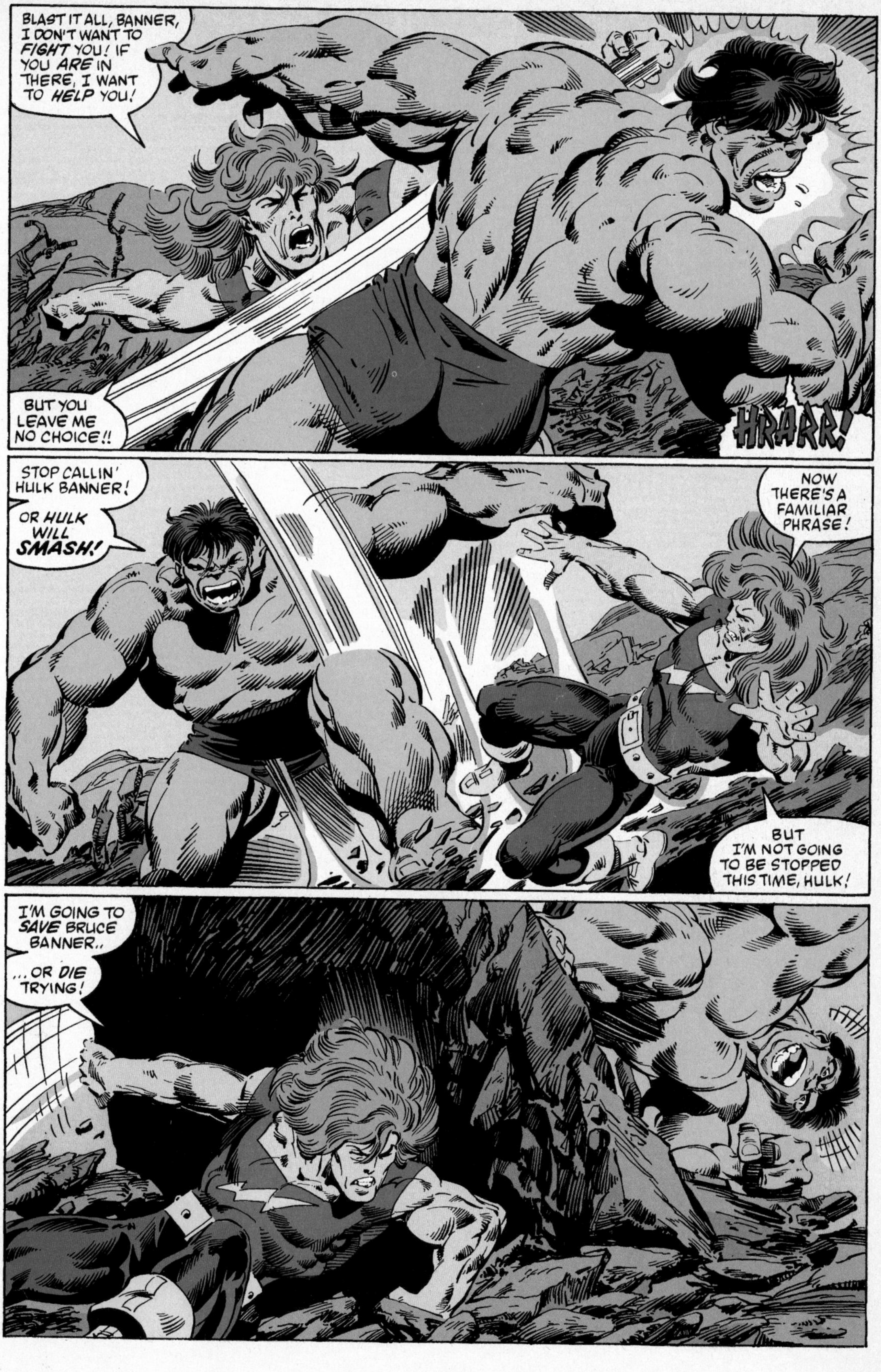
BLAST IT ALL, BANNER, I DON'T WANT TO FIGHT YOU! IF YOU ARE IN THERE, I WANT TO HELP YOU!
BUT YOU LEAVE ME NO CHOICE!!
HRARR!
STOP CALLIN' HULK BANNER!
OR HULK WILL SMASH!
NOW THERE'S A FAMILIAR PHRASE!
BUT I'M NOT GOING TO BE STOPPED THIS TIME, HULK!
I'M GOING TO SAVE BRUCE BANNER..
...OR DIE TRYING!

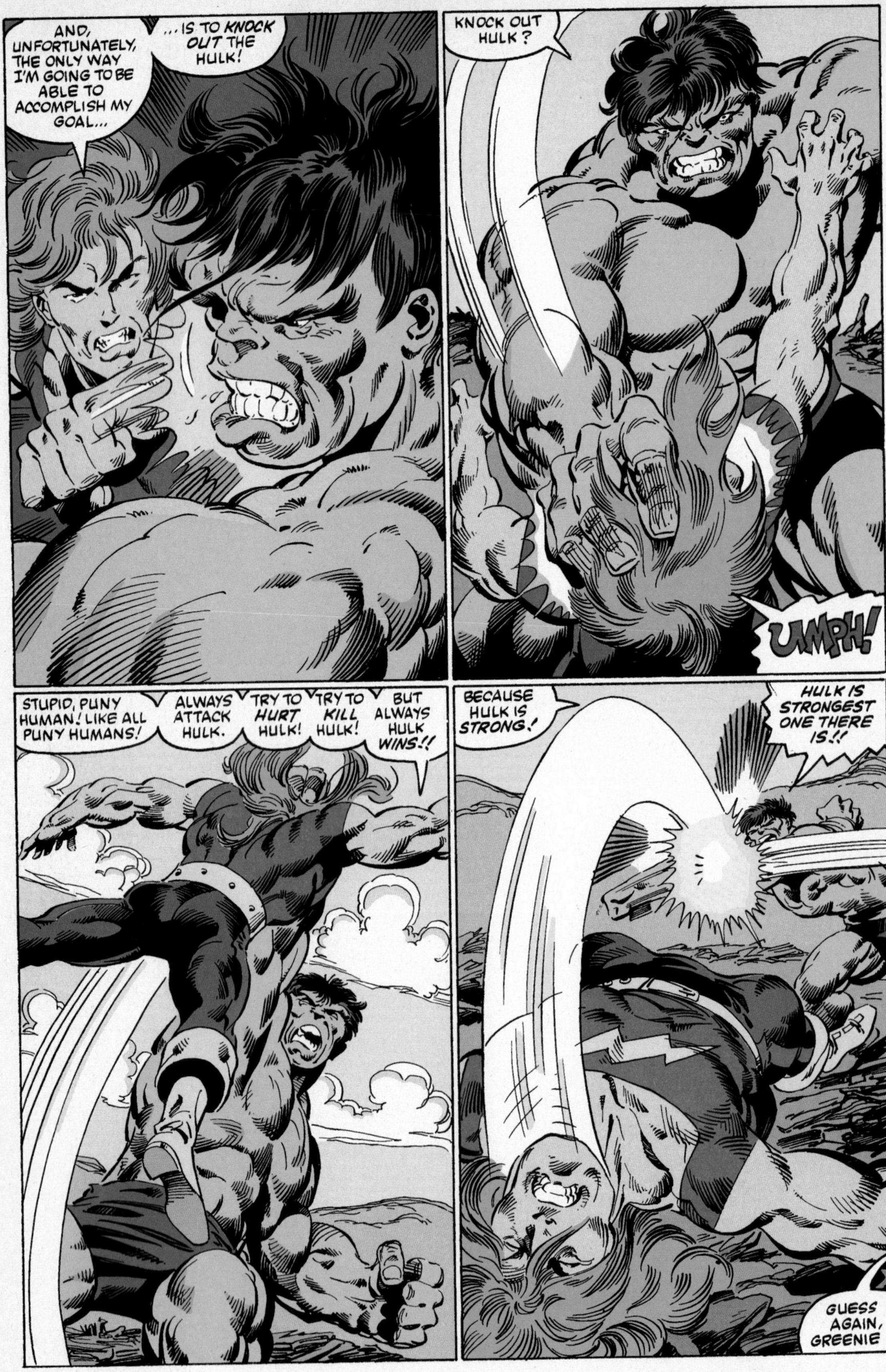
AND, UNFORTUNATELY, THE ONLY WAY I'M GOING TO BE ABLE TO ACCOMPLISH MY GOAL...
...IS TO KNOCK OUT THE HULK!
KNOCK OUT HULK?
UMPH!
STUPID, PUNY HUMAN! LIKE ALL PUNY HUMANS!
ALWAYS ATTACK HULK.
TRY TO HURT HULK!
TRY TO KILL HULK!
BUT ALWAYS HULK WINS!!
BECAUSE HULK IS STRONG!
HULK IS STRONGEST ONE THERE IS!!
GUESS AGAIN, GREENIE

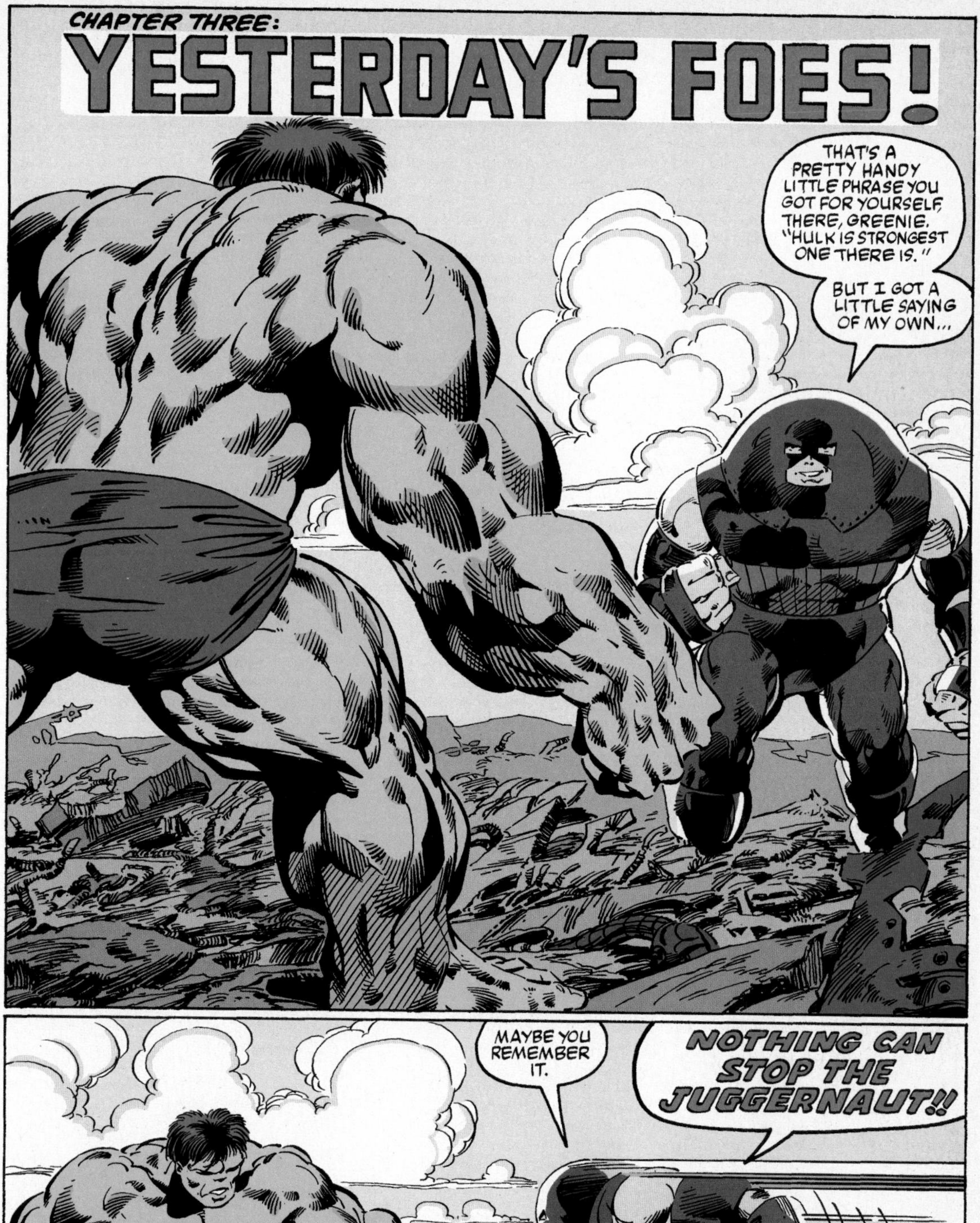
CHAPTER THREE:
YESTERDAY'S FOES!
THAT'S A PRETTY HANDY LITTLE PHRASE YOU GOT FOR YOURSELF, THERE, GREENIE. "HULK IS STRONGEST ONE THERE IS."
BUT I GOT A LITTLE SAYING OF MY OWN...

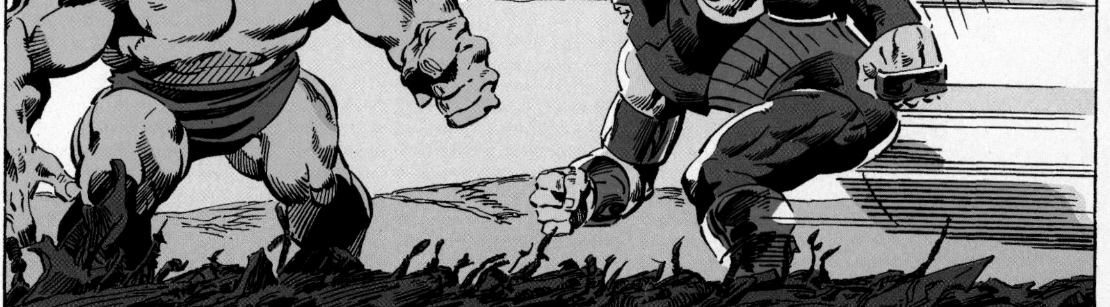
MAYBE YOU REMEMBER IT.
NOTHING CAN STOP THE JUGGERNAUT!!
15

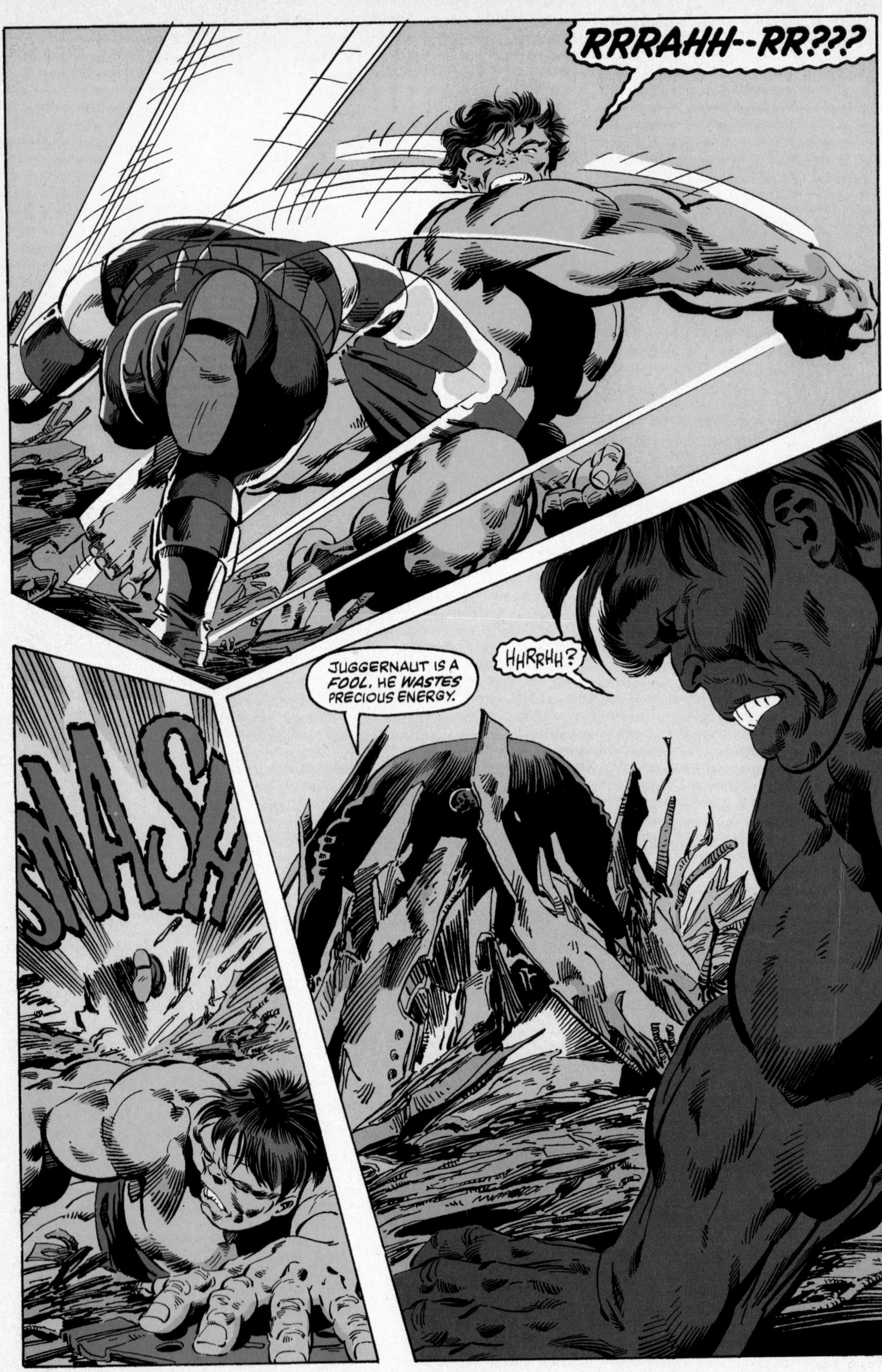
RRRAHH--RR???
SMASH
JUGGERNAUT IS A FOOL. HE WASTES PRECIOUS ENERGY.
HHRRHH?

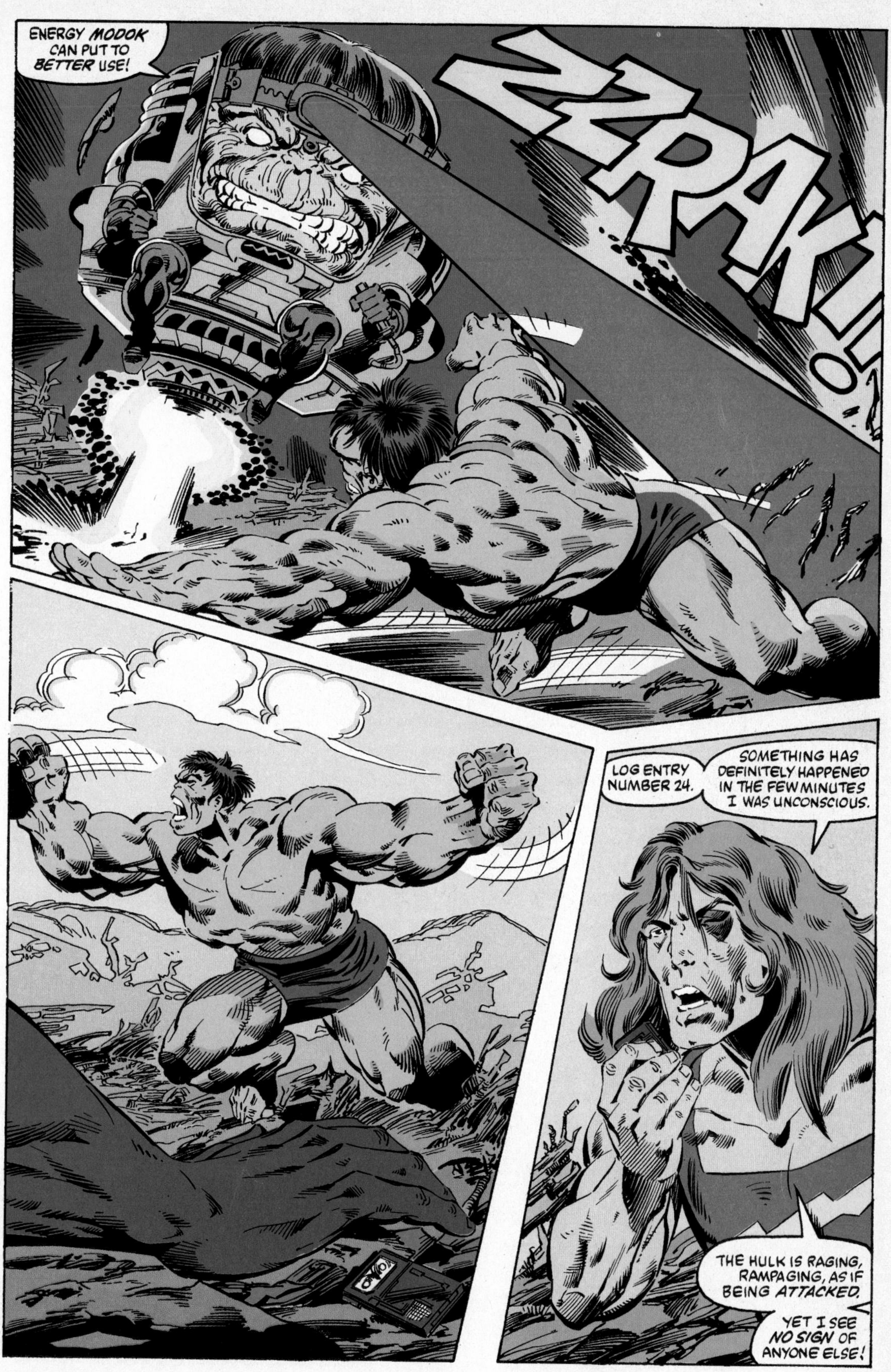
ENERGY MODOK CAN PUT TO BETTER USE!
ZZRAK!!
LOG ENTRY NUMBER 24.
SOMETHING HAS DEFINITELY HAPPENED IN THE FEW MINUTES I WAS UNCONSCIOUS.
THE HULK IS RAGING, RAMPAGING, AS IF BEING ATTACKED.
YET I SEE NO SIGN OF ANYONE ELSE!

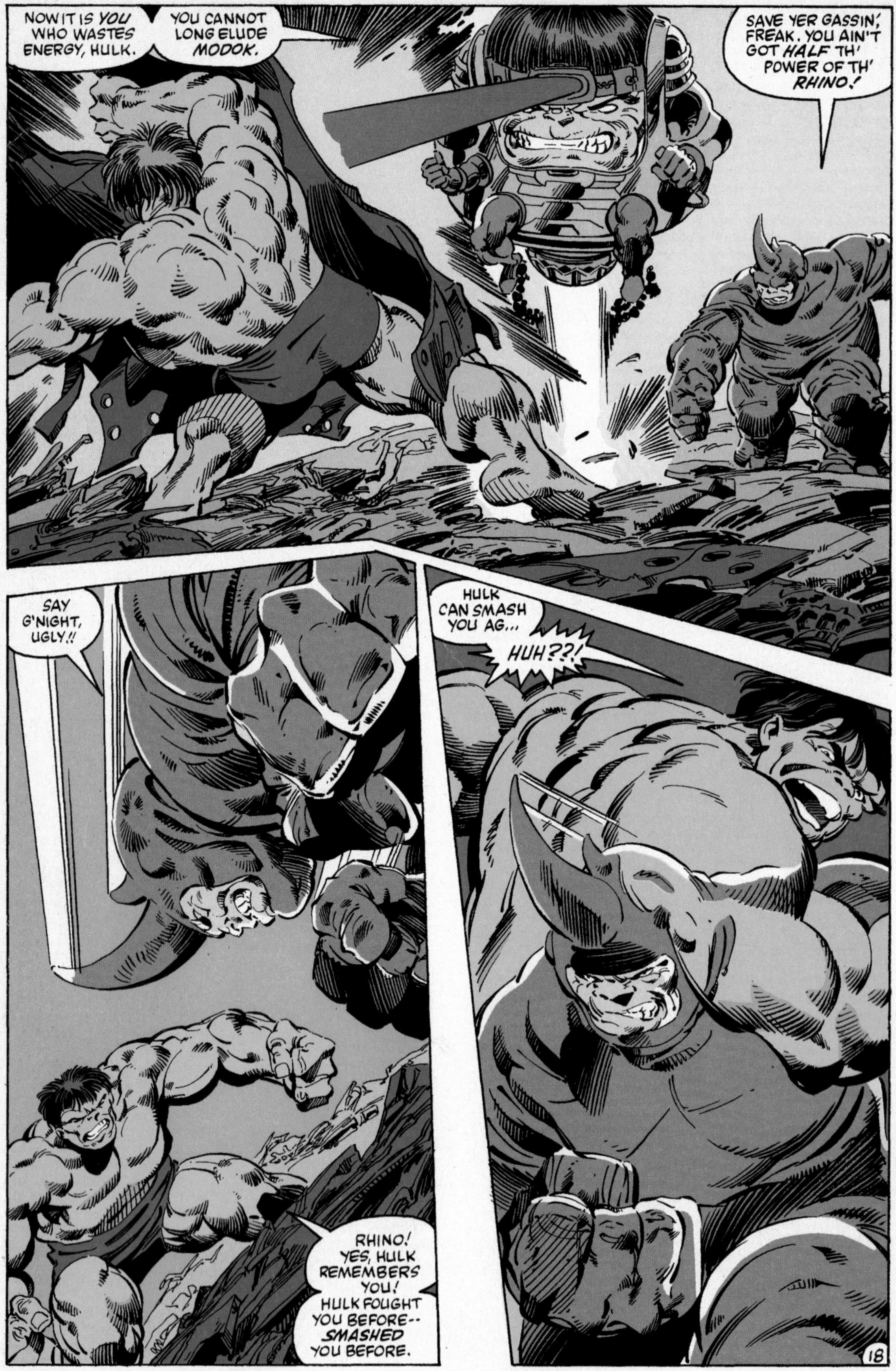
NOW IT IS *YOU* WHO WASTES ENERGY, HULK.
YOU CANNOT LONG ELUDE *MODOK*.
SAVE YER GASSIN', FREAK. YOU AIN'T GOT *HALF* TH' POWER OF TH' *RHINO!*
SAY G'NIGHT, UGLY!!
RHINO! YES, HULK REMEMBERS YOU! HULK FOUGHT YOU BEFORE-- *SMASHED* YOU BEFORE.
HULK CAN SMASH YOU AG...
HUH??!
18

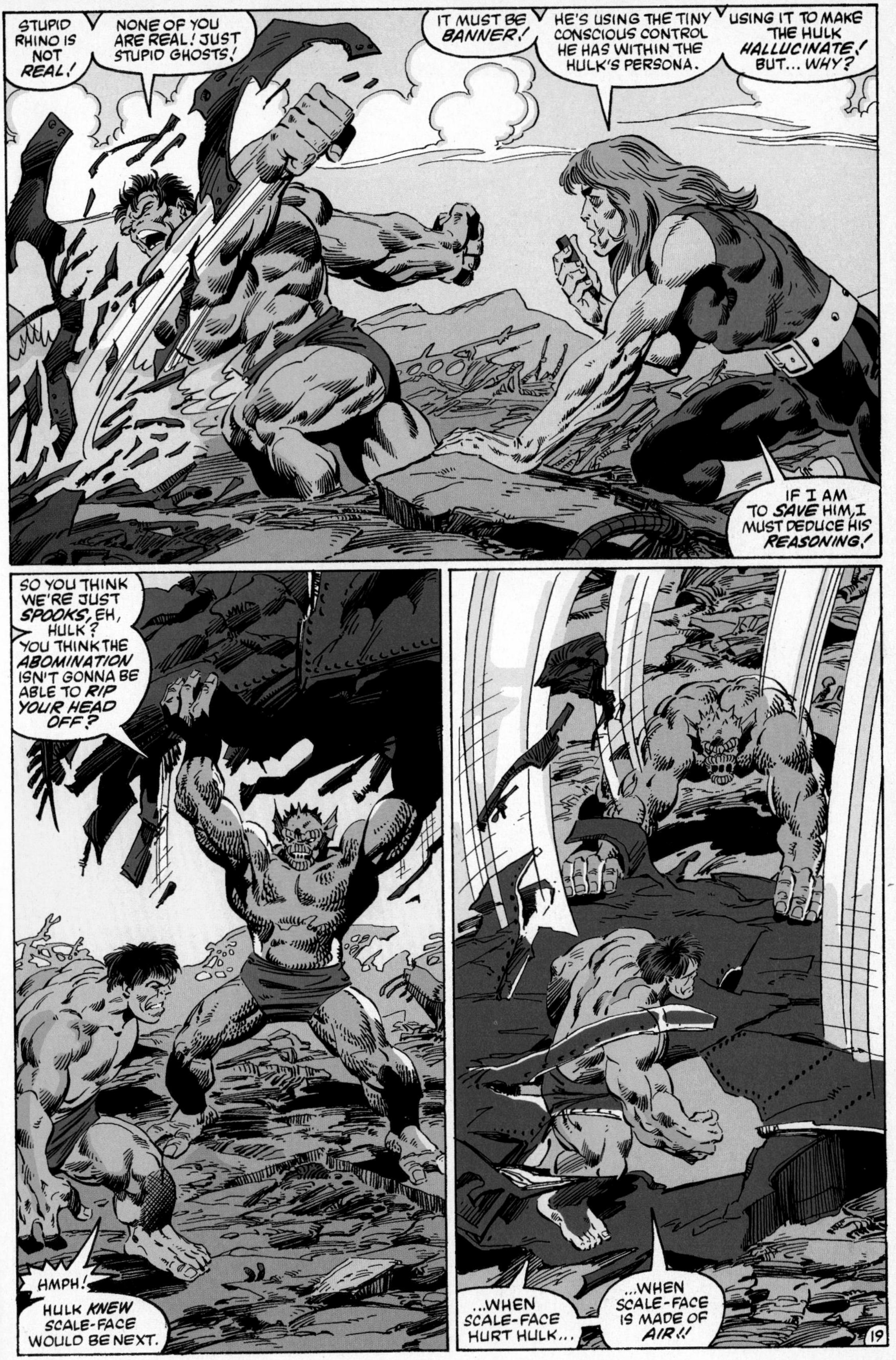
STUPID RHINO IS NOT REAL!
NONE OF YOU ARE REAL! JUST STUPID GHOSTS!
IT MUST BE BANNER!
HE'S USING THE TINY CONSCIOUS CONTROL HE HAS WITHIN THE HULK'S PERSONA.
USING IT TO MAKE THE HULK HALLUCINATE! BUT... WHY?
IF I AM TO SAVE HIM, I MUST DEDUCE HIS REASONING!
SO YOU THINK WE'RE JUST SPOOKS, EH, HULK? YOU THINK THE ABOMINATION ISN'T GONNA BE ABLE TO RIP YOUR HEAD OFF?
HMPH!
HULK KNEW SCALE-FACE WOULD BE NEXT.
...WHEN SCALE-FACE HURT HULK...
...WHEN SCALE-FACE IS MADE OF AIR!!
19

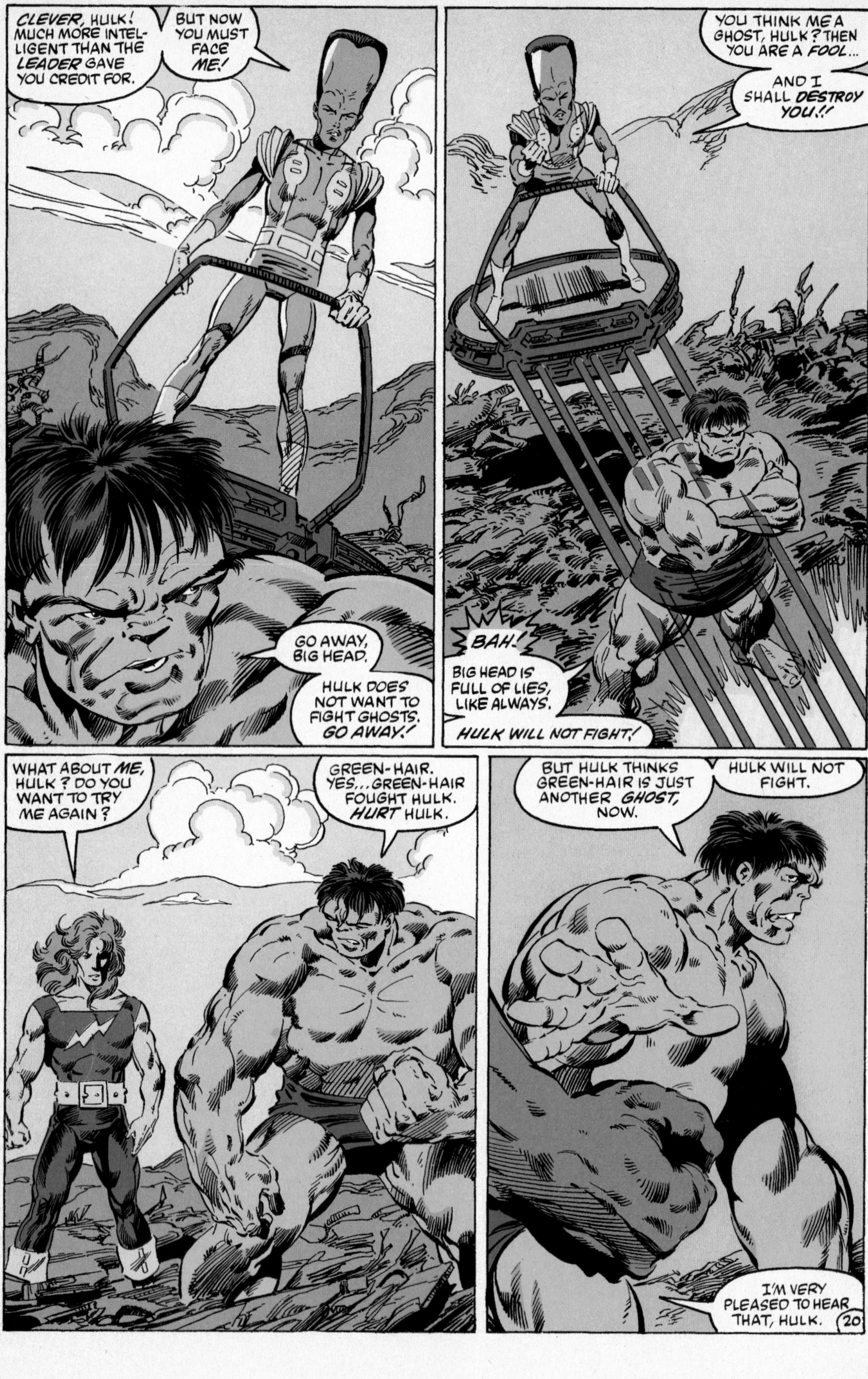

CLEVER, HULK! MUCH MORE INTELLIGENT THAN THE LEADER GAVE YOU CREDIT FOR.
BUT NOW YOU MUST FACE ME!
GO AWAY, BIG HEAD.
HULK DOES NOT WANT TO FIGHT GHOSTS. GO AWAY!
YOU THINK ME A GHOST, HULK? THEN YOU ARE A FOOL...
AND I SHALL DESTROY YOU!!
BAH!
BIG HEAD IS FULL OF LIES, LIKE ALWAYS.
HULK WILL NOT FIGHT!
WHAT ABOUT ME, HULK? DO YOU WANT TO TRY ME AGAIN?
GREEN-HAIR. YES... GREEN-HAIR FOUGHT HULK. HURT HULK.
BUT HULK THINKS GREEN-HAIR IS JUST ANOTHER GHOST, NOW.
HULK WILL NOT FIGHT.
I'M VERY PLEASED TO HEAR THAT, HULK.
20

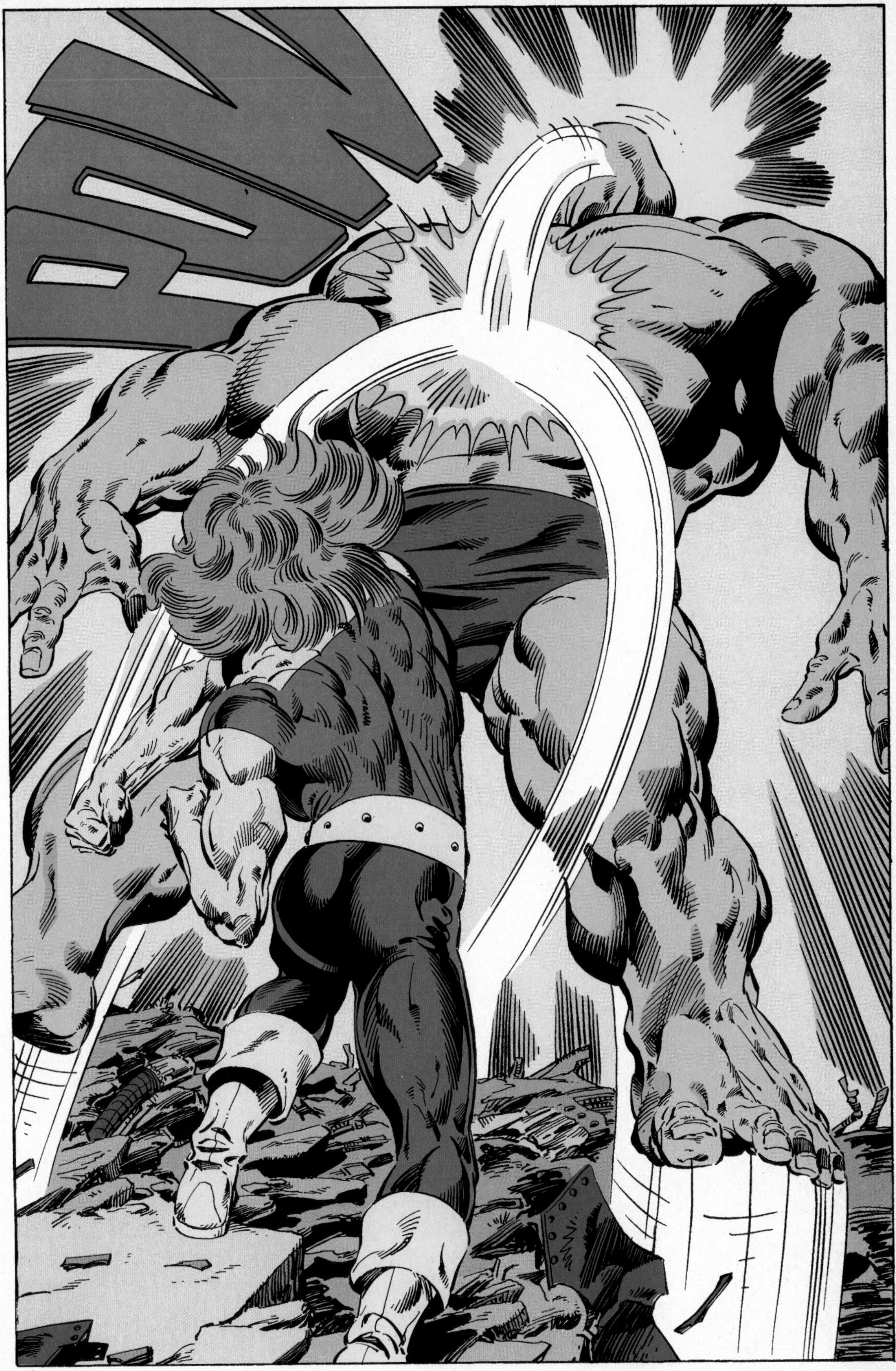

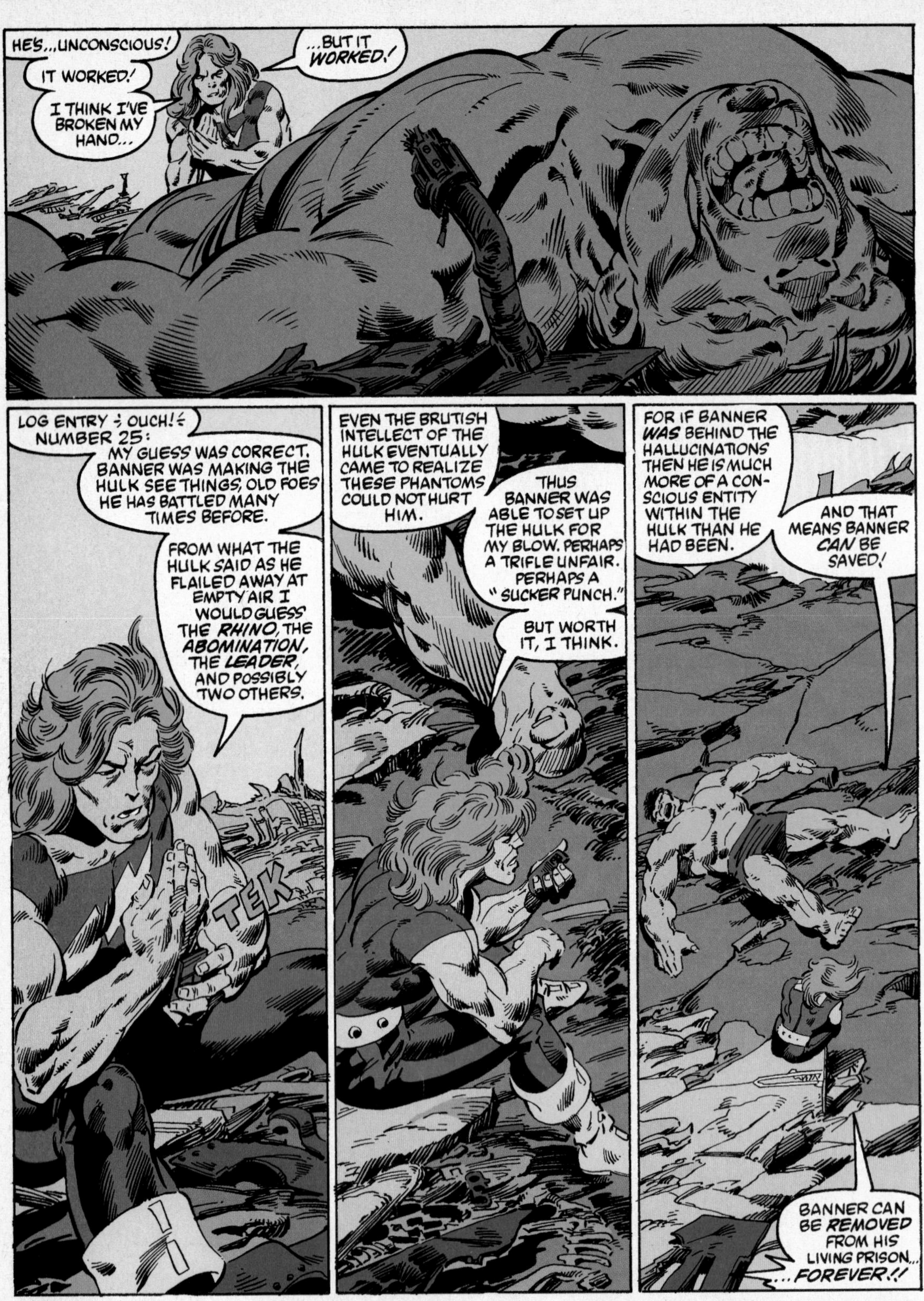
HE'S...UNCONSCIOUS!
IT WORKED!
I THINK I'VE BROKEN MY HAND...
...BUT IT WORKED!
LOG ENTRY ÷ OUCH! ÷ NUMBER 25:
MY GUESS WAS CORRECT. BANNER WAS MAKING THE HULK SEE THINGS, OLD FOES HE HAS BATTLED MANY TIMES BEFORE.
FROM WHAT THE HULK SAID AS HE FLAILED AWAY AT EMPTY AIR I WOULD GUESS THE RHINO, THE ABOMINATION, THE LEADER, AND POSSIBLY TWO OTHERS.
EVEN THE BRUTISH INTELLECT OF THE HULK EVENTUALLY CAME TO REALIZE THESE PHANTOMS COULD NOT HURT HIM.
THUS BANNER WAS ABLE TO SET UP THE HULK FOR MY BLOW. PERHAPS A TRIFLE UNFAIR. PERHAPS A "SUCKER PUNCH."
BUT WORTH IT, I THINK.
FOR IF BANNER WAS BEHIND THE HALLUCINATIONS THEN HE IS MUCH MORE OF A CONSCIOUS ENTITY WITHIN THE HULK THAN HE HAD BEEN.
AND THAT MEANS BANNER CAN BE SAVED!
TEK
BANNER CAN BE REMOVED FROM HIS LIVING PRISON...
...FOREVER!!
NEXT ISSUE:
WHAT IS DOC SAMSON'S PLAN? CAN IT SUCCEED? CAN BRUCE BANNER BE FREED FROM THE HULK? ...AND WHO WAS THAT LADY? FIND OUT IN...
A HULK DIVIDED
...IN THIRTY DAYS!

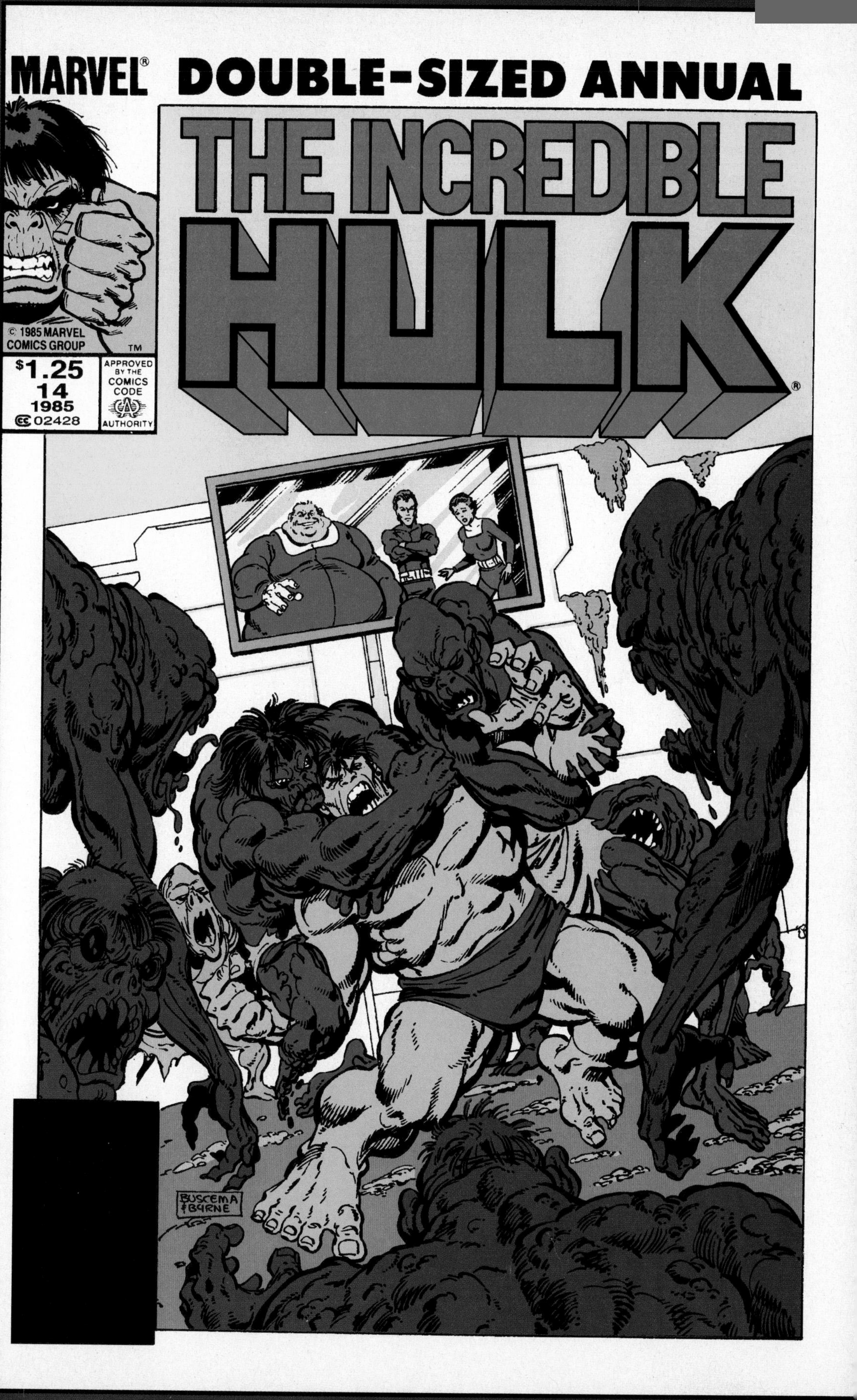
MARVEL®
DOUBLE-SIZED ANNUAL
THE INCREDIBLE HULK®
© 1985 MARVEL COMICS GROUP
TM
$1.25
14
1985
CC 02428
APPROVED BY THE COMICS CODE AUTHORITY
BUSCEMA & BYRNE

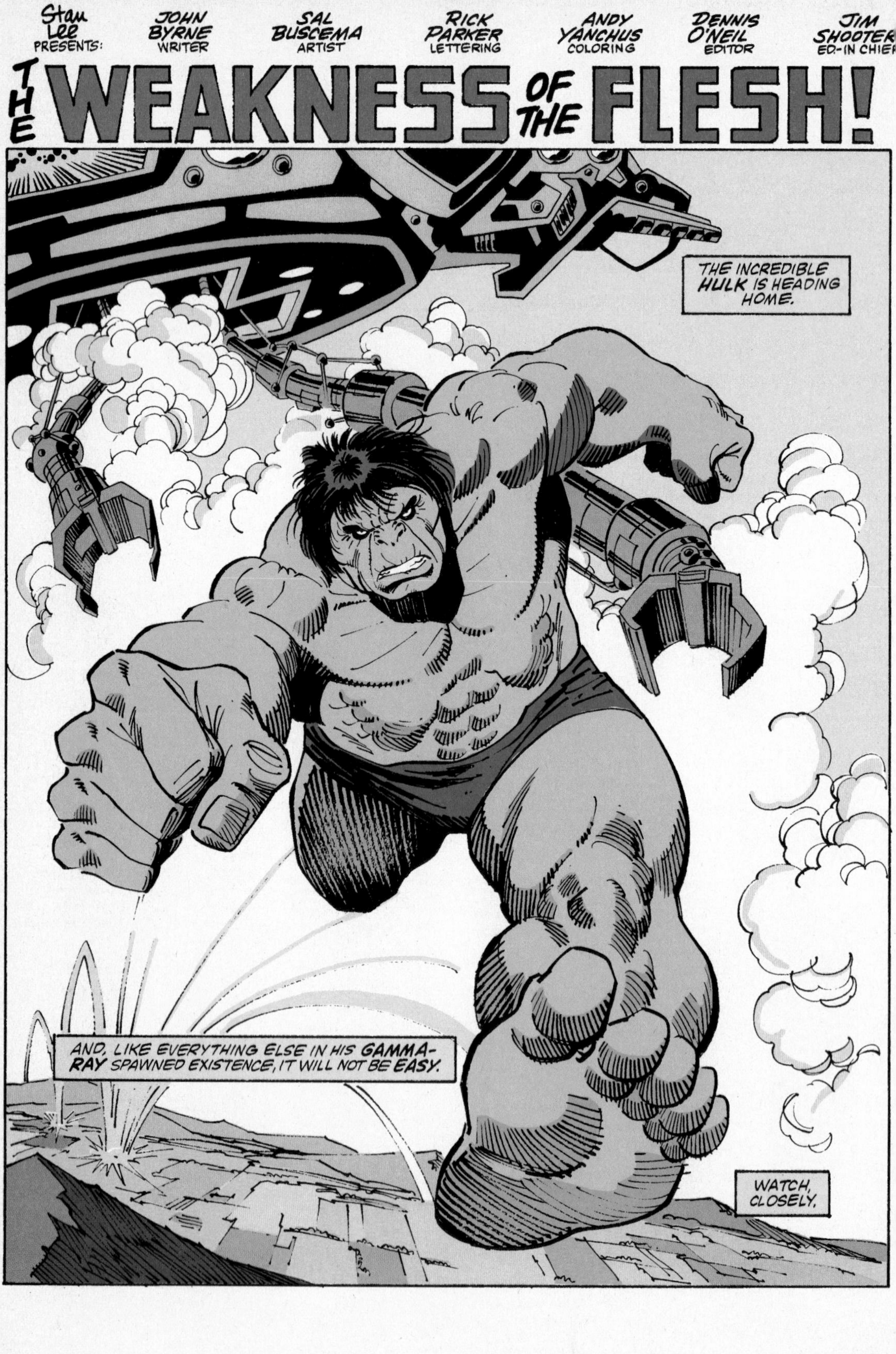
Stan Lee PRESENTS:
JOHN BYRNE WRITER
SAL BUSCEMA ARTIST
RICK PARKER LETTERING
ANDY YANCHUS COLORING
DENNIS O'NEIL EDITOR
JIM SHOOTER ED.-IN CHIEF
THE WEAKNESS OF THE FLESH!
THE INCREDIBLE HULK IS HEADING HOME.
AND, LIKE EVERYTHING ELSE IN HIS GAMMA-RAY SPAWNED EXISTENCE, IT WILL NOT BE EASY.
WATCH, CLOSELY.

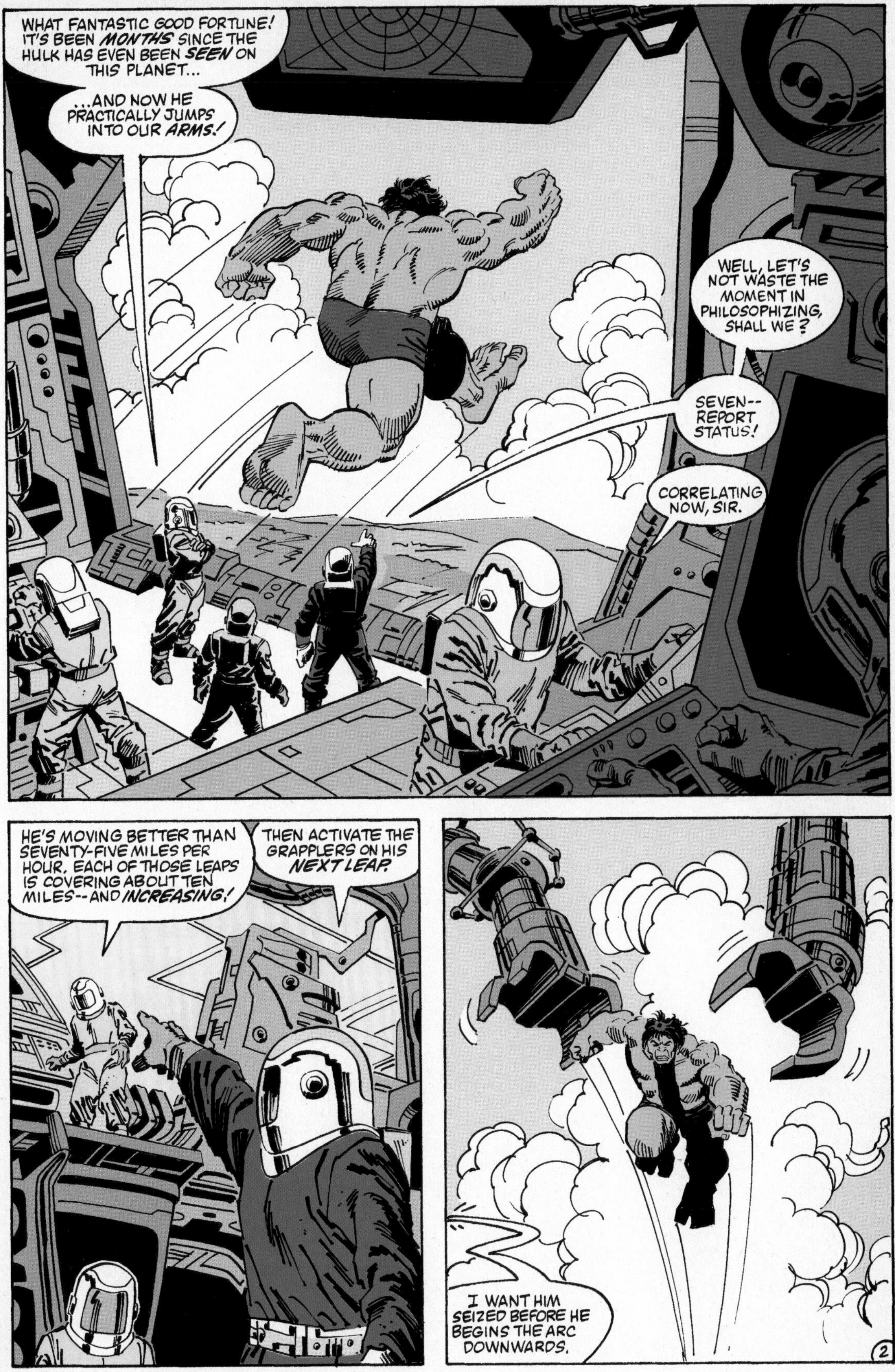
WHAT FANTASTIC GOOD FORTUNE! IT'S BEEN MONTHS SINCE THE HULK HAS EVEN BEEN SEEN ON THIS PLANET...
...AND NOW HE PRACTICALLY JUMPS INTO OUR ARMS!
WELL, LET'S NOT WASTE THE MOMENT IN PHILOSOPHIZING, SHALL WE?
SEVEN-- REPORT STATUS!
CORRELATING NOW, SIR.
HE'S MOVING BETTER THAN SEVENTY-FIVE MILES PER HOUR. EACH OF THOSE LEAPS IS COVERING ABOUT TEN MILES--AND INCREASING!
THEN ACTIVATE THE GRAPPLERS ON HIS NEXT LEAP.
I WANT HIM SEIZED BEFORE HE BEGINS THE ARC DOWNWARDS.
2

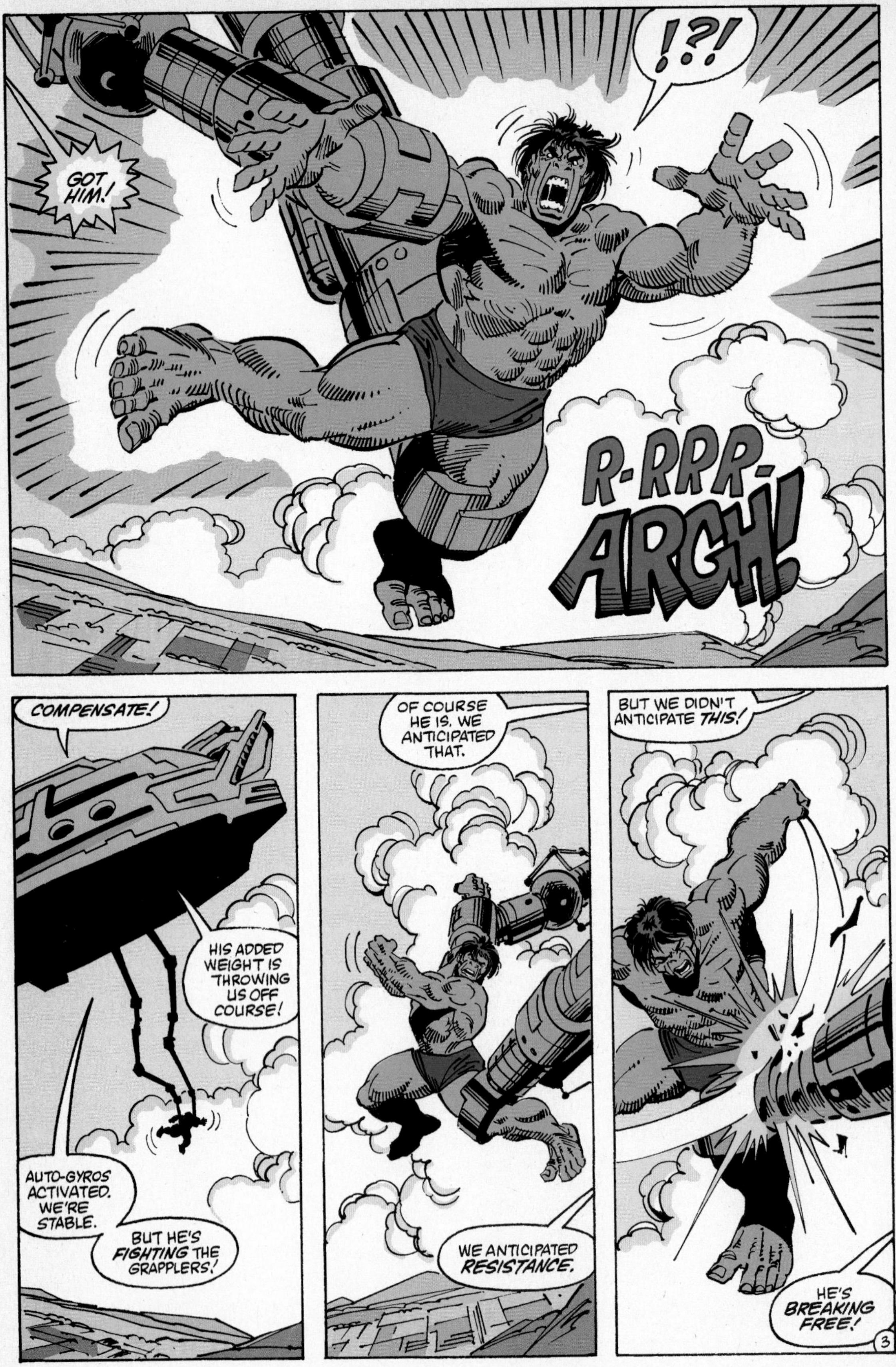
!?!
GOT HIM!
R-RRR-ARGH!
COMPENSATE!
HIS ADDED WEIGHT IS THROWING US OFF COURSE!
AUTO-GYROS ACTIVATED. WE'RE STABLE.
BUT HE'S FIGHTING THE GRAPPLERS!
OF COURSE HE IS. WE ANTICIPATED THAT.
WE ANTICIPATED RESISTANCE.
BUT WE DIDN'T ANTICIPATE THIS!
HE'S BREAKING FREE!
3

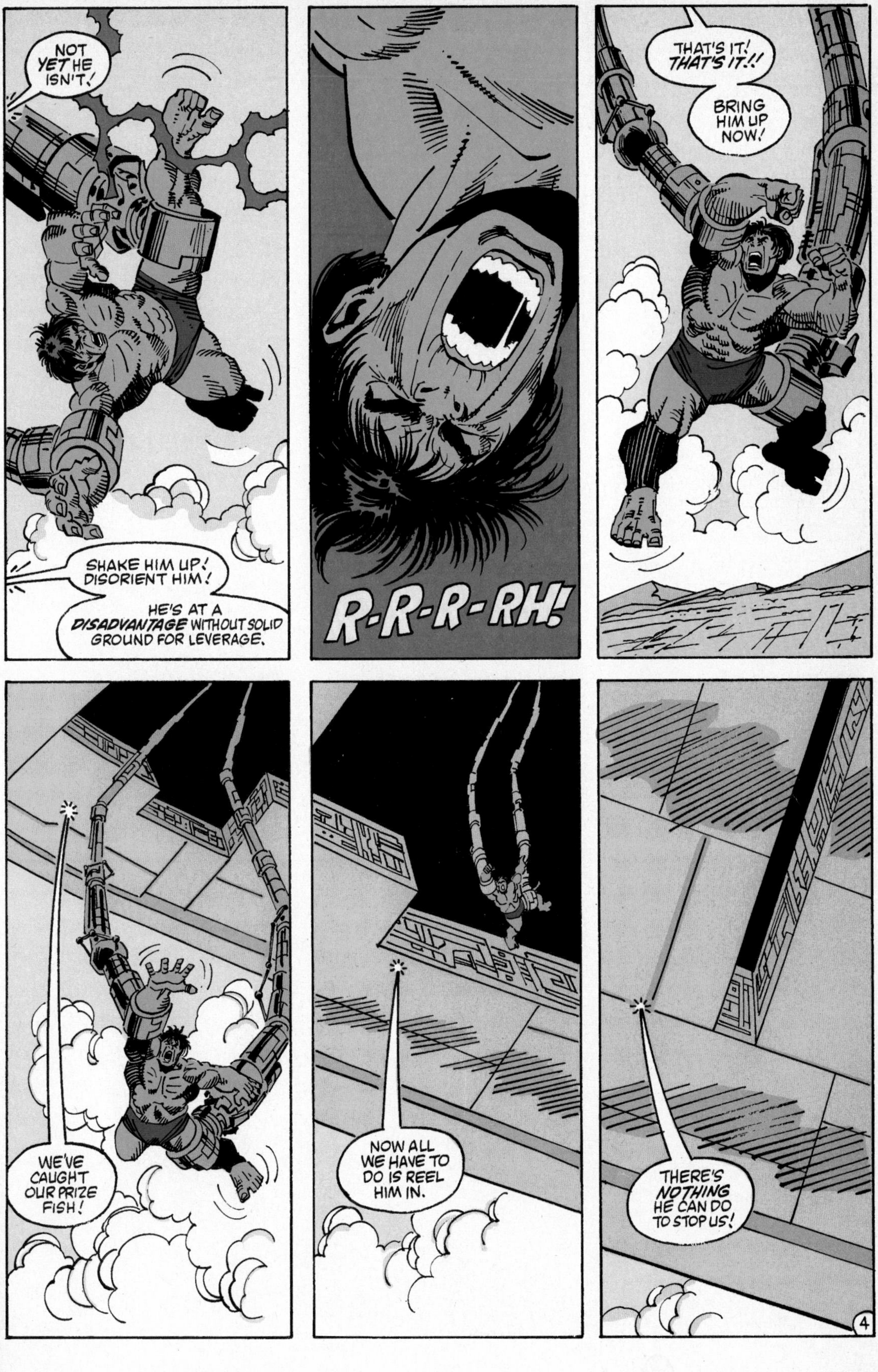
NOT YET HE ISN'T!
SHAKE HIM UP! DISORIENT HIM!
HE'S AT A DISADVANTAGE WITHOUT SOLID GROUND FOR LEVERAGE.
R-R-R-RH!
THAT'S IT! THAT'S IT!!
BRING HIM UP NOW!
WE'VE CAUGHT OUR PRIZE FISH!
NOW ALL WE HAVE TO DO IS REEL HIM IN.
THERE'S NOTHING HE CAN DO TO STOP US!
4

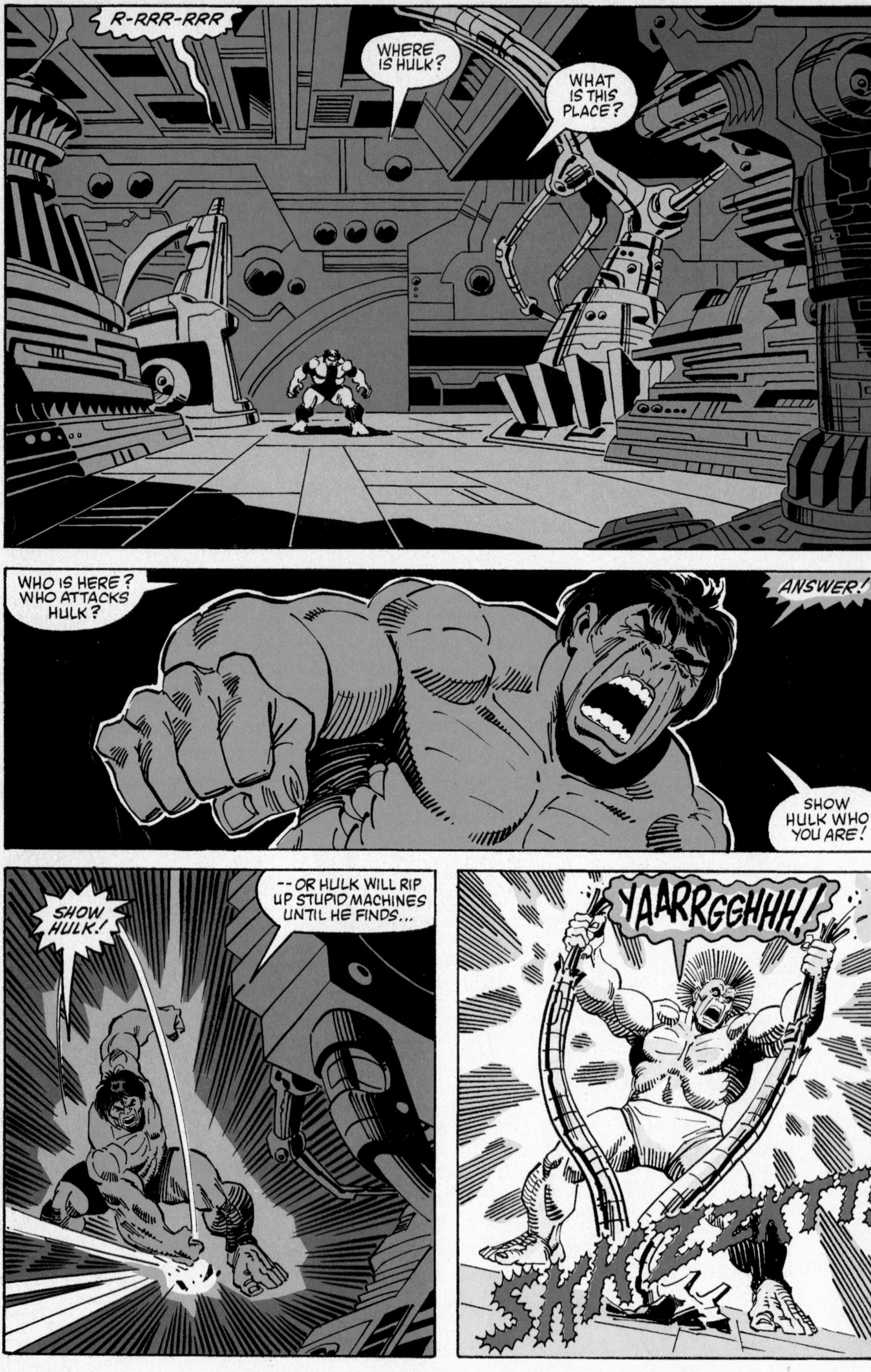

R-RRR-RRR
WHERE IS HULK?
WHAT IS THIS PLACE?
WHO IS HERE? WHO ATTACKS HULK?
ANSWER!
SHOW HULK WHO YOU ARE!
SHOW HULK!
-- OR HULK WILL RIP UP STUPID MACHINES UNTIL HE FINDS...
YAARRGGHHH!!
SHKKZZKTT!

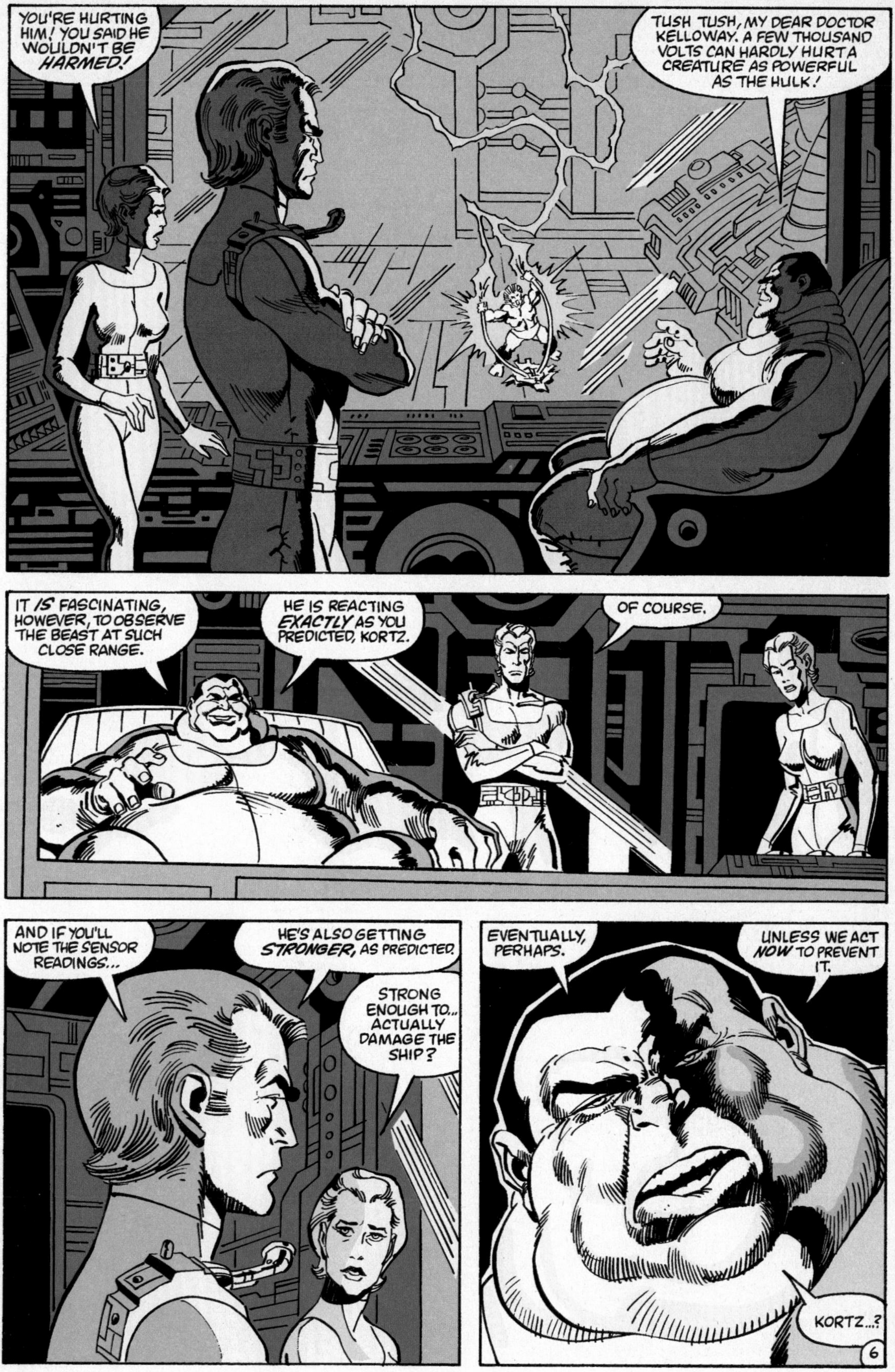
YOU'RE HURTING HIM! YOU SAID HE WOULDN'T BE HARMED!
TUSH TUSH, MY DEAR DOCTOR KELLOWAY. A FEW THOUSAND VOLTS CAN HARDLY HURT A CREATURE AS POWERFUL AS THE HULK!
IT IS FASCINATING, HOWEVER, TO OBSERVE THE BEAST AT SUCH CLOSE RANGE.
HE IS REACTING EXACTLY AS YOU PREDICTED, KORTZ.
OF COURSE.
AND IF YOU'LL NOTE THE SENSOR READINGS...
HE'S ALSO GETTING STRONGER, AS PREDICTED.
STRONG ENOUGH TO... ACTUALLY DAMAGE THE SHIP?
EVENTUALLY, PERHAPS.
UNLESS WE ACT NOW TO PREVENT IT.
KORTZ...?
6

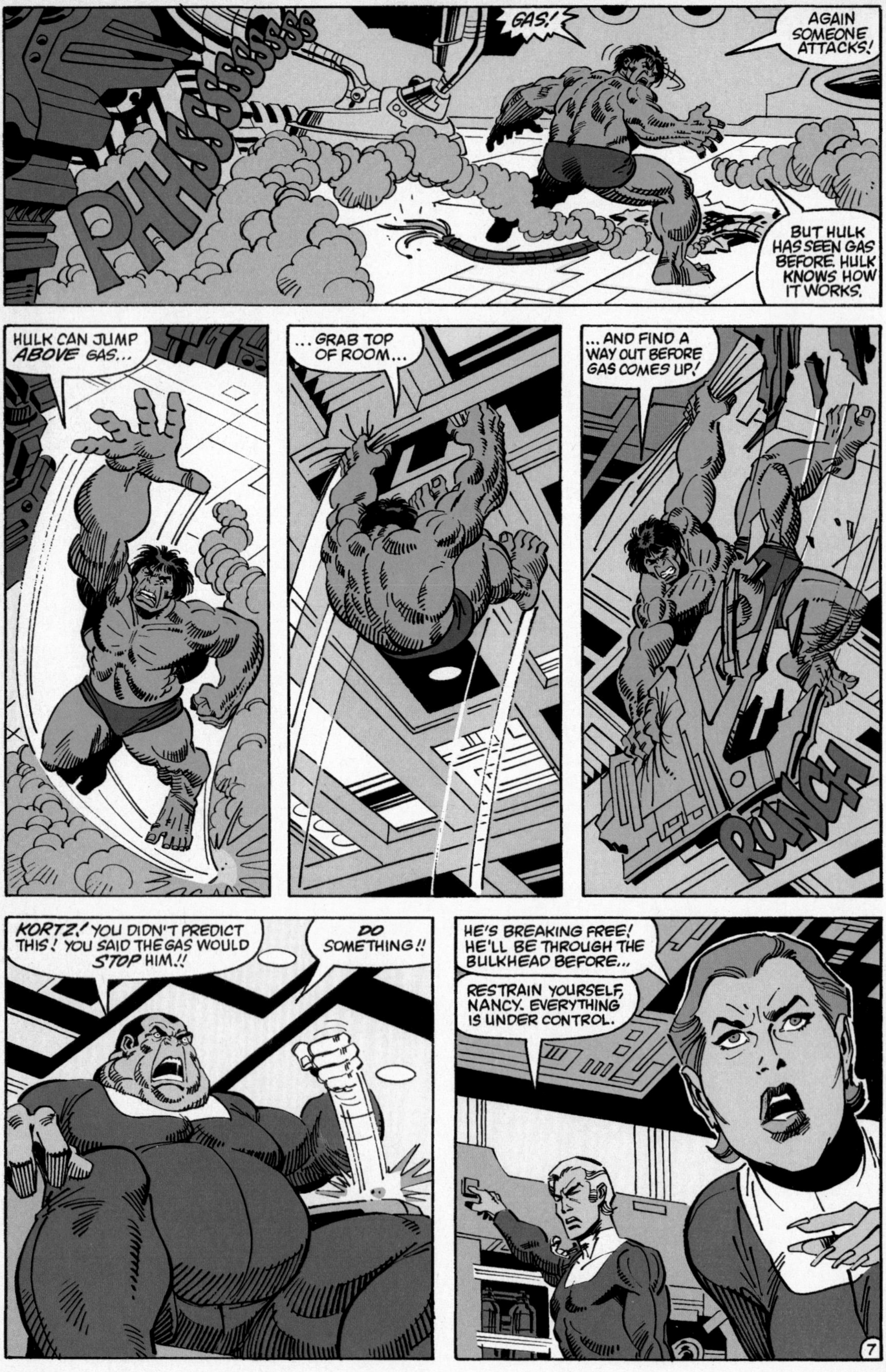
PHSSSSSSSSS
GAS!
AGAIN SOMEONE ATTACKS!
BUT HULK HAS SEEN GAS BEFORE. HULK KNOWS HOW IT WORKS.
HULK CAN JUMP ABOVE GAS...
...GRAB TOP OF ROOM...
...AND FIND A WAY OUT BEFORE GAS COMES UP!
RUNCH
KORTZ! YOU DIDN'T PREDICT THIS! YOU SAID THE GAS WOULD STOP HIM!!
DO SOMETHING!!
HE'S BREAKING FREE! HE'LL BE THROUGH THE BULKHEAD BEFORE...
RESTRAIN YOURSELF, NANCY. EVERYTHING IS UNDER CONTROL.
7

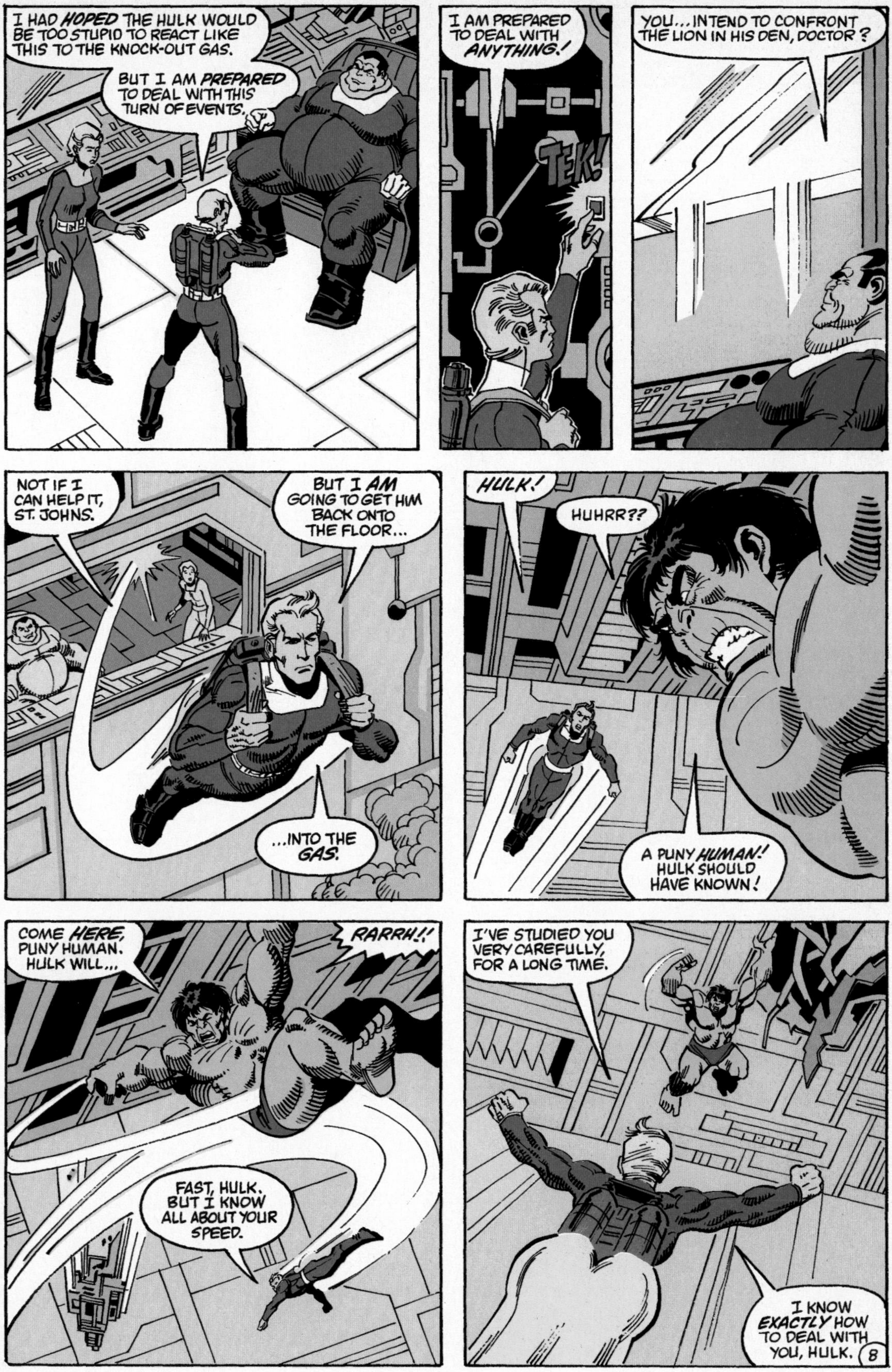
I HAD HOPED THE HULK WOULD BE TOO STUPID TO REACT LIKE THIS TO THE KNOCK-OUT GAS.
BUT I AM PREPARED TO DEAL WITH THIS TURN OF EVENTS.
I AM PREPARED TO DEAL WITH ANYTHING.!
TEK!
YOU... INTEND TO CONFRONT THE LION IN HIS DEN, DOCTOR?
NOT IF I CAN HELP IT, ST. JOHNS.
BUT I AM GOING TO GET HIM BACK ONTO THE FLOOR...
...INTO THE GAS.
HULK!
HUHRR??
A PUNY HUMAN! HULK SHOULD HAVE KNOWN!
COME HERE, PUNY HUMAN. HULK WILL...
RARRH!!
FAST, HULK. BUT I KNOW ALL ABOUT YOUR SPEED.
I'VE STUDIED YOU VERY CAREFULLY, FOR A LONG TIME.
I KNOW EXACTLY HOW TO DEAL WITH YOU, HULK.
8

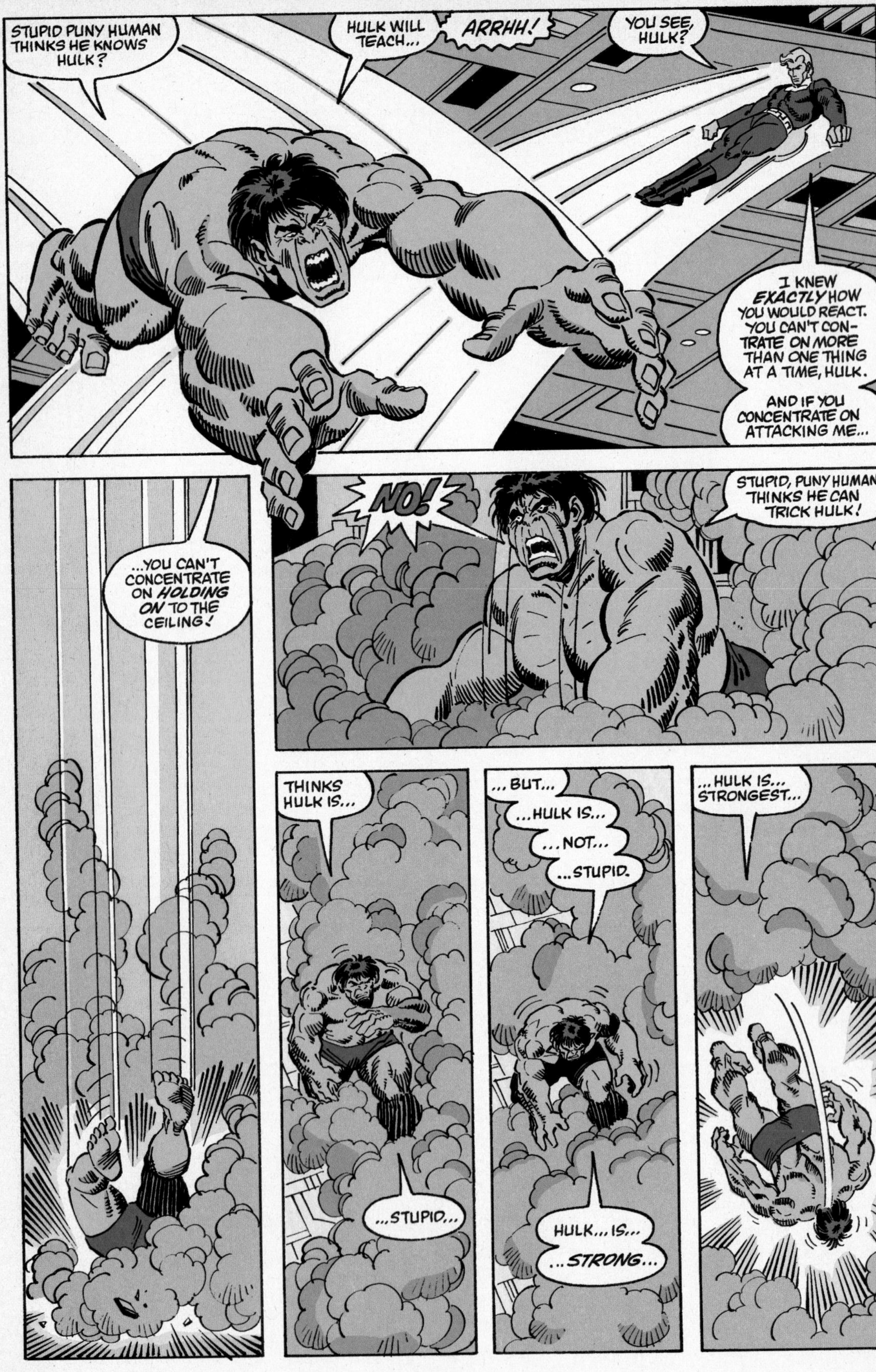
STUPID PUNY HUMAN THINKS HE KNOWS HULK?
HULK WILL TEACH...
ARRHH!
YOU SEE, HULK?
I KNEW EXACTLY HOW YOU WOULD REACT. YOU CAN'T CONTRATE ON MORE THAN ONE THING AT A TIME, HULK.
AND IF YOU CONCENTRATE ON ATTACKING ME...
...YOU CAN'T CONCENTRATE ON HOLDING ON TO THE CEILING!
NO!
STUPID, PUNY HUMAN THINKS HE CAN TRICK HULK!
THINKS HULK IS...
...STUPID...
...BUT...
...HULK IS...
...NOT...
...STUPID.
HULK... IS...
...STRONG...
...HULK IS... STRONGEST...

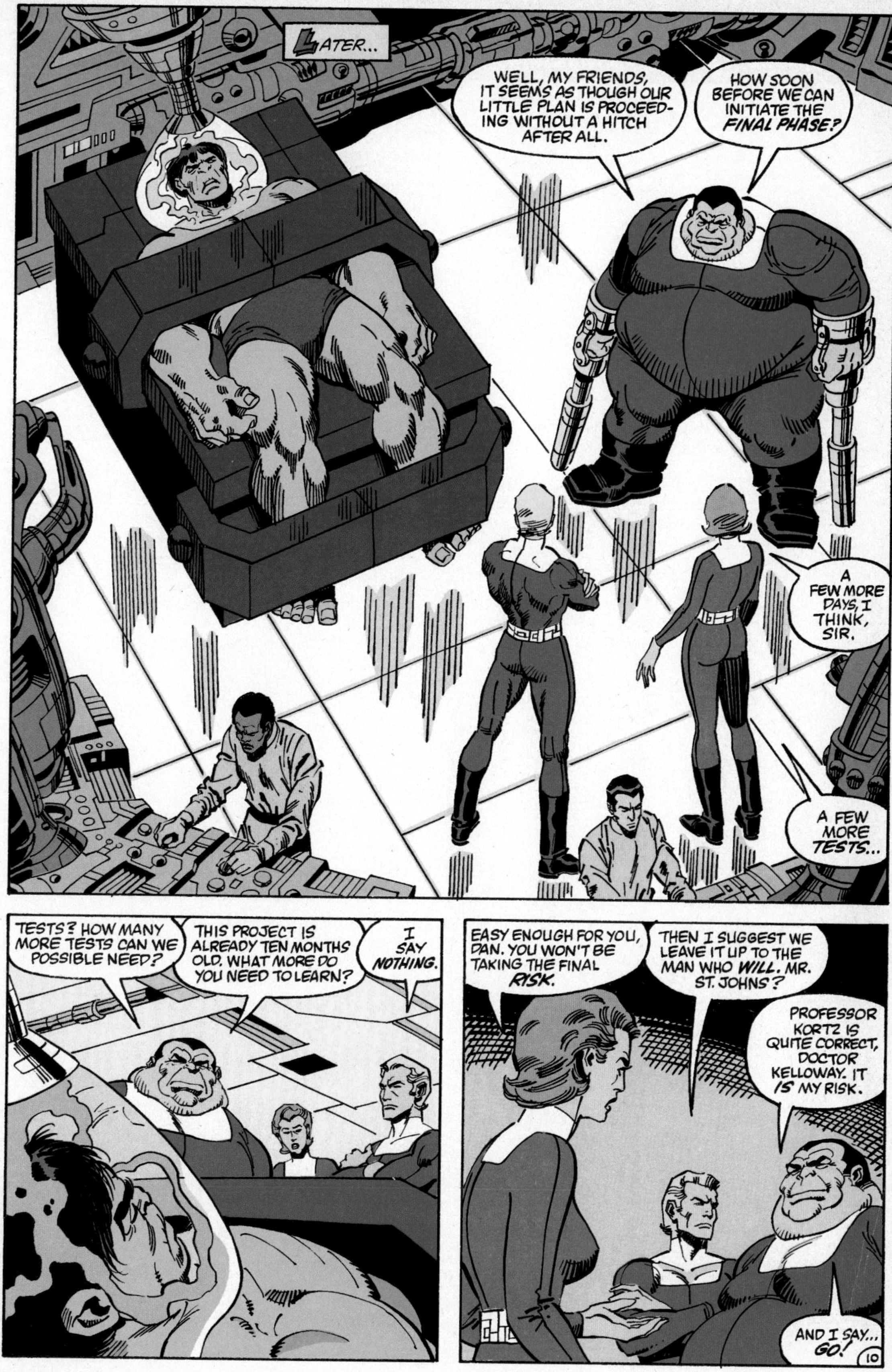
LATER...
WELL, MY FRIENDS, IT SEEMS AS THOUGH OUR LITTLE PLAN IS PROCEEDING WITHOUT A HITCH AFTER ALL.
HOW SOON BEFORE WE CAN INITIATE THE FINAL PHASE?
A FEW MORE DAYS, I THINK, SIR.
A FEW MORE TESTS...
TESTS? HOW MANY MORE TESTS CAN WE POSSIBLE NEED?
THIS PROJECT IS ALREADY TEN MONTHS OLD. WHAT MORE DO YOU NEED TO LEARN?
I SAY NOTHING.
EASY ENOUGH FOR YOU, DAN. YOU WON'T BE TAKING THE FINAL RISK.
THEN I SUGGEST WE LEAVE IT UP TO THE MAN WHO WILL. MR. ST. JOHNS?
PROFESSOR KORTZ IS QUITE CORRECT, DOCTOR KELLOWAY. IT IS MY RISK.
AND I SAY... GO!
10

MR. ST. JOHNS! THE HULK IS WAKING UP!

EXCELLENT! EXCELLENT! I WOULD *PREFER* HIM TO BE AWARE OF WHAT IS ABOUT TO HAPPEN.

BUT PERHAPS NOT *TOO* AWARE. INCREASE THE GAS CONCENTRATION WITHIN THE HELMET. KEEP HIM GROGGY.

AND NOW, WE MEET AT LAST, MY OLD FRIEND.

YOU *DO* SEEM LIKE AN OLD FRIEND, HULK, DO YOU REALIZE THAT? EVEN THOUGH WE HAVE NEVER MET.

FOR I HAVE STUDIED YOU VERY CAREFULLY, VERY HARD, FOR A LONG, LONG TIME.

YOU SEE, I FEEL THAT YOUR *PRISON* MAY BE THE *KEY* TO *MINE!*

rrrrrr

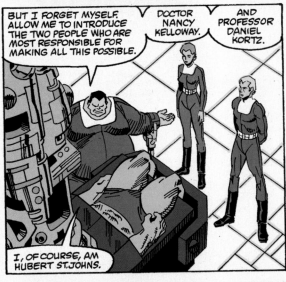

BUT I FORGET MYSELF. ALLOW ME TO INTRODUCE THE TWO PEOPLE WHO ARE MOST RESPONSIBLE FOR MAKING ALL THIS POSSIBLE.

DOCTOR NANCY KELLOWAY.

AND PROFESSOR DANIEL KORTZ.

I, OF COURSE, AM HUBERT ST. JOHNS.

BUT, I FEAR, GOOD MANNERS ARE WASTED ON YOU, HULK. PROCEED, KORTZ.

YES. I'LL CONFESS, THIS IS A MOMENT I HAVE LONG LOOKED FORWARD TO, ST. JOHNS.

UNTIL NOW, IT'S ALL BEEN THEORETICAL, ALL BEEN GUESS-WORK.

NOW IT BECOMES *REAL!*

11

NO NEED TO STERILIZE THE POINT OF PUNCTURE, OF COURSE.

THERE'S NOT A MICROBE ON EARTH THAT COULD LIVE MORE THAN HALF A MICROSECOND IN THE HULK'S BLOODSTREAM.

SPARE US THE LECTURE, KORTZ. AND *BE CAREFUL!*

THAT MICRO-TIPPED NEEDLE TOOK A YEAR TO PRODUCE AND A FORTUNE TO...

AHHGHH!

STOP IT! STOP HURTING HIM!!

YOU ASTOUND ME, NANCY. YOU REALLY DO.

WHEN I WAS A STUDENT IN YOUR CLASSES I THOUGHT YOU WERE MADE OF STERN-ER STUFF.

YES,...

I HOPE THIS SUDDEN... HUMANITARIANISM IS NOT GOING TO INTERFERE WITH YOUR PERFORMING YOUR *DUTY,* DOCTOR.

N-NO.

IT'S ONLY THAT... YOU PROMISED...

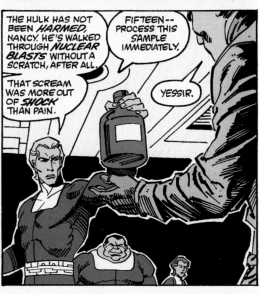

THE HULK HAS NOT BEEN *HARMED,* NANCY. HE'S WALKED THROUGH *NUCLEAR BLASTS* WITHOUT A SCRATCH, AFTER ALL.

THAT SCREAM WAS MORE OUT OF *SHOCK* THAN PAIN.

FIFTEEN -- PROCESS THIS SAMPLE IMMEDIATELY.

YESSIR.

THAT SHOULD TAKE ABOUT AN HOUR. ENOUGH FOR A REST AND A MEAL, I THINK.

A LAST MEAL, YES. BEFORE I NEVER NEED TO *EAT* AGAIN!!

12

TECHNICIAN THIRTEEN, HOURLY REPORT.

THE HULK IS STILL AWAKE, BUT REMAINS GROGGY. THE EFFECT OF THE GAS SHOULD BE ENOUGH NOW TO RISK MOVING HIM INTO THE HOLDING CHAMBER.

GAS LINE DETACHING.

ACTIVATING TABLE-MOTIVATOR CIRCUITS.

OPENING CHAMBER DOORS.

rrrrr...

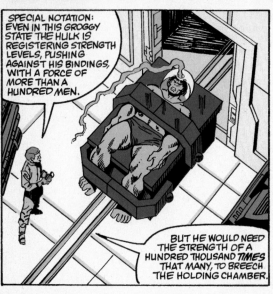

SPECIAL NOTATION: EVEN IN THIS GROGGY STATE THE HULK IS REGISTERING STRENGTH LEVELS, PUSHING AGAINST HIS BINDINGS, WITH A FORCE OF MORE THAN A HUNDRED MEN.

BUT HE WOULD NEED THE STRENGTH OF A HUNDRED THOUSAND *TIMES* THAT MANY, TO BREECH THE HOLDING CHAMBER.

FOR THE FIRST TIME IN HIS EXISTENCE, THE HULK IS TRULY A PRISONER, TRULY HELPLESS.

I WONDER HOW HE *FEELS?* 13

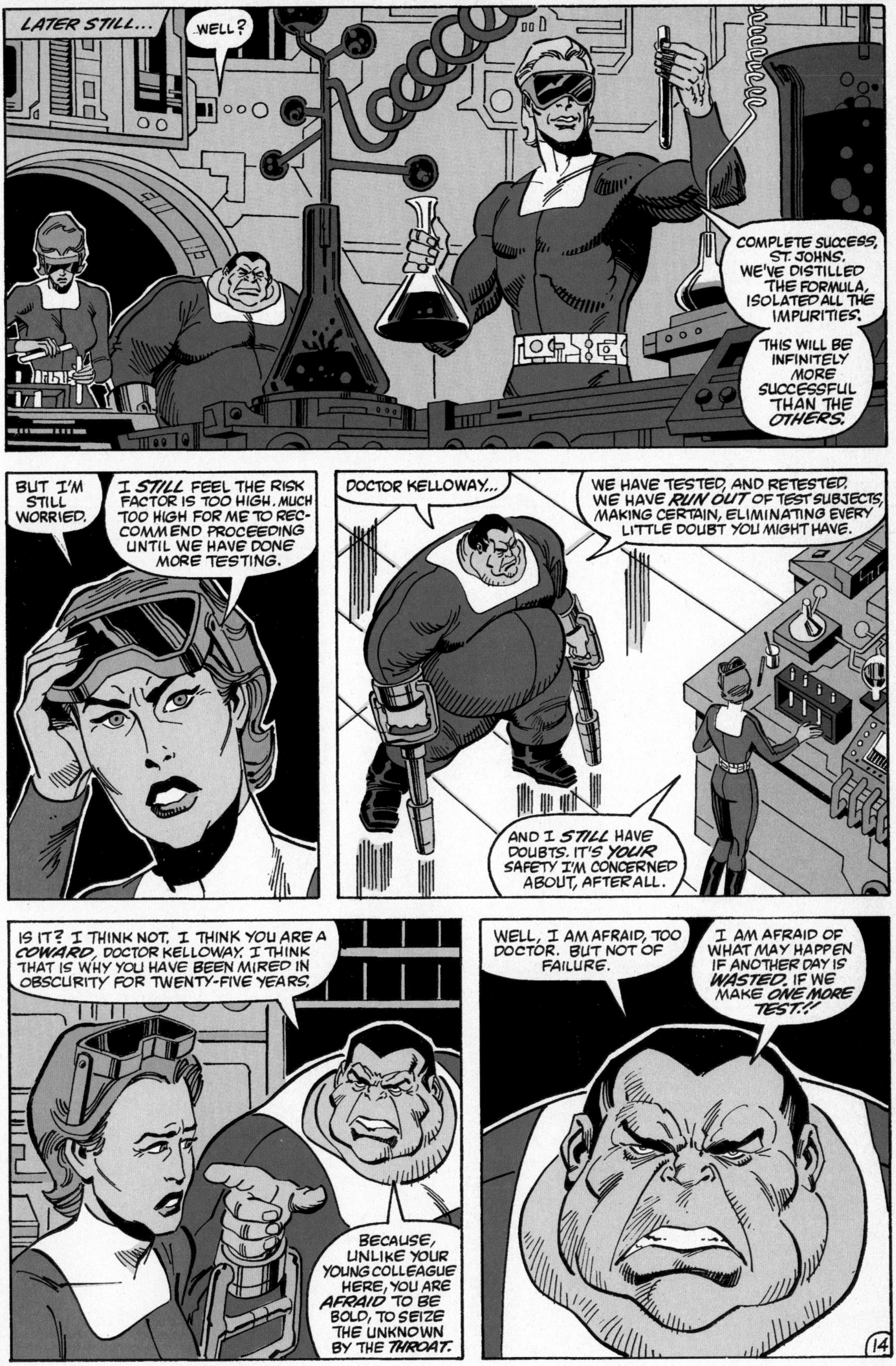
LATER STILL...
WELL?
COMPLETE SUCCESS, ST. JOHNS. WE'VE DISTILLED THE FORMULA, ISOLATED ALL THE IMPURITIES.
THIS WILL BE INFINITELY MORE SUCCESSFUL THAN THE OTHERS.
BUT I'M STILL WORRIED.
I STILL FEEL THE RISK FACTOR IS TOO HIGH. MUCH TOO HIGH FOR ME TO RECOMMEND PROCEEDING UNTIL WE HAVE DONE MORE TESTING.
DOCTOR KELLOWAY...
WE HAVE TESTED, AND RETESTED. WE HAVE RUN OUT OF TEST SUBJECTS, MAKING CERTAIN, ELIMINATING EVERY LITTLE DOUBT YOU MIGHT HAVE.
AND I STILL HAVE DOUBTS. IT'S YOUR SAFETY I'M CONCERNED ABOUT, AFTER ALL.
IS IT? I THINK NOT. I THINK YOU ARE A COWARD, DOCTOR KELLOWAY. I THINK THAT IS WHY YOU HAVE BEEN MIRED IN OBSCURITY FOR TWENTY-FIVE YEARS,
BECAUSE, UNLIKE YOUR YOUNG COLLEAGUE HERE, YOU ARE AFRAID TO BE BOLD, TO SEIZE THE UNKNOWN BY THE THROAT.
WELL, I AM AFRAID, TOO DOCTOR. BUT NOT OF FAILURE.
I AM AFRAID OF WHAT MAY HAPPEN IF ANOTHER DAY IS WASTED. IF WE MAKE ONE MORE TEST!!
14

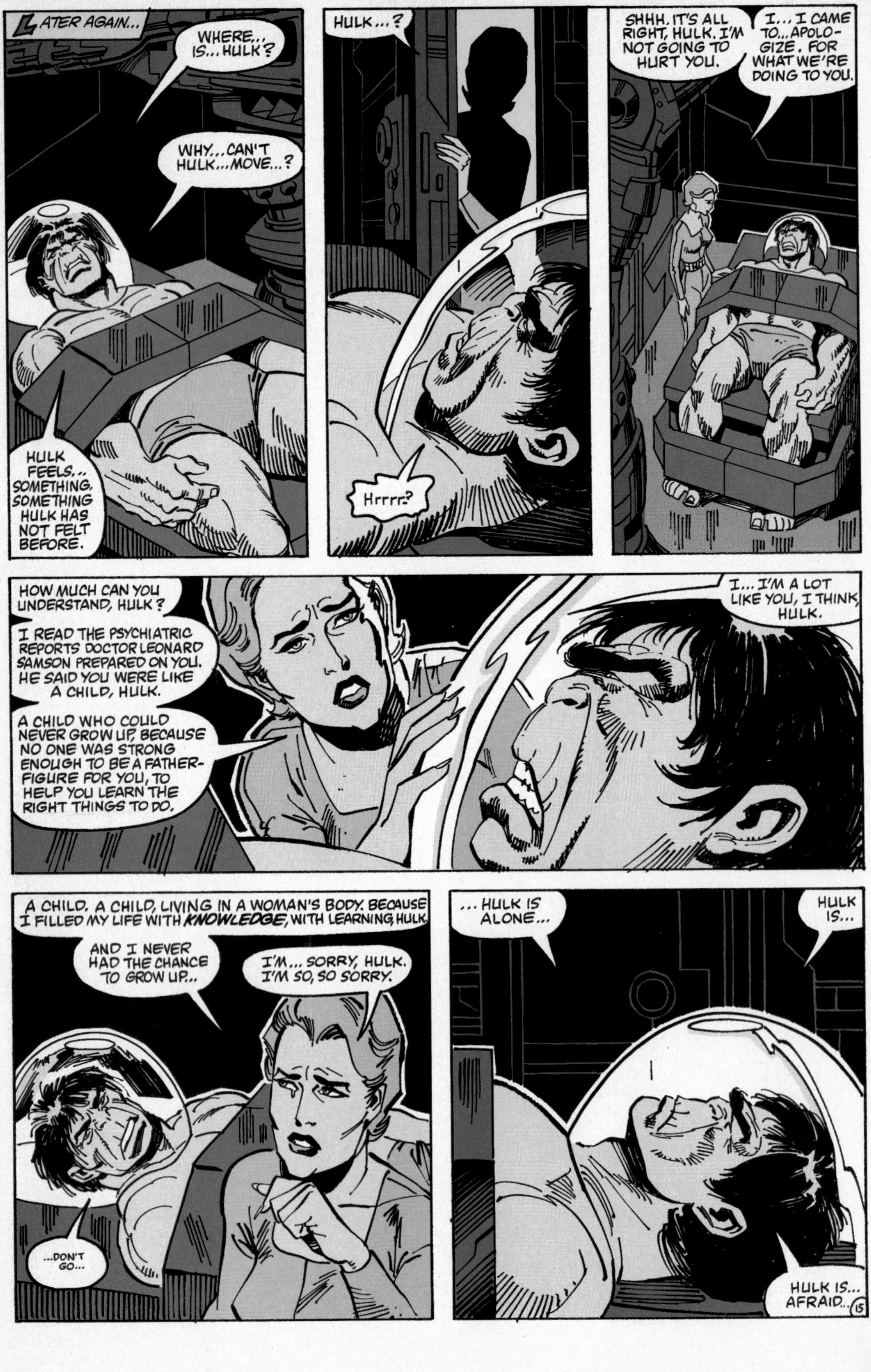
LATER AGAIN...
WHERE... IS... HULK?
WHY... CAN'T HULK... MOVE...?
HULK FEELS... SOMETHING. SOMETHING HULK HAS NOT FELT BEFORE.
HULK...?
Hrrrr?
SHHH. IT'S ALL RIGHT, HULK. I'M NOT GOING TO HURT YOU.
I... I CAME TO... APOLOGIZE. FOR WHAT WE'RE DOING TO YOU.
HOW MUCH CAN YOU UNDERSTAND, HULK?
I READ THE PSYCHIATRIC REPORTS DOCTOR LEONARD SAMSON PREPARED ON YOU. HE SAID YOU WERE LIKE A CHILD, HULK.
A CHILD WHO COULD NEVER GROW UP, BECAUSE NO ONE WAS STRONG ENOUGH TO BE A FATHER-FIGURE FOR YOU, TO HELP YOU LEARN THE RIGHT THINGS TO DO.
I... I'M A LOT LIKE YOU, I THINK, HULK.
A CHILD. A CHILD, LIVING IN A WOMAN'S BODY. BECAUSE I FILLED MY LIFE WITH KNOWLEDGE, WITH LEARNING, HULK.
AND I NEVER HAD THE CHANCE TO GROW UP...
I'M... SORRY, HULK. I'M SO, SO SORRY.
...DON'T GO...
...HULK IS ALONE...
HULK IS...
HULK IS... AFRAID...
15

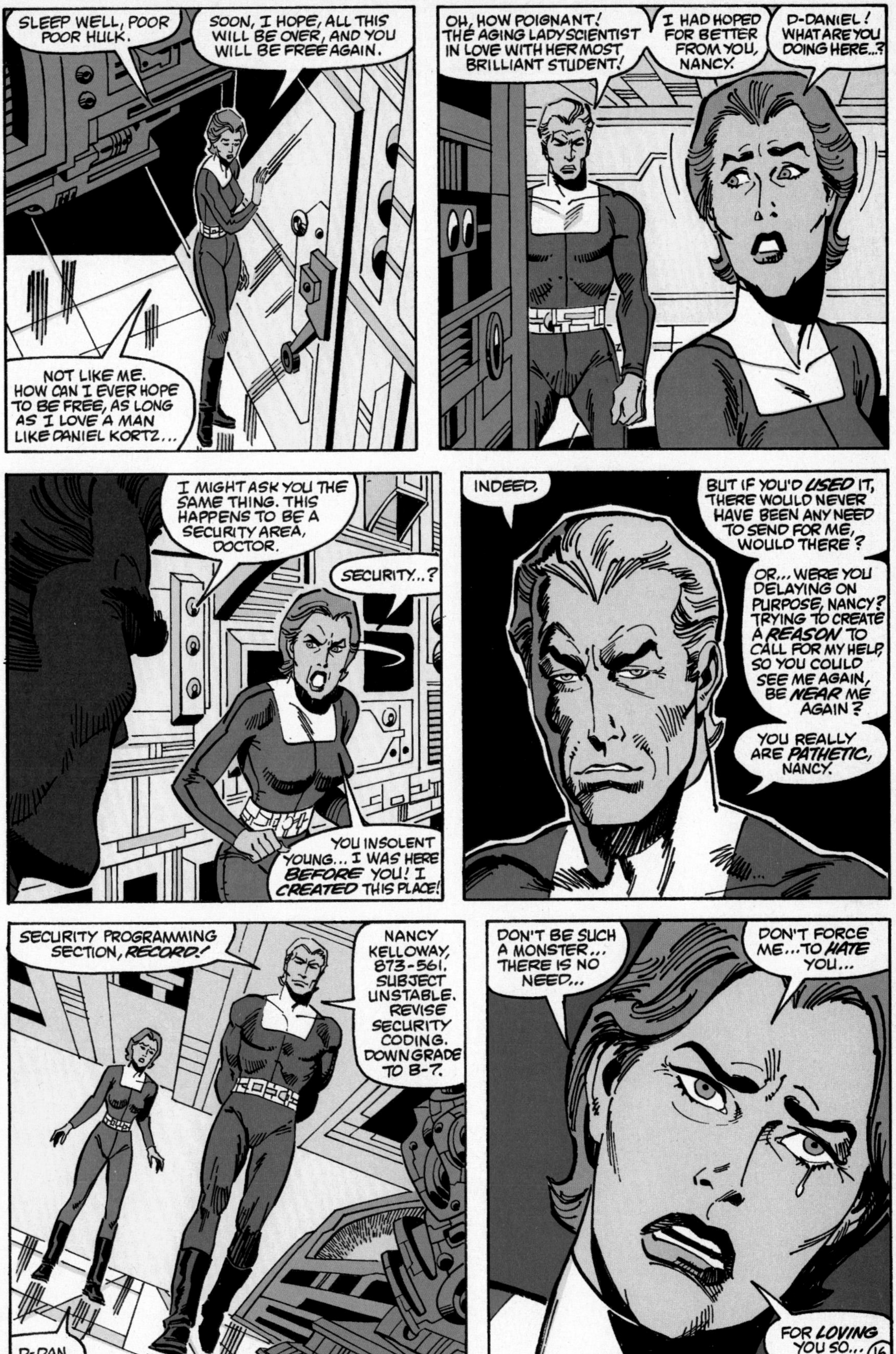
SLEEP WELL, POOR POOR HULK.
SOON, I HOPE, ALL THIS WILL BE OVER, AND YOU WILL BE FREE AGAIN.
NOT LIKE ME. HOW CAN I EVER HOPE TO BE FREE, AS LONG AS I LOVE A MAN LIKE DANIEL KORTZ...
OH, HOW POIGNANT! THE AGING LADY SCIENTIST IN LOVE WITH HER MOST BRILLIANT STUDENT!
I HAD HOPED FOR BETTER FROM YOU, NANCY.
D-DANIEL! WHAT ARE YOU DOING HERE...?
I MIGHT ASK YOU THE SAME THING. THIS HAPPENS TO BE A SECURITY AREA, DOCTOR.
SECURITY...?
YOU INSOLENT YOUNG... I WAS HERE BEFORE YOU! I CREATED THIS PLACE!
INDEED.
BUT IF YOU'D USED IT, THERE WOULD NEVER HAVE BEEN ANY NEED TO SEND FOR ME, WOULD THERE?
OR... WERE YOU DELAYING ON PURPOSE, NANCY? TRYING TO CREATE A REASON TO CALL FOR MY HELP, SO YOU COULD SEE ME AGAIN, BE NEAR ME AGAIN?
YOU REALLY ARE PATHETIC, NANCY.
SECURITY PROGRAMMING SECTION, RECORD!
NANCY KELLOWAY, 873-561. SUBJECT UNSTABLE. REVISE SECURITY CODING. DOWNGRADE TO B-7.
D-DAN.
DON'T BE SUCH A MONSTER... THERE IS NO NEED...
DON'T FORCE ME... TO HATE YOU...
FOR LOVING YOU SO...
16

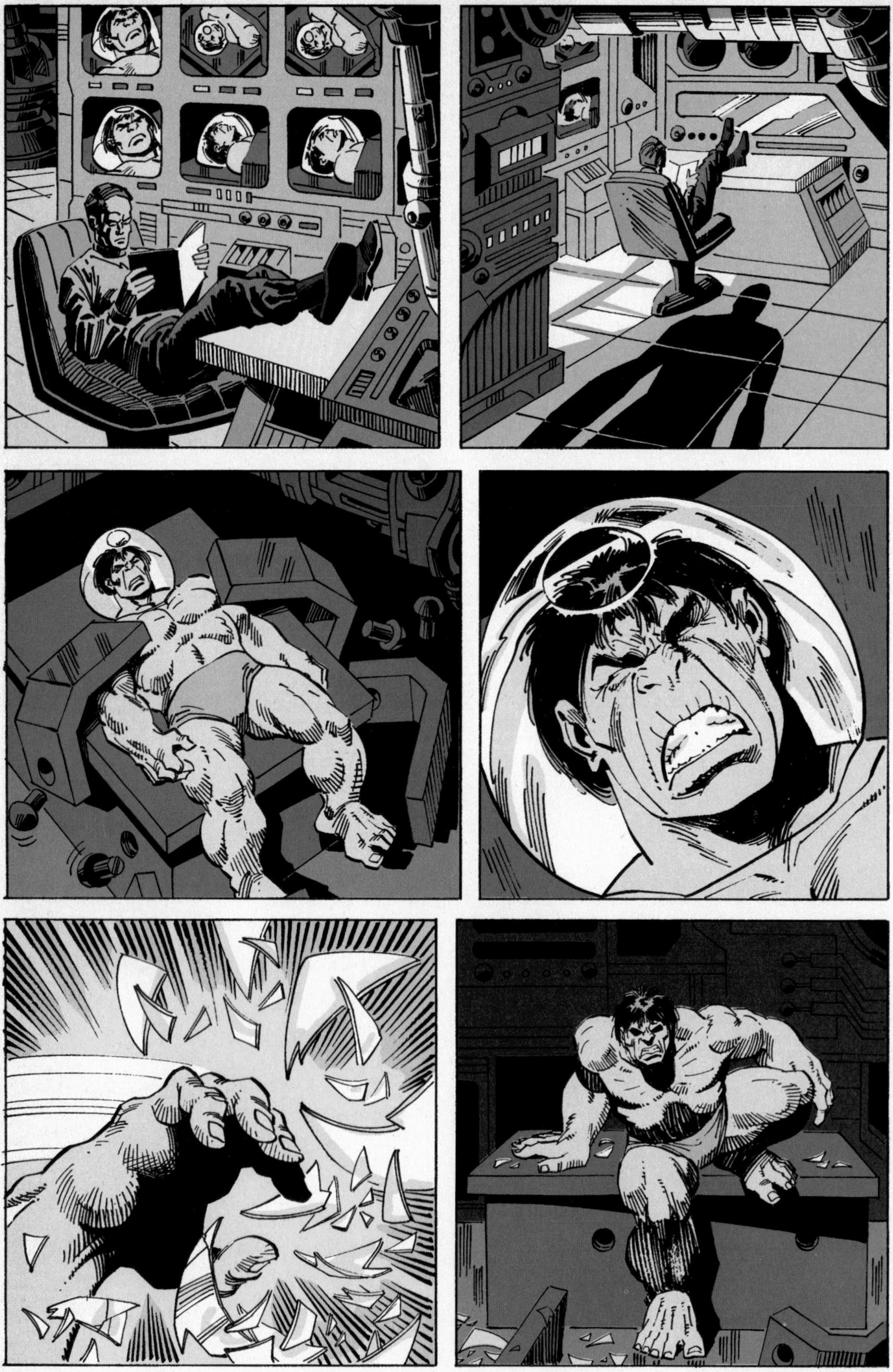

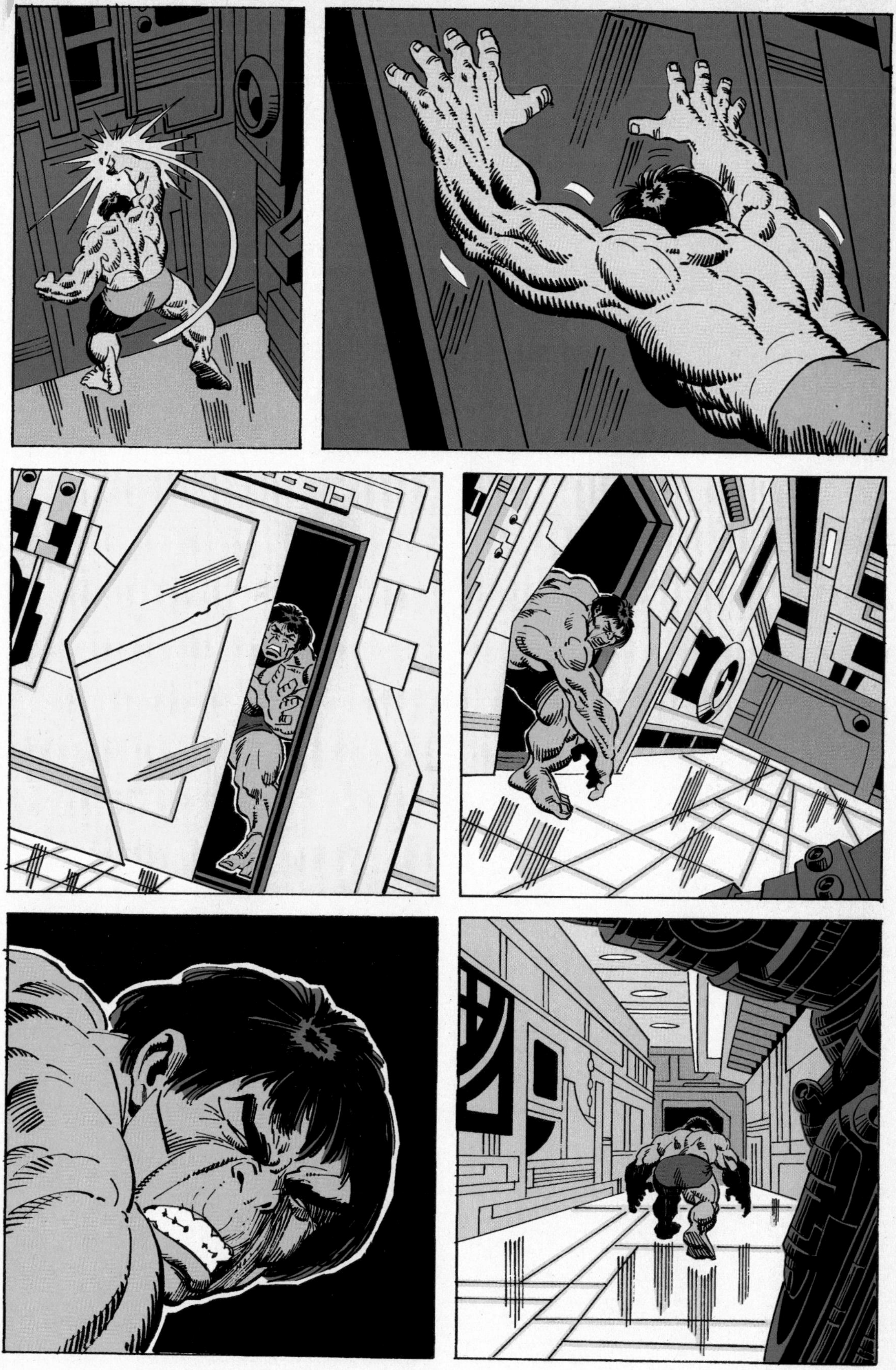

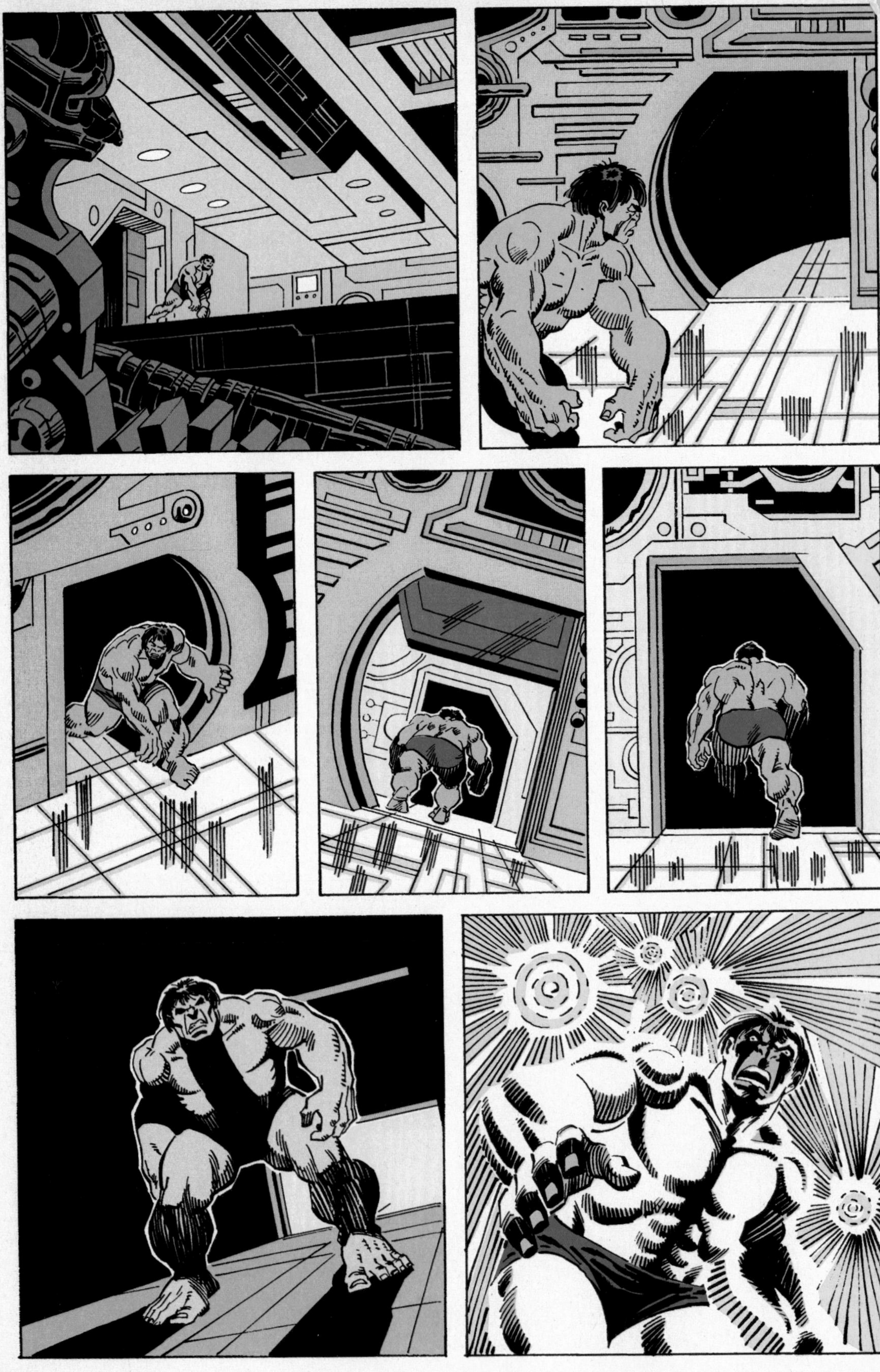

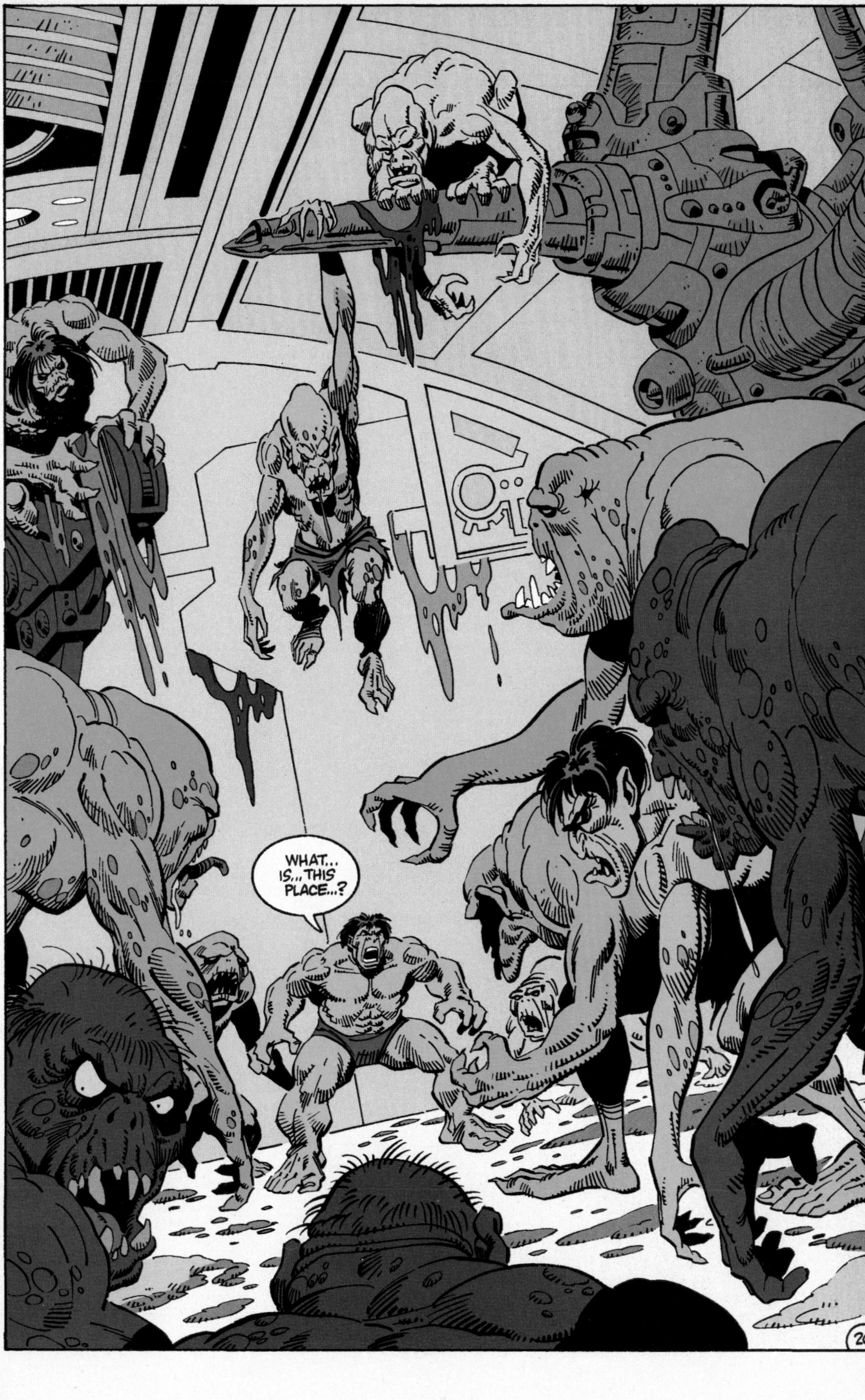
WHAT... IS... THIS PLACE...?
20

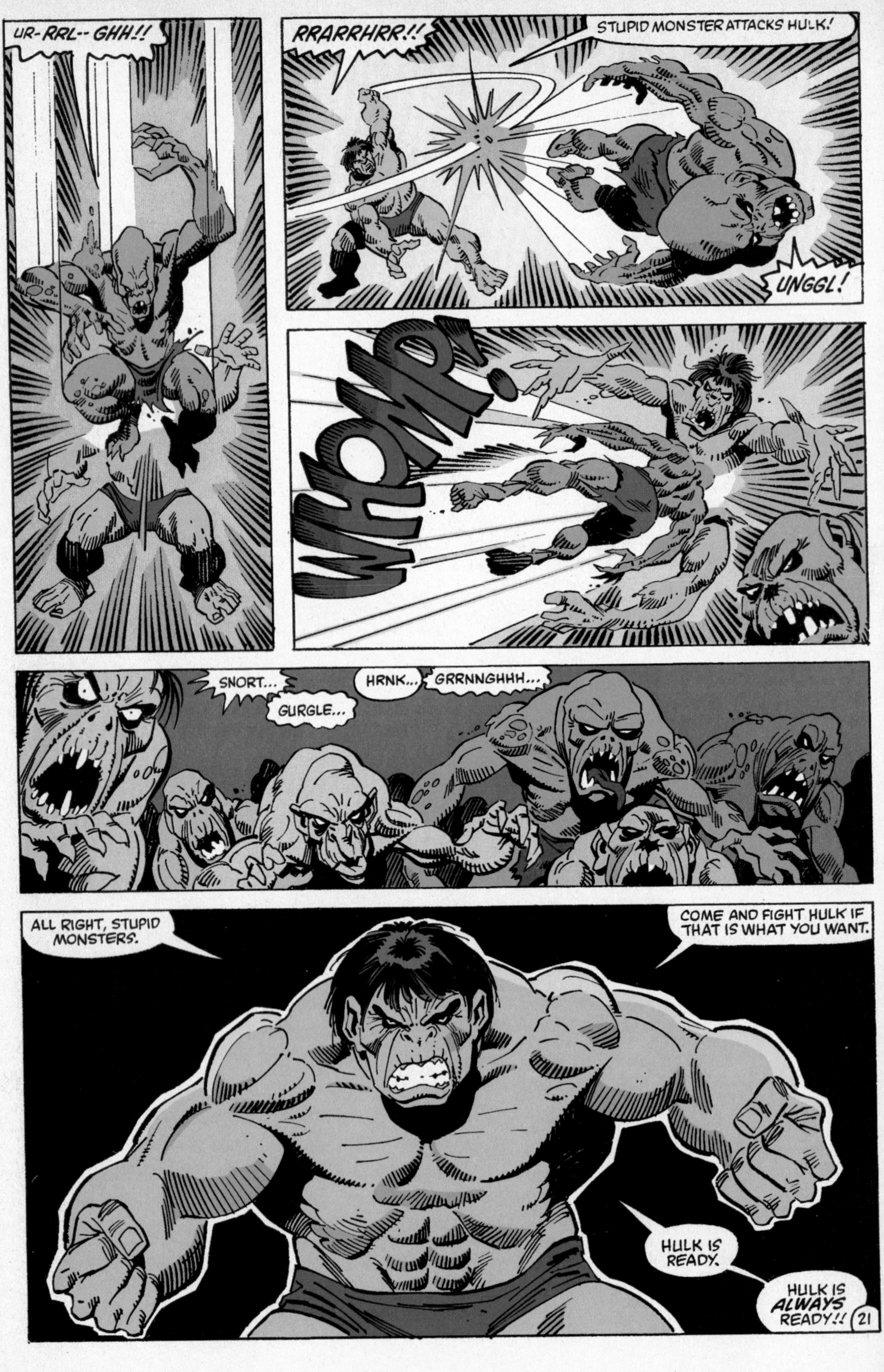

UR-RRL-- GHH!!
RRARRHRR!!
STUPID MONSTER ATTACKS HULK!
UNGGL!
WHOMP!
SNORT...
GURGLE...
HRNK...
GRRNNGHHH...
ALL RIGHT, STUPID MONSTERS.
COME AND FIGHT HULK IF THAT IS WHAT YOU WANT.
HULK IS READY.
HULK IS ALWAYS READY!!
21

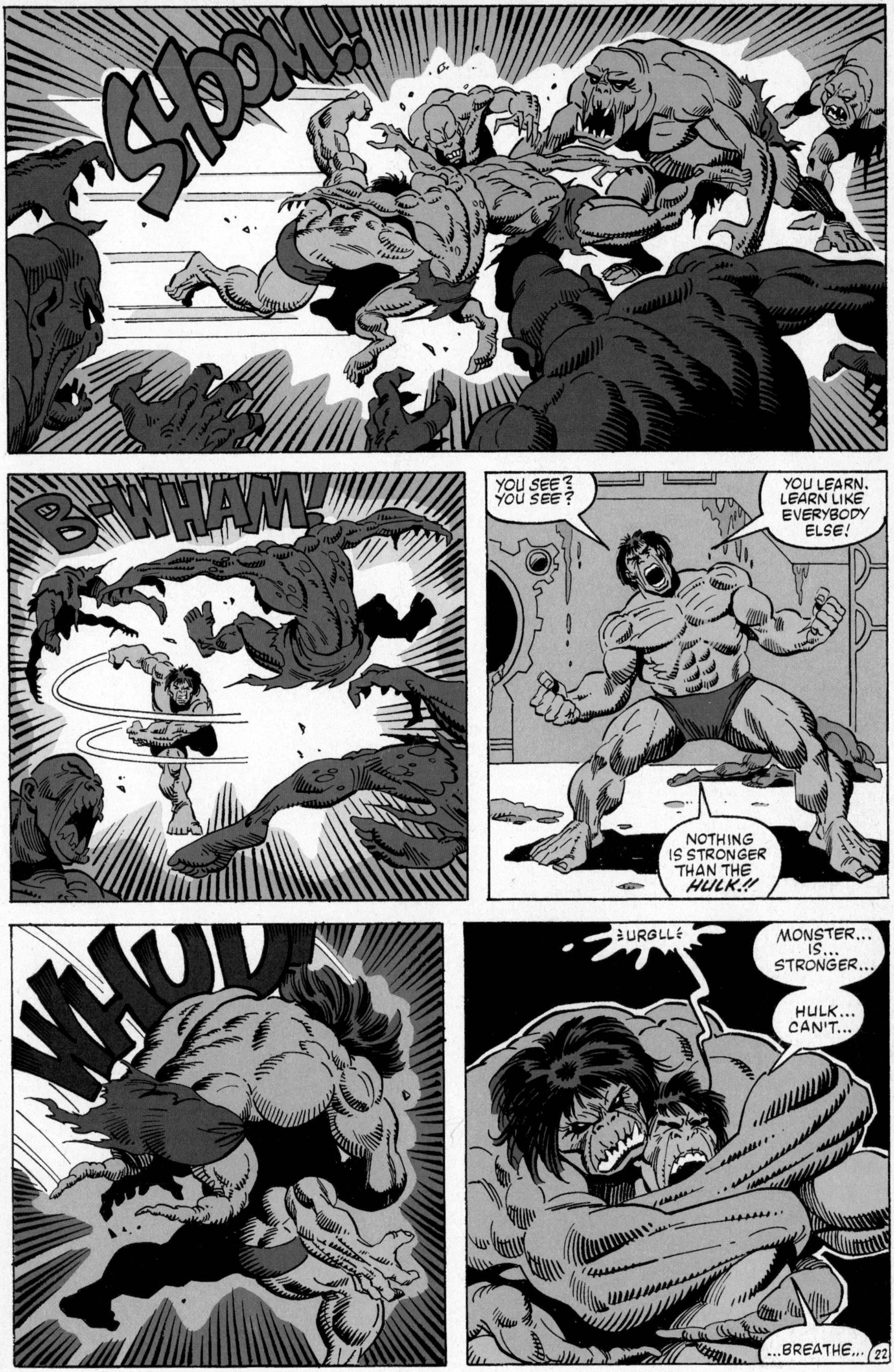
SHOOM!!
B-WHAM!
YOU SEE? YOU SEE?
YOU LEARN. LEARN LIKE EVERYBODY ELSE!
NOTHING IS STRONGER THAN THE HULK!!
WHUD
URGLL
MONSTER... IS... STRONGER...
HULK... CAN'T...
...BREATHE...
22

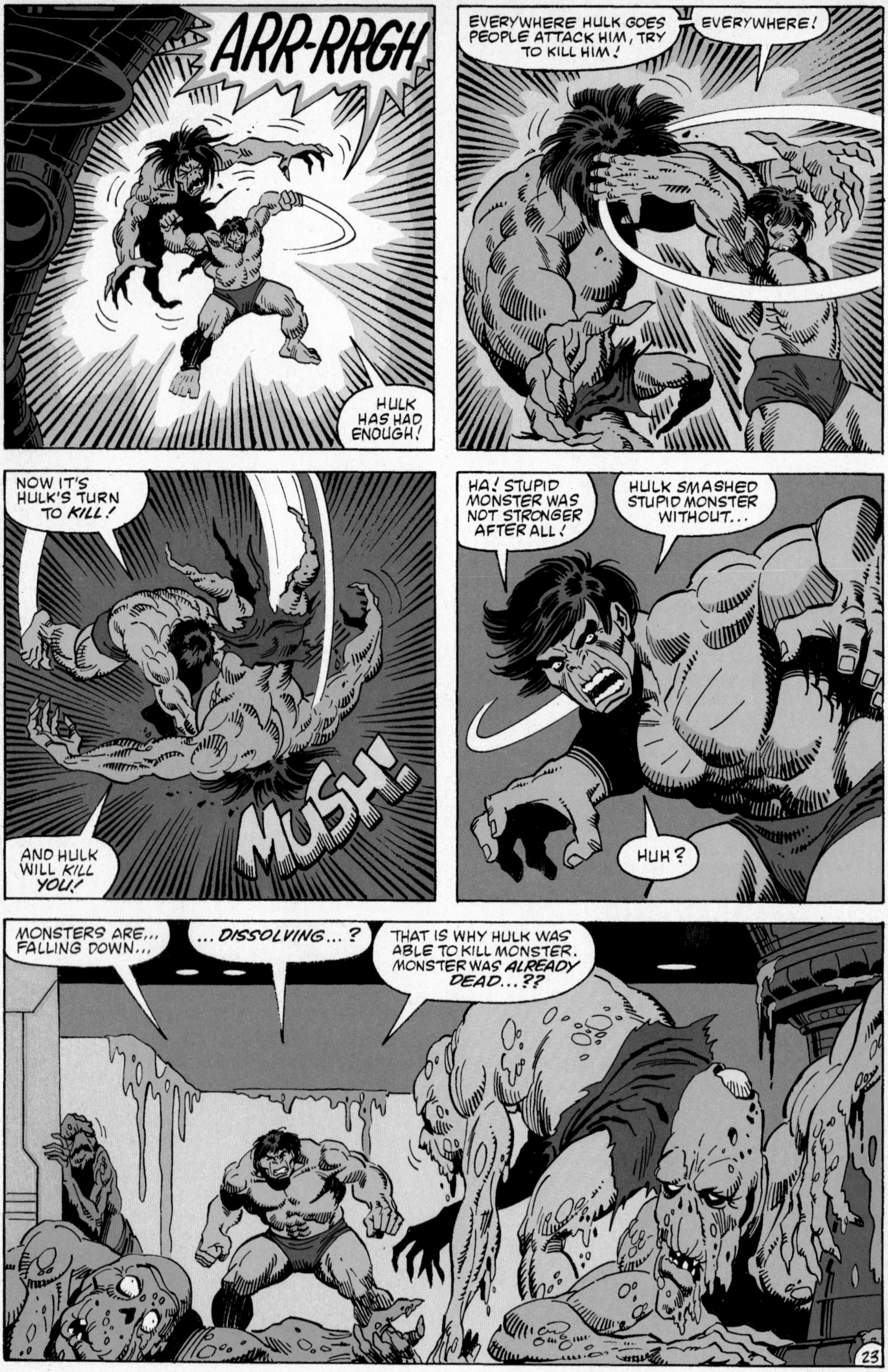
ARR-RRGH
HULK HAS HAD ENOUGH!
EVERYWHERE HULK GOES PEOPLE ATTACK HIM, TRY TO KILL HIM!
EVERYWHERE!
NOW IT'S HULK'S TURN TO KILL!
MUSH!
AND HULK WILL KILL YOU!
HA! STUPID MONSTER WAS NOT STRONGER AFTER ALL!
HULK SMASHED STUPID MONSTER WITHOUT...
HUH?
MONSTERS ARE... FALLING DOWN...
...DISSOLVING...?
THAT IS WHY HULK WAS ABLE TO KILL MONSTER. MONSTER WAS ALREADY DEAD...??
23

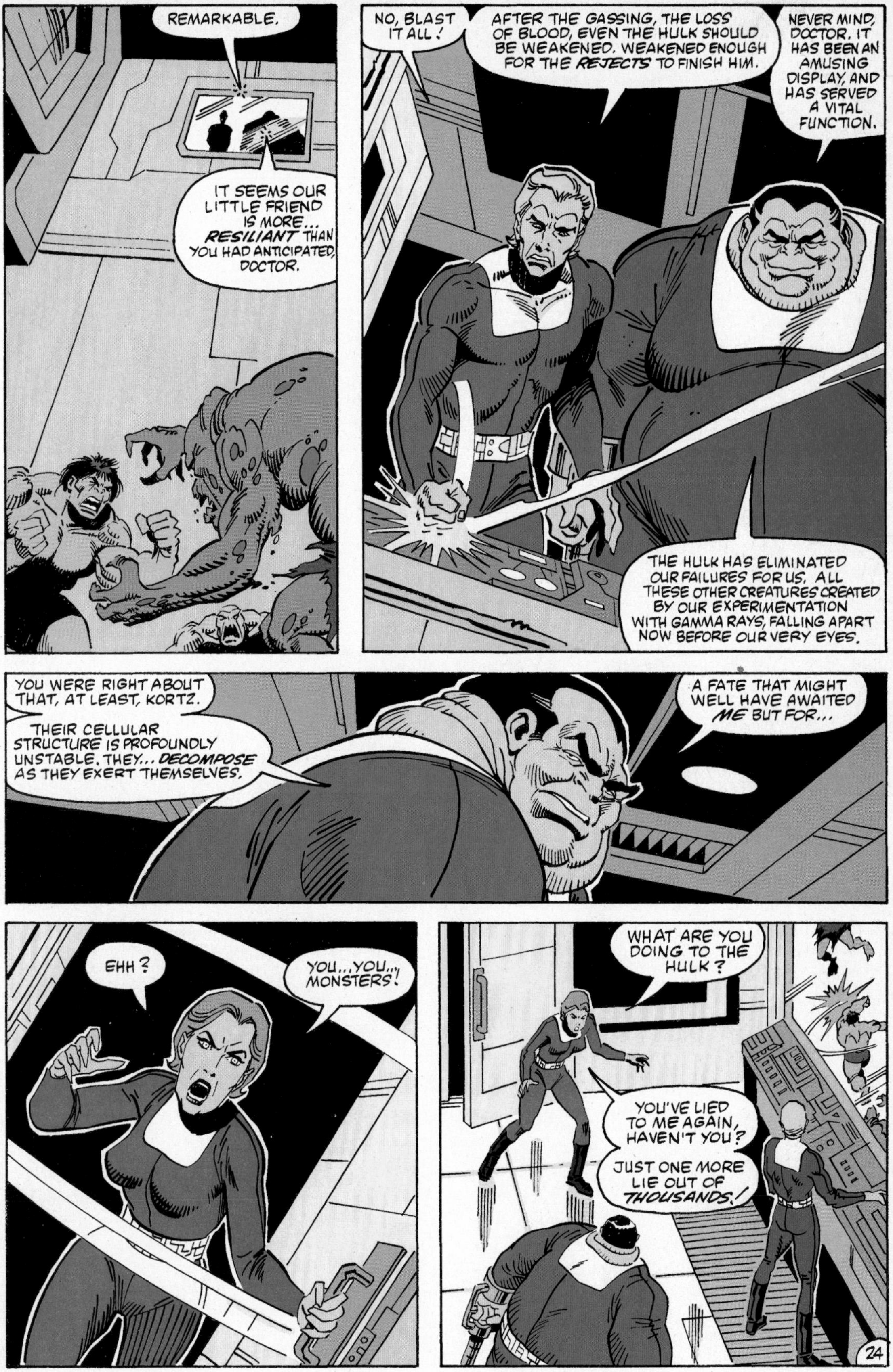
REMARKABLE.
IT SEEMS OUR LITTLE FRIEND IS MORE... RESILIANT THAN YOU HAD ANTICIPATED, DOCTOR.
NO, BLAST IT ALL!
AFTER THE GASSING, THE LOSS OF BLOOD, EVEN THE HULK SHOULD BE WEAKENED. WEAKENED ENOUGH FOR THE REJECTS TO FINISH HIM.
NEVER MIND, DOCTOR. IT HAS BEEN AN AMUSING DISPLAY, AND HAS SERVED A VITAL FUNCTION.
THE HULK HAS ELIMINATED OUR FAILURES FOR US. ALL THESE OTHER CREATURES CREATED BY OUR EXPERIMENTATION WITH GAMMA RAYS, FALLING APART NOW BEFORE OUR VERY EYES.
YOU WERE RIGHT ABOUT THAT, AT LEAST, KORTZ.
THEIR CELLULAR STRUCTURE IS PROFOUNDLY UNSTABLE. THEY... DECOMPOSE AS THEY EXERT THEMSELVES.
A FATE THAT MIGHT WELL HAVE AWAITED ME BUT FOR...
EHH?
YOU... YOU... MONSTERS!
WHAT ARE YOU DOING TO THE HULK?
YOU'VE LIED TO ME AGAIN, HAVEN'T YOU?
JUST ONE MORE LIE OUT OF THOUSANDS!
24

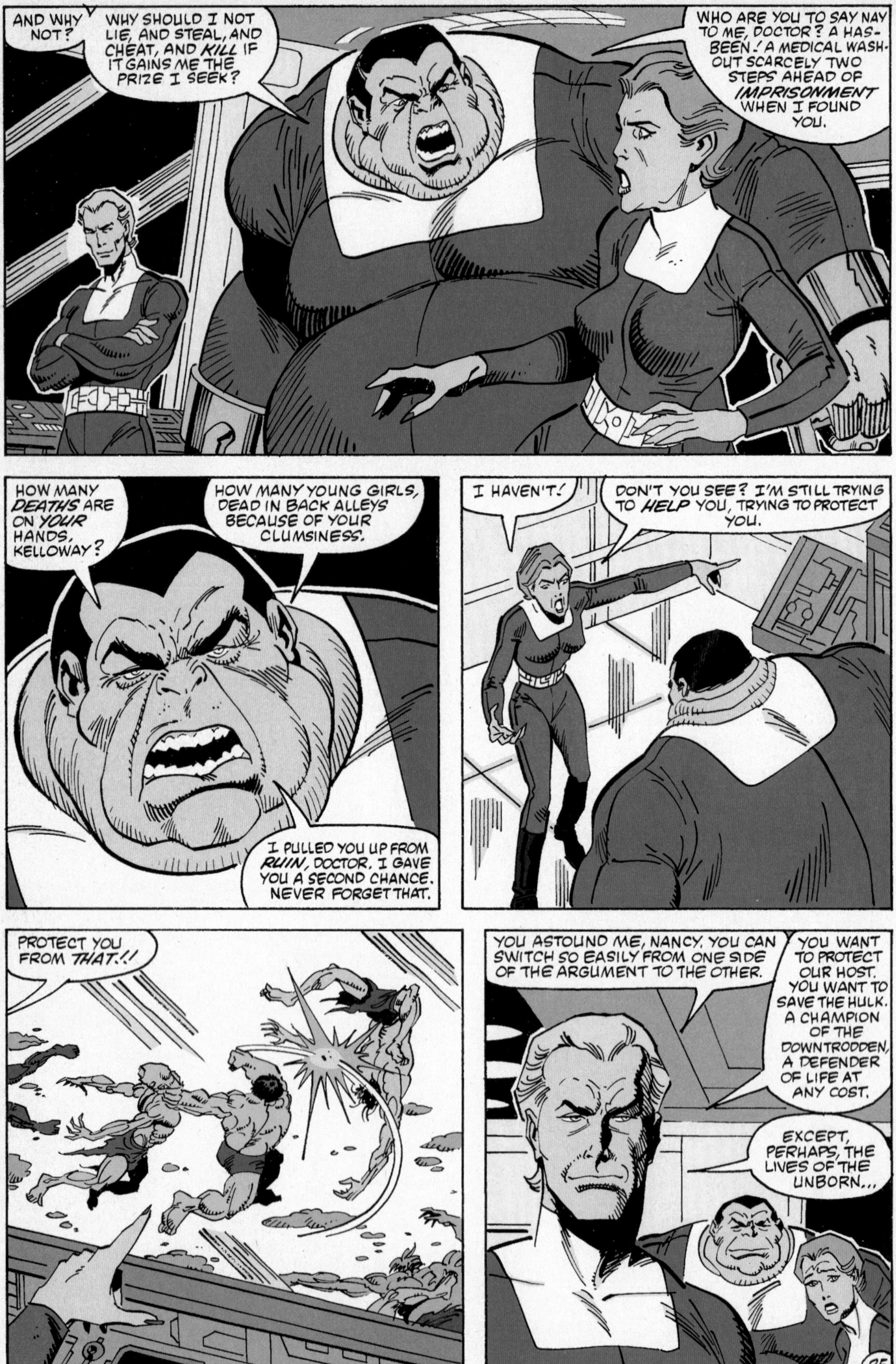
AND WHY NOT?
WHY SHOULD I NOT LIE, AND STEAL, AND CHEAT, AND KILL IF IT GAINS ME THE PRIZE I SEEK?
WHO ARE YOU TO SAY NAY TO ME, DOCTOR? A HAS-BEEN! A MEDICAL WASH-OUT SCARCELY TWO STEPS AHEAD OF IMPRISONMENT WHEN I FOUND YOU.
HOW MANY DEATHS ARE ON YOUR HANDS, KELLOWAY?
HOW MANY YOUNG GIRLS, DEAD IN BACK ALLEYS BECAUSE OF YOUR CLUMSINESS.
I PULLED YOU UP FROM RUIN, DOCTOR. I GAVE YOU A SECOND CHANCE. NEVER FORGET THAT.
I HAVEN'T!
DON'T YOU SEE? I'M STILL TRYING TO HELP YOU, TRYING TO PROTECT YOU.
PROTECT YOU FROM THAT!!!
YOU ASTOUND ME, NANCY. YOU CAN SWITCH SO EASILY FROM ONE SIDE OF THE ARGUMENT TO THE OTHER.
YOU WANT TO PROTECT OUR HOST. YOU WANT TO SAVE THE HULK. A CHAMPION OF THE DOWNTRODDEN, A DEFENDER OF LIFE AT ANY COST.
EXCEPT, PERHAPS, THE LIVES OF THE UNBORN...
25

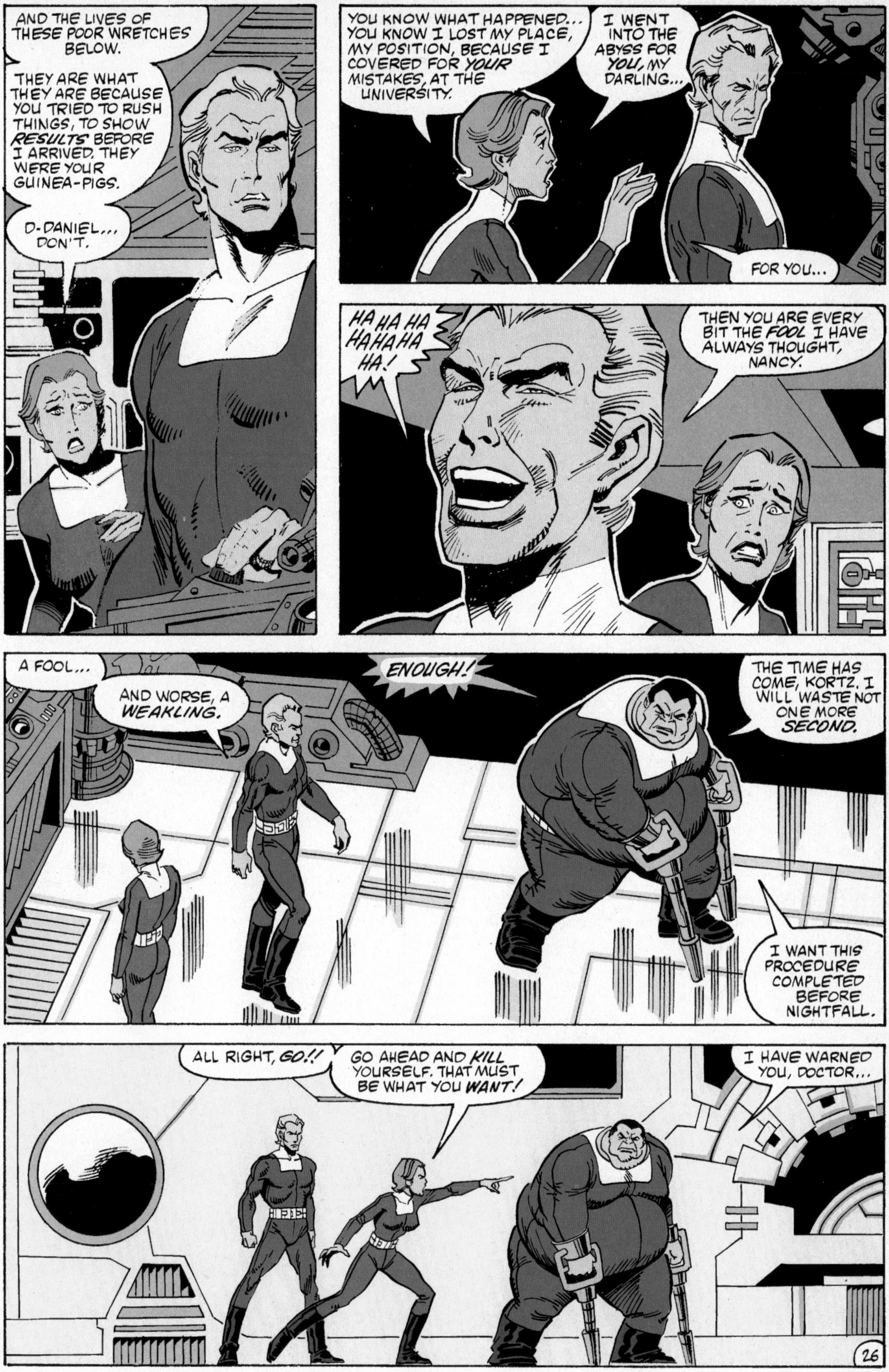
AND THE LIVES OF THESE POOR WRETCHES BELOW.
THEY ARE WHAT THEY ARE BECAUSE YOU TRIED TO RUSH THINGS, TO SHOW RESULTS BEFORE I ARRIVED. THEY WERE YOUR GUINEA-PIGS.
D-DANIEL... DON'T.
YOU KNOW WHAT HAPPENED... YOU KNOW I LOST MY PLACE, MY POSITION, BECAUSE I COVERED FOR YOUR MISTAKES, AT THE UNIVERSITY.
I WENT INTO THE ABYSS FOR YOU, MY DARLING...
FOR YOU...
HA HA HA HAHAHA HA!
THEN YOU ARE EVERY BIT THE FOOL I HAVE ALWAYS THOUGHT, NANCY.
A FOOL...
AND WORSE, A WEAKLING.
ENOUGH!
THE TIME HAS COME, KORTZ. I WILL WASTE NOT ONE MORE SECOND.
I WANT THIS PROCEDURE COMPLETED BEFORE NIGHTFALL.
ALL RIGHT, GO!!
GO AHEAD AND KILL YOURSELF. THAT MUST BE WHAT YOU WANT!
I HAVE WARNED YOU, DOCTOR...
26

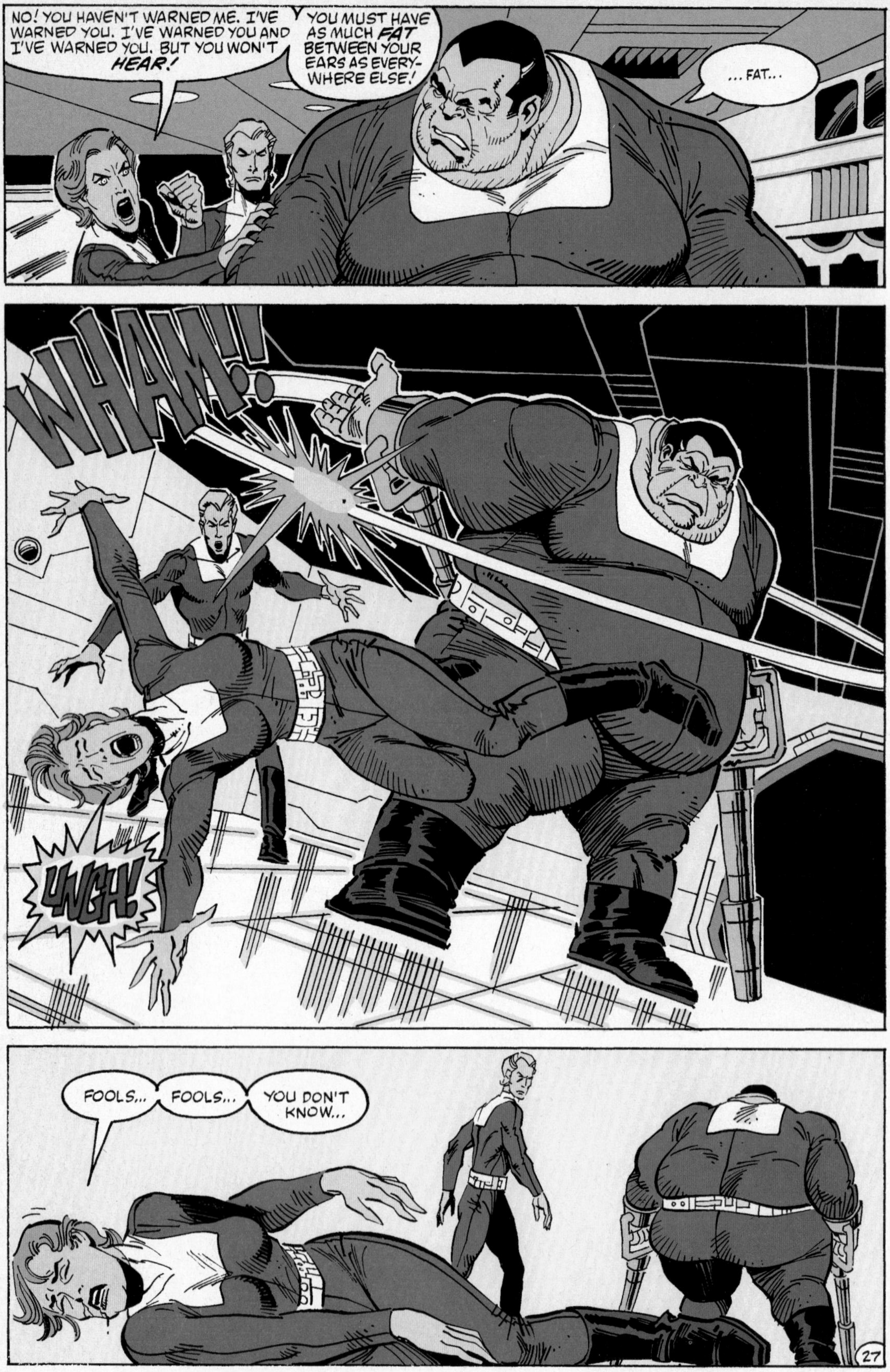
NO! YOU HAVEN'T WARNED ME. I'VE WARNED YOU. I'VE WARNED YOU AND I'VE WARNED YOU. BUT YOU WON'T HEAR!
YOU MUST HAVE AS MUCH FAT BETWEEN YOUR EARS AS EVERY-WHERE ELSE!
...FAT...
WHAM!!
UNGH!
FOOLS...
FOOLS...
YOU DON'T KNOW...
27

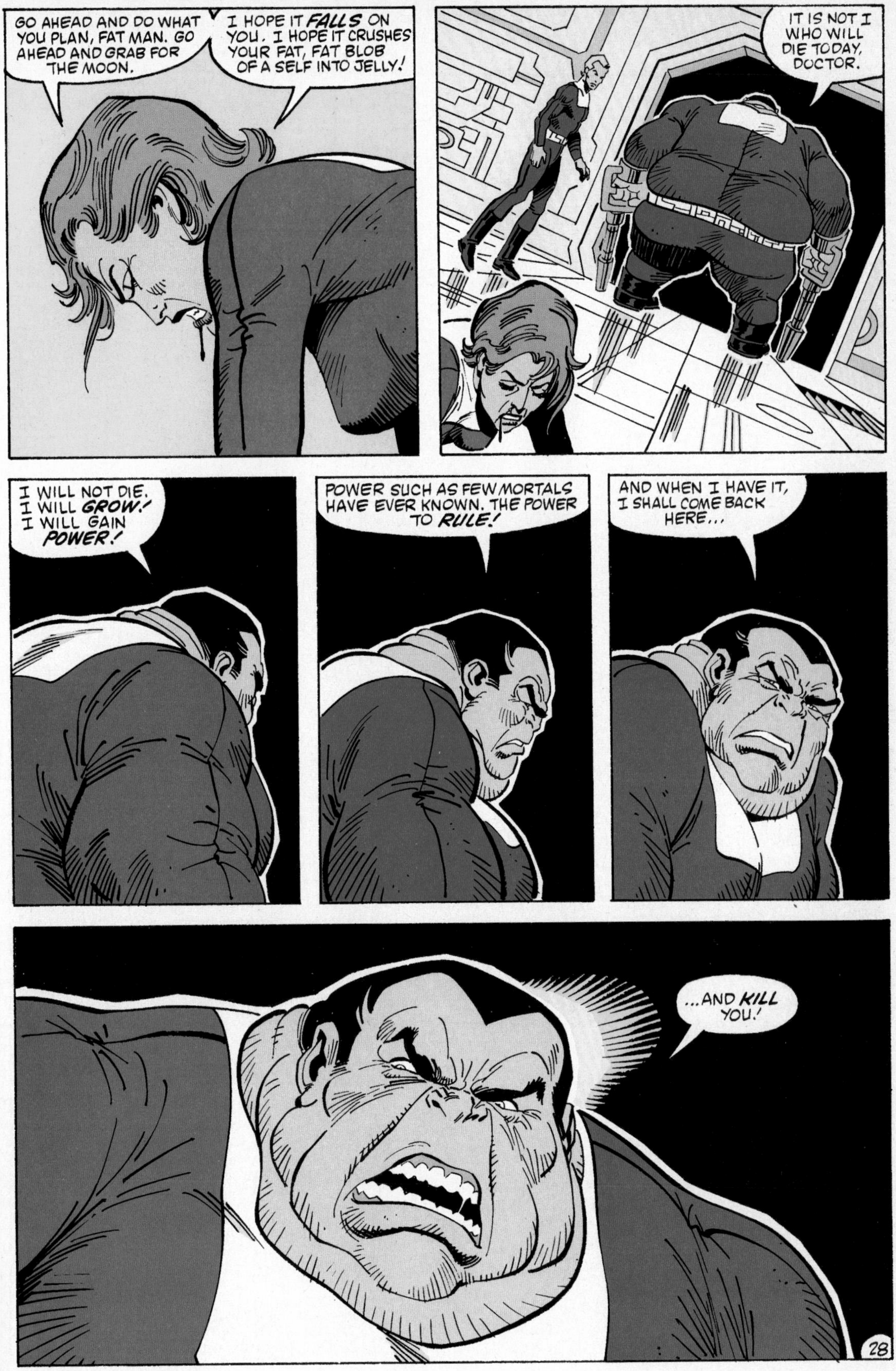
GO AHEAD AND DO WHAT YOU PLAN, FAT MAN. GO AHEAD AND GRAB FOR THE MOON.
I HOPE IT FALLS ON YOU. I HOPE IT CRUSHES YOUR FAT, FAT BLOB OF A SELF INTO JELLY!
IT IS NOT I WHO WILL DIE TODAY, DOCTOR.
I WILL NOT DIE. I WILL GROW! I WILL GAIN POWER!
POWER SUCH AS FEW MORTALS HAVE EVER KNOWN. THE POWER TO RULE!
AND WHEN I HAVE IT, I SHALL COME BACK HERE...
...AND KILL YOU!
28

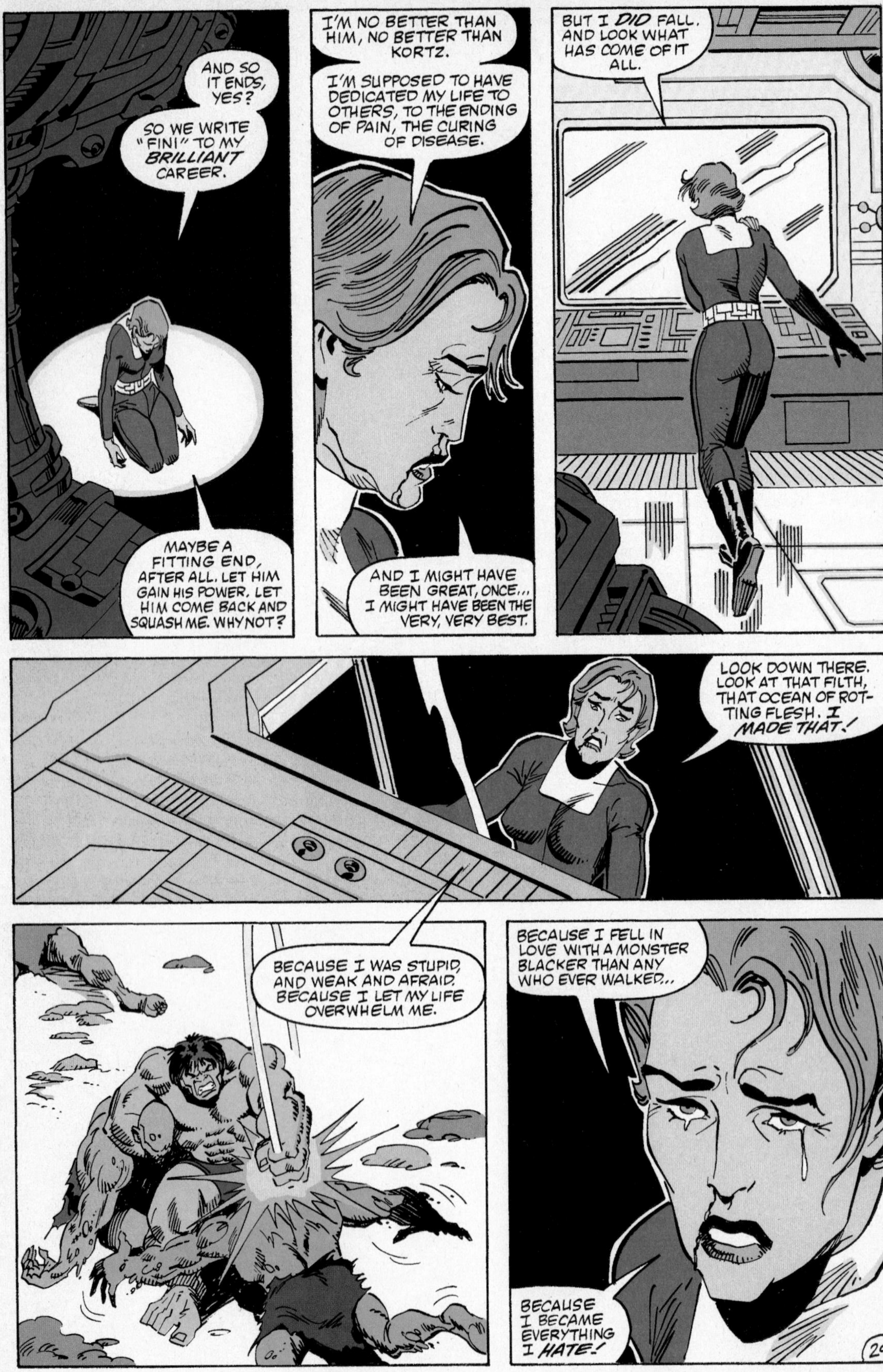
AND SO IT ENDS, YES?
SO WE WRITE "FINI" TO MY BRILLIANT CAREER.
MAYBE A FITTING END, AFTER ALL. LET HIM GAIN HIS POWER. LET HIM COME BACK AND SQUASH ME. WHY NOT?
I'M NO BETTER THAN HIM, NO BETTER THAN KORTZ.
I'M SUPPOSED TO HAVE DEDICATED MY LIFE TO OTHERS, TO THE ENDING OF PAIN, THE CURING OF DISEASE.
AND I MIGHT HAVE BEEN GREAT, ONCE... I MIGHT HAVE BEEN THE VERY, VERY BEST.
BUT I DID FALL. AND LOOK WHAT HAS COME OF IT ALL.
LOOK DOWN THERE. LOOK AT THAT FILTH, THAT OCEAN OF ROTTING FLESH. I MADE THAT!
BECAUSE I WAS STUPID, AND WEAK AND AFRAID. BECAUSE I LET MY LIFE OVERWHELM ME.
BECAUSE I FELL IN LOVE WITH A MONSTER BLACKER THAN ANY WHO EVER WALKED...
BECAUSE I BECAME EVERYTHING I HATE!
29

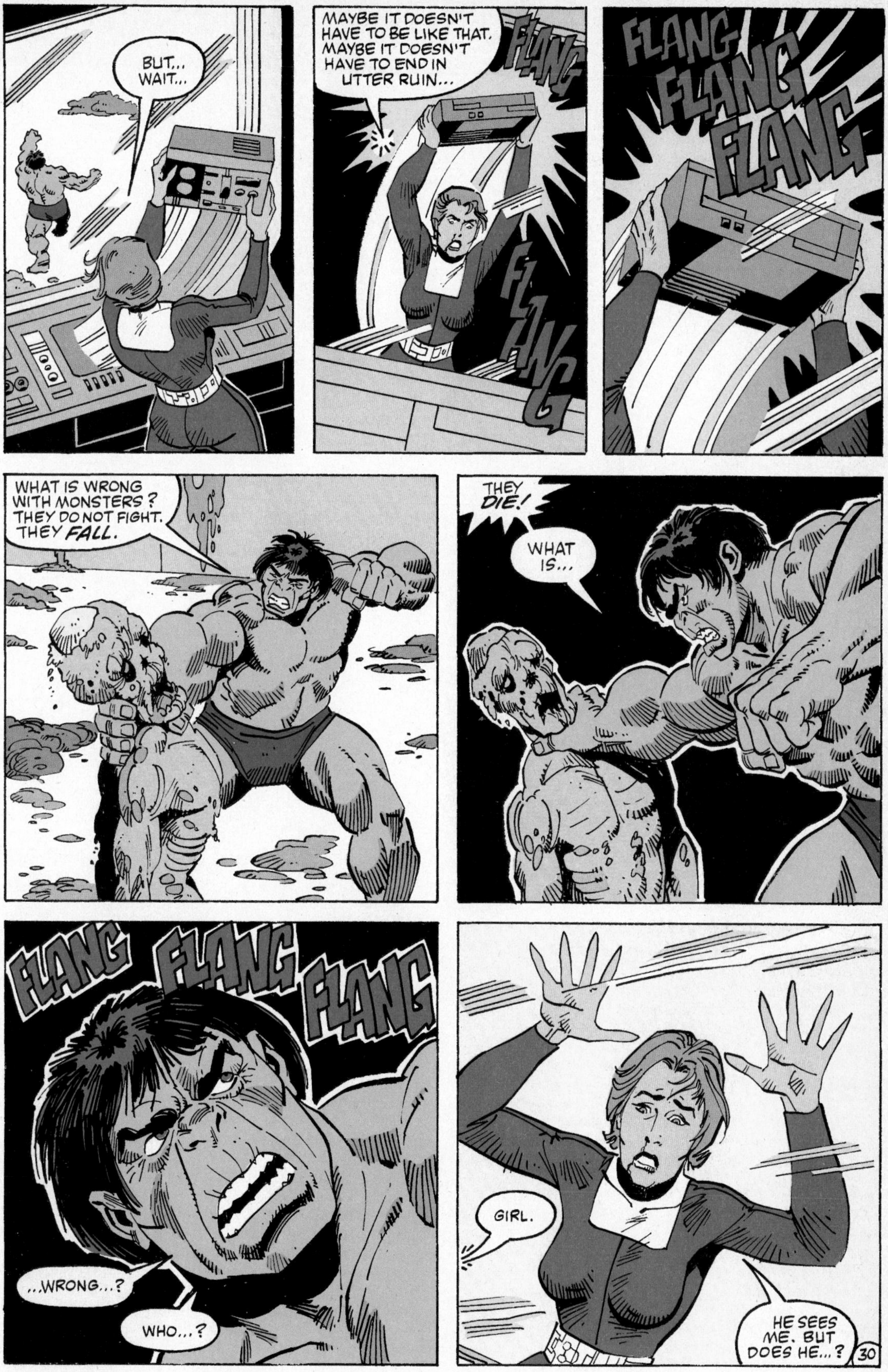
BUT... WAIT...
MAYBE IT DOESN'T HAVE TO BE LIKE THAT. MAYBE IT DOESN'T HAVE TO END IN UTTER RUIN...
FLANG
FLANG
FLANG FLANG FLANG
WHAT IS WRONG WITH MONSTERS? THEY DO NOT FIGHT. THEY FALL.
THEY DIE!
WHAT IS...
FLANG FLANG FLANG
...WRONG...?
WHO...?
GIRL.
HE SEES ME. BUT DOES HE...?
30

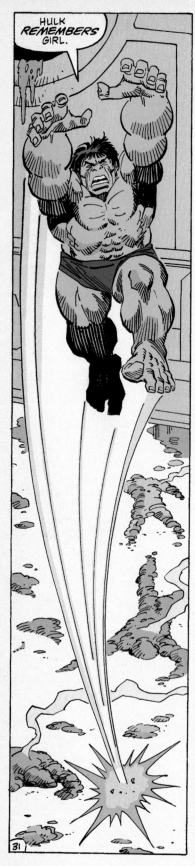

HULK *REMEMBERS* GIRL.

I THINK IT'S GOING TO...

CRUNCH!

...WORK...

SK-RASH!

GIRL...

HULK... *REMEMBERS* YOU...

YOU WERE...

...*FRIEND...?*

YES! OH, YES!

I'M YOUR *FRIEND*, HULK. I TRIED TO *HELP* YOU.

HELP.. HULK...

YES, AND NOW... I NEED YOU TO HELP *ME*...

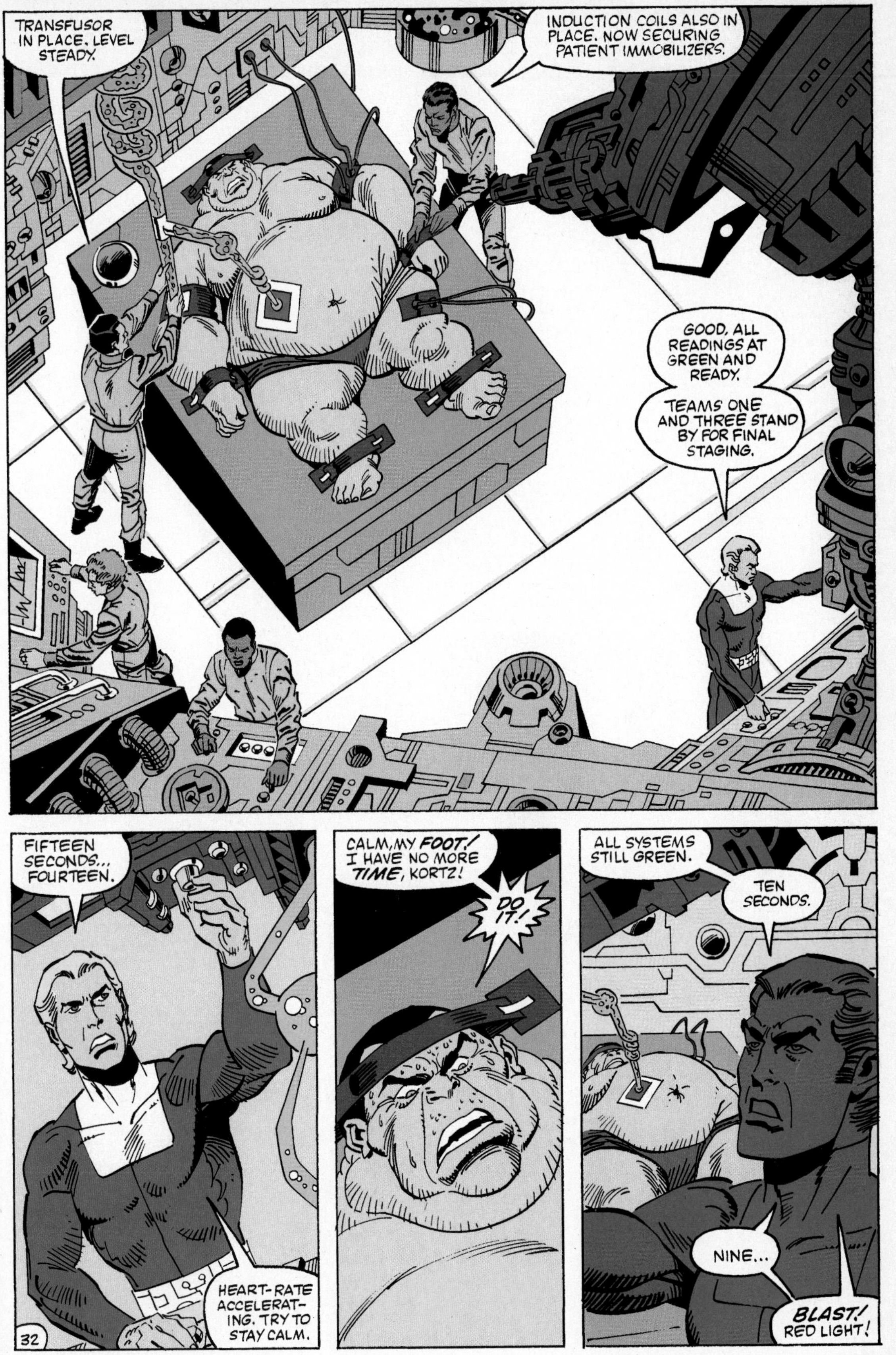
TRANSFUSOR IN PLACE. LEVEL STEADY.
INDUCTION COILS ALSO IN PLACE. NOW SECURING PATIENT IMMOBILIZERS.
GOOD, ALL READINGS AT GREEN AND READY.
TEAMS ONE AND THREE STAND BY FOR FINAL STAGING.
FIFTEEN SECONDS... FOURTEEN.
HEART-RATE ACCELERATING. TRY TO STAY CALM.
32
CALM, MY FOOT! I HAVE NO MORE TIME, KORTZ!
DO IT!
ALL SYSTEMS STILL GREEN.
TEN SECONDS.
NINE...
BLAST! RED LIGHT!

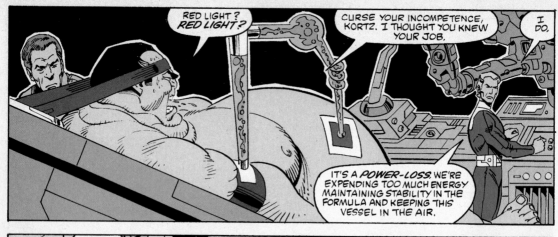

RED LIGHT? *RED LIGHT?*

CURSE YOUR INCOMPETENCE, KORTZ. I THOUGHT YOU KNEW YOUR JOB.

I DO.

IT'S A *POWER-LOSS*. WE'RE EXPENDING TOO MUCH ENERGY MAINTAINING STABILITY IN THE FORMULA AND KEEPING THIS VESSEL IN THE AIR.

THEN LAND!

DO I HAVE TO THINK OF EVERYTHING.

DON'T YOU HAVE EVEN THE GLIMMER OF A NOTION OF HOW LONG I HAVE WAITED FOR THIS MOMENT, KORTZ?

SINCE THE DAY IT WAS REVEALED TO THE WORLD THAT *BRUE BANNER* HAD BEEN TRANSFORMED INTO THE HULK. THAT WAS THE DAY I REALIZED WHAT HAD HAPPENED TO HIM WAS THE KEY TO MY PRISON OF FLESH.

ALL THESE LONG YEARS I HAVE WAITED, AND NOW YOU RISK *EVERYTHING* FOR THE SAKE OF A FEW *SECONDS!*

GET ON WITH IT, KORTZ!

THIS PROJECT HAS COST *BILLIONS* OF DOLLARS. *HUNDREDS* OF LIVES.

I'LL NOT SEE IT COST A SINGLE *NANO-SECOND* MORE!

AS YOU WISH.

TWENTY-ONE, OVER-RIDE CIRCUITS B-73 AND DG-18.

GET ME MAXIMUM POWER ON ALL SYSTEMS, *NOW!!*

YESSIR........

OVER-RIDING...

33

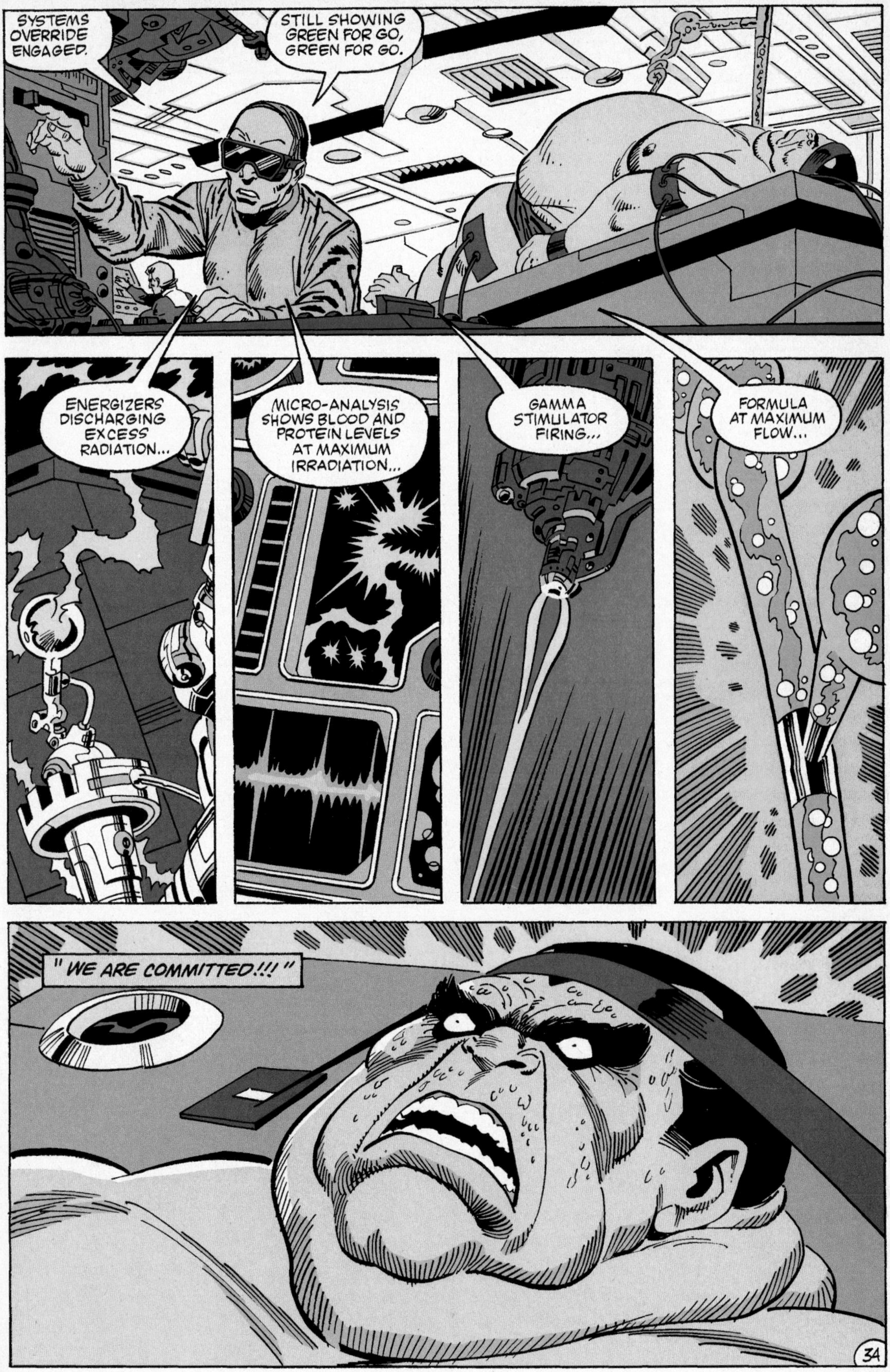
SYSTEMS OVERRIDE ENGAGED.
STILL SHOWING GREEN FOR GO, GREEN FOR GO.
ENERGIZERS DISCHARGING EXCESS RADIATION...
MICRO-ANALYSIS SHOWS BLOOD AND PROTEIN LEVELS AT MAXIMUM IRRADIATION...
GAMMA STIMULATOR FIRING...
FORMULA AT MAXIMUM FLOW...
"WE ARE COMMITTED!!!"
34

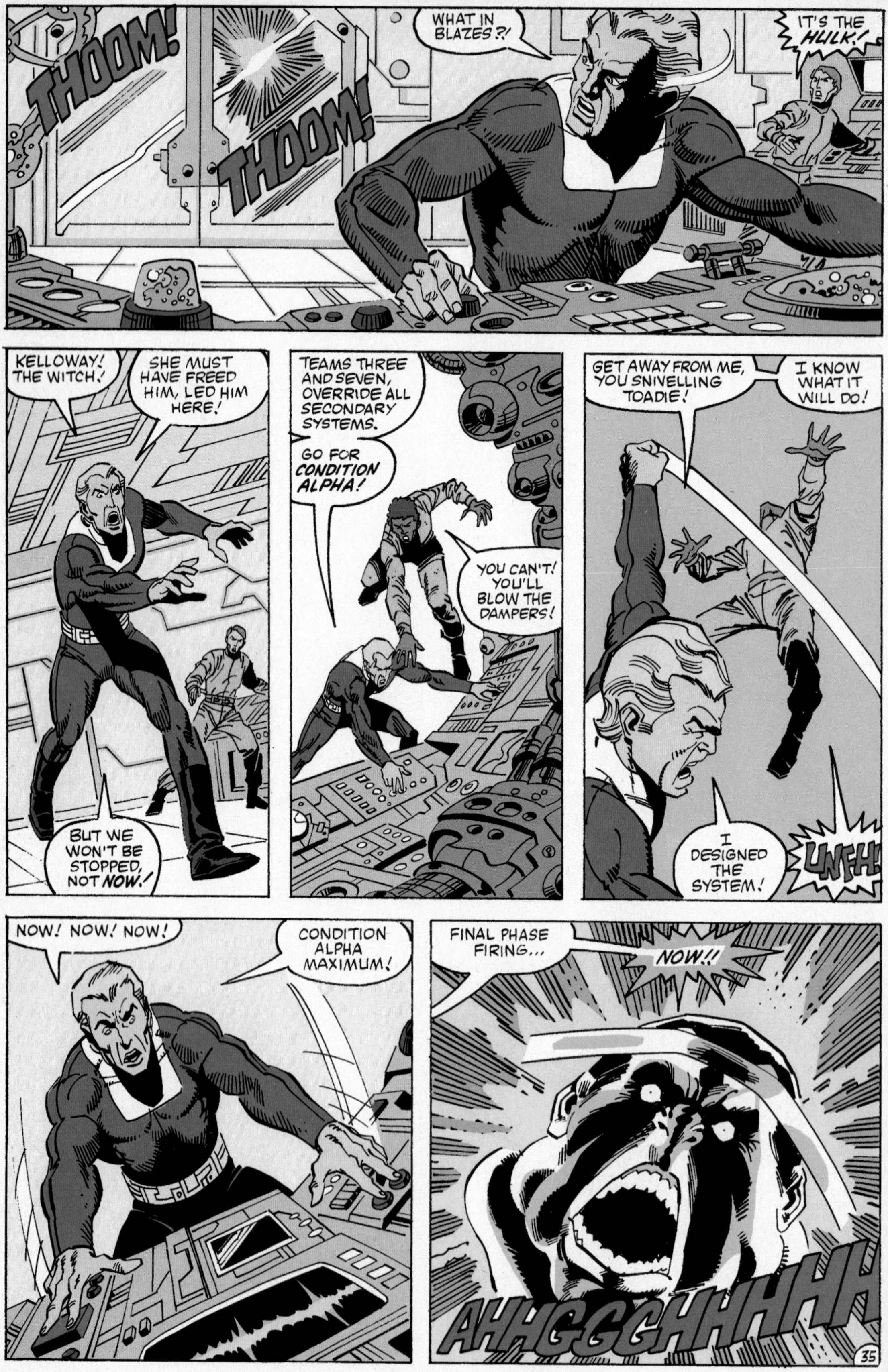
THOOM!
THOOM!
WHAT IN BLAZES ?!
IT'S THE HULK!
KELLOWAY! THE WITCH!
SHE MUST HAVE FREED HIM, LED HIM HERE!
BUT WE WON'T BE STOPPED, NOT NOW!
TEAMS THREE AND SEVEN, OVERRIDE ALL SECONDARY SYSTEMS.
GO FOR CONDITION ALPHA!
YOU CAN'T! YOU'LL BLOW THE DAMPERS!
GET AWAY FROM ME, YOU SNIVELLING TOADIE!
I KNOW WHAT IT WILL DO!
I DESIGNED THE SYSTEM!
UNH!
NOW! NOW! NOW!
CONDITION ALPHA MAXIMUM!
FINAL PHASE FIRING...
NOW!!
AHHGGGHHHHH
35

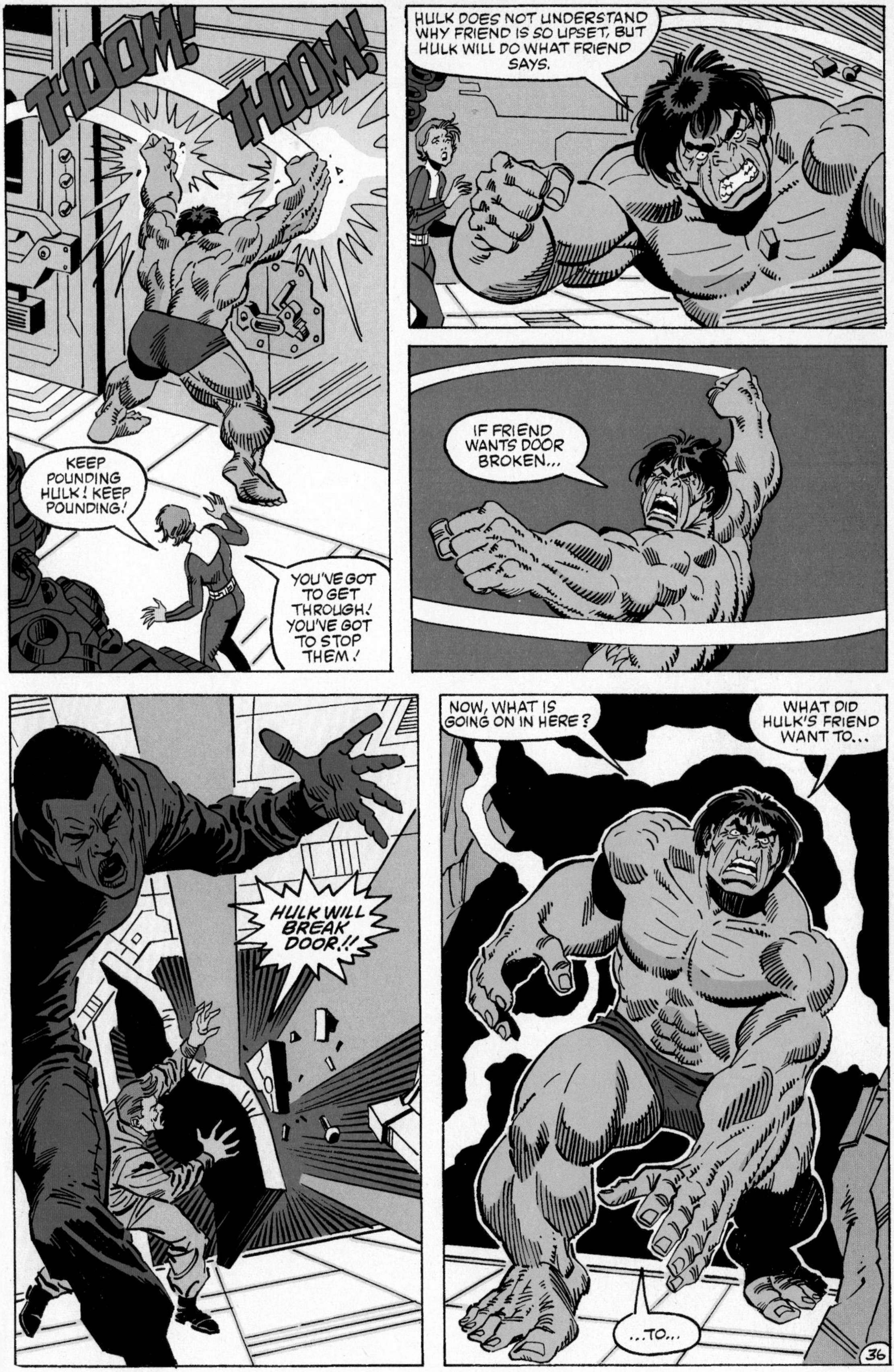
THOOM!
THOOM!
KEEP POUNDING HULK! KEEP POUNDING!
YOU'VE GOT TO GET THROUGH! YOU'VE GOT TO STOP THEM!
HULK DOES NOT UNDERSTAND WHY FRIEND IS SO UPSET, BUT HULK WILL DO WHAT FRIEND SAYS.
IF FRIEND WANTS DOOR BROKEN...
HULK WILL BREAK DOOR!!
NOW, WHAT IS GOING ON IN HERE?
WHAT DID HULK'S FRIEND WANT TO...
...TO...
36

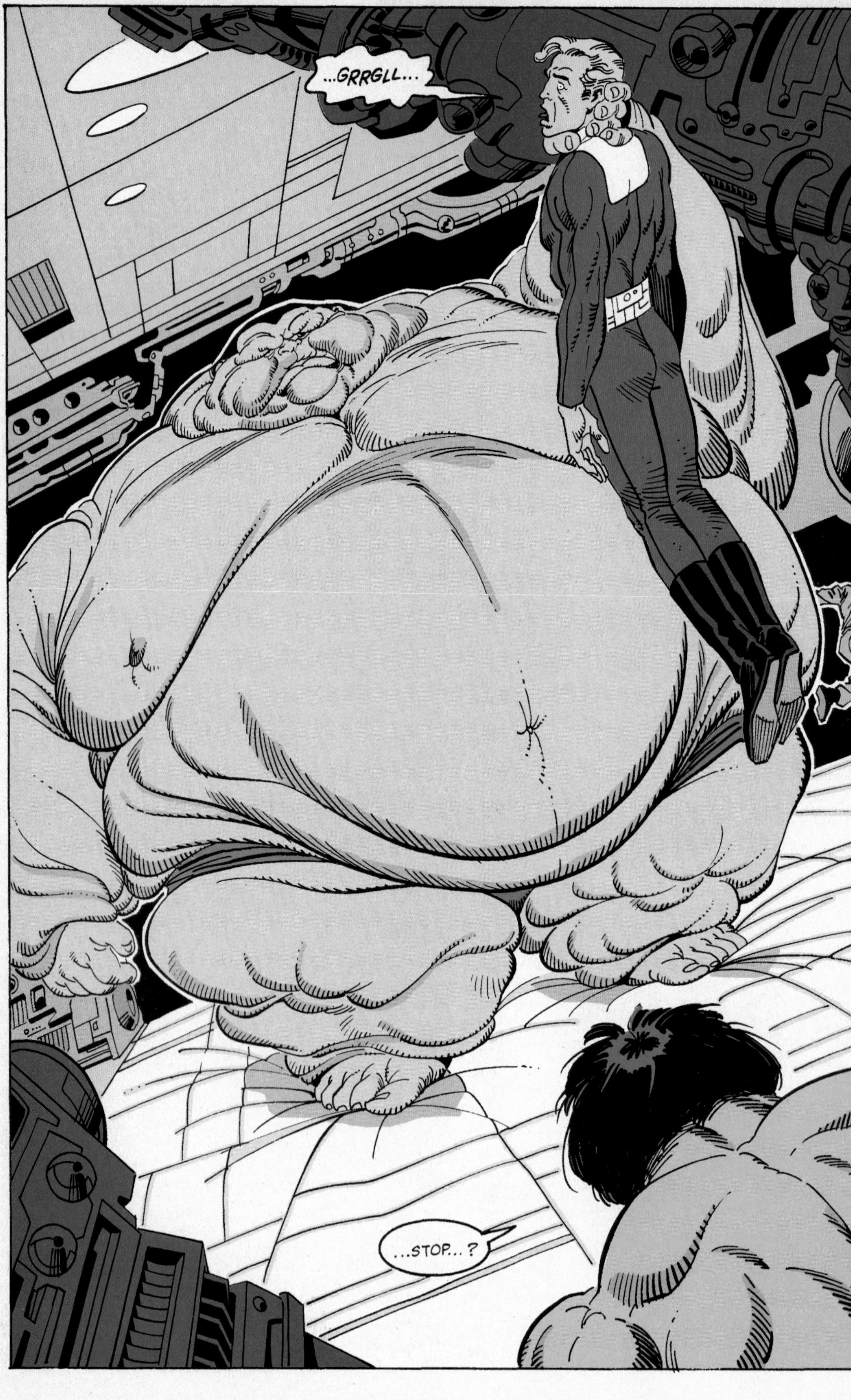
...GRRGLL...
...STOP...?
37

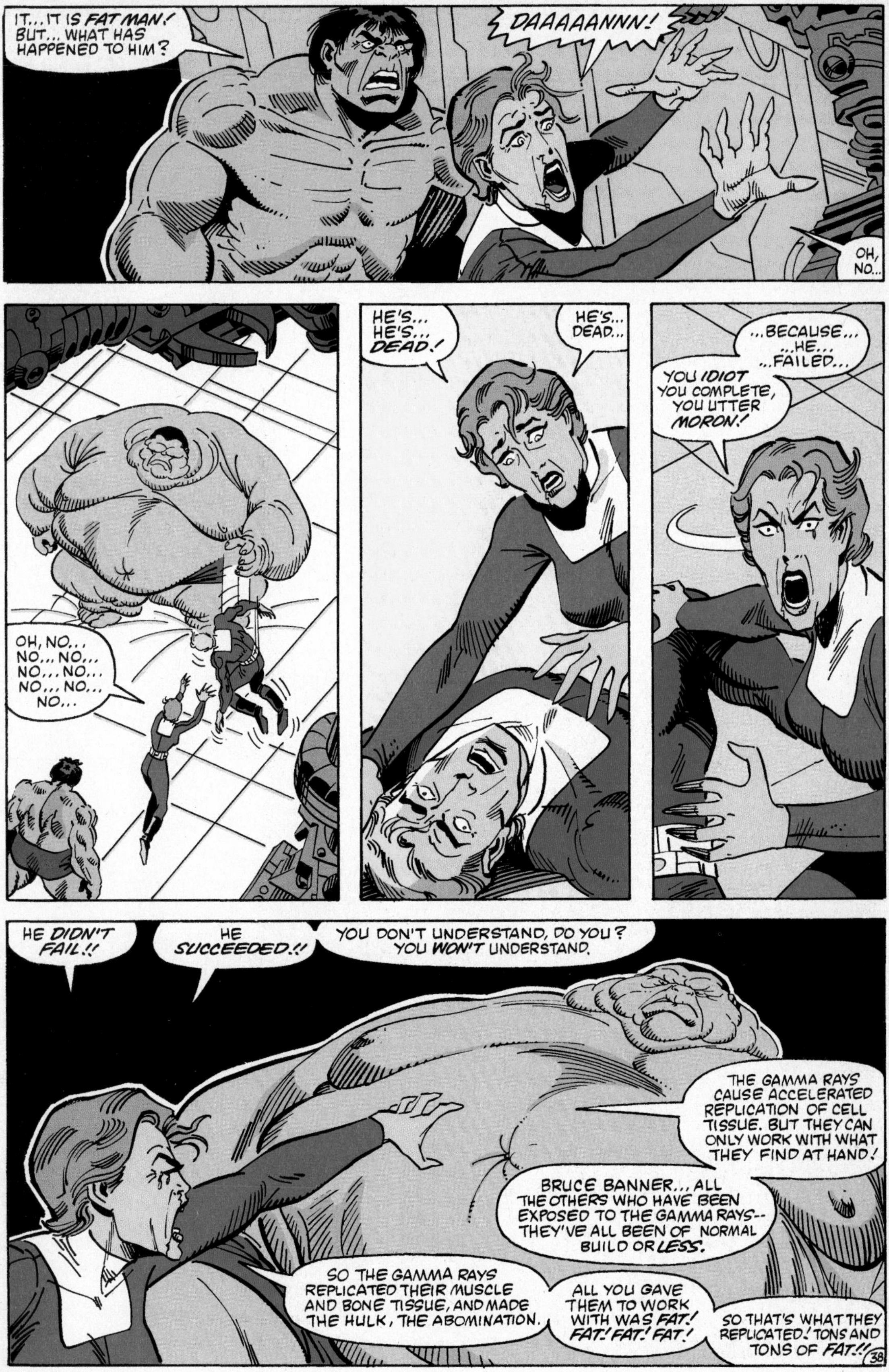
IT... IT IS FAT MAN! BUT... WHAT HAS HAPPENED TO HIM?
DAAAAAANNN!
OH, NO...
OH, NO... NO... NO... NO... NO... NO... NO... NO...
HE'S... HE'S... DEAD!
HE'S... DEAD...
...BECAUSE... ...HE... ...FAILED...
YOU IDIOT YOU COMPLETE, YOU UTTER MORON!
HE DIDN'T FAIL!!
HE SUCCEEDED!!
YOU DON'T UNDERSTAND, DO YOU? YOU WON'T UNDERSTAND.
THE GAMMA RAYS CAUSE ACCELERATED REPLICATION OF CELL TISSUE. BUT THEY CAN ONLY WORK WITH WHAT THEY FIND AT HAND!
BRUCE BANNER... ALL THE OTHERS WHO HAVE BEEN EXPOSED TO THE GAMMA RAYS-- THEY'VE ALL BEEN OF NORMAL BUILD OR LESS.
SO THE GAMMA RAYS REPLICATED THEIR MUSCLE AND BONE TISSUE, AND MADE THE HULK, THE ABOMINATION.
ALL YOU GAVE THEM TO WORK WITH WAS FAT! FAT! FAT! FAT!
SO THAT'S WHAT THEY REPLICATED! TONS AND TONS OF FAT!!
38

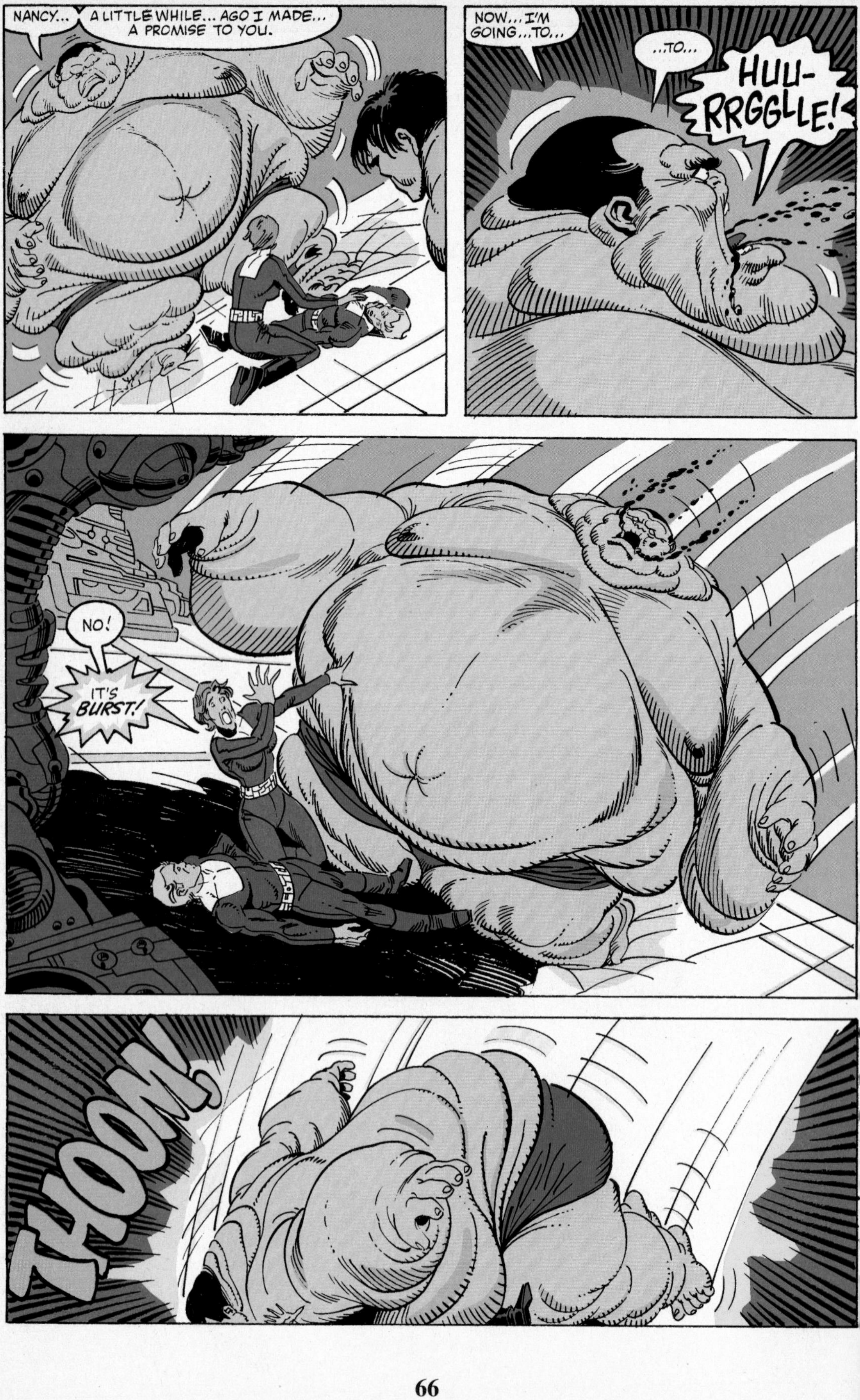

NANCY...
A LITTLE WHILE... AGO I MADE... A PROMISE TO YOU.
NOW... I'M GOING... TO...
...TO...
HUU-RRGGLLE!
NO!
IT'S BURST!
THOOM!

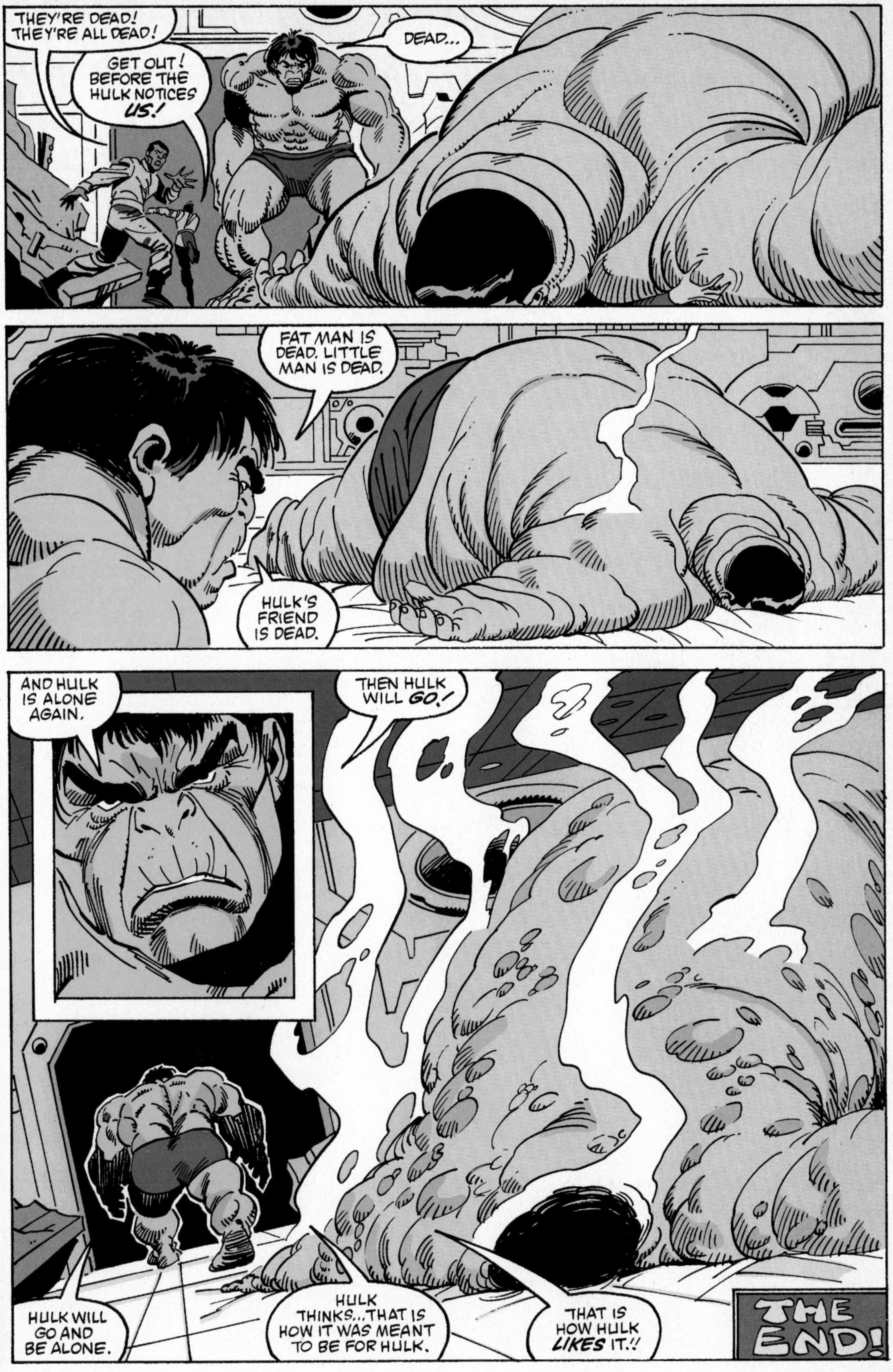
THEY'RE DEAD! THEY'RE ALL DEAD!
GET OUT! BEFORE THE HULK NOTICES US!
DEAD...
FAT MAN IS DEAD. LITTLE MAN IS DEAD.
HULK'S FRIEND IS DEAD.
AND HULK IS ALONE AGAIN.
THEN HULK WILL GO.!
HULK WILL GO AND BE ALONE.
HULK THINKS...THAT IS HOW IT WAS MEANT TO BE FOR HULK.
THAT IS HOW HULK LIKES IT.!!
THE END!

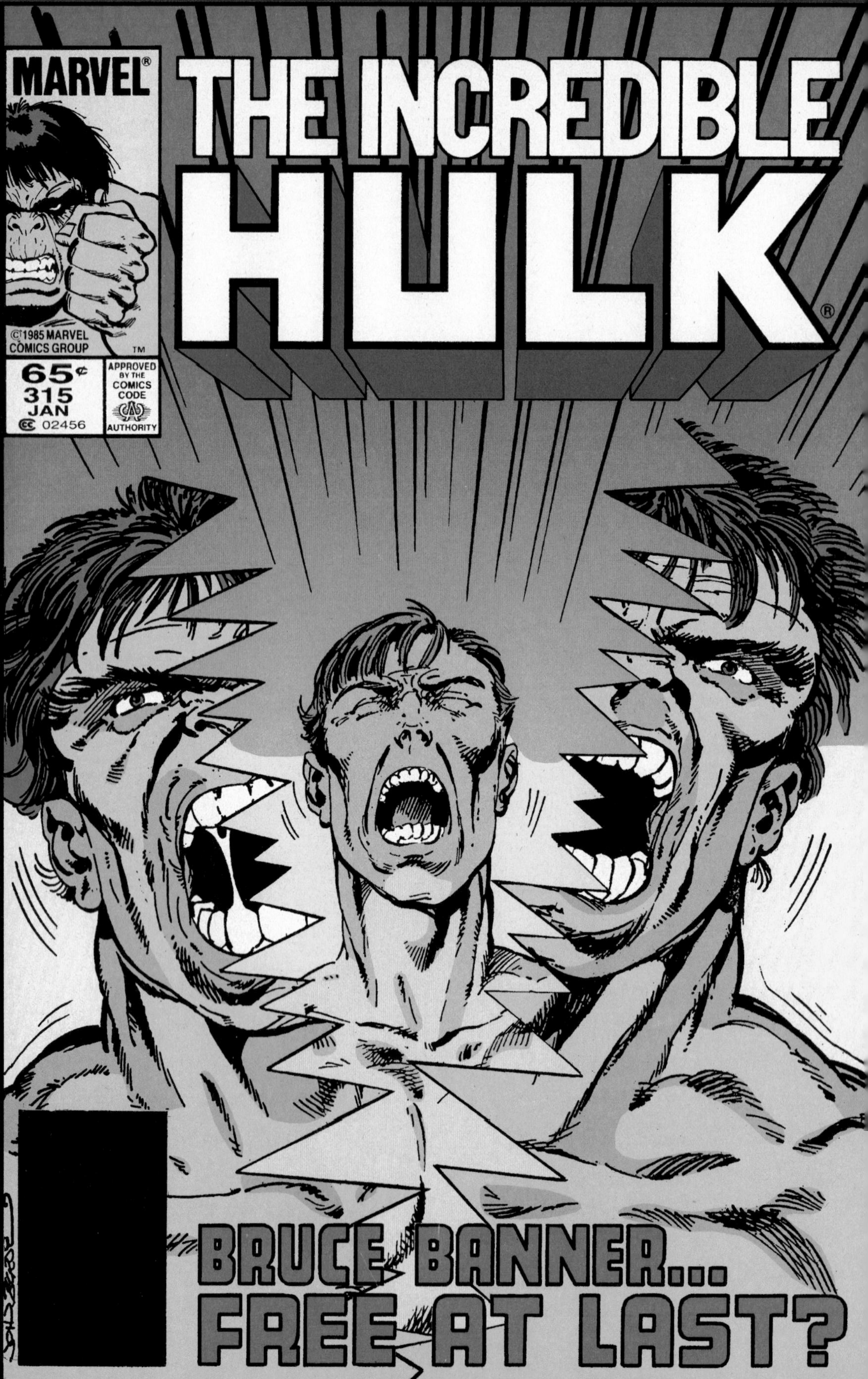
MARVEL®
THE INCREDIBLE
HULK®
©1985 MARVEL COMICS GROUP
TM
65¢
315
JAN
CC 02456
APPROVED BY THE COMICS CODE AUTHORITY
BRUCE BANNER...
FREE AT LAST?

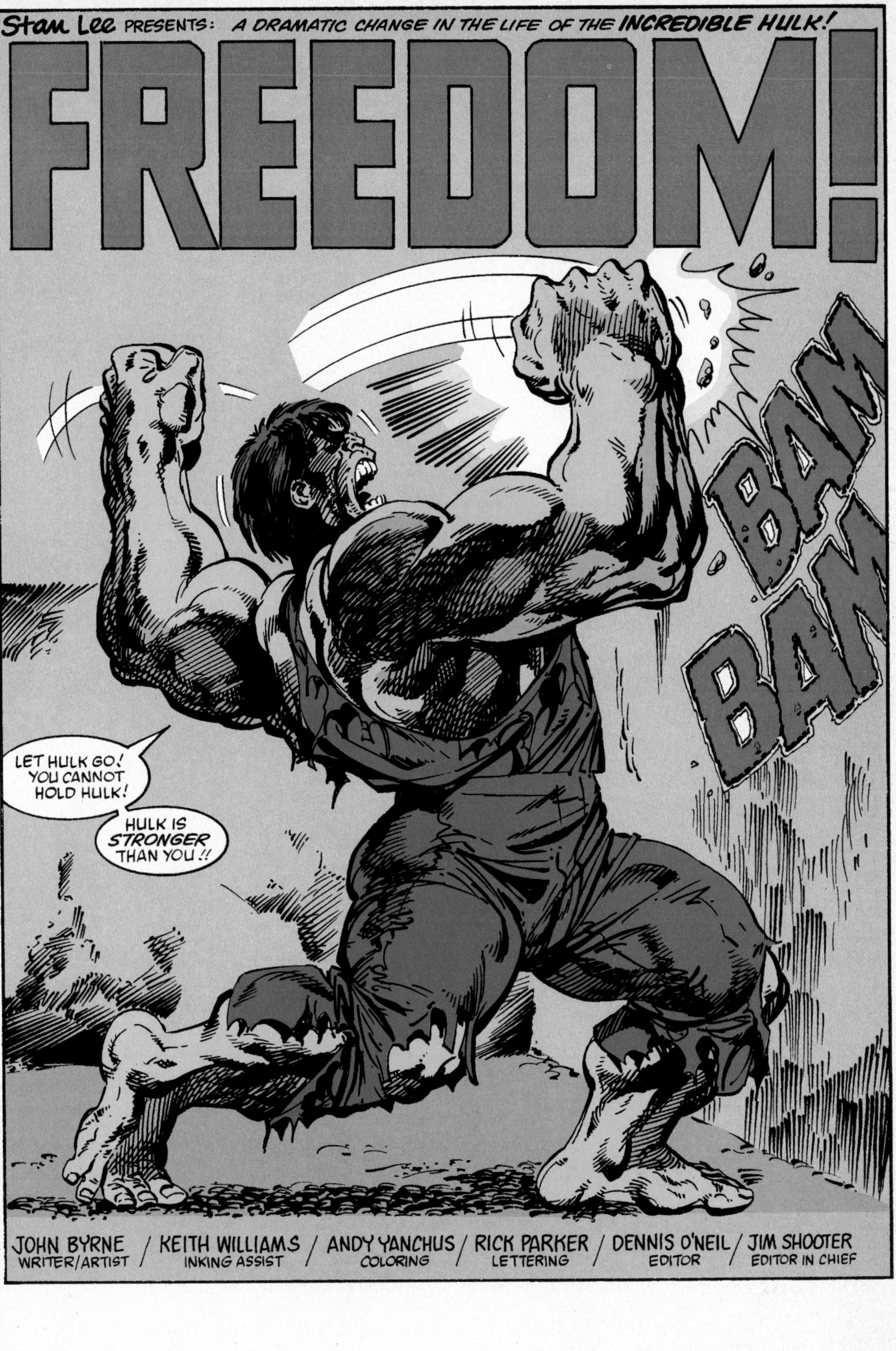

Stan Lee PRESENTS: A DRAMATIC CHANGE IN THE LIFE OF THE INCREDIBLE HULK!
FREEDOM!
BAM BAM
LET HULK GO! YOU CANNOT HOLD HULK!
HULK IS STRONGER THAN YOU!!
JOHN BYRNE WRITER/ARTIST / KEITH WILLIAMS INKING ASSIST / ANDY YANCHUS COLORING / RICK PARKER LETTERING / DENNIS O'NEIL EDITOR / JIM SHOOTER EDITOR IN CHIEF

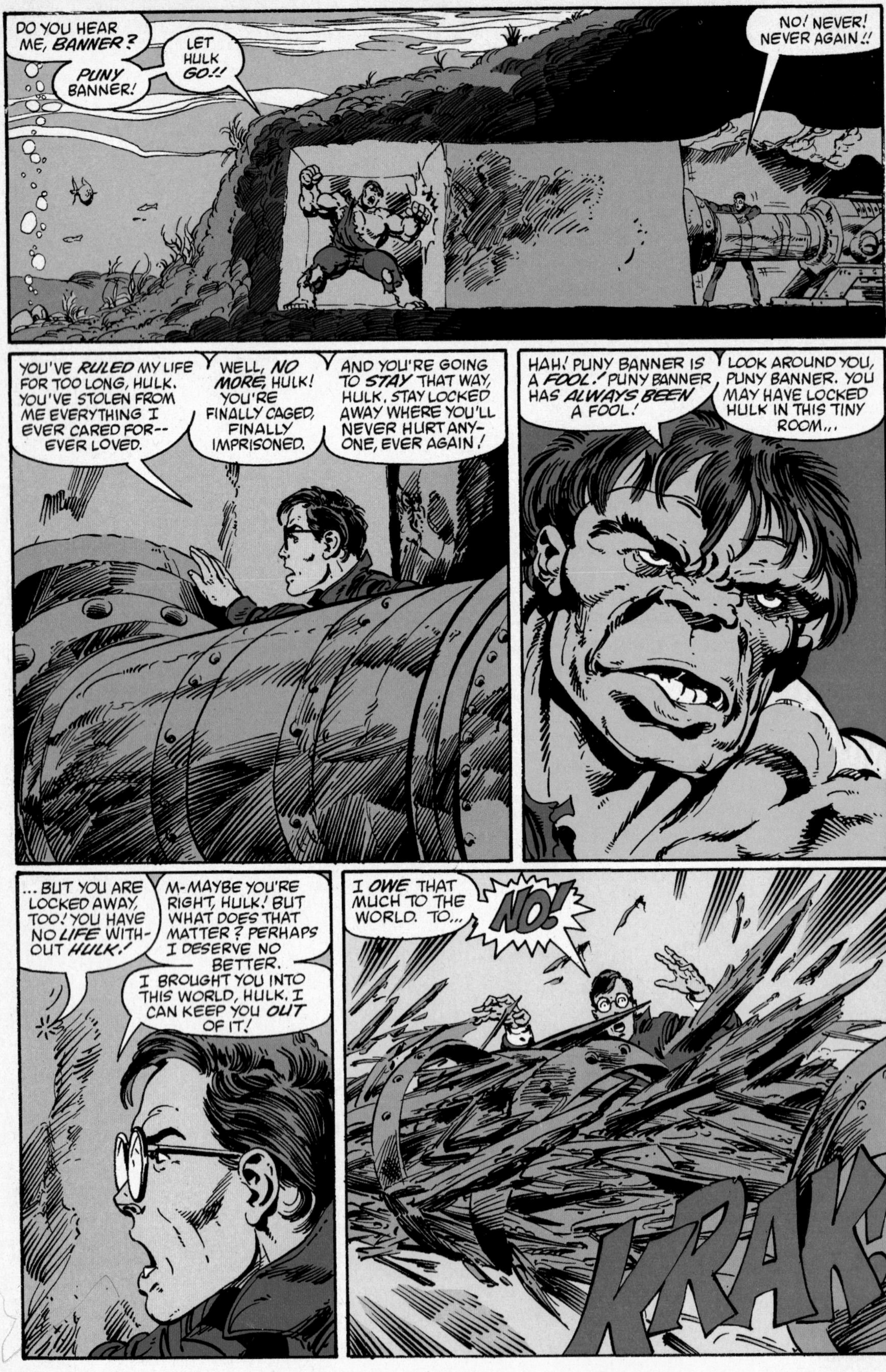
DO YOU HEAR ME, BANNER?
PUNY BANNER!
LET HULK GO!!
NO! NEVER! NEVER AGAIN!!
YOU'VE RULED MY LIFE FOR TOO LONG, HULK. YOU'VE STOLEN FROM ME EVERYTHING I EVER CARED FOR-- EVER LOVED.
WELL, NO MORE, HULK! YOU'RE FINALLY CAGED, FINALLY IMPRISONED.
AND YOU'RE GOING TO STAY THAT WAY, HULK. STAY LOCKED AWAY WHERE YOU'LL NEVER HURT ANYONE, EVER AGAIN!
HAH! PUNY BANNER IS A FOOL! PUNY BANNER HAS ALWAYS BEEN A FOOL!
LOOK AROUND YOU, PUNY BANNER. YOU MAY HAVE LOCKED HULK IN THIS TINY ROOM...
...BUT YOU ARE LOCKED AWAY, TOO! YOU HAVE NO LIFE WITHOUT HULK!
M-MAYBE YOU'RE RIGHT, HULK! BUT WHAT DOES THAT MATTER? PERHAPS I DESERVE NO BETTER.
I BROUGHT YOU INTO THIS WORLD, HULK. I CAN KEEP YOU OUT OF IT!
I OWE THAT MUCH TO THE WORLD. TO...
NO!
KRAK!

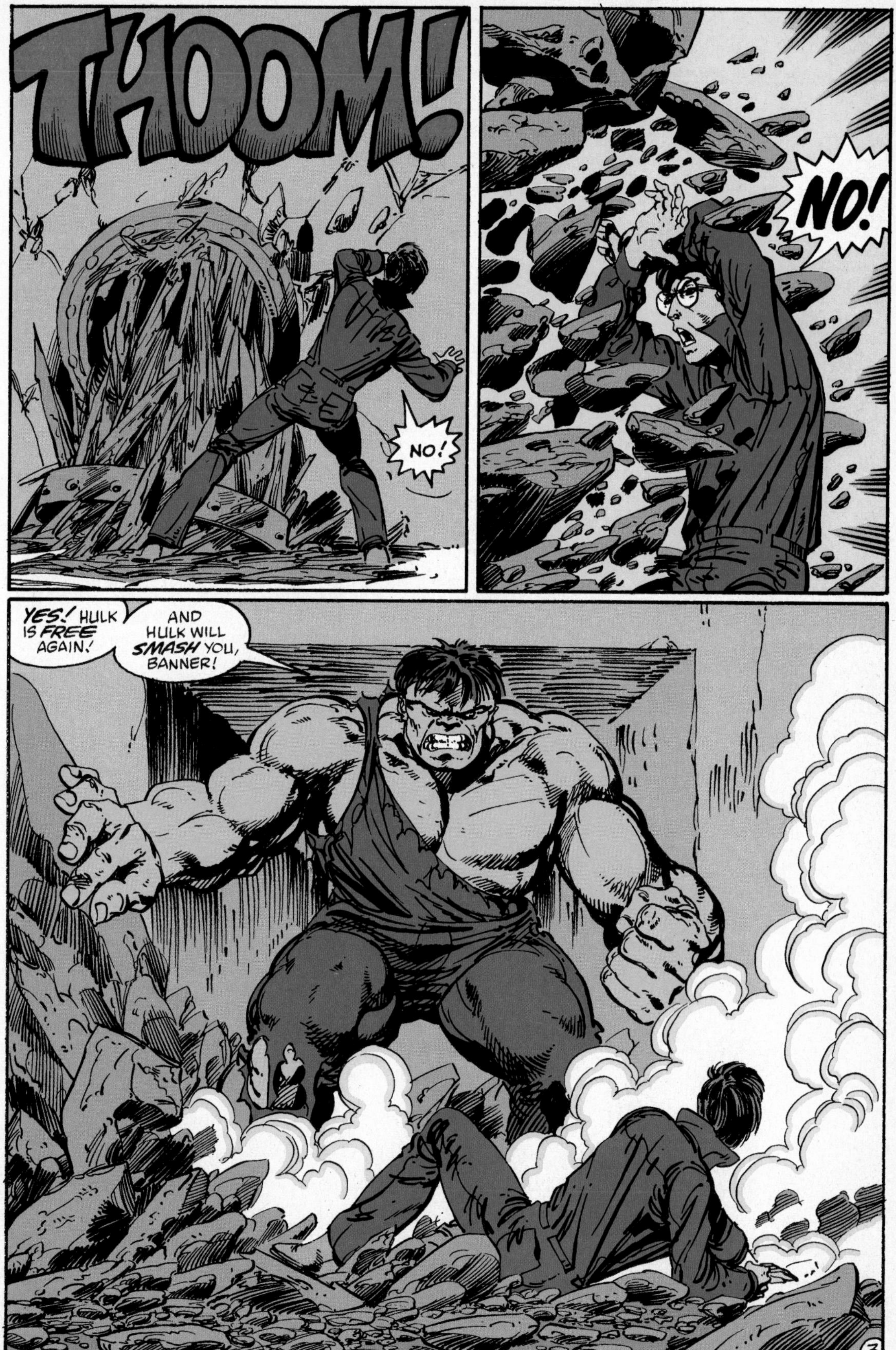
THOOM!
NO!
NO!
YES! HULK IS FREE AGAIN!
AND HULK WILL SMASH YOU, BANNER!
3

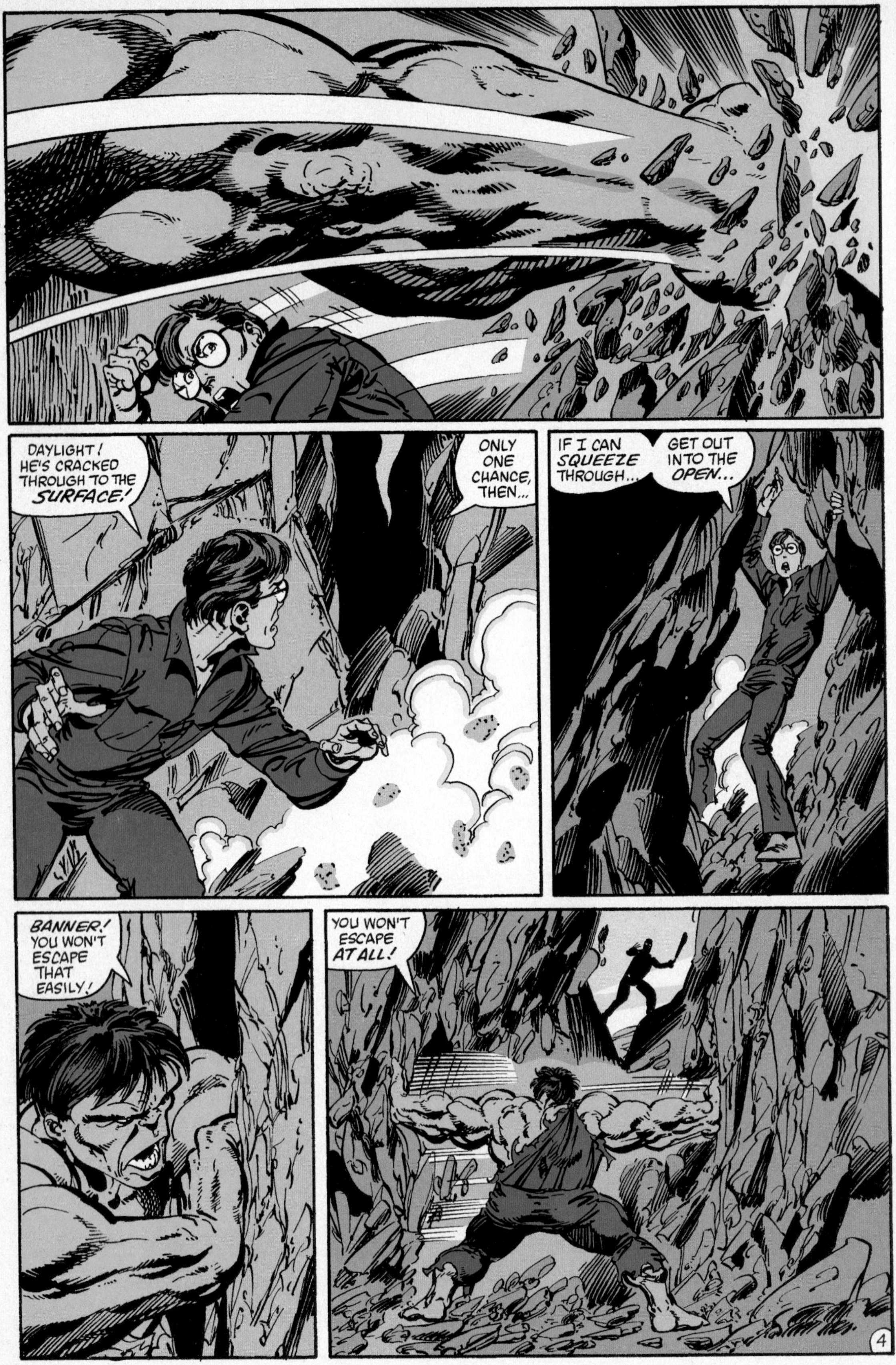
DAYLIGHT! HE'S CRACKED THROUGH TO THE SURFACE!
ONLY ONE CHANCE, THEN...
IF I CAN SQUEEZE THROUGH...
GET OUT INTO THE OPEN...
BANNER! YOU WON'T ESCAPE THAT EASILY!
YOU WON'T ESCAPE AT ALL!
4

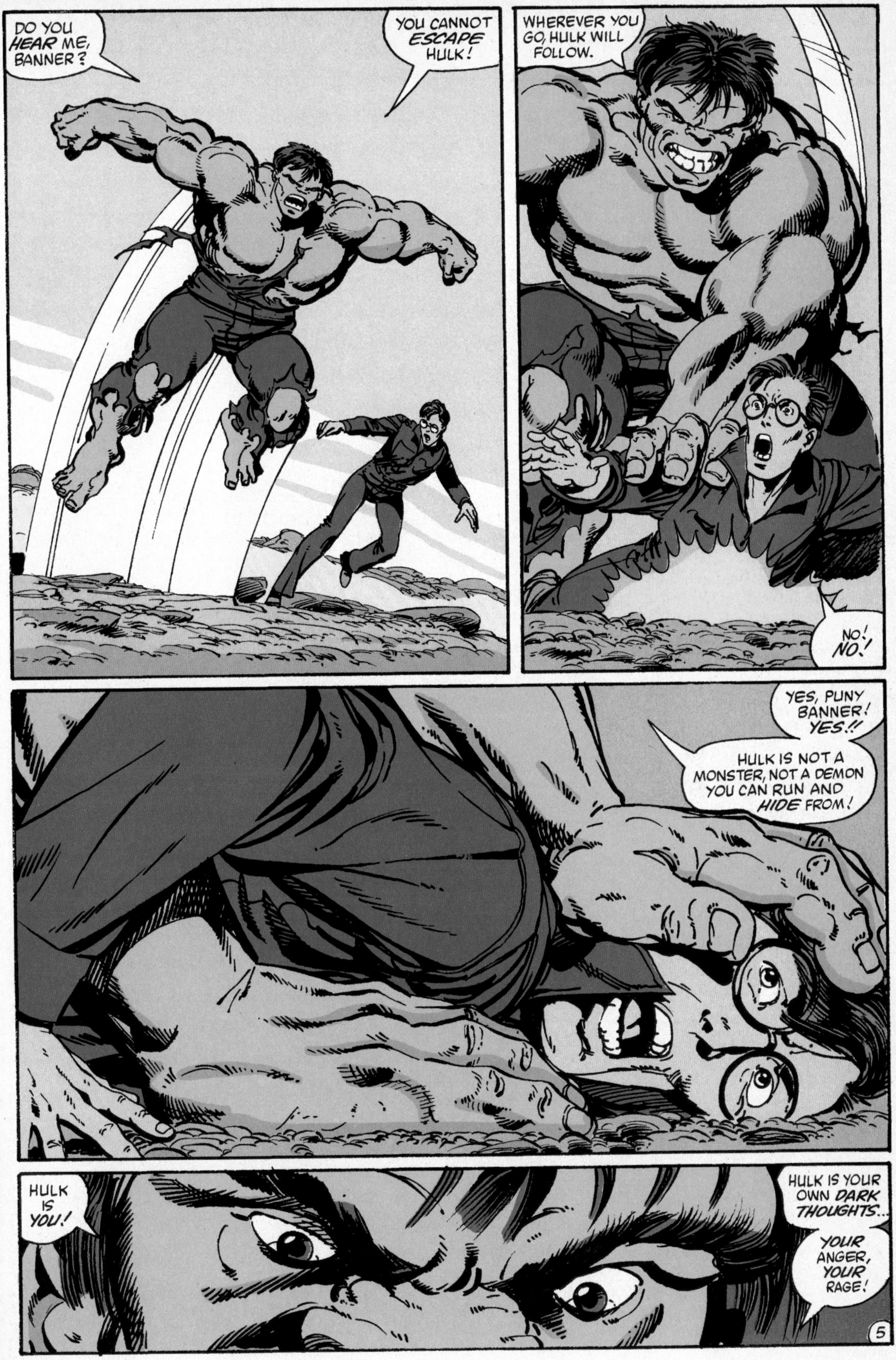

DO YOU HEAR ME, BANNER?
YOU CANNOT ESCAPE HULK!
WHEREVER YOU GO, HULK WILL FOLLOW.
NO! NO!
YES, PUNY BANNER! YES!!
HULK IS NOT A MONSTER, NOT A DEMON YOU CAN RUN AND HIDE FROM!
HULK IS YOU!
HULK IS YOUR OWN DARK THOUGHTS...
YOUR ANGER, YOUR RAGE!
5

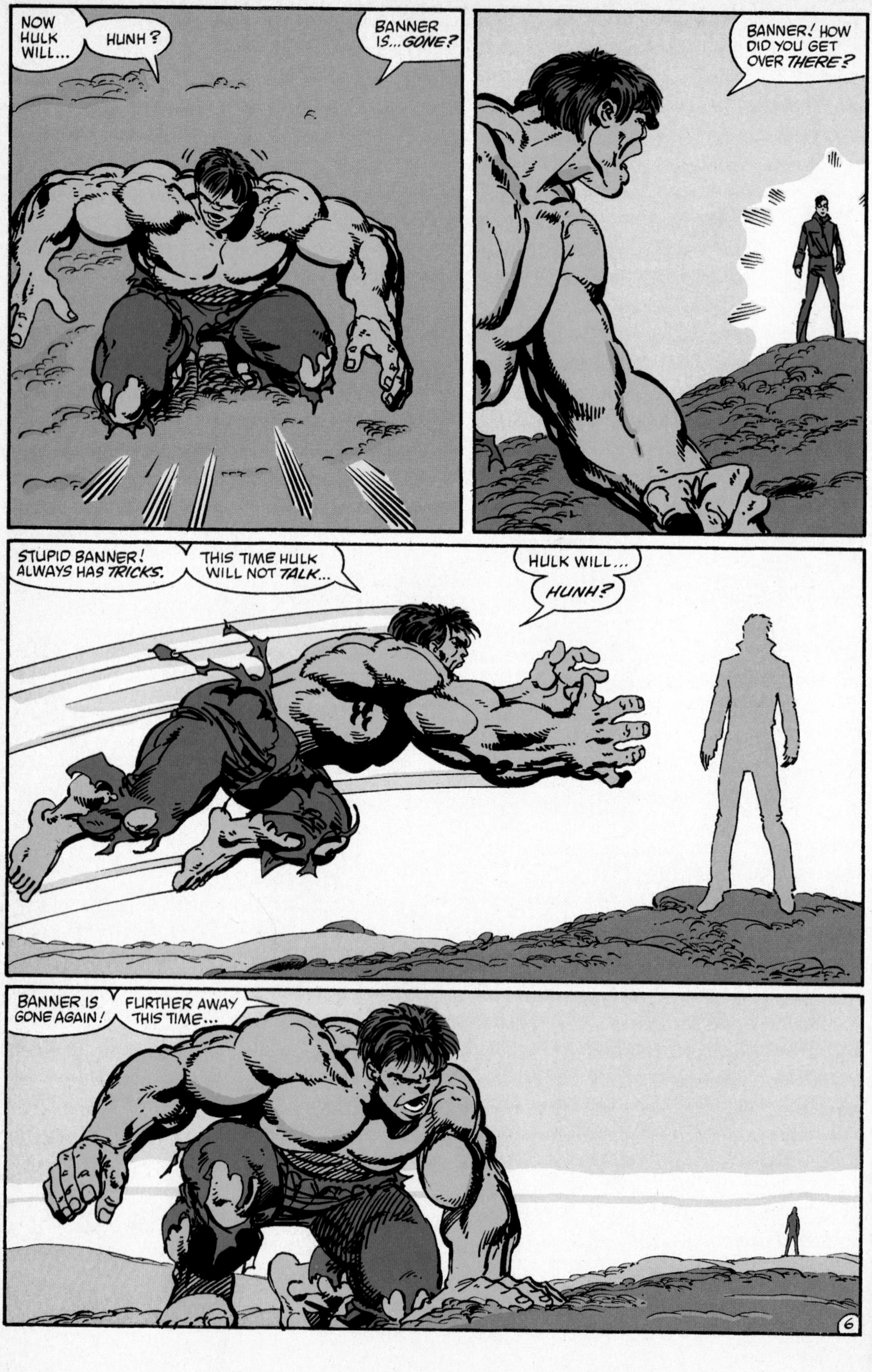
NOW HULK WILL...
HUNH?
BANNER IS... GONE?
BANNER! HOW DID YOU GET OVER THERE?
STUPID BANNER! ALWAYS HAS TRICKS.
THIS TIME HULK WILL NOT TALK...
HULK WILL...
HUNH?
BANNER IS GONE AGAIN!
FURTHER AWAY THIS TIME...
6

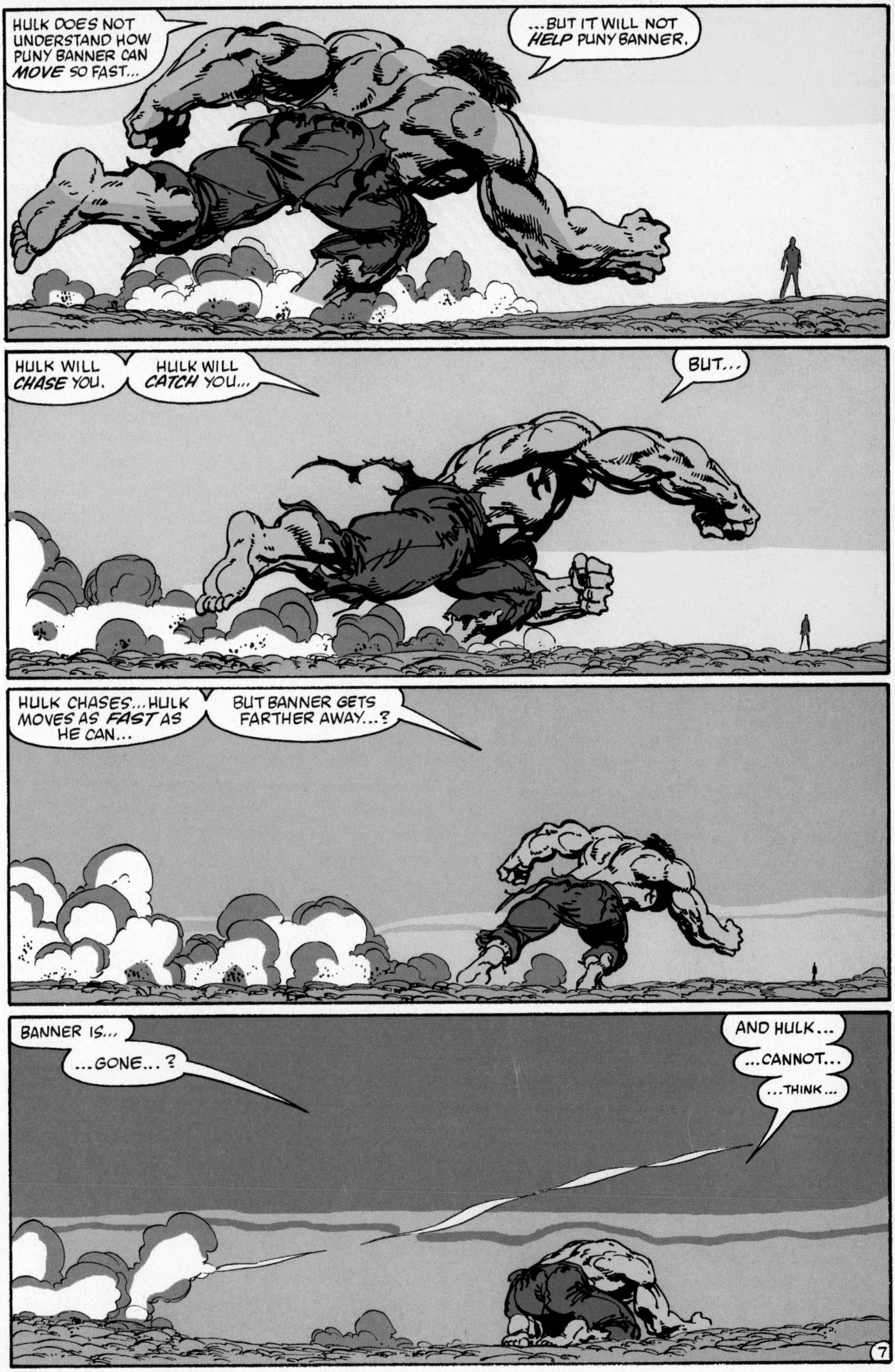

HULK DOES NOT UNDERSTAND HOW PUNY BANNER CAN MOVE SO FAST...
...BUT IT WILL NOT HELP PUNY BANNER.
HULK WILL CHASE YOU.
HULK WILL CATCH YOU...
BUT...
HULK CHASES...HULK MOVES AS FAST AS HE CAN...
BUT BANNER GETS FARTHER AWAY...?
BANNER IS...
...GONE...?
AND HULK...
...CANNOT...
...THINK...
7

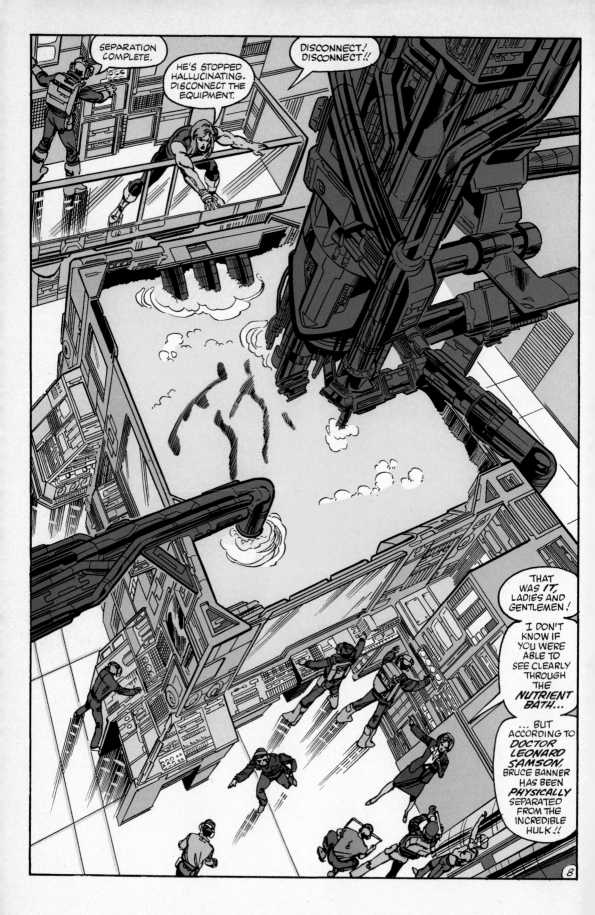

SEPARATION COMPLETE.

HE'S STOPPED HALLUCINATING. DISCONNECT THE EQUIPMENT.

DISCONNECT! DISCONNECT!!

THAT WAS *IT*, LADIES AND GENTLEMEN!

I DON'T KNOW IF YOU WERE ABLE TO SEE CLEARLY THROUGH THE *NUTRIENT BATH*...

...BUT ACCORDING TO *DOCTOR LEONARD SAMSON*, BRUCE BANNER HAS BEEN *PHYSICALLY* SEPARATED FROM THE INCREDIBLE HULK!!

8

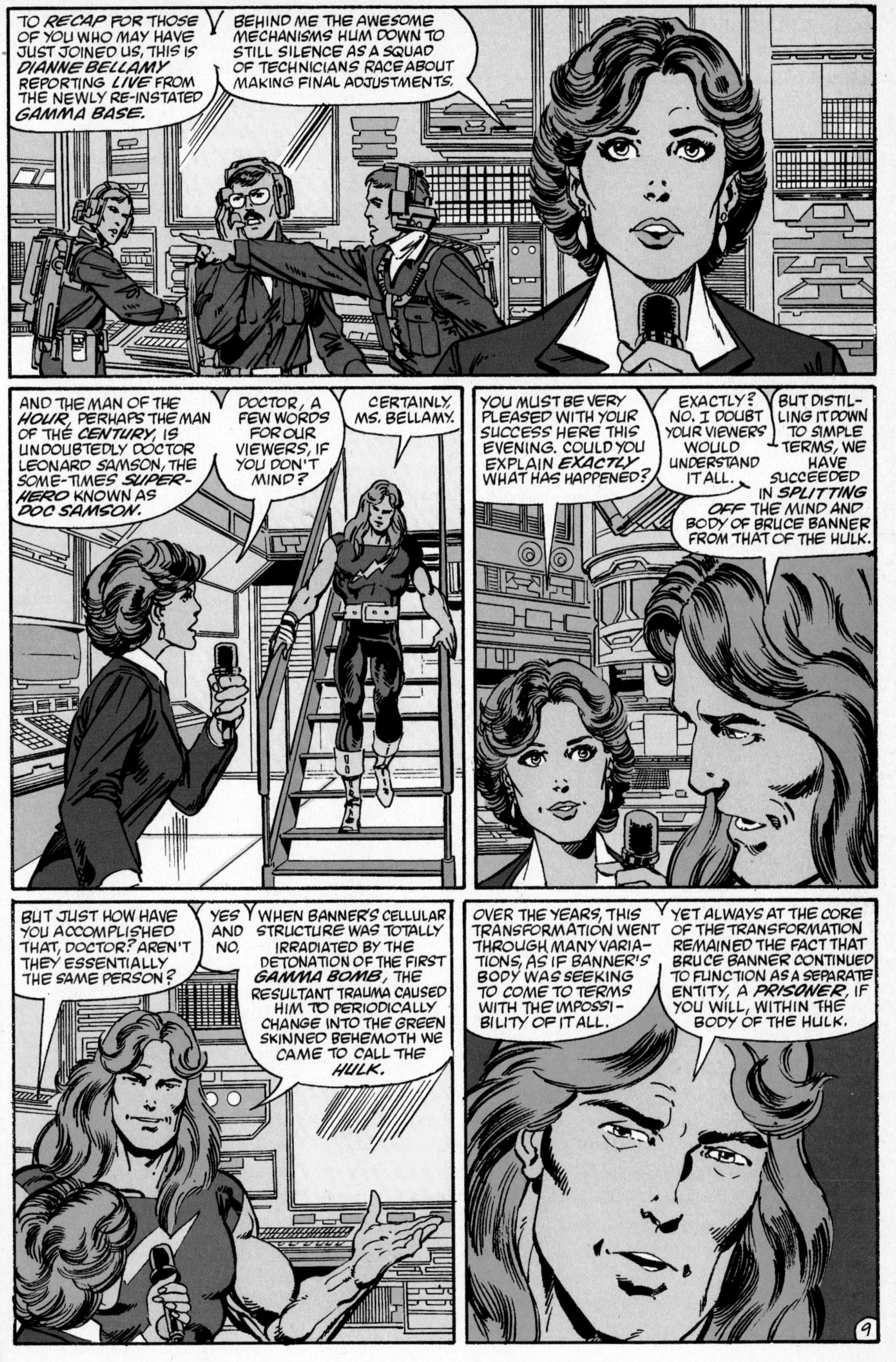
TO RECAP FOR THOSE OF YOU WHO MAY HAVE JUST JOINED US, THIS IS DIANNE BELLAMY REPORTING LIVE FROM THE NEWLY RE-INSTATED GAMMA BASE.
BEHIND ME THE AWESOME MECHANISMS HUM DOWN TO STILL SILENCE AS A SQUAD OF TECHNICIANS RACE ABOUT MAKING FINAL ADJUSTMENTS.
AND THE MAN OF THE HOUR, PERHAPS THE MAN OF THE CENTURY, IS UNDOUBTEDLY DOCTOR LEONARD SAMSON, THE SOME-TIMES SUPER-HERO KNOWN AS DOC SAMSON.
DOCTOR, A FEW WORDS FOR OUR VIEWERS, IF YOU DON'T MIND?
CERTAINLY, MS. BELLAMY.
YOU MUST BE VERY PLEASED WITH YOUR SUCCESS HERE THIS EVENING. COULD YOU EXPLAIN EXACTLY WHAT HAS HAPPENED?
EXACTLY? NO. I DOUBT YOUR VIEWERS WOULD UNDERSTAND IT ALL.
BUT DISTIL-LING IT DOWN TO SIMPLE TERMS, WE HAVE SUCCEEDED IN SPLITTING OFF THE MIND AND BODY OF BRUCE BANNER FROM THAT OF THE HULK.
BUT JUST HOW HAVE YOU ACCOMPLISHED THAT, DOCTOR? AREN'T THEY ESSENTIALLY THE SAME PERSON?
YES AND NO,
WHEN BANNER'S CELLULAR STRUCTURE WAS TOTALLY IRRADIATED BY THE DETONATION OF THE FIRST GAMMA BOMB, THE RESULTANT TRAUMA CAUSED HIM TO PERIODICALLY CHANGE INTO THE GREEN SKINNED BEHEMOTH WE CAME TO CALL THE HULK.
OVER THE YEARS, THIS TRANSFORMATION WENT THROUGH MANY VARIA-TIONS, AS IF BANNER'S BODY WAS SEEKING TO COME TO TERMS WITH THE IMPOSSI-BILITY OF IT ALL.
YET ALWAYS AT THE CORE OF THE TRANSFORMATION REMAINED THE FACT THAT BRUCE BANNER CONTINUED TO FUNCTION AS A SEPARATE ENTITY, A PRISONER, IF YOU WILL, WITHIN THE BODY OF THE HULK.
9

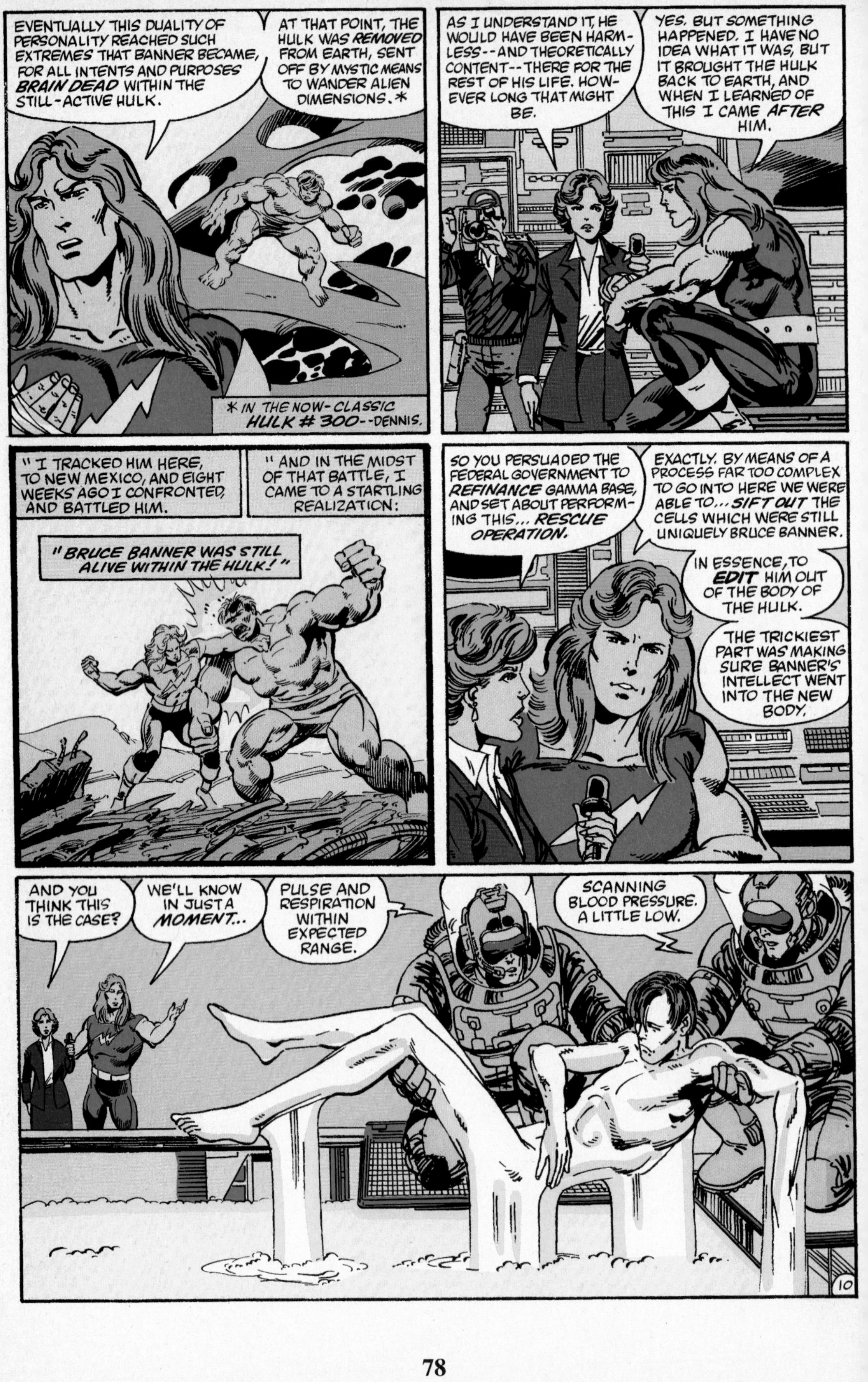
EVENTUALLY THIS DUALITY OF PERSONALITY REACHED SUCH EXTREMES THAT BANNER BECAME, FOR ALL INTENTS AND PURPOSES BRAIN DEAD WITHIN THE STILL-ACTIVE HULK.
AT THAT POINT, THE HULK WAS REMOVED FROM EARTH, SENT OFF BY MYSTIC MEANS TO WANDER ALIEN DIMENSIONS.*
*IN THE NOW-CLASSIC HULK #300--DENNIS.
AS I UNDERSTAND IT, HE WOULD HAVE BEEN HARMLESS--AND THEORETICALLY CONTENT--THERE FOR THE REST OF HIS LIFE. HOWEVER LONG THAT MIGHT BE.
YES. BUT SOMETHING HAPPENED. I HAVE NO IDEA WHAT IT WAS, BUT IT BROUGHT THE HULK BACK TO EARTH, AND WHEN I LEARNED OF THIS I CAME AFTER HIM.
"I TRACKED HIM HERE, TO NEW MEXICO, AND EIGHT WEEKS AGO I CONFRONTED, AND BATTLED HIM.
"AND IN THE MIDST OF THAT BATTLE, I CAME TO A STARTLING REALIZATION:
"BRUCE BANNER WAS STILL ALIVE WITHIN THE HULK!"
SO YOU PERSUADED THE FEDERAL GOVERNMENT TO REFINANCE GAMMA BASE, AND SET ABOUT PERFORMING THIS... RESCUE OPERATION.
EXACTLY. BY MEANS OF A PROCESS FAR TOO COMPLEX TO GO INTO HERE WE WERE ABLE TO... SIFT OUT THE CELLS WHICH WERE STILL UNIQUELY BRUCE BANNER.
IN ESSENCE, TO EDIT HIM OUT OF THE BODY OF THE HULK.
THE TRICKIEST PART WAS MAKING SURE BANNER'S INTELLECT WENT INTO THE NEW BODY.
AND YOU THINK THIS IS THE CASE?
WE'LL KNOW IN JUST A MOMENT...
PULSE AND RESPIRATION WITHIN EXPECTED RANGE.
SCANNING BLOOD PRESSURE. A LITTLE LOW.
10

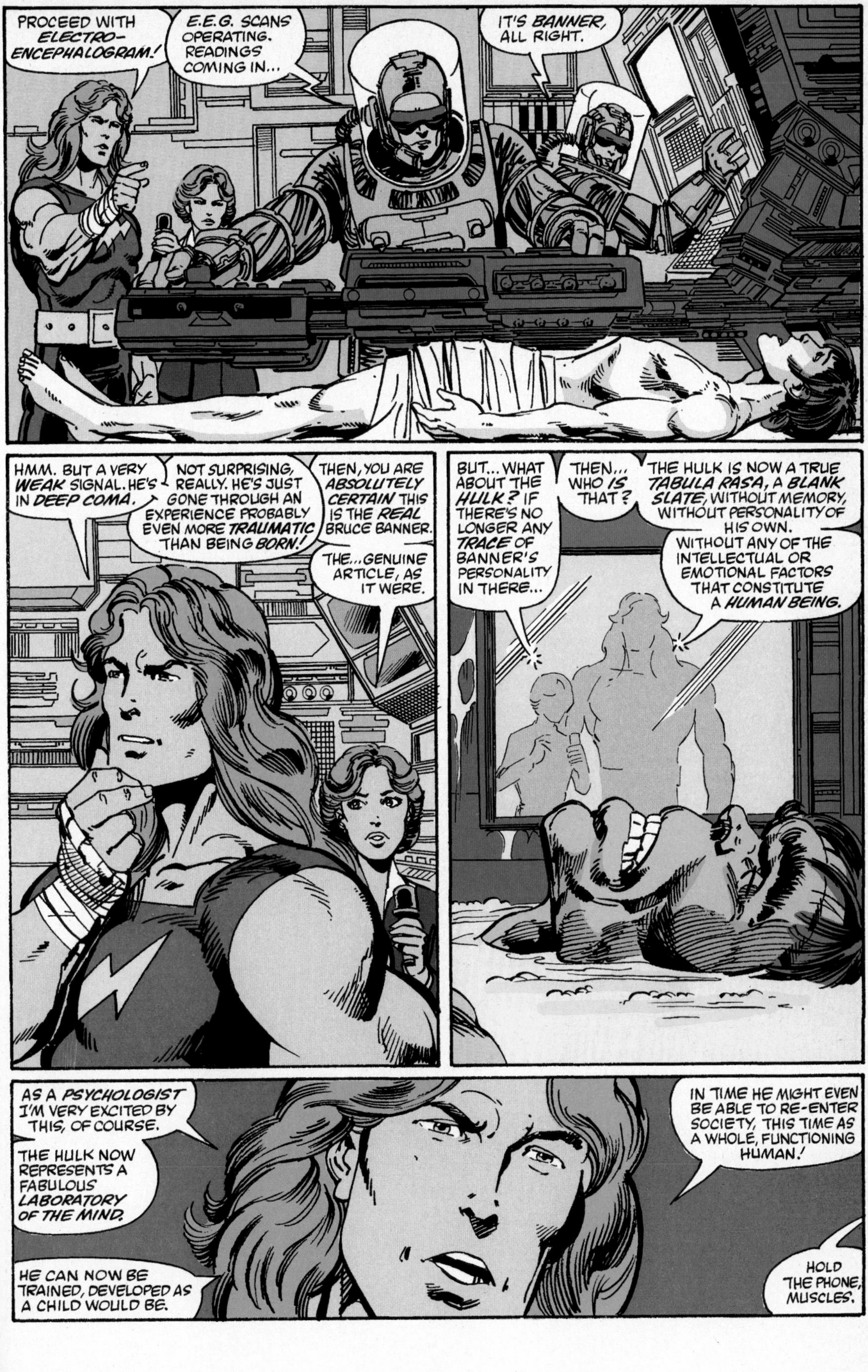
PROCEED WITH ELECTRO-ENCEPHALOGRAM!
E.E.G. SCANS OPERATING. READINGS COMING IN...
IT'S BANNER, ALL RIGHT.
HMM. BUT A VERY WEAK SIGNAL. HE'S IN DEEP COMA.
NOT SURPRISING, REALLY. HE'S JUST GONE THROUGH AN EXPERIENCE PROBABLY EVEN MORE TRAUMATIC THAN BEING BORN!
THEN, YOU ARE ABSOLUTELY CERTAIN THIS IS THE REAL BRUCE BANNER.
THE...GENUINE ARTICLE, AS IT WERE.
BUT... WHAT ABOUT THE HULK? IF THERE'S NO LONGER ANY TRACE OF BANNER'S PERSONALITY IN THERE...
THEN... WHO IS THAT?
THE HULK IS NOW A TRUE TABULA RASA, A BLANK SLATE, WITHOUT MEMORY, WITHOUT PERSONALITY OF HIS OWN.
WITHOUT ANY OF THE INTELLECTUAL OR EMOTIONAL FACTORS THAT CONSTITUTE A HUMAN BEING.
AS A PSYCHOLOGIST I'M VERY EXCITED BY THIS, OF COURSE.
THE HULK NOW REPRESENTS A FABULOUS LABORATORY OF THE MIND.
HE CAN NOW BE TRAINED, DEVELOPED AS A CHILD WOULD BE.
IN TIME HE MIGHT EVEN BE ABLE TO RE-ENTER SOCIETY, THIS TIME AS A WHOLE, FUNCTIONING HUMAN!
HOLD THE PHONE, MUSCLES.

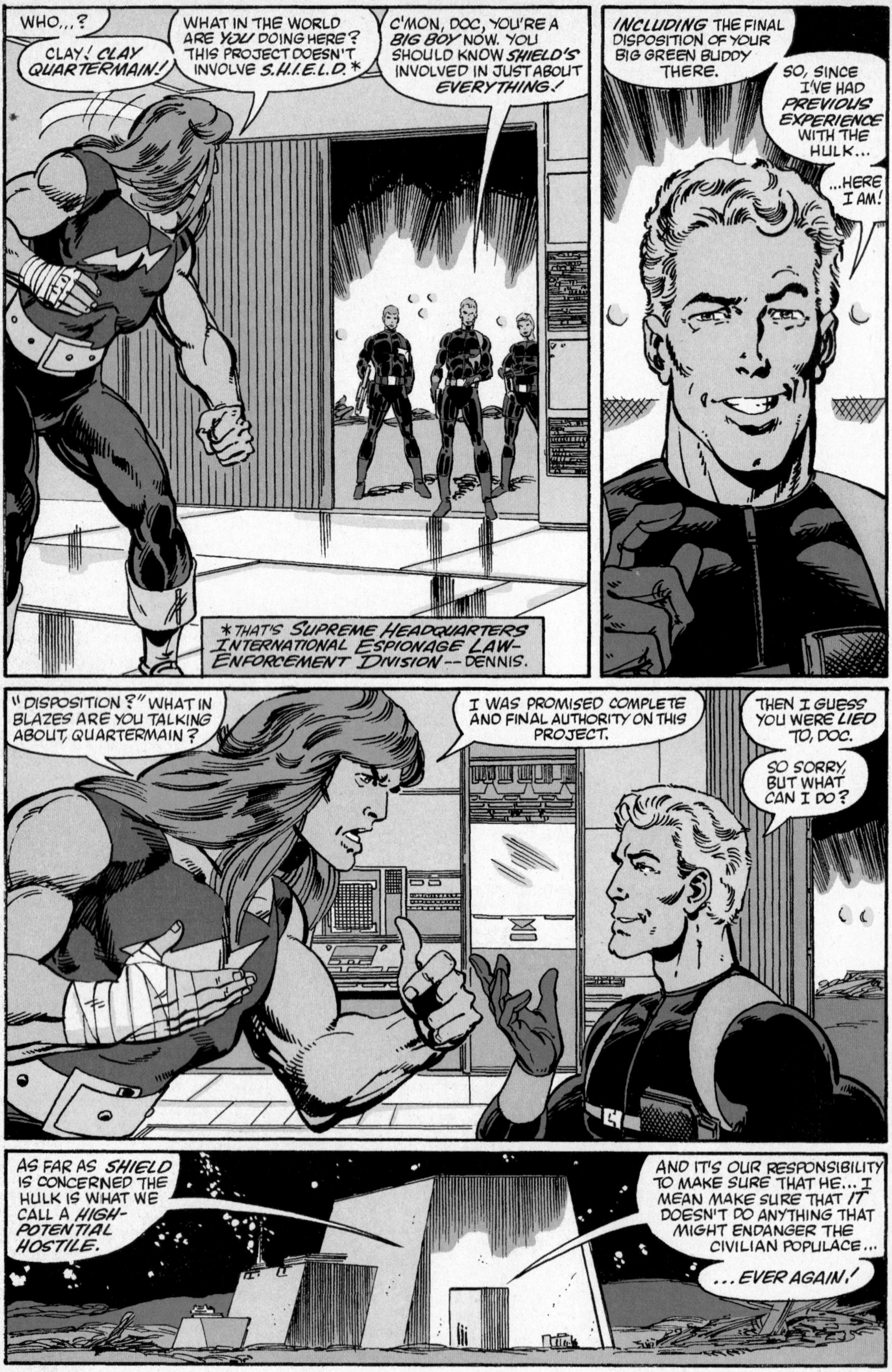
WHO...?
CLAY! CLAY QUARTERMAIN!
WHAT IN THE WORLD ARE YOU DOING HERE? THIS PROJECT DOESN'T INVOLVE S.H.I.E.L.D.*
C'MON, DOC, YOU'RE A BIG BOY NOW. YOU SHOULD KNOW SHIELD'S INVOLVED IN JUST ABOUT EVERYTHING!
*THAT'S SUPREME HEADQUARTERS INTERNATIONAL ESPIONAGE LAW-ENFORCEMENT DIVISION -- DENNIS.
INCLUDING THE FINAL DISPOSITION OF YOUR BIG GREEN BUDDY THERE.
SO, SINCE I'VE HAD PREVIOUS EXPERIENCE WITH THE HULK...
...HERE I AM!
"DISPOSITION?" WHAT IN BLAZES ARE YOU TALKING ABOUT, QUARTERMAIN?
I WAS PROMISED COMPLETE AND FINAL AUTHORITY ON THIS PROJECT.
THEN I GUESS YOU WERE LIED TO, DOC.
SO SORRY, BUT WHAT CAN I DO?
AS FAR AS SHIELD IS CONCERNED THE HULK IS WHAT WE CALL A HIGH-POTENTIAL HOSTILE.
AND IT'S OUR RESPONSIBILITY TO MAKE SURE THAT HE... I MEAN MAKE SURE THAT IT DOESN'T DO ANYTHING THAT MIGHT ENDANGER THE CIVILIAN POPULACE...
...EVER AGAIN!

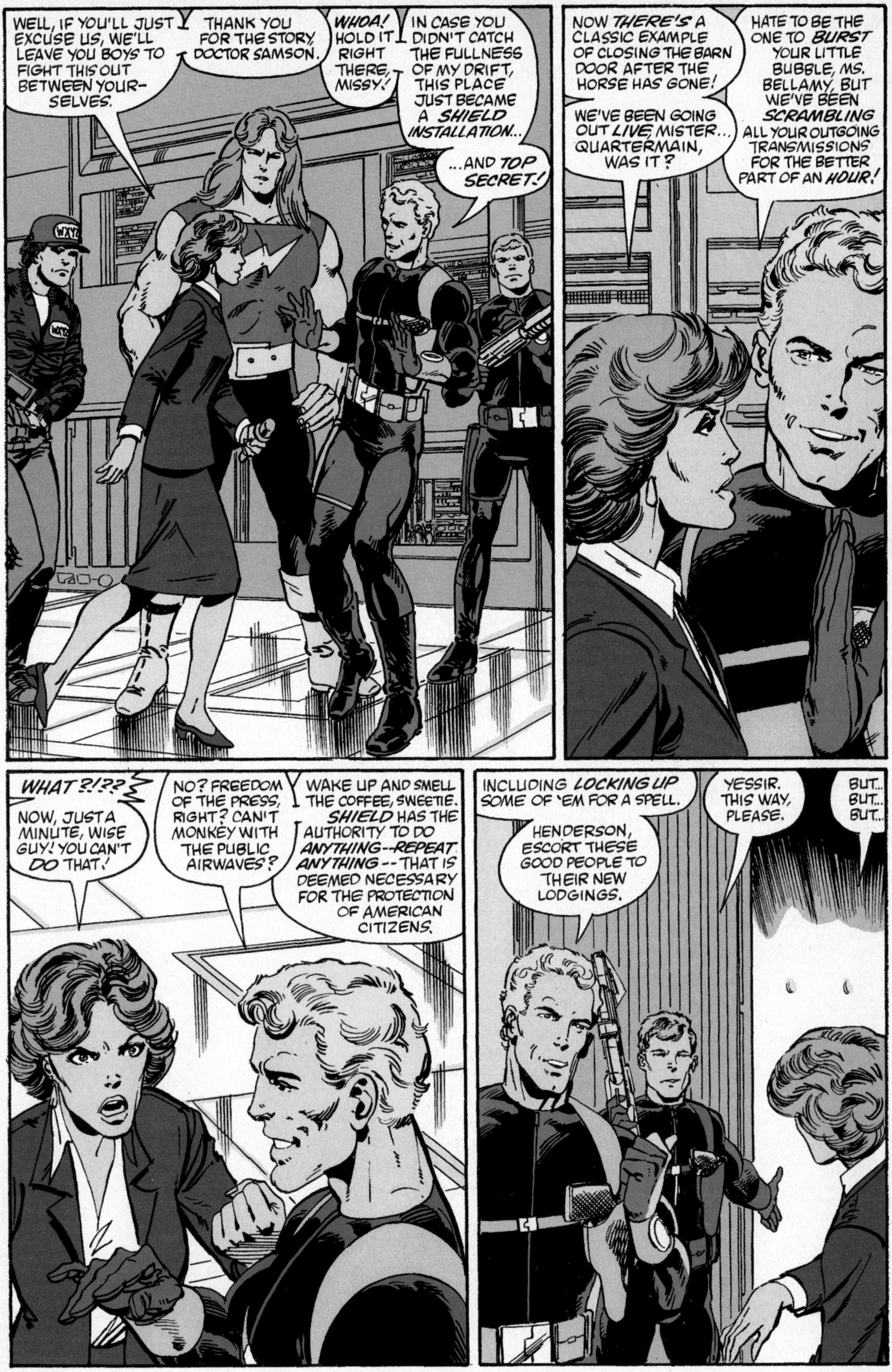
WELL, IF YOU'LL JUST EXCUSE US, WE'LL LEAVE YOU BOYS TO FIGHT THIS OUT BETWEEN YOURSELVES.
THANK YOU FOR THE STORY, DOCTOR SAMSON.
WHOA! HOLD IT RIGHT THERE, MISSY!
IN CASE YOU DIDN'T CATCH THE FULLNESS OF MY DRIFT, THIS PLACE JUST BECAME A SHIELD INSTALLATION...
...AND TOP SECRET!
NOW THERE'S A CLASSIC EXAMPLE OF CLOSING THE BARN DOOR AFTER THE HORSE HAS GONE!
WE'VE BEEN GOING OUT LIVE, MISTER... QUARTERMAIN, WAS IT?
HATE TO BE THE ONE TO BURST YOUR LITTLE BUBBLE, MS. BELLAMY, BUT WE'VE BEEN SCRAMBLING ALL YOUR OUTGOING TRANSMISSIONS FOR THE BETTER PART OF AN HOUR!
WHAT?!??
NOW, JUST A MINUTE, WISE GUY! YOU CAN'T DO THAT!
NO? FREEDOM OF THE PRESS, RIGHT? CAN'T MONKEY WITH THE PUBLIC AIRWAVES?
WAKE UP AND SMELL THE COFFEE, SWEETIE. SHIELD HAS THE AUTHORITY TO DO ANYTHING--REPEAT ANYTHING--THAT IS DEEMED NECESSARY FOR THE PROTECTION OF AMERICAN CITIZENS.
INCLUDING LOCKING UP SOME OF 'EM FOR A SPELL.
HENDERSON, ESCORT THESE GOOD PEOPLE TO THEIR NEW LODGINGS.
YESSIR. THIS WAY, PLEASE.
BUT... BUT... BUT...

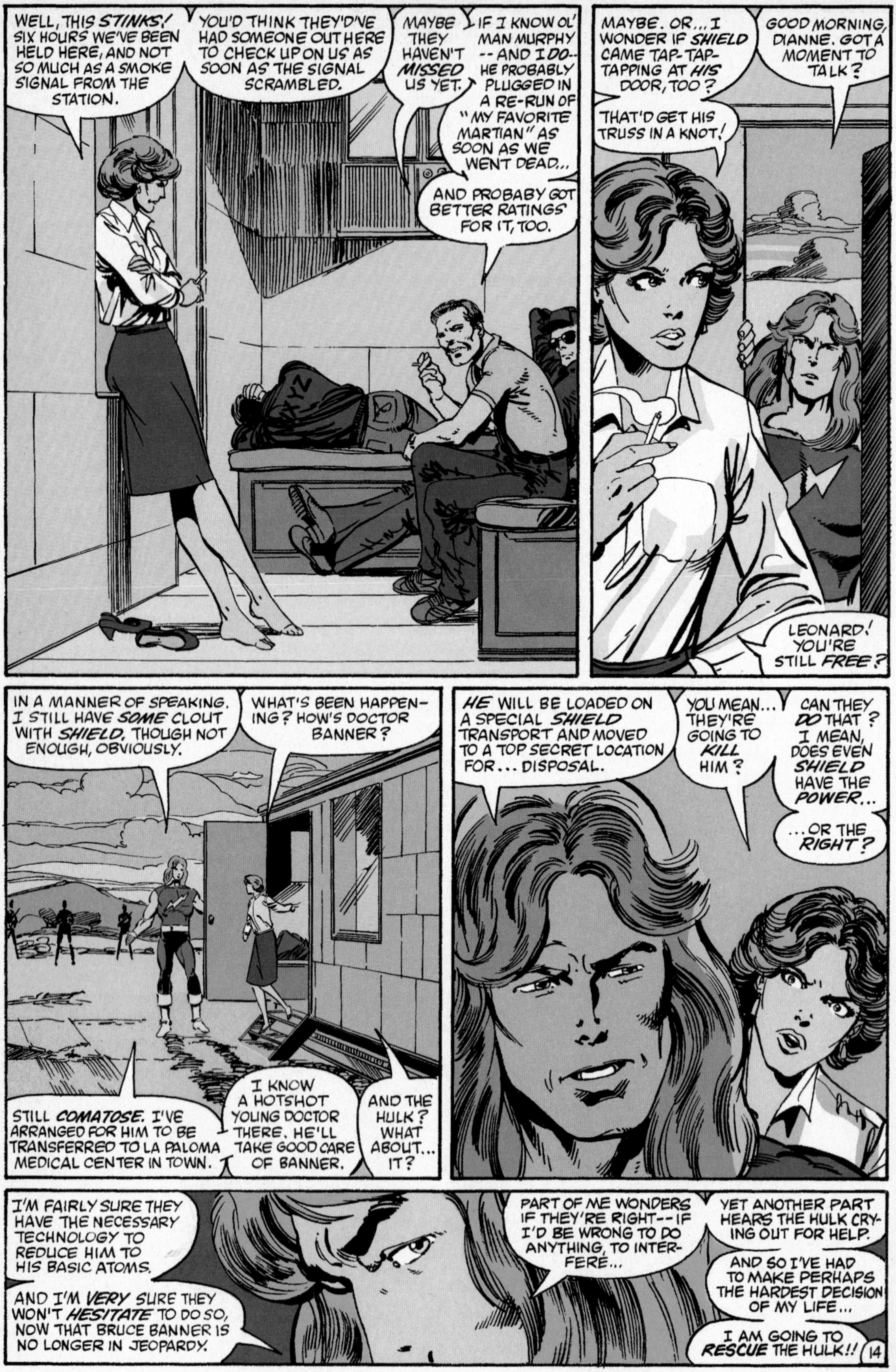
WELL, THIS STINKS! SIX HOURS WE'VE BEEN HELD HERE, AND NOT SO MUCH AS A SMOKE SIGNAL FROM THE STATION.
YOU'D THINK THEY'D'VE HAD SOMEONE OUT HERE TO CHECK UP ON US AS SOON AS THE SIGNAL SCRAMBLED.
MAYBE THEY HAVEN'T MISSED US YET.
IF I KNOW OL' MAN MURPHY -- AND I DO-- HE PROBABLY PLUGGED IN A RE-RUN OF "MY FAVORITE MARTIAN" AS SOON AS WE WENT DEAD...
AND PROBABY GOT BETTER RATINGS FOR IT, TOO.
MAYBE. OR... I WONDER IF SHIELD CAME TAP-TAP-TAPPING AT HIS DOOR, TOO?
THAT'D GET HIS TRUSS IN A KNOT!
GOOD MORNING, DIANNE. GOT A MOMENT TO TALK?
LEONARD! YOU'RE STILL FREE?
IN A MANNER OF SPEAKING. I STILL HAVE SOME CLOUT WITH SHIELD, THOUGH NOT ENOUGH, OBVIOUSLY.
WHAT'S BEEN HAPPENING? HOW'S DOCTOR BANNER?
STILL COMATOSE. I'VE ARRANGED FOR HIM TO BE TRANSFERRED TO LA PALOMA MEDICAL CENTER IN TOWN.
I KNOW A HOTSHOT YOUNG DOCTOR THERE. HE'LL TAKE GOOD CARE OF BANNER.
AND THE HULK? WHAT ABOUT... IT?
HE WILL BE LOADED ON A SPECIAL SHIELD TRANSPORT AND MOVED TO A TOP SECRET LOCATION FOR... DISPOSAL.
YOU MEAN... THEY'RE GOING TO KILL HIM?
CAN THEY DO THAT? I MEAN, DOES EVEN SHIELD HAVE THE POWER...
...OR THE RIGHT?
I'M FAIRLY SURE THEY HAVE THE NECESSARY TECHNOLOGY TO REDUCE HIM TO HIS BASIC ATOMS.
AND I'M VERY SURE THEY WON'T HESITATE TO DO SO, NOW THAT BRUCE BANNER IS NO LONGER IN JEOPARDY.
PART OF ME WONDERS IF THEY'RE RIGHT-- IF I'D BE WRONG TO DO ANYTHING, TO INTERFERE...
YET ANOTHER PART HEARS THE HULK CRYING OUT FOR HELP.
AND SO I'VE HAD TO MAKE PERHAPS THE HARDEST DECISION OF MY LIFE...
I AM GOING TO RESCUE THE HULK!!
14

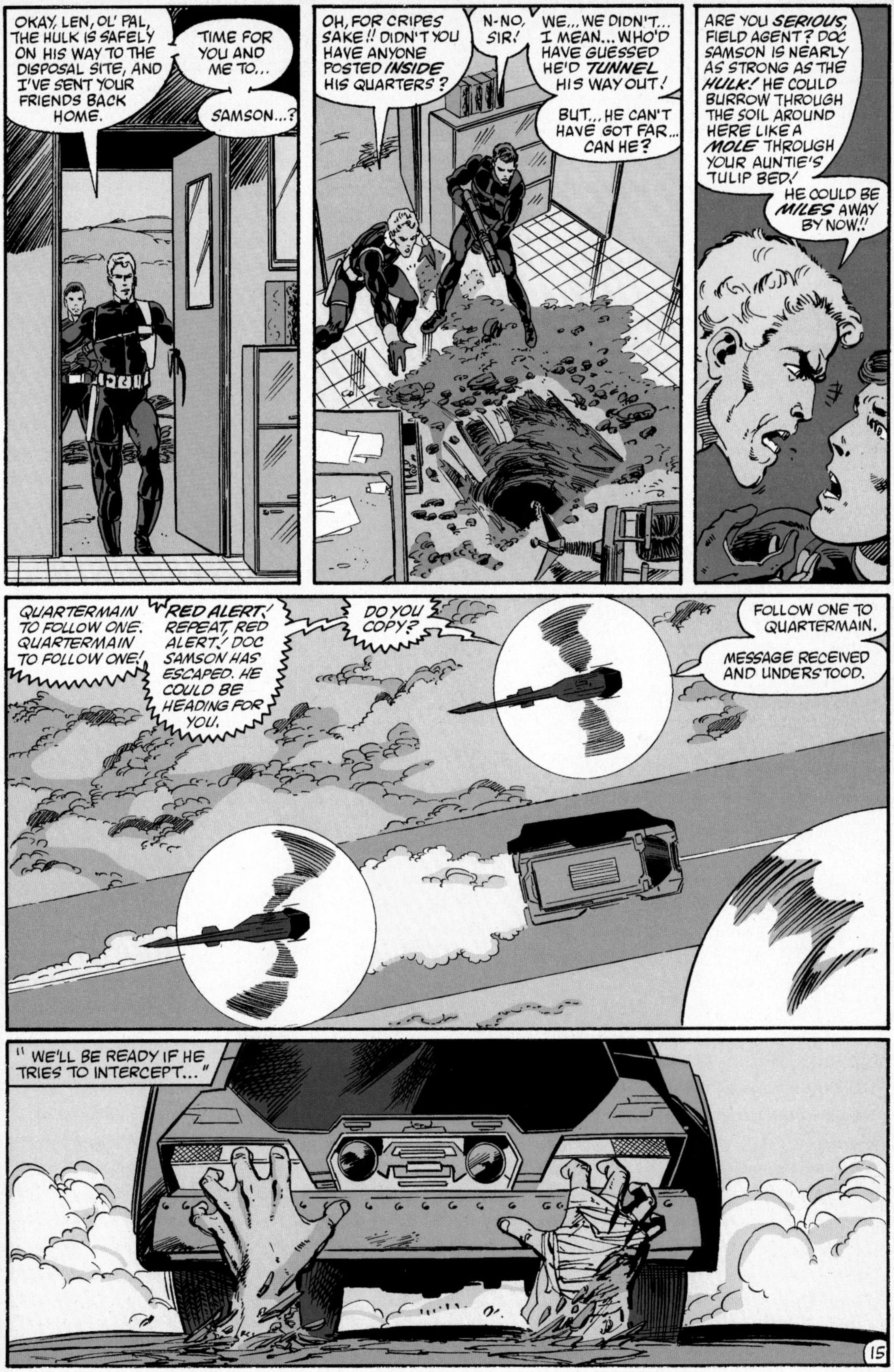

OKAY, LEN, OL' PAL, THE HULK IS SAFELY ON HIS WAY TO THE DISPOSAL SITE, AND I'VE SENT YOUR FRIENDS BACK HOME.
TIME FOR YOU AND ME TO...
SAMSON...?
OH, FOR CRIPES SAKE!! DIDN'T YOU HAVE ANYONE POSTED INSIDE HIS QUARTERS?
N-NO, SIR!
WE... WE DIDN'T... I MEAN... WHO'D HAVE GUESSED HE'D TUNNEL HIS WAY OUT!
BUT... HE CAN'T HAVE GOT FAR... CAN HE?
ARE YOU SERIOUS, FIELD AGENT? DOC SAMSON IS NEARLY AS STRONG AS THE HULK! HE COULD BURROW THROUGH THE SOIL AROUND HERE LIKE A MOLE THROUGH YOUR AUNTIE'S TULIP BED!
HE COULD BE MILES AWAY BY NOW!!
QUARTERMAIN TO FOLLOW ONE. QUARTERMAIN TO FOLLOW ONE!
RED ALERT! REPEAT, RED ALERT! DOC SAMSON HAS ESCAPED. HE COULD BE HEADING FOR YOU.
DO YOU COPY?
FOLLOW ONE TO QUARTERMAIN.
MESSAGE RECEIVED AND UNDERSTOOD.
"WE'LL BE READY IF HE TRIES TO INTERCEPT..."
15

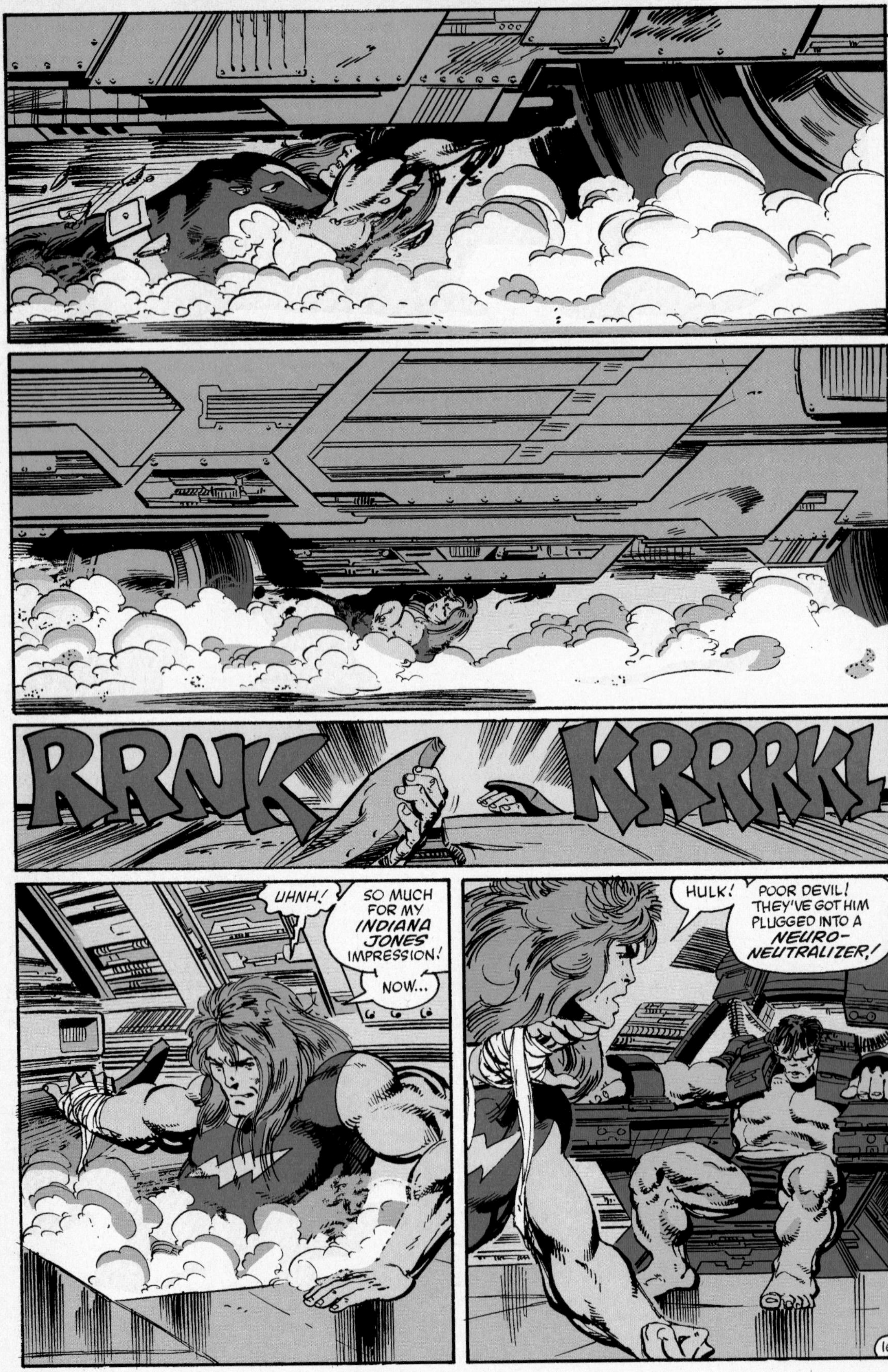
RRNK
KRRRKL
UHNH!
SO MUCH FOR MY INDIANA JONES IMPRESSION!
NOW...
HULK!
POOR DEVIL! THEY'VE GOT HIM PLUGGED INTO A NEURO-NEUTRALIZER!
16

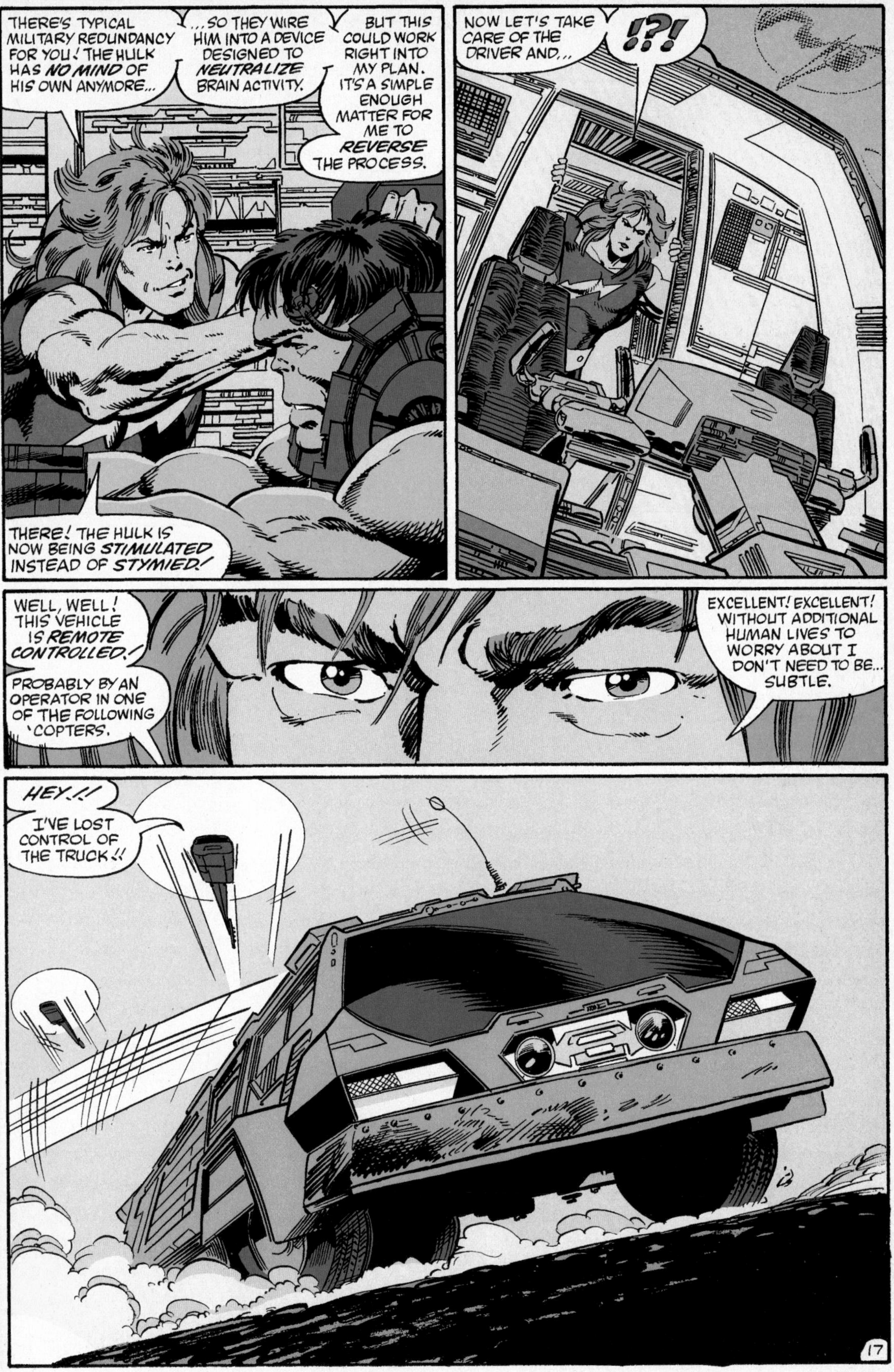

THERE'S TYPICAL MILITARY REDUNDANCY FOR YOU! THE HULK HAS NO MIND OF HIS OWN ANYMORE...
...SO THEY WIRE HIM INTO A DEVICE DESIGNED TO NEUTRALIZE BRAIN ACTIVITY.
BUT THIS COULD WORK RIGHT INTO MY PLAN. IT'S A SIMPLE ENOUGH MATTER FOR ME TO REVERSE THE PROCESS.
THERE! THE HULK IS NOW BEING STIMULATED INSTEAD OF STYMIED!
NOW LET'S TAKE CARE OF THE DRIVER AND...
!?!
WELL, WELL! THIS VEHICLE IS REMOTE CONTROLLED!
PROBABLY BY AN OPERATOR IN ONE OF THE FOLLOWING 'COPTERS.
EXCELLENT! EXCELLENT! WITHOUT ADDITIONAL HUMAN LIVES TO WORRY ABOUT I DON'T NEED TO BE... SUBTLE.
HEY!!!
I'VE LOST CONTROL OF THE TRUCK!!
17

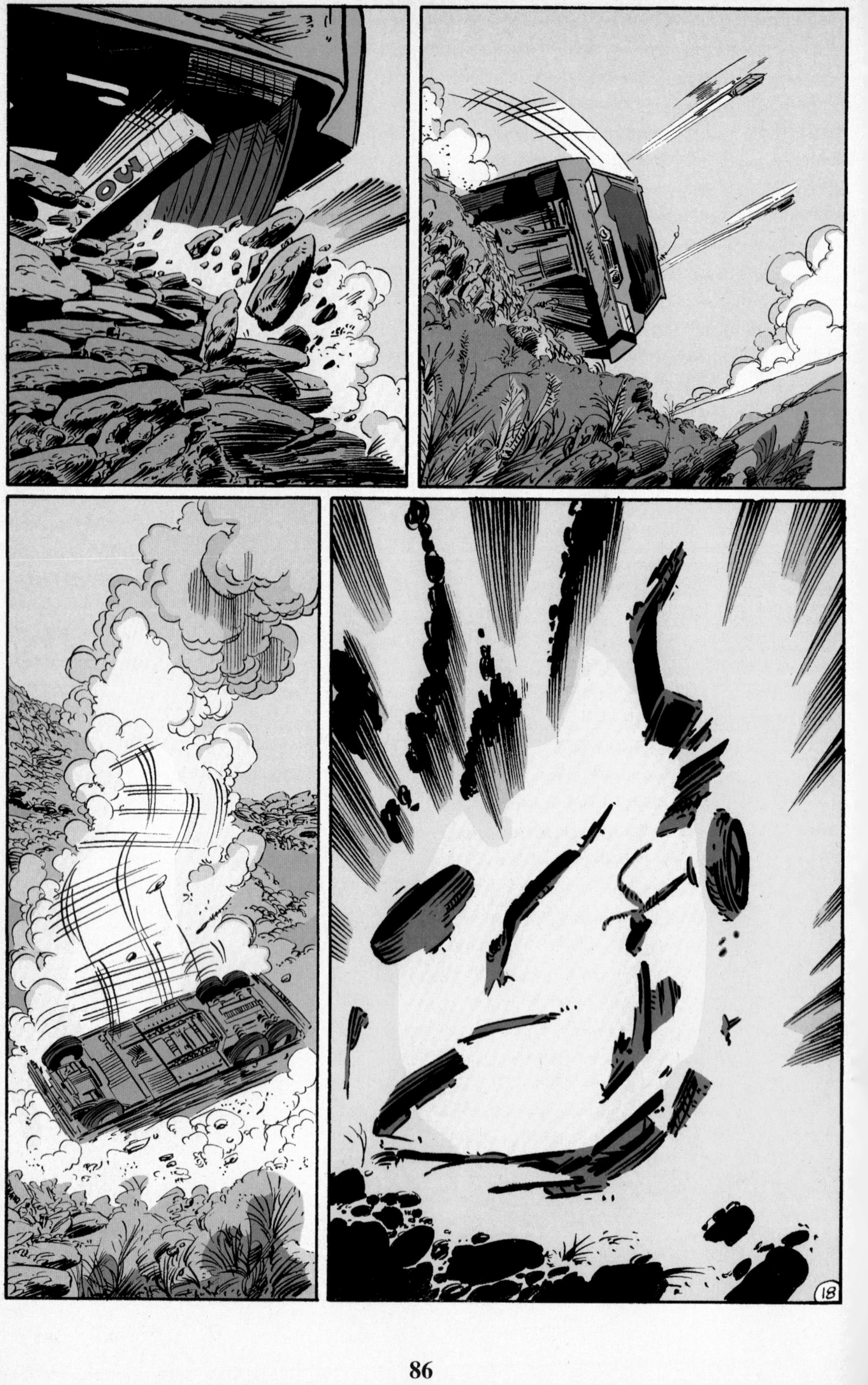

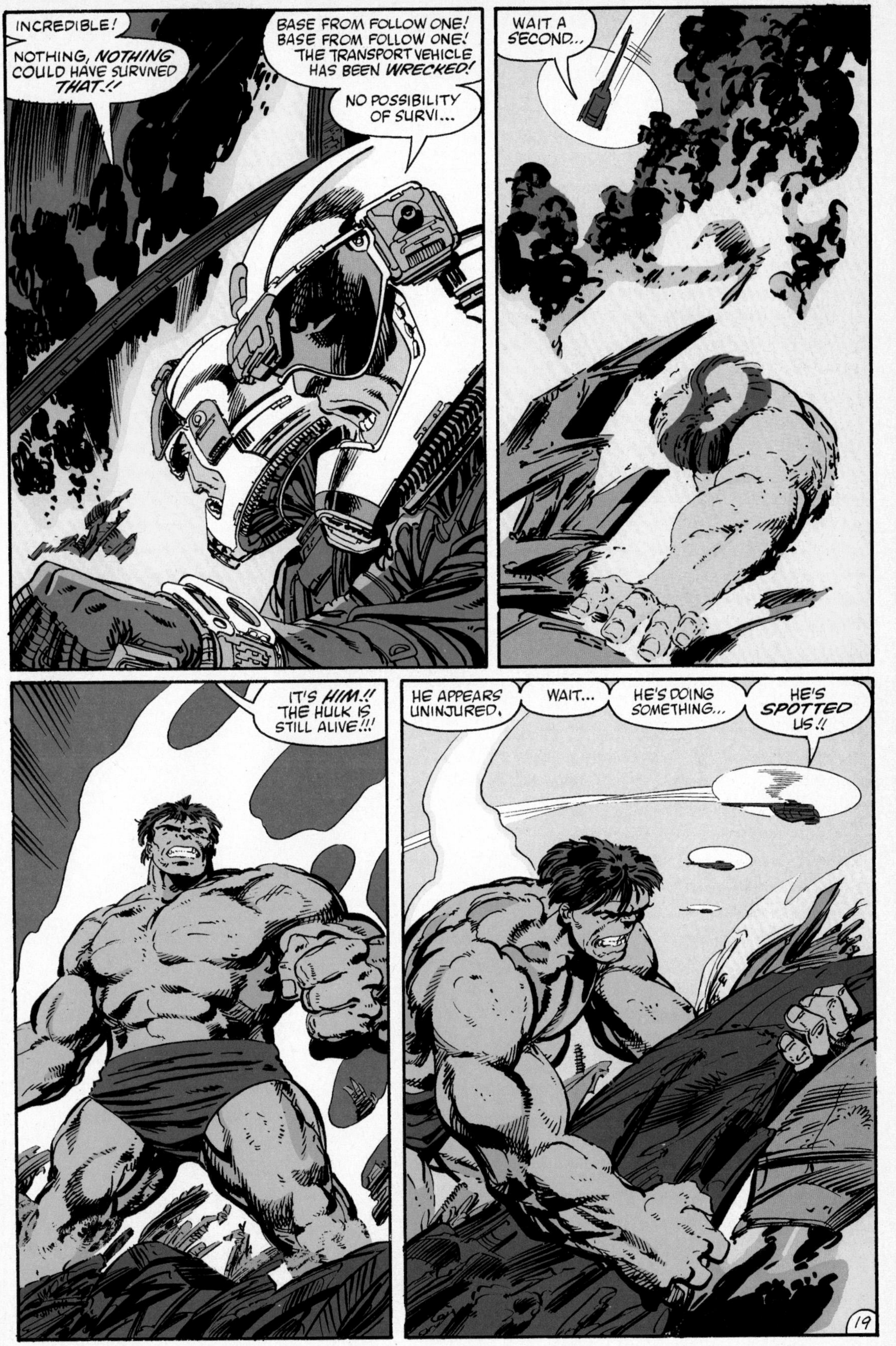
INCREDIBLE!
NOTHING, NOTHING COULD HAVE SURVIVED THAT!!
BASE FROM FOLLOW ONE! BASE FROM FOLLOW ONE! THE TRANSPORT VEHICLE HAS BEEN WRECKED!
NO POSSIBILITY OF SURVI...
WAIT A SECOND...
IT'S HIM!! THE HULK IS STILL ALIVE!!!
HE APPEARS UNINJURED.
WAIT...
HE'S DOING SOMETHING...
HE'S SPOTTED US!!
19

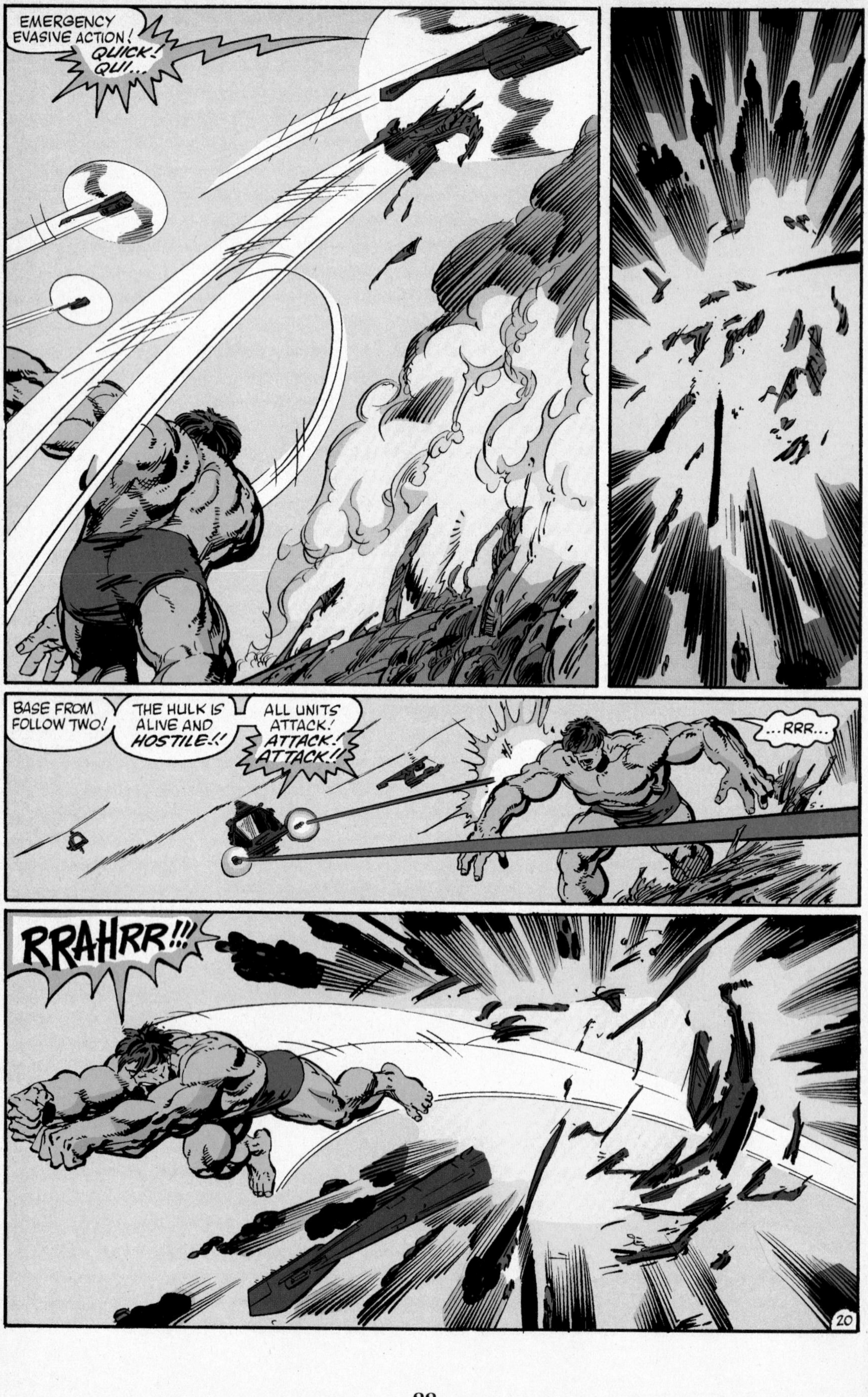

EMERGENCY EVASIVE ACTION! QUICK! QU!...
BASE FROM FOLLOW TWO!
THE HULK IS ALIVE AND HOSTILE!!
ALL UNITS ATTACK! ATTACK! ATTACK!!
...RRR...
RRAHRR!!!
20

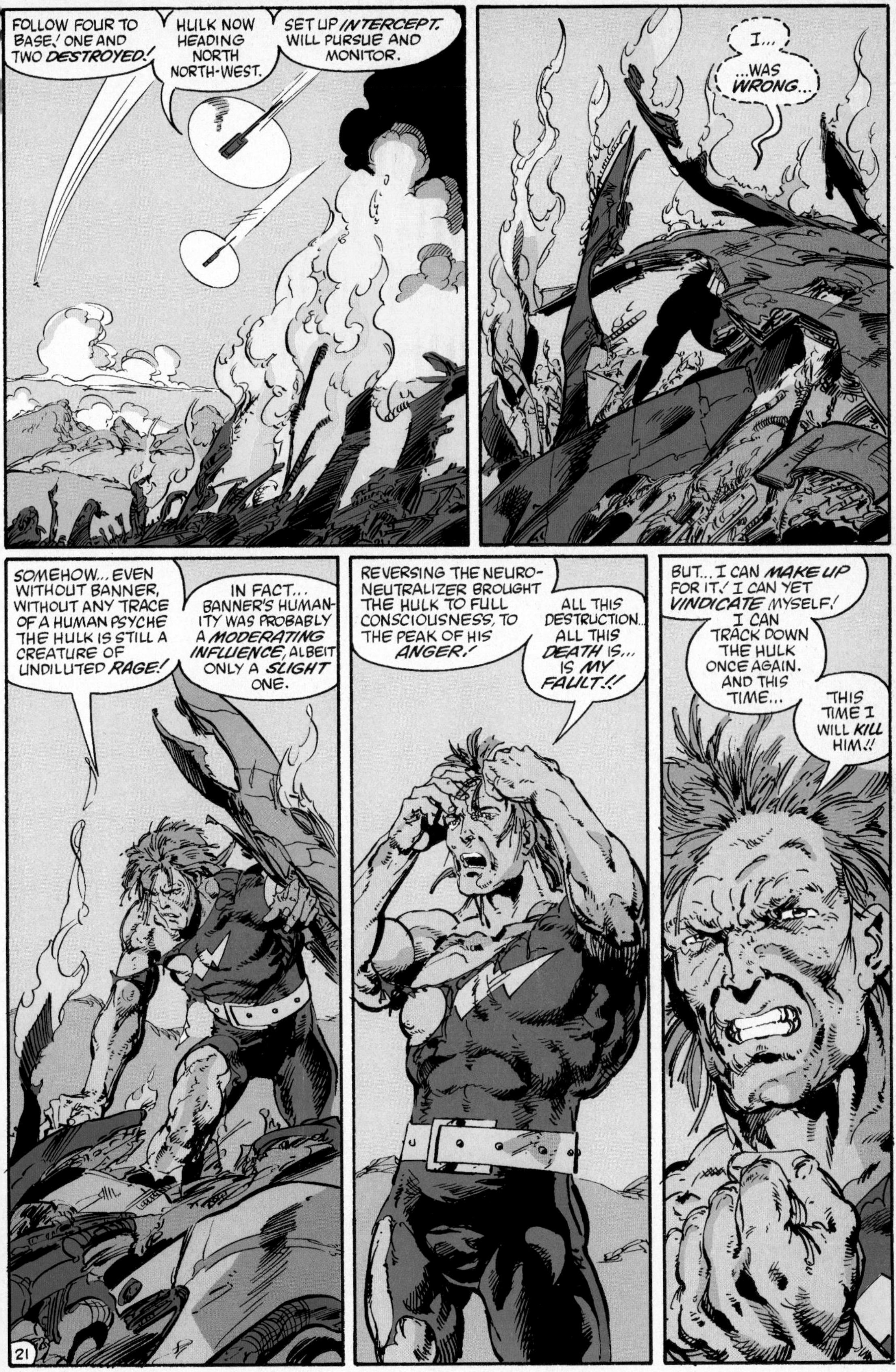
FOLLOW FOUR TO BASE! ONE AND TWO DESTROYED!
HULK NOW HEADING NORTH NORTH-WEST.
SET UP INTERCEPT. WILL PURSUE AND MONITOR.
I...
...WAS WRONG...
SOMEHOW... EVEN WITHOUT BANNER, WITHOUT ANY TRACE OF A HUMAN PSYCHE THE HULK IS STILL A CREATURE OF UNDILUTED RAGE!
IN FACT... BANNER'S HUMANITY WAS PROBABLY A MODERATING INFLUENCE, ALBEIT ONLY A SLIGHT ONE.
21
REVERSING THE NEURO-NEUTRALIZER BROUGHT THE HULK TO FULL CONSCIOUSNESS, TO THE PEAK OF HIS ANGER!
ALL THIS DESTRUCTION... ALL THIS DEATH IS... IS MY FAULT!!
BUT... I CAN MAKE UP FOR IT! I CAN YET VINDICATE MYSELF!
I CAN TRACK DOWN THE HULK ONCE AGAIN. AND THIS TIME...
THIS TIME I WILL KILL HIM!!

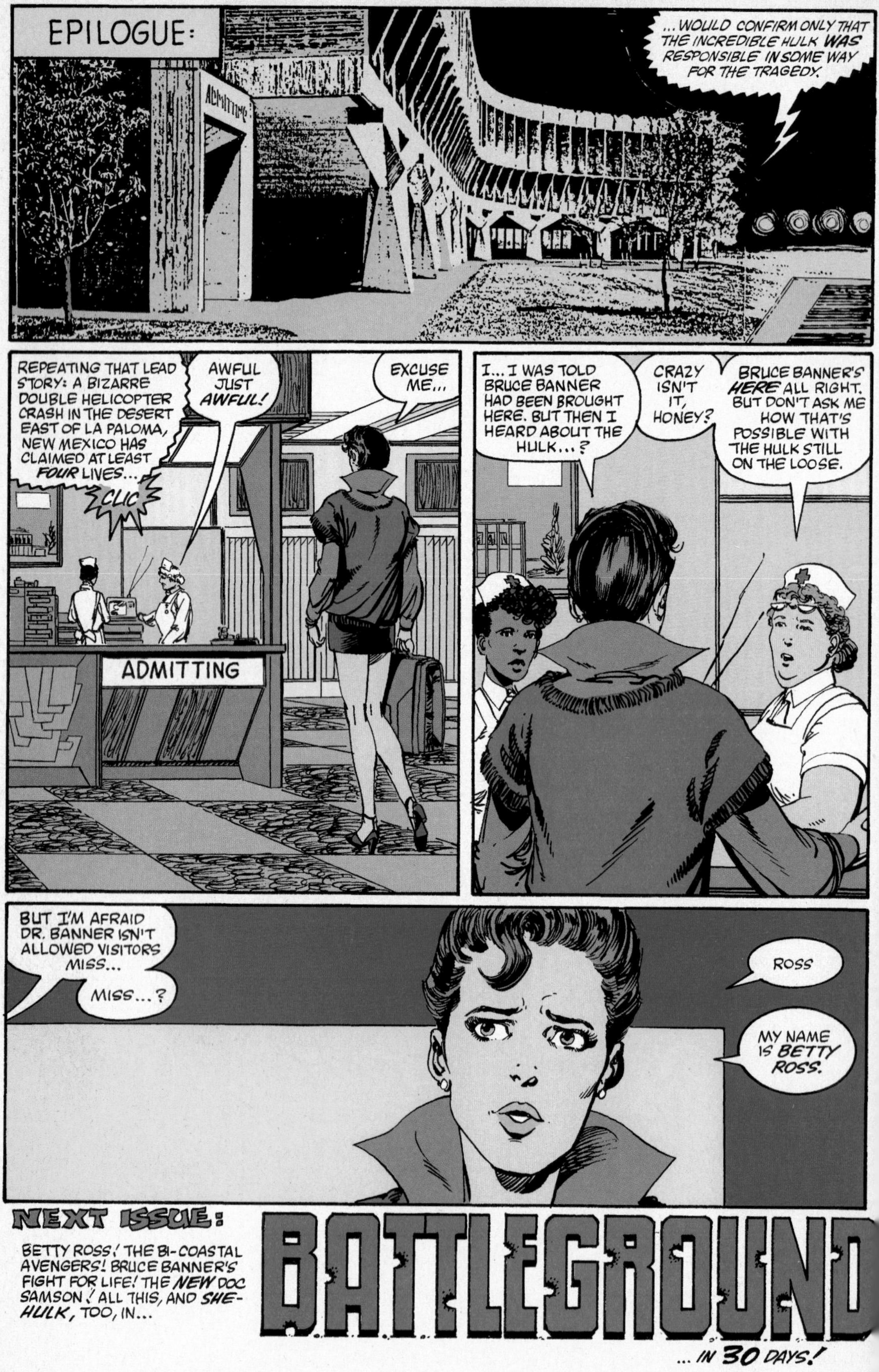
EPILOGUE:
ADMITTING
...WOULD CONFIRM ONLY THAT THE INCREDIBLE HULK WAS RESPONSIBLE IN SOME WAY FOR THE TRAGEDY.
REPEATING THAT LEAD STORY: A BIZARRE DOUBLE HELICOPTER CRASH IN THE DESERT EAST OF LA PALOMA, NEW MEXICO HAS CLAIMED AT LEAST FOUR LIVES...
CLIC
AWFUL JUST AWFUL!
EXCUSE ME...
ADMITTING
I... I WAS TOLD BRUCE BANNER HAD BEEN BROUGHT HERE. BUT THEN I HEARD ABOUT THE HULK...?
CRAZY ISN'T IT, HONEY?
BRUCE BANNER'S HERE ALL RIGHT. BUT DON'T ASK ME HOW THAT'S POSSIBLE WITH THE HULK STILL ON THE LOOSE.
BUT I'M AFRAID DR. BANNER ISN'T ALLOWED VISITORS MISS...
MISS...?
ROSS
MY NAME IS BETTY ROSS.
NEXT ISSUE:
BETTY ROSS! THE BI-COASTAL AVENGERS! BRUCE BANNER'S FIGHT FOR LIFE! THE NEW DOC SAMSON! ALL THIS, AND SHE-HULK, TOO, IN...
BATTLEGROUND
...IN 30 DAYS!

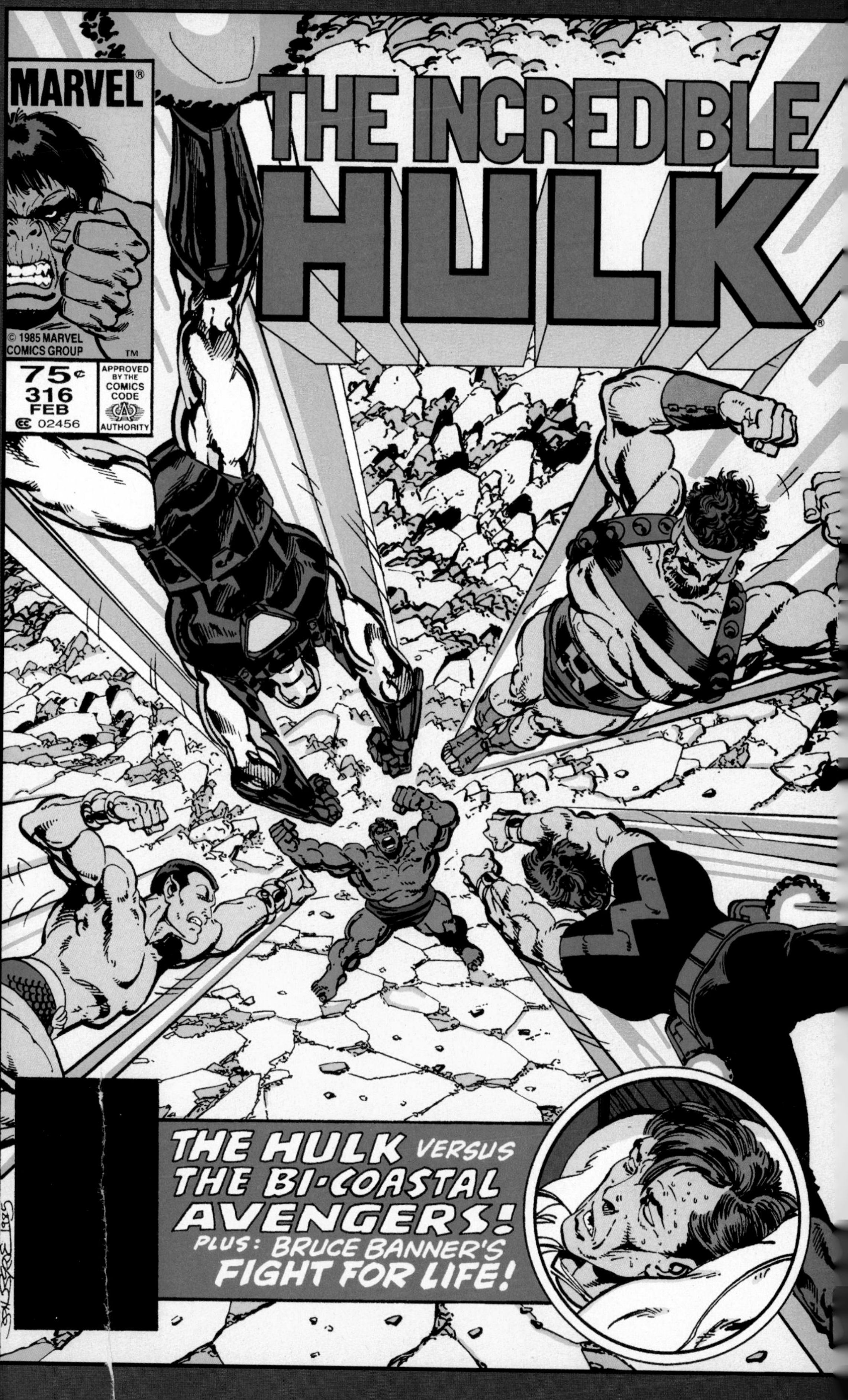
MARVEL®
THE INCREDIBLE HULK®
© 1985 MARVEL COMICS GROUP
TM
75¢
316
FEB
02456
APPROVED BY THE COMICS CODE AUTHORITY
THE HULK VERSUS THE BI-COASTAL AVENGERS!
PLUS: BRUCE BANNER'S FIGHT FOR LIFE!

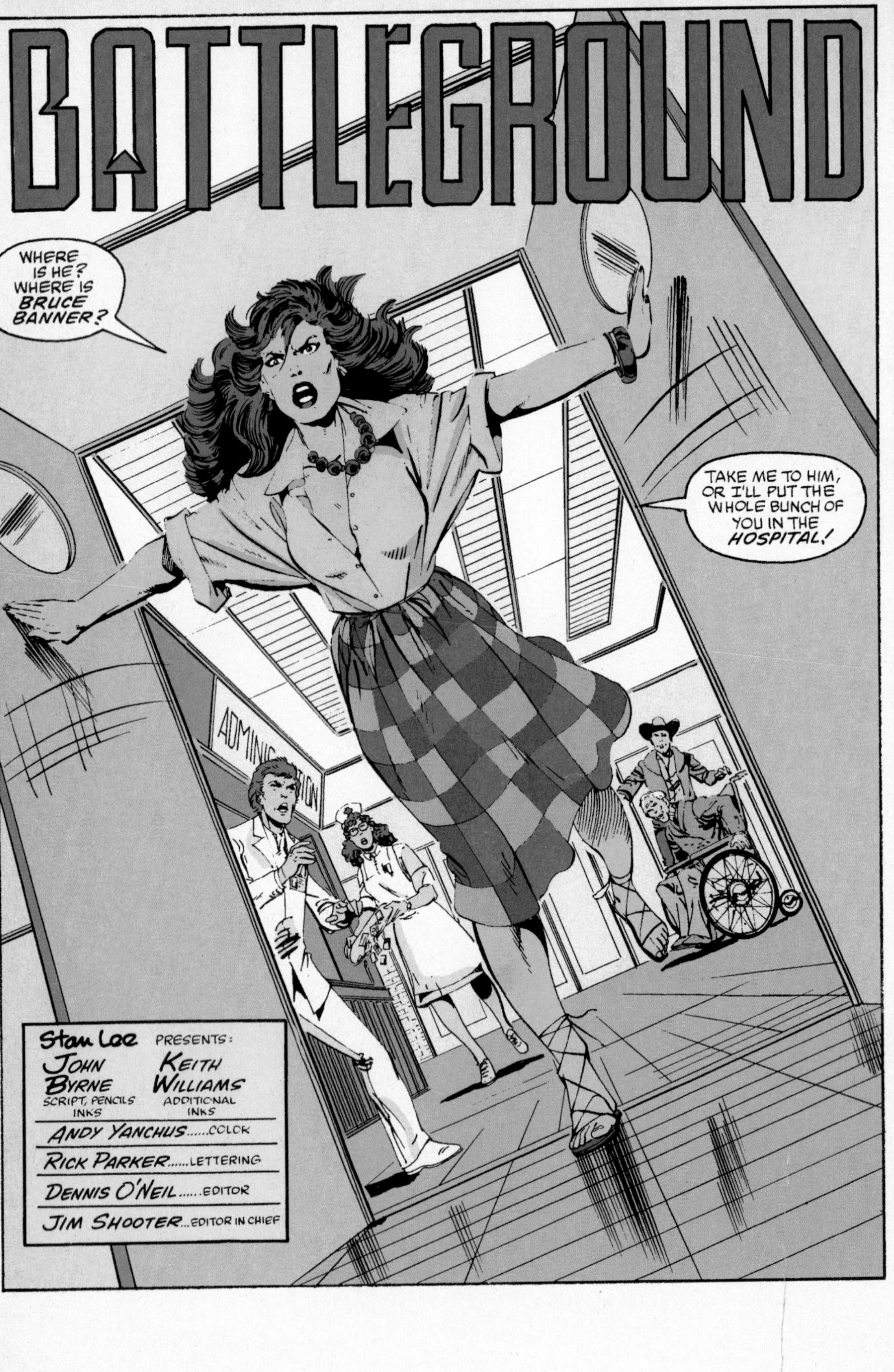
BATTLEGROUND
WHERE IS HE? WHERE IS BRUCE BANNER?
TAKE ME TO HIM, OR I'LL PUT THE WHOLE BUNCH OF YOU IN THE HOSPITAL!
ADMINISTRATION
Stan Lee PRESENTS:
JOHN BYRNE SCRIPT, PENCILS INKS
KEITH WILLIAMS ADDITIONAL INKS
ANDY YANCHUS......COLOR
RICK PARKER......LETTERING
DENNIS O'NEIL......EDITOR
JIM SHOOTER...EDITOR IN CHIEF

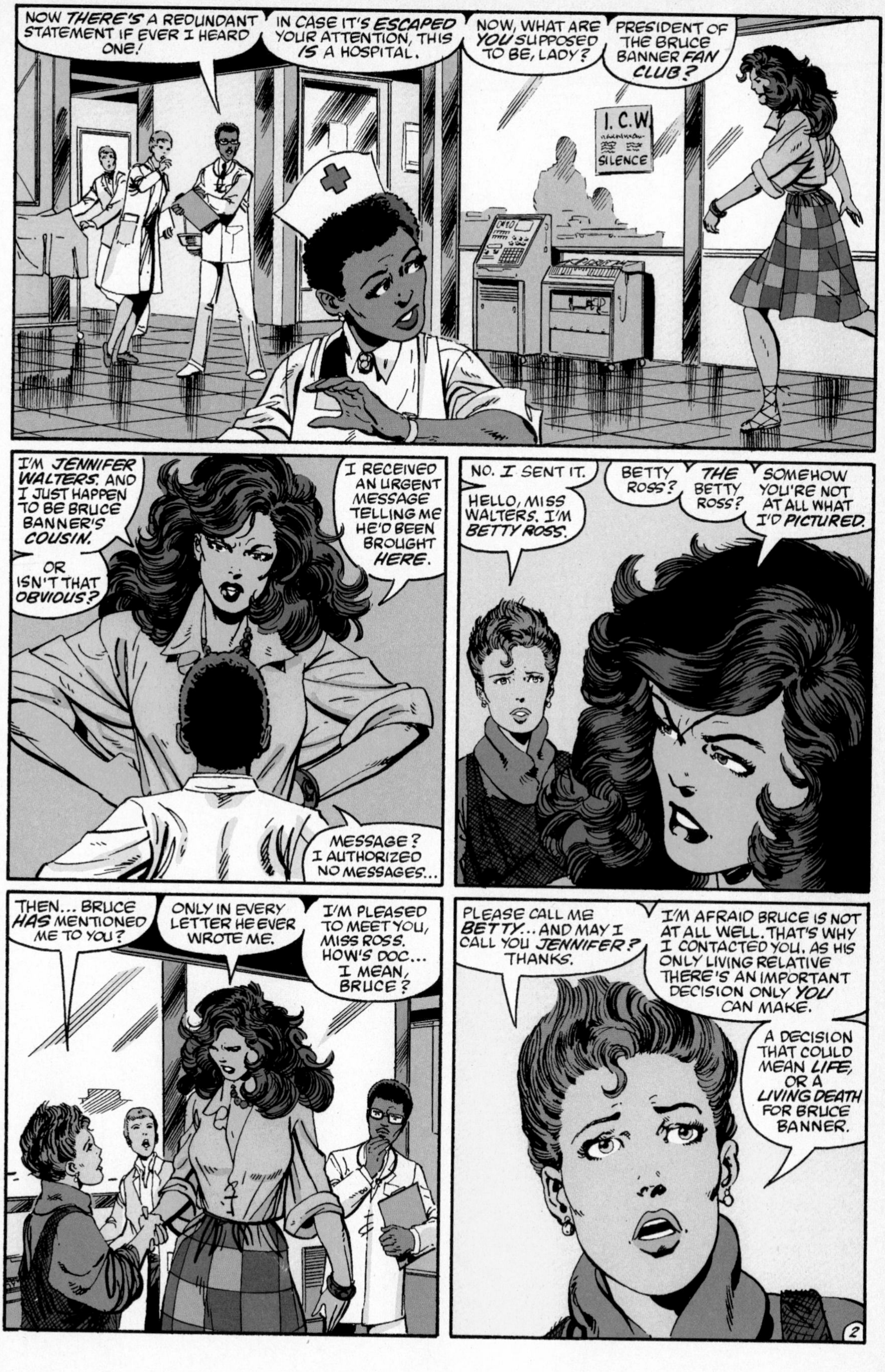

NOW THERE'S A REDUNDANT STATEMENT IF EVER I HEARD ONE!
IN CASE IT'S ESCAPED YOUR ATTENTION, THIS IS A HOSPITAL.
NOW, WHAT ARE YOU SUPPOSED TO BE, LADY?
PRESIDENT OF THE BRUCE BANNER FAN CLUB?
I.C.W
SILENCE
I'M JENNIFER WALTERS. AND I JUST HAPPEN TO BE BRUCE BANNER'S COUSIN.
OR ISN'T THAT OBVIOUS?
I RECEIVED AN URGENT MESSAGE TELLING ME HE'D BEEN BROUGHT HERE.
MESSAGE? I AUTHORIZED NO MESSAGES...
NO. I SENT IT.
HELLO, MISS WALTERS. I'M BETTY ROSS.
BETTY ROSS?
THE BETTY ROSS?
SOMEHOW YOU'RE NOT AT ALL WHAT I'D PICTURED.
THEN... BRUCE HAS MENTIONED ME TO YOU?
ONLY IN EVERY LETTER HE EVER WROTE ME.
I'M PLEASED TO MEET YOU, MISS ROSS. HOW'S DOC... I MEAN, BRUCE?
PLEASE CALL ME BETTY... AND MAY I CALL YOU JENNIFER? THANKS.
I'M AFRAID BRUCE IS NOT AT ALL WELL. THAT'S WHY I CONTACTED YOU. AS HIS ONLY LIVING RELATIVE THERE'S AN IMPORTANT DECISION ONLY YOU CAN MAKE.
A DECISION THAT COULD MEAN LIFE, OR A LIVING DEATH FOR BRUCE BANNER.
2

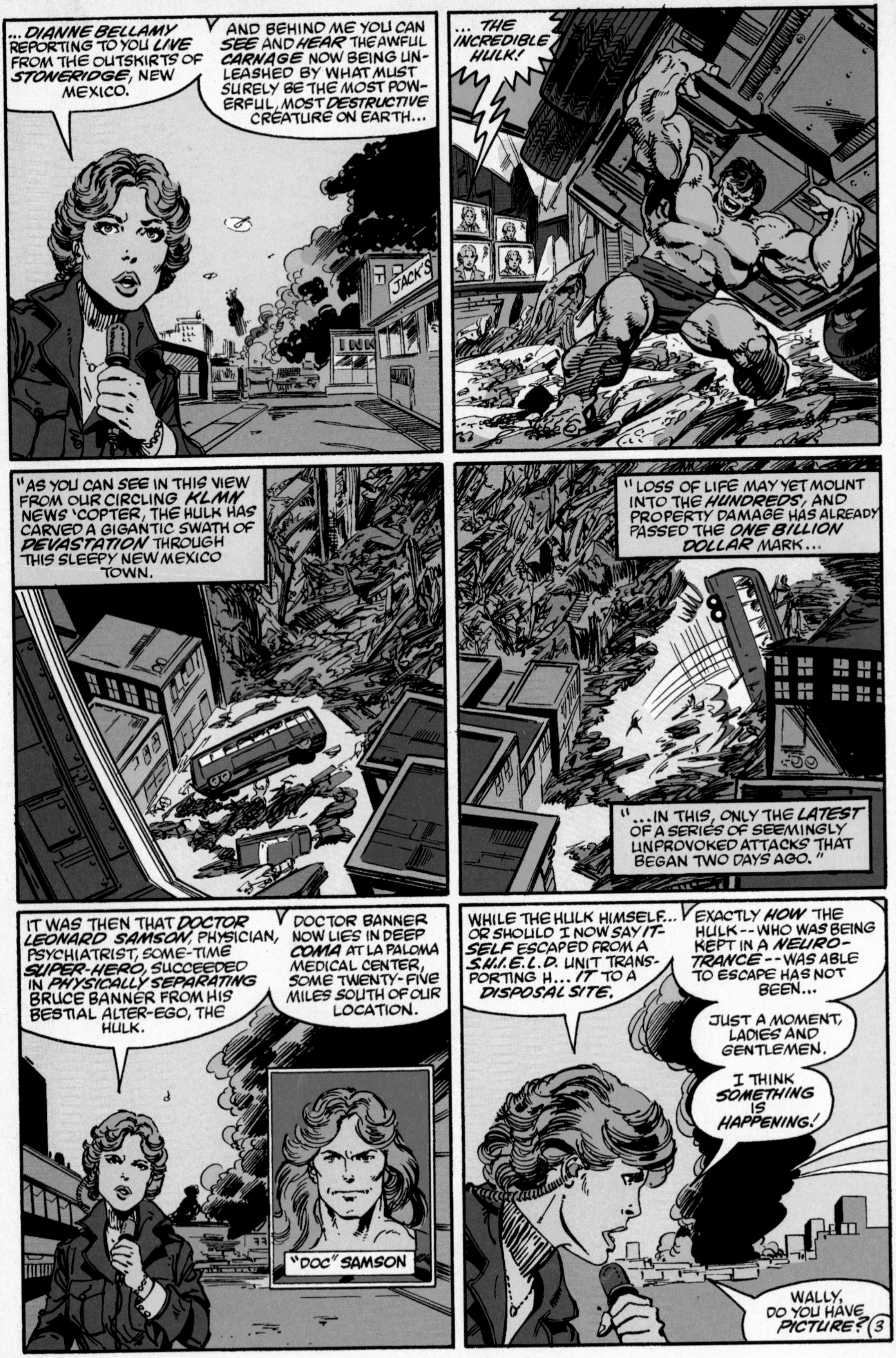
...DIANNE BELLAMY REPORTING TO YOU LIVE FROM THE OUTSKIRTS OF STONERIDGE, NEW MEXICO.
AND BEHIND ME YOU CAN SEE AND HEAR THE AWFUL CARNAGE NOW BEING UNLEASHED BY WHAT MUST SURELY BE THE MOST POWERFUL, MOST DESTRUCTIVE CREATURE ON EARTH...
JACK'S
INK
... THE INCREDIBLE HULK!
"AS YOU CAN SEE IN THIS VIEW FROM OUR CIRCLING KLMN NEWS 'COPTER, THE HULK HAS CARVED A GIGANTIC SWATH OF DEVASTATION THROUGH THIS SLEEPY NEW MEXICO TOWN.
"LOSS OF LIFE MAY YET MOUNT INTO THE HUNDREDS, AND PROPERTY DAMAGE HAS ALREADY PASSED THE ONE BILLION DOLLAR MARK...
"...IN THIS, ONLY THE LATEST OF A SERIES OF SEEMINGLY UNPROVOKED ATTACKS THAT BEGAN TWO DAYS AGO."
IT WAS THEN THAT DOCTOR LEONARD SAMSON, PHYSICIAN, PSYCHIATRIST, SOME-TIME SUPER-HERO, SUCCEEDED IN PHYSICALLY SEPARATING BRUCE BANNER FROM HIS BESTIAL ALTER-EGO, THE HULK.
DOCTOR BANNER NOW LIES IN DEEP COMA AT LA PALOMA MEDICAL CENTER, SOME TWENTY-FIVE MILES SOUTH OF OUR LOCATION.
"DOC" SAMSON
WHILE THE HULK HIMSELF... OR SHOULD I NOW SAY IT-SELF ESCAPED FROM A S.H.I.E.L.D. UNIT TRANSPORTING H... IT TO A DISPOSAL SITE.
EXACTLY HOW THE HULK--WHO WAS BEING KEPT IN A NEURO-TRANCE--WAS ABLE TO ESCAPE HAS NOT BEEN...
JUST A MOMENT, LADIES AND GENTLEMEN.
I THINK SOMETHING IS HAPPENING!
WALLY, DO YOU HAVE PICTURE?
3

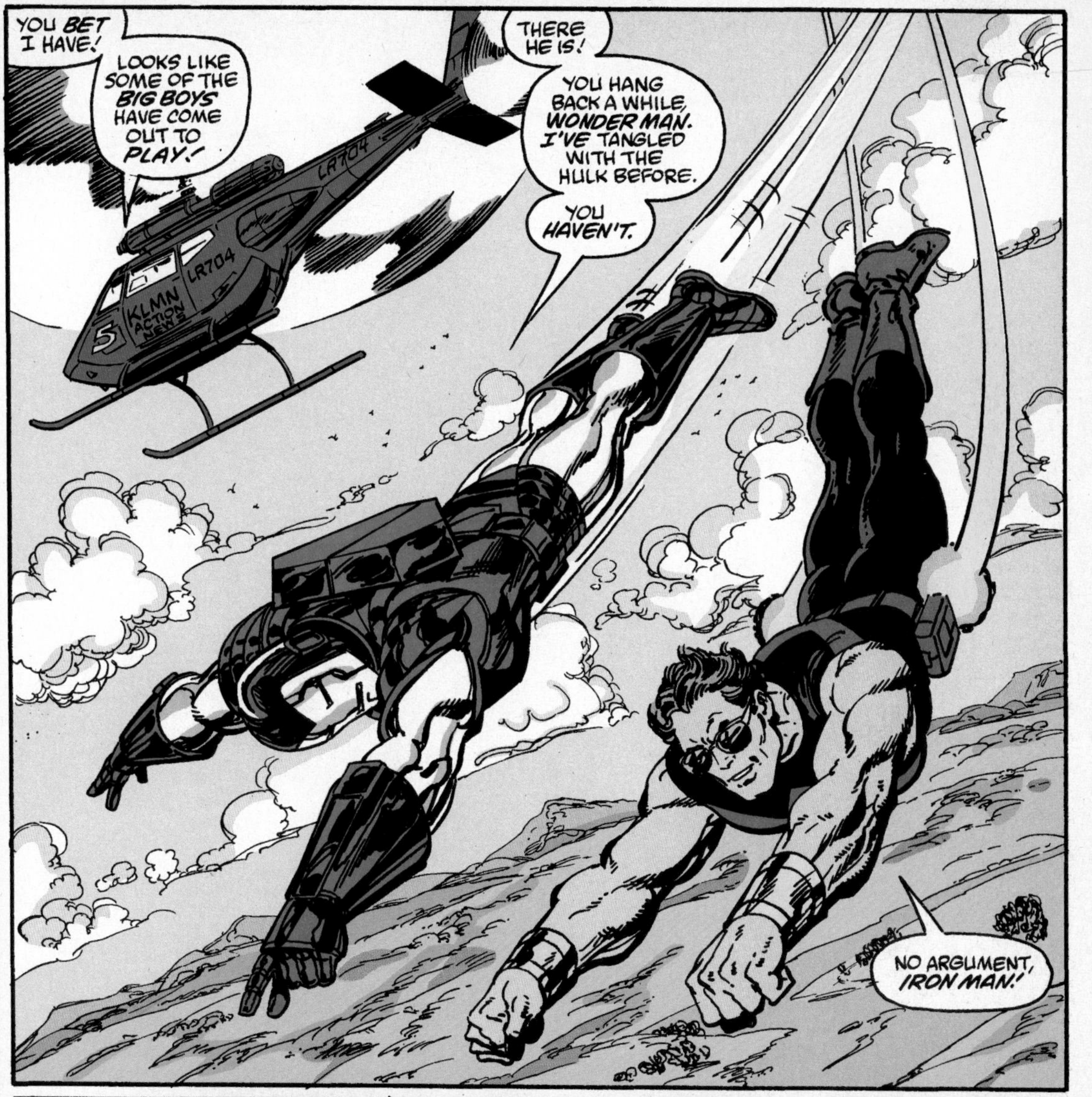
YOU BET I HAVE!
LOOKS LIKE SOME OF THE BIG BOYS HAVE COME OUT TO PLAY!
THERE HE IS!
YOU HANG BACK A WHILE, WONDER MAN. I'VE TANGLED WITH THE HULK BEFORE.
YOU HAVEN'T.
NO ARGUMENT, IRON MAN!
KLMN ACTION NEWS
LR704

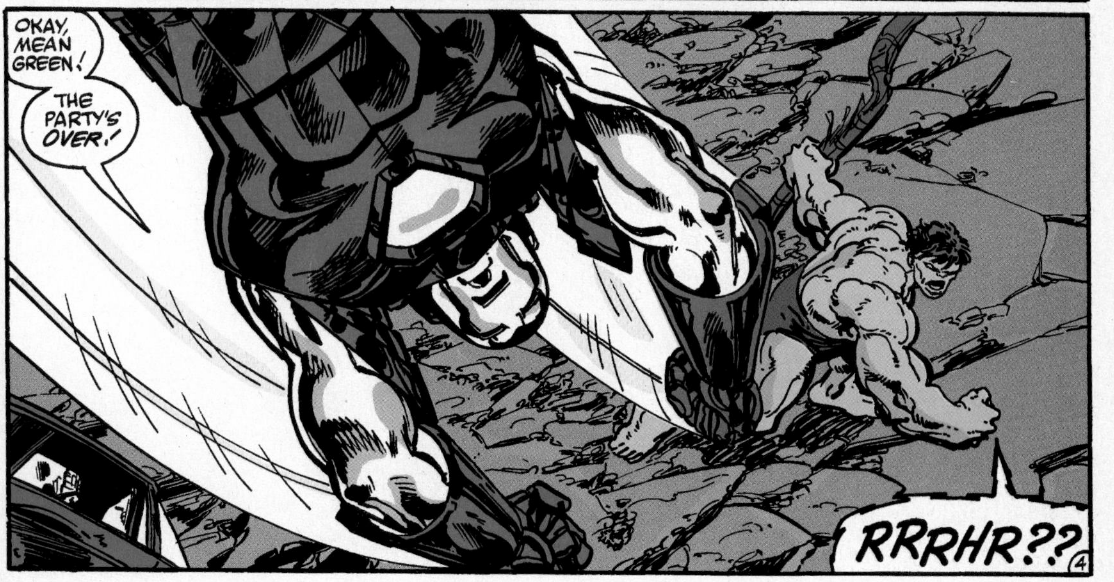
OKAY, MEAN GREEN!
THE PARTY'S OVER!
RRRHR??
4

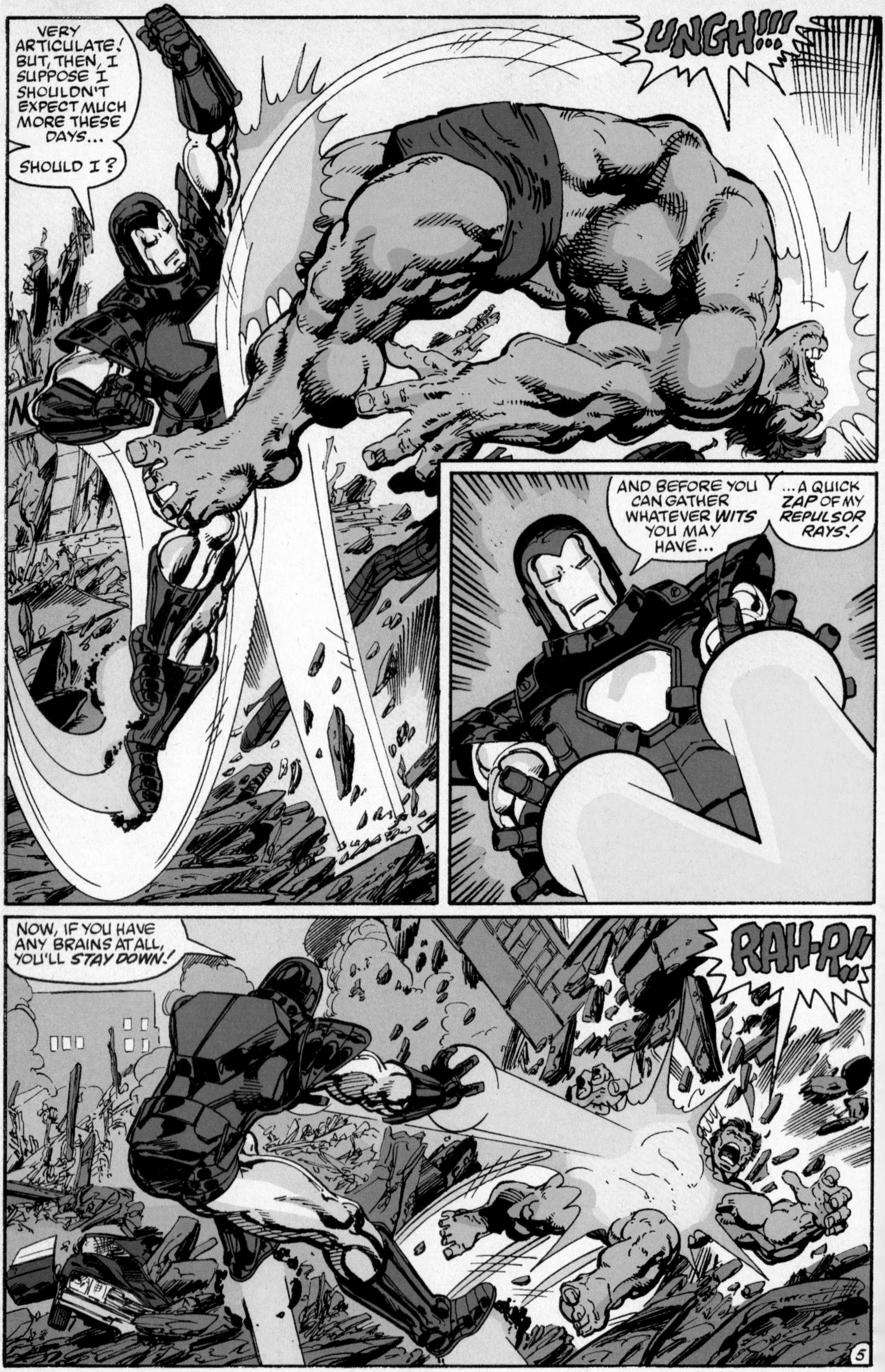
VERY ARTICULATE! BUT, THEN, I SUPPOSE I SHOULDN'T EXPECT MUCH MORE THESE DAYS...
SHOULD I?
UNGH!!!
AND BEFORE YOU CAN GATHER WHATEVER WITS YOU MAY HAVE...
...A QUICK ZAP OF MY REPULSOR RAYS!
NOW, IF YOU HAVE ANY BRAINS AT ALL, YOU'LL STAY DOWN!
RAH-R!!
5

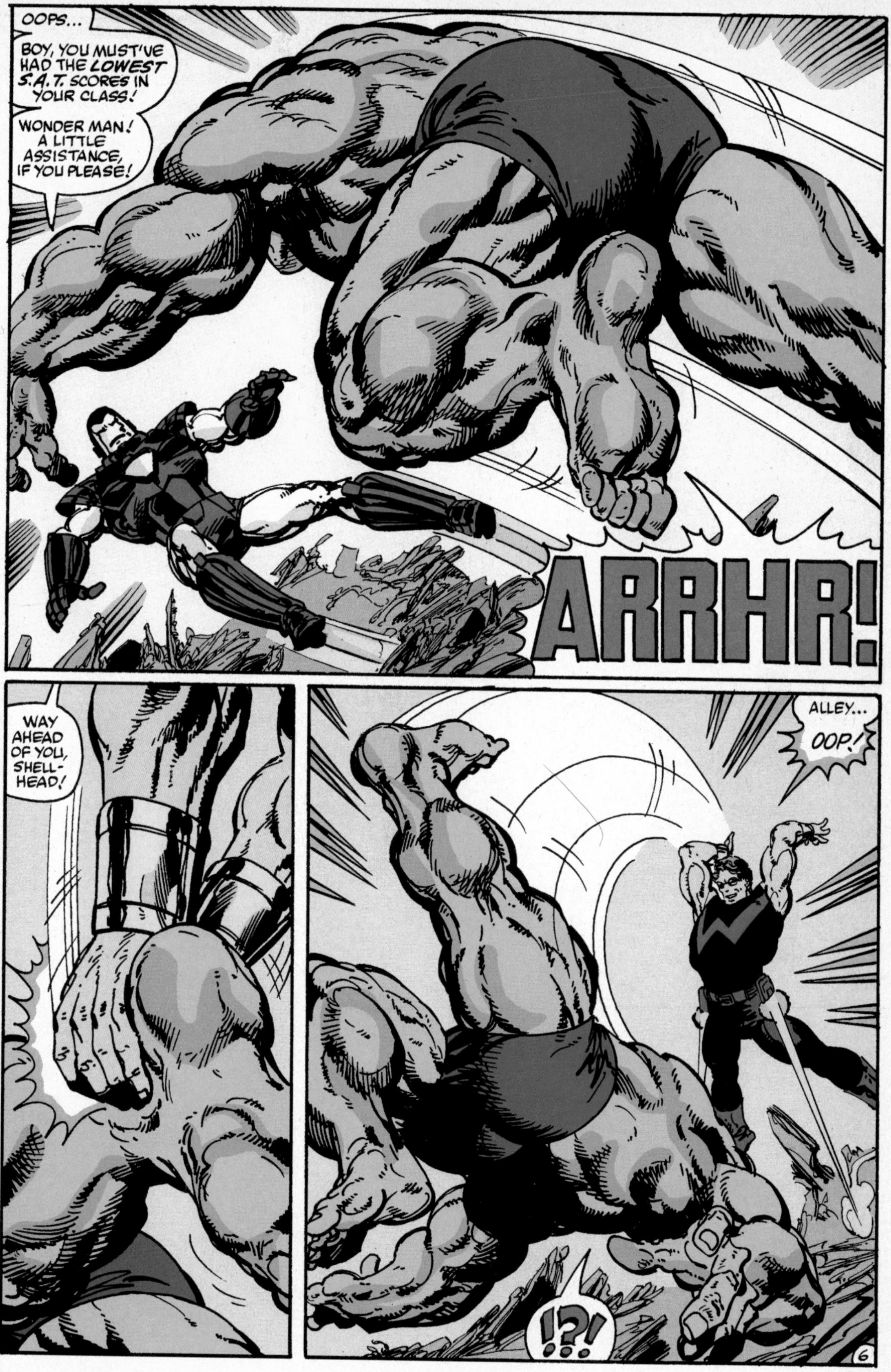
OOPS...
BOY, YOU MUST'VE HAD THE LOWEST S.A.T. SCORES IN YOUR CLASS!
WONDER MAN! A LITTLE ASSISTANCE, IF YOU PLEASE!
ARRHR!
WAY AHEAD OF YOU, SHELL-HEAD!
ALLEY...
OOP!
!?!
6

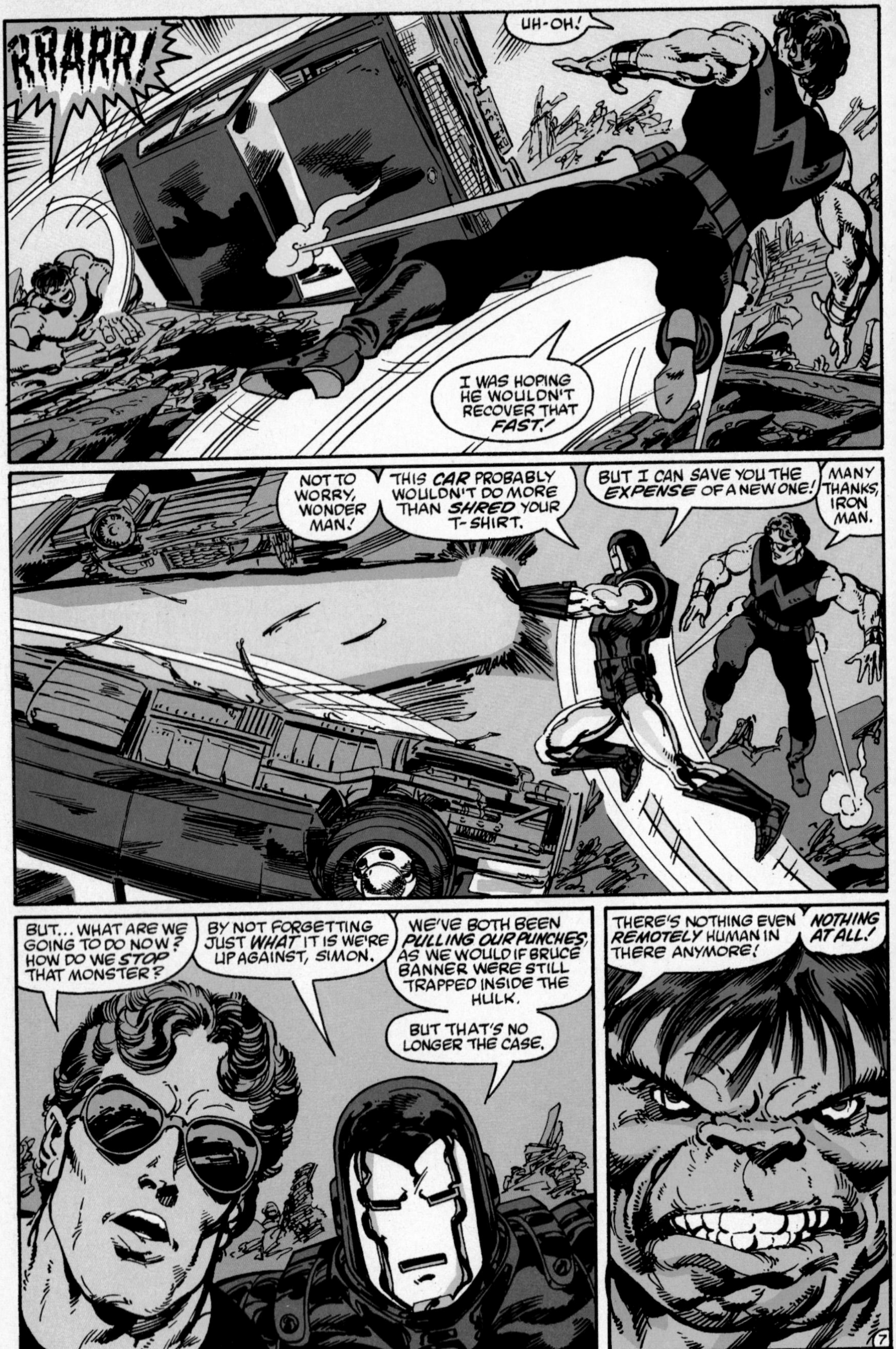
RRARR!
UH-OH!
I WAS HOPING HE WOULDN'T RECOVER THAT FAST!
NOT TO WORRY, WONDER MAN!
THIS CAR PROBABLY WOULDN'T DO MORE THAN SHRED YOUR T-SHIRT.
BUT I CAN SAVE YOU THE EXPENSE OF A NEW ONE!
MANY THANKS, IRON MAN.
BUT... WHAT ARE WE GOING TO DO NOW? HOW DO WE STOP THAT MONSTER?
BY NOT FORGETTING JUST WHAT IT IS WE'RE UP AGAINST, SIMON.
WE'VE BOTH BEEN PULLING OUR PUNCHES, AS WE WOULD IF BRUCE BANNER WERE STILL TRAPPED INSIDE THE HULK.
BUT THAT'S NO LONGER THE CASE.
THERE'S NOTHING EVEN REMOTELY HUMAN IN THERE ANYMORE!
NOTHING AT ALL!
7

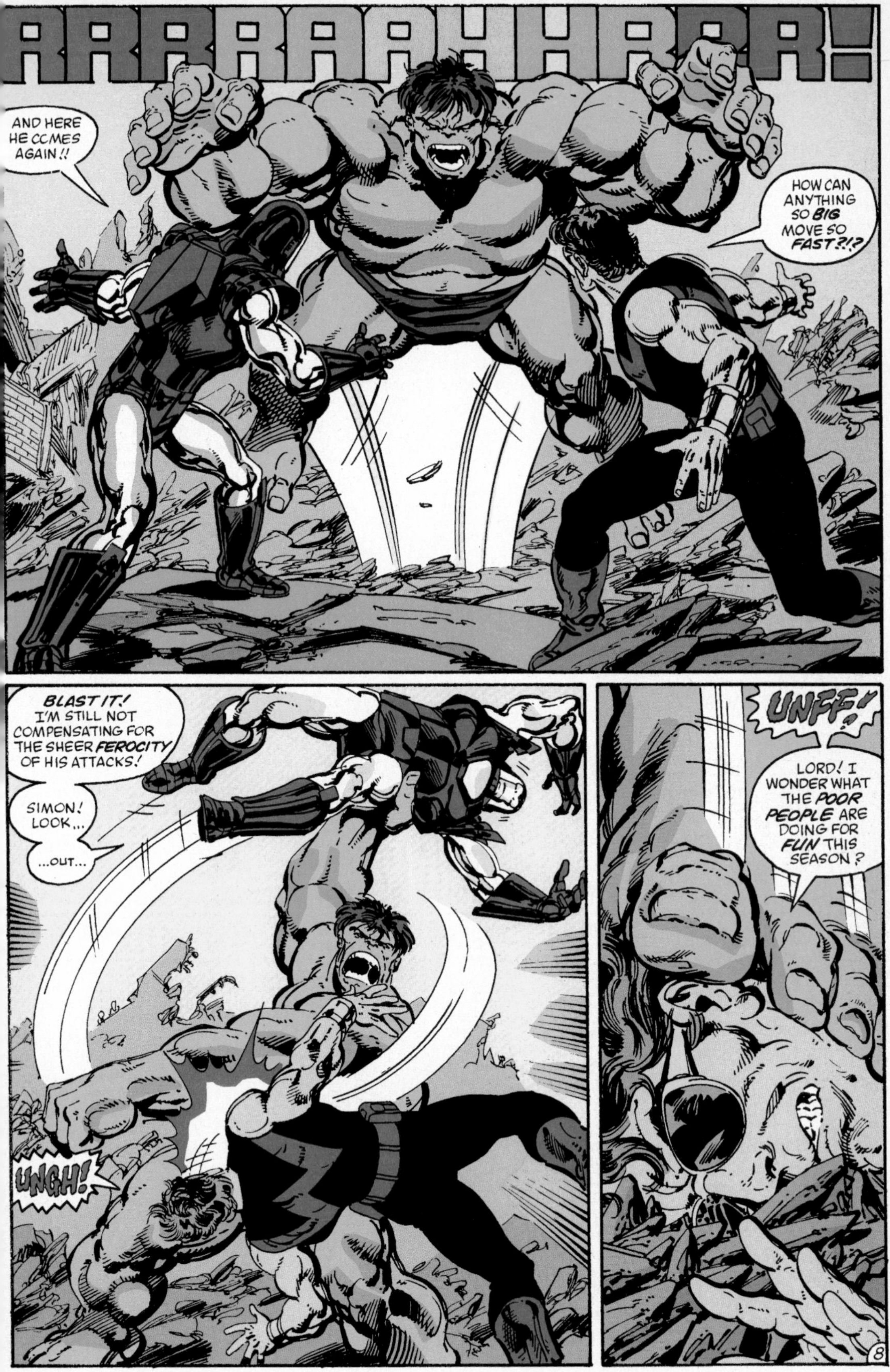

RRRRRAAHHRRR!
AND HERE HE COMES AGAIN!!
HOW CAN ANYTHING SO BIG MOVE SO FAST?!?
BLAST IT! I'M STILL NOT COMPENSATING FOR THE SHEER FEROCITY OF HIS ATTACKS!
SIMON! LOOK... ...OUT...
UNGH!
UNFF!
LORD! I WONDER WHAT THE POOR PEOPLE ARE DOING FOR FUN THIS SEASON?
8

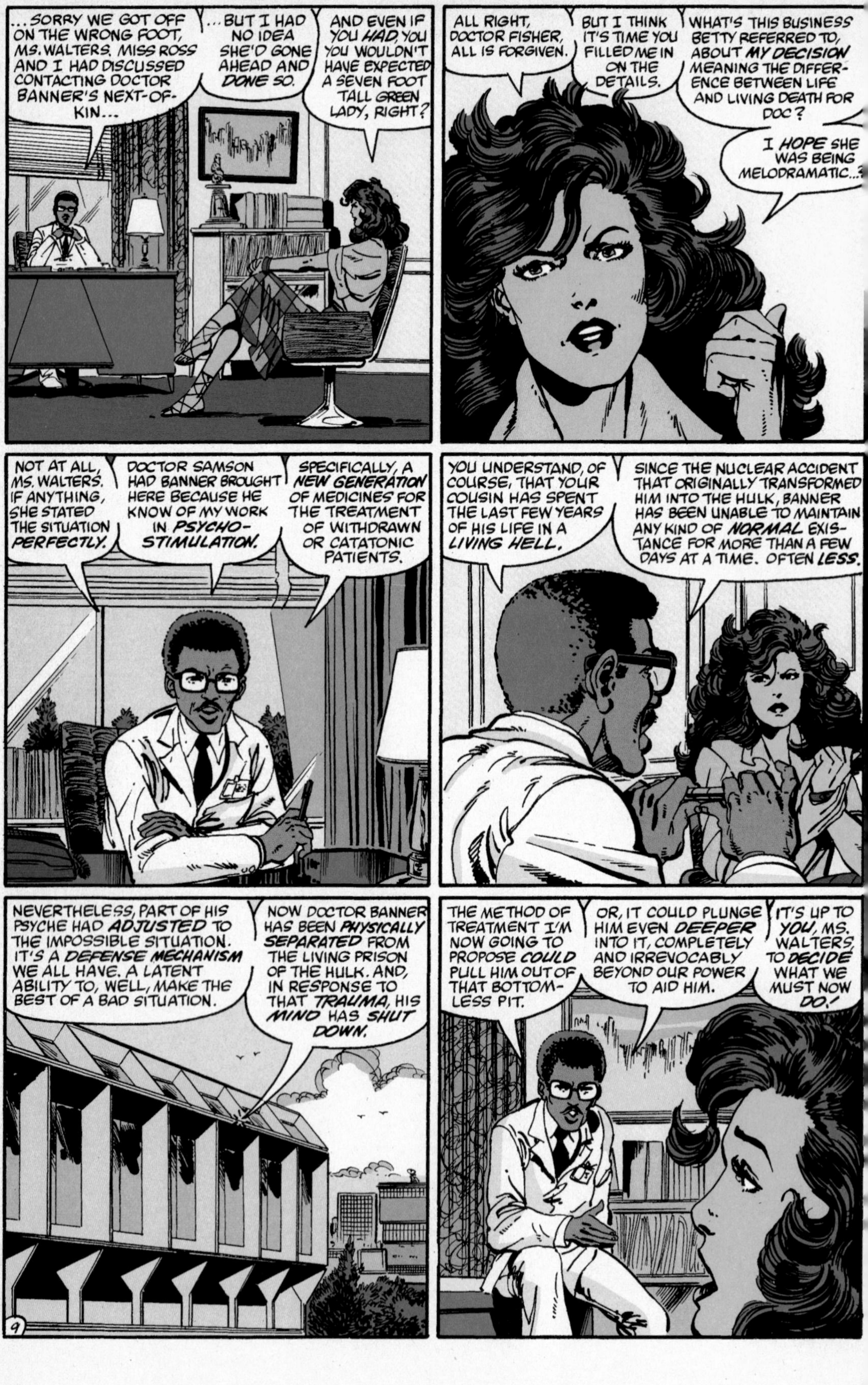
...SORRY WE GOT OFF ON THE WRONG FOOT, MS. WALTERS. MISS ROSS AND I HAD DISCUSSED CONTACTING DOCTOR BANNER'S NEXT-OF-KIN...
...BUT I HAD NO IDEA SHE'D GONE AHEAD AND DONE SO.
AND EVEN IF YOU HAD, YOU YOU WOULDN'T HAVE EXPECTED A SEVEN FOOT TALL GREEN LADY, RIGHT?
ALL RIGHT, DOCTOR FISHER, ALL IS FORGIVEN.
BUT I THINK IT'S TIME YOU FILLED ME IN ON THE DETAILS.
WHAT'S THIS BUSINESS BETTY REFERRED TO, ABOUT MY DECISION MEANING THE DIFFERENCE BETWEEN LIFE AND LIVING DEATH FOR DOC?
I HOPE SHE WAS BEING MELODRAMATIC...?
NOT AT ALL, MS. WALTERS. IF ANYTHING, SHE STATED THE SITUATION PERFECTLY.
DOCTOR SAMSON HAD BANNER BROUGHT HERE BECAUSE HE KNOW OF MY WORK IN PSYCHO-STIMULATION.
SPECIFICALLY, A NEW GENERATION OF MEDICINES FOR THE TREATMENT OF WITHDRAWN OR CATATONIC PATIENTS.
YOU UNDERSTAND, OF COURSE, THAT YOUR COUSIN HAS SPENT THE LAST FEW YEARS OF HIS LIFE IN A LIVING HELL.
SINCE THE NUCLEAR ACCIDENT THAT ORIGINALLY TRANSFORMED HIM INTO THE HULK, BANNER HAS BEEN UNABLE TO MAINTAIN ANY KIND OF NORMAL EXISTANCE FOR MORE THAN A FEW DAYS AT A TIME. OFTEN LESS.
NEVERTHELESS, PART OF HIS PSYCHE HAD ADJUSTED TO THE IMPOSSIBLE SITUATION. IT'S A DEFENSE MECHANISM WE ALL HAVE. A LATENT ABILITY TO, WELL, MAKE THE BEST OF A BAD SITUATION.
NOW DOCTOR BANNER HAS BEEN PHYSICALLY SEPARATED FROM THE LIVING PRISON OF THE HULK. AND, IN RESPONSE TO THAT TRAUMA, HIS MIND HAS SHUT DOWN.
THE METHOD OF TREATMENT I'M NOW GOING TO PROPOSE COULD PULL HIM OUT OF THAT BOTTOMLESS PIT.
OR, IT COULD PLUNGE HIM EVEN DEEPER INTO IT, COMPLETELY AND IRREVOCABLY BEYOND OUR POWER TO AID HIM.
IT'S UP TO YOU, MS. WALTERS, TO DECIDE WHAT WE MUST NOW DO!
9

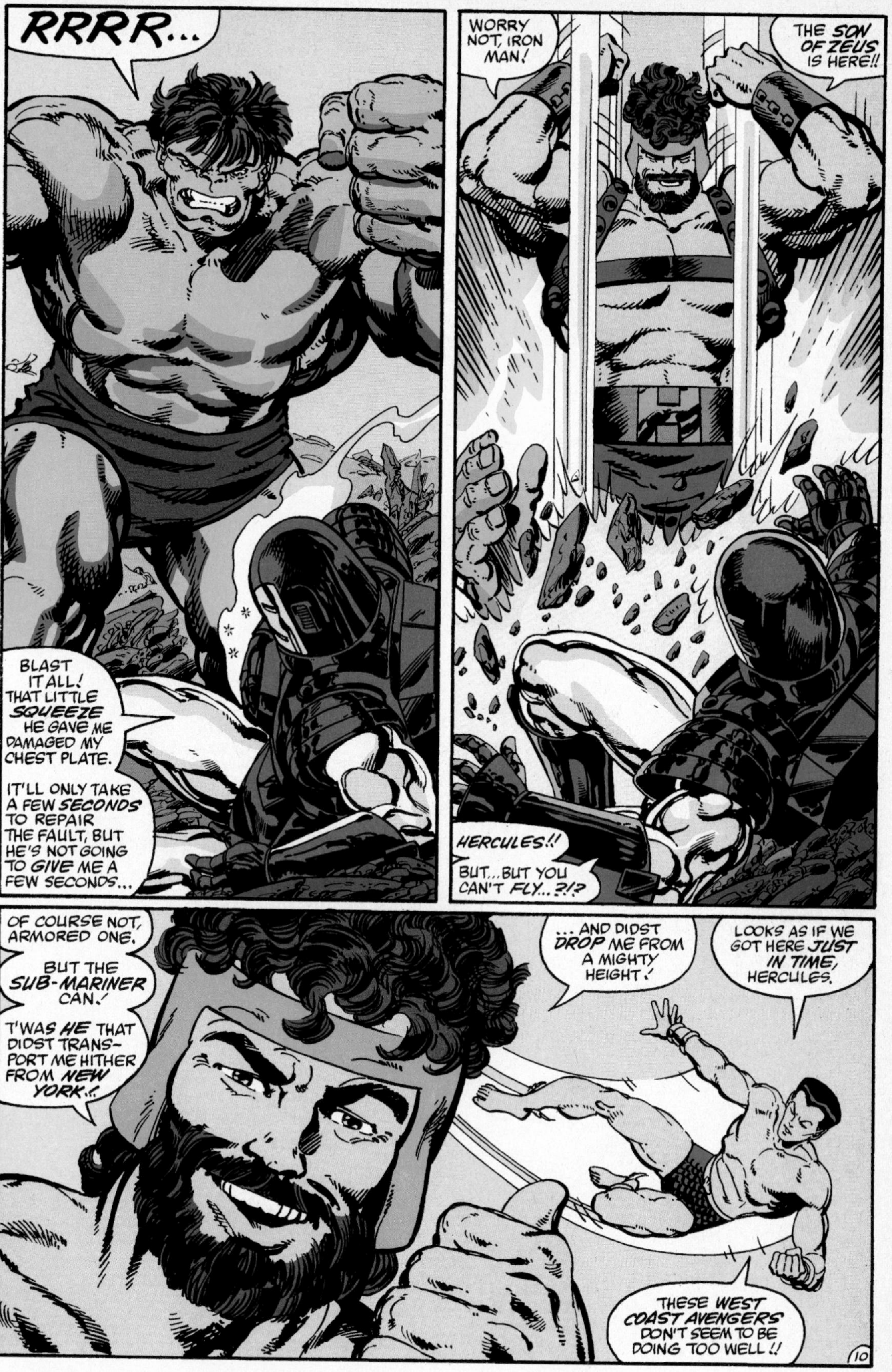
RRRR...
WORRY NOT, IRON MAN!
THE SON OF ZEUS IS HERE!!
BLAST IT ALL! THAT LITTLE SQUEEZE HE GAVE ME DAMAGED MY CHEST PLATE.
IT'LL ONLY TAKE A FEW SECONDS TO REPAIR THE FAULT, BUT HE'S NOT GOING TO GIVE ME A FEW SECONDS...
HERCULES!!
BUT...BUT YOU CAN'T FLY...?!?
OF COURSE NOT, ARMORED ONE.
BUT THE SUB-MARINER CAN!
T'WAS HE THAT DIDST TRANSPORT ME HITHER FROM NEW YORK!...
...AND DIDST DROP ME FROM A MIGHTY HEIGHT!
LOOKS AS IF WE GOT HERE JUST IN TIME, HERCULES.
THESE WEST COAST AVENGERS DON'T SEEM TO BE DOING TOO WELL!!
10

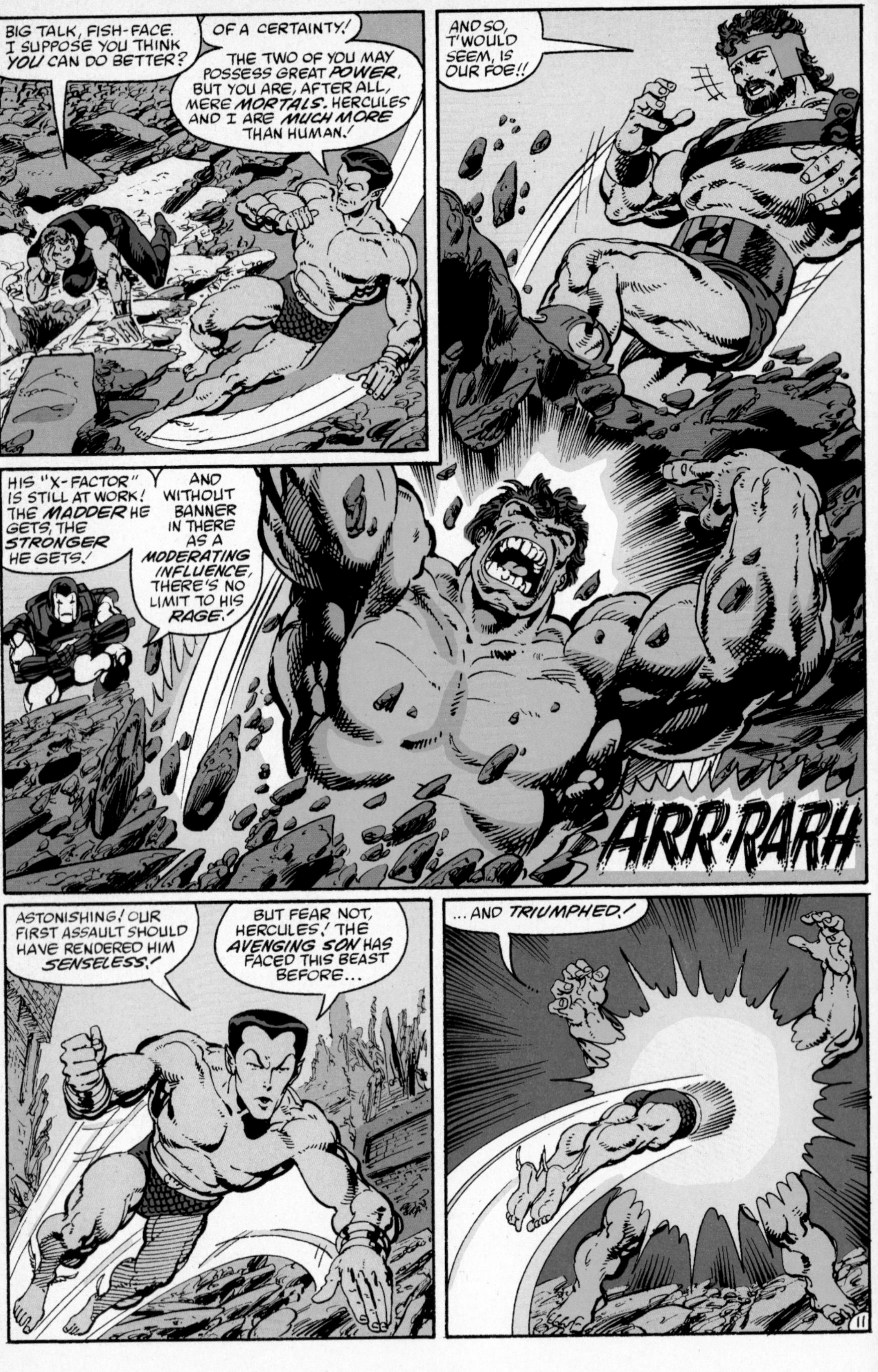
BIG TALK, FISH-FACE. I SUPPOSE YOU THINK YOU CAN DO BETTER?
OF A CERTAINTY!
THE TWO OF YOU MAY POSSESS GREAT POWER, BUT YOU ARE, AFTER ALL, MERE MORTALS. HERCULES AND I ARE MUCH MORE THAN HUMAN!
AND SO, T'WOULD SEEM, IS OUR FOE!!
HIS "X-FACTOR" IS STILL AT WORK! THE MADDER HE GETS, THE STRONGER HE GETS!
AND WITHOUT BANNER IN THERE AS A MODERATING INFLUENCE, THERE'S NO LIMIT TO HIS RAGE!
ARR-RARH
ASTONISHING! OUR FIRST ASSAULT SHOULD HAVE RENDERED HIM SENSELESS!
BUT FEAR NOT, HERCULES! THE AVENGING SON HAS FACED THIS BEAST BEFORE...
...AND TRIUMPHED!
11

AH-RR!

UNGH!

BEARD OF MY FATHER!! HE DIDST TOSS ASIDE SUB-MARINER AS IF HE WERE BUT THISTLE-DOWN!

VERILY, THIS JADE-HUED TITAN MAY WELL DEMAND THE LOOSING OF THE GREATEST POWER ON EARTH, BEFORE HE *FALLS!*

'TIS FORTUNATE THEN THAT *HERCULES* POSSESSES SUCH POWER!

RRRRR...?

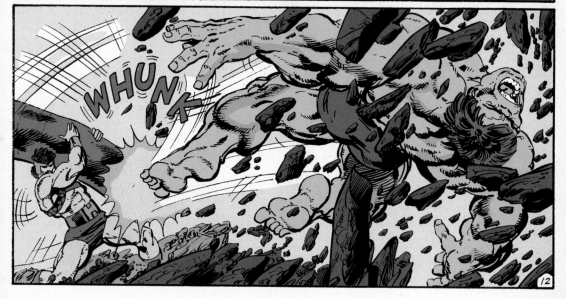

WHUNK

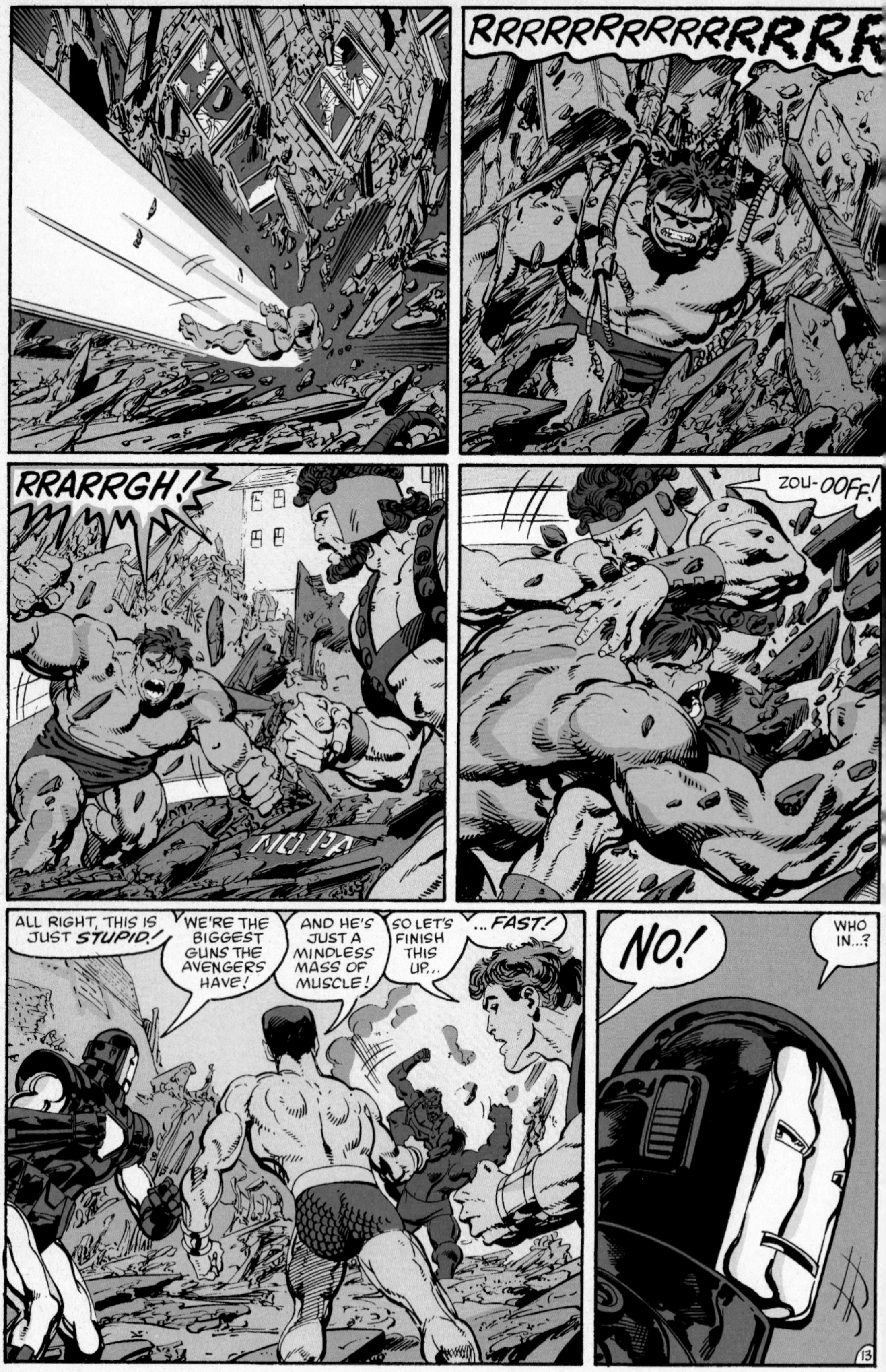
RRRRRRRRRRRRRR
RRARRGH!
ZOU-OOFF!
NO:PA
ALL RIGHT, THIS IS JUST STUPID!
WE'RE THE BIGGEST GUNS THE AVENGERS HAVE!
AND HE'S JUST A MINDLESS MASS OF MUSCLE!
SO LET'S FINISH THIS UP...
...FAST!
NO!
WHO IN...?
13

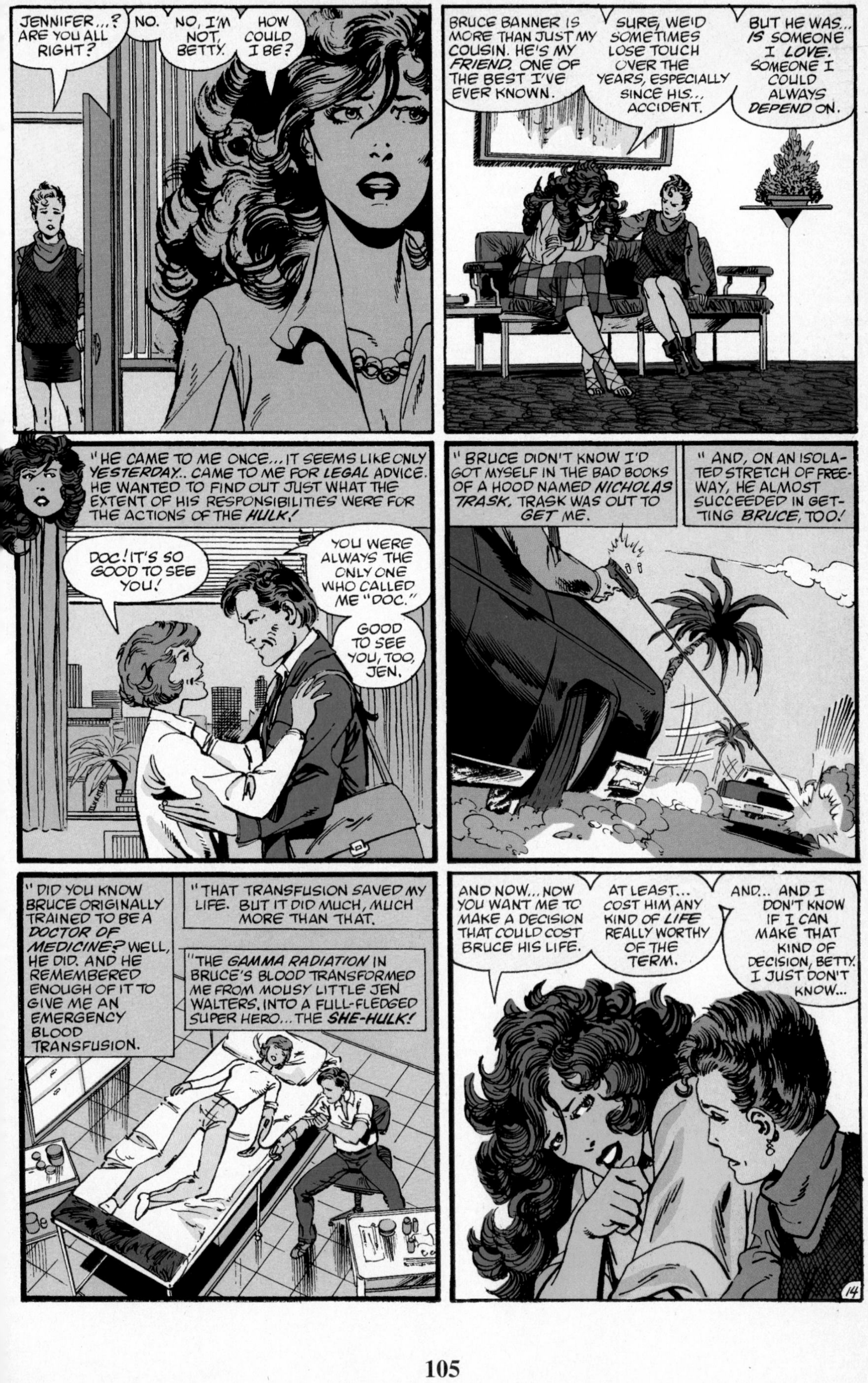
JENNIFER...? ARE YOU ALL RIGHT?
NO.
NO, I'M NOT, BETTY.
HOW COULD I BE?
BRUCE BANNER IS MORE THAN JUST MY COUSIN. HE'S MY FRIEND, ONE OF THE BEST I'VE EVER KNOWN.
SURE, WE'D SOMETIMES LOSE TOUCH OVER THE YEARS, ESPECIALLY SINCE HIS... ACCIDENT.
BUT HE WAS... IS SOMEONE I LOVE. SOMEONE I COULD ALWAYS DEPEND ON.
"HE CAME TO ME ONCE... IT SEEMS LIKE ONLY YESTERDAY... CAME TO ME FOR LEGAL ADVICE. HE WANTED TO FIND OUT JUST WHAT THE EXTENT OF HIS RESPONSIBILITIES WERE FOR THE ACTIONS OF THE HULK!
DOC! IT'S SO GOOD TO SEE YOU!
YOU WERE ALWAYS THE ONLY ONE WHO CALLED ME "DOC."
GOOD TO SEE YOU, TOO, JEN.
"BRUCE DIDN'T KNOW I'D GOT MYSELF IN THE BAD BOOKS OF A HOOD NAMED NICHOLAS TRASK. TRASK WAS OUT TO GET ME.
"AND, ON AN ISOLATED STRETCH OF FREEWAY, HE ALMOST SUCCEEDED IN GETTING BRUCE, TOO!
"DID YOU KNOW BRUCE ORIGINALLY TRAINED TO BE A DOCTOR OF MEDICINE? WELL, HE DID. AND HE REMEMBERED ENOUGH OF IT TO GIVE ME AN EMERGENCY BLOOD TRANSFUSION.
"THAT TRANSFUSION SAVED MY LIFE. BUT IT DID MUCH, MUCH MORE THAN THAT.
"THE GAMMA RADIATION IN BRUCE'S BLOOD TRANSFORMED ME FROM MOUSY LITTLE JEN WALTERS, INTO A FULL-FLEDGED SUPER HERO... THE SHE-HULK!
AND NOW... NOW YOU WANT ME TO MAKE A DECISION THAT COULD COST BRUCE HIS LIFE.
AT LEAST... COST HIM ANY KIND OF LIFE REALLY WORTHY OF THE TERM.
AND... AND I DON'T KNOW IF I CAN MAKE THAT KIND OF DECISION, BETTY. I JUST DON'T KNOW...
14

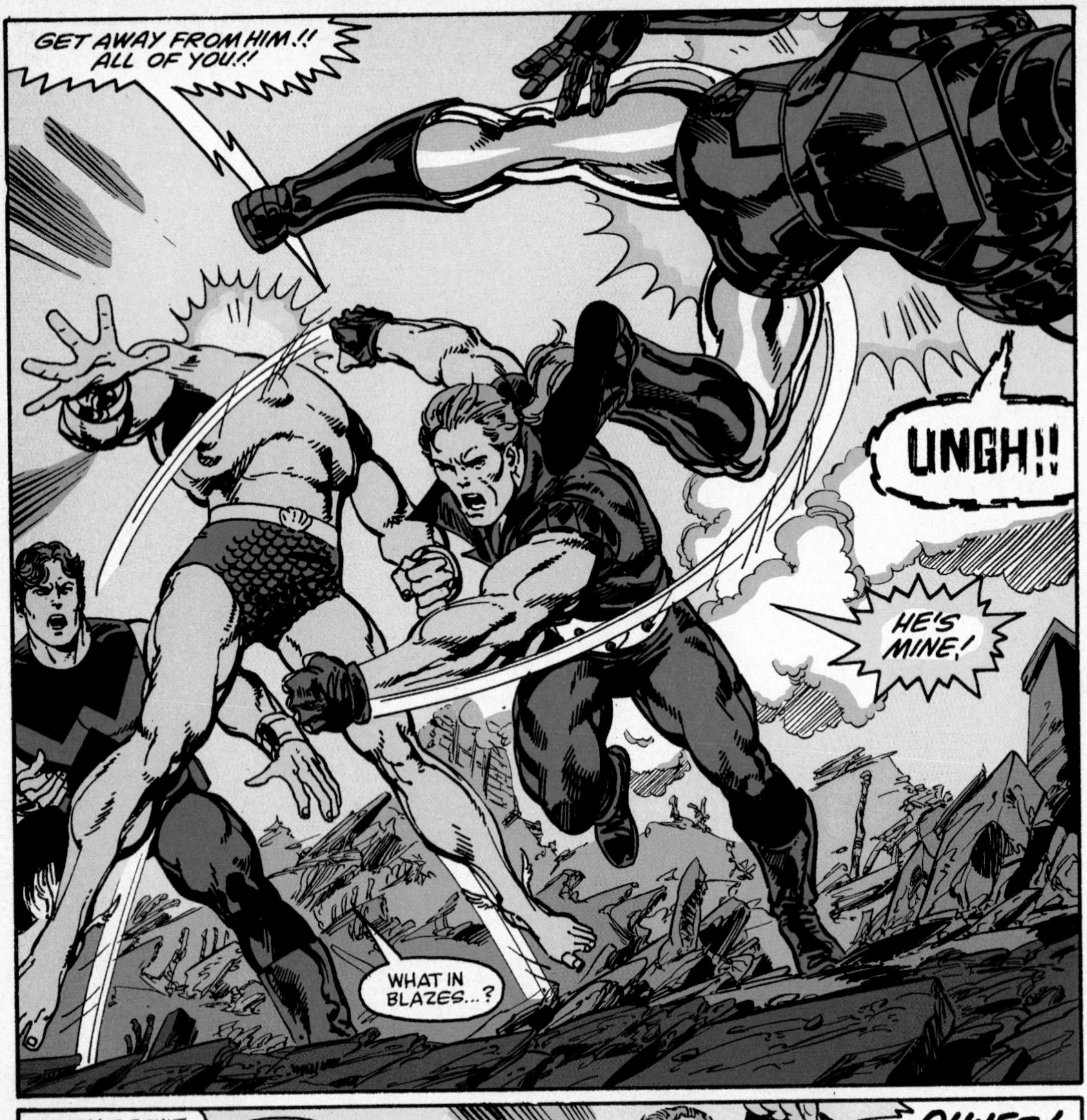
GET AWAY FROM HIM!! ALL OF YOU!!
UNGH!!
HE'S MINE!
WHAT IN BLAZES...?

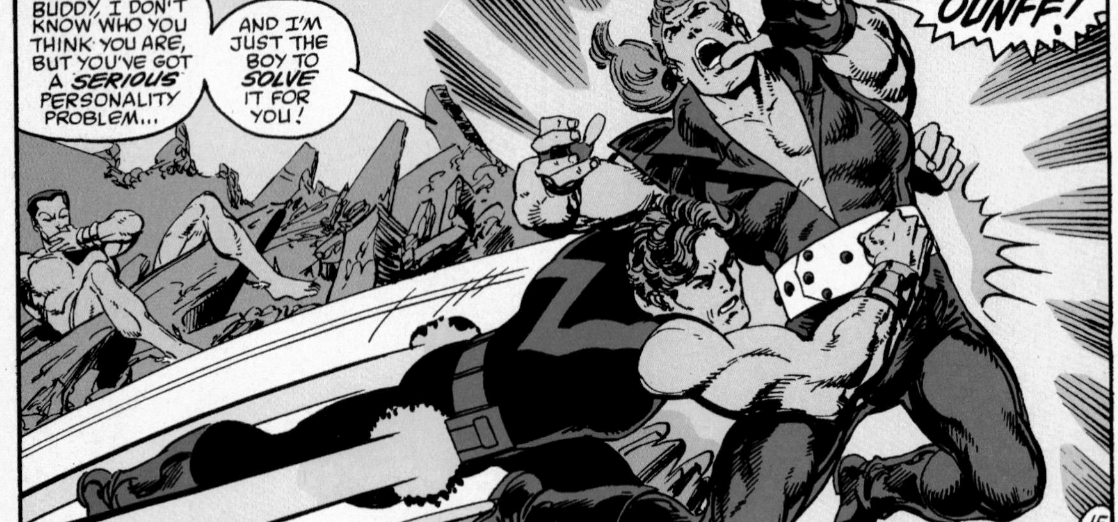
BUDDY, I DON'T KNOW WHO YOU THINK YOU ARE, BUT YOU'VE GOT A SERIOUS PERSONALITY PROBLEM...
AND I'M JUST THE BOY TO SOLVE IT FOR YOU!
OUNFF!
15

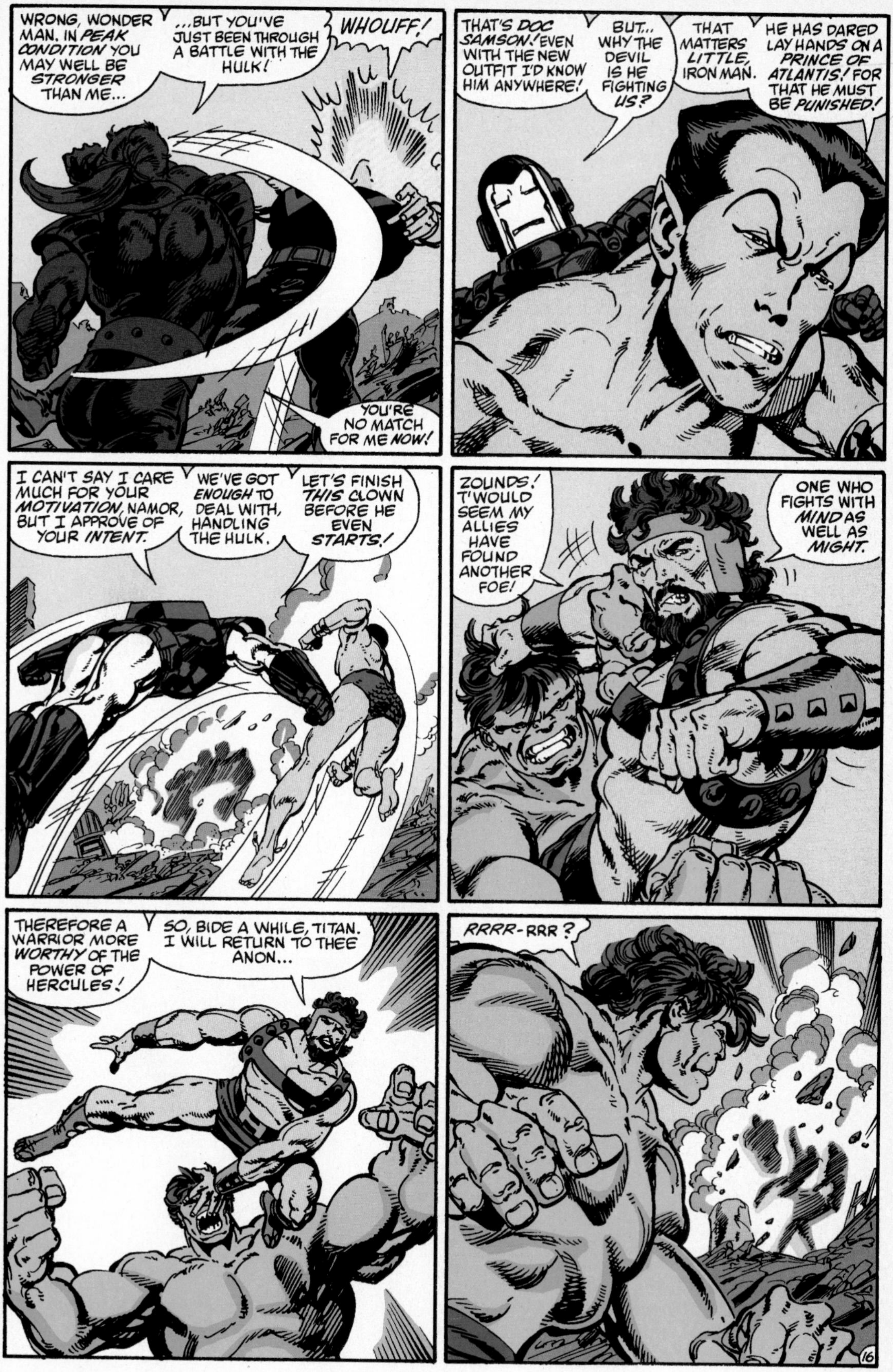
WRONG, WONDER MAN. IN PEAK CONDITION YOU MAY WELL BE STRONGER THAN ME...
...BUT YOU'VE JUST BEEN THROUGH A BATTLE WITH THE HULK!
WHOUFF!
YOU'RE NO MATCH FOR ME NOW!
THAT'S DOC SAMSON! EVEN WITH THE NEW OUTFIT I'D KNOW HIM ANYWHERE!
BUT... WHY THE DEVIL IS HE FIGHTING US?
THAT MATTERS LITTLE, IRON MAN.
HE HAS DARED LAY HANDS ON A PRINCE OF ATLANTIS! FOR THAT HE MUST BE PUNISHED!
I CAN'T SAY I CARE MUCH FOR YOUR MOTIVATION, NAMOR, BUT I APPROVE OF YOUR INTENT.
WE'VE GOT ENOUGH TO DEAL WITH, HANDLING THE HULK.
LET'S FINISH THIS CLOWN BEFORE HE EVEN STARTS!
ZOUNDS! T'WOULD SEEM MY ALLIES HAVE FOUND ANOTHER FOE!
ONE WHO FIGHTS WITH MIND AS WELL AS MIGHT.
THEREFORE A WARRIOR MORE WORTHY OF THE POWER OF HERCULES!
SO, BIDE A WHILE, TITAN. I WILL RETURN TO THEE ANON...
RRRR-RRR?
16

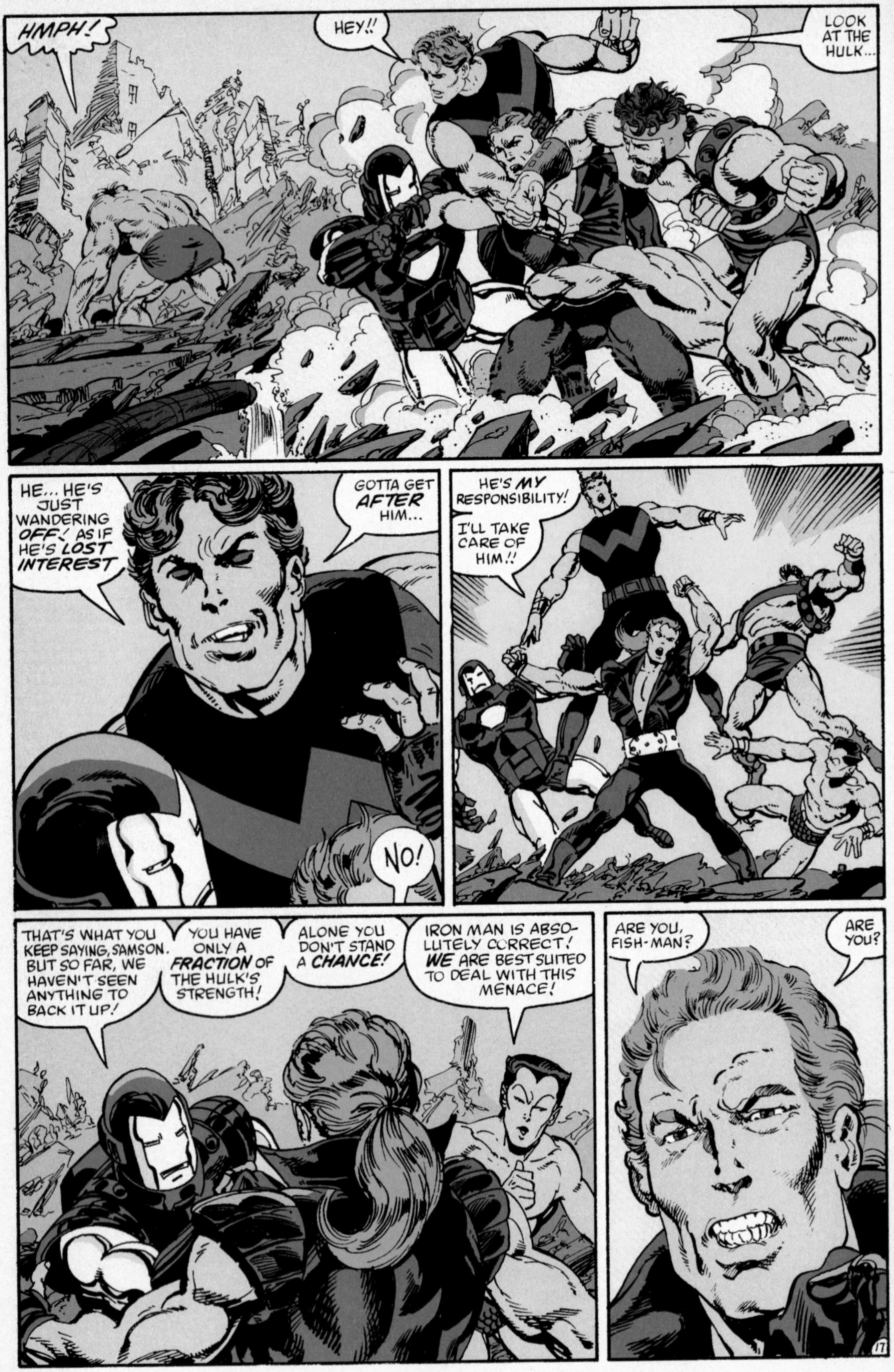
HMPH!
HEY!!
LOOK AT THE HULK...
HE... HE'S JUST WANDERING OFF! AS IF HE'S LOST INTEREST
GOTTA GET AFTER HIM...
NO!
HE'S MY RESPONSIBILITY!
I'LL TAKE CARE OF HIM!!
THAT'S WHAT YOU KEEP SAYING, SAMSON. BUT SO FAR, WE HAVEN'T SEEN ANYTHING TO BACK IT UP!
YOU HAVE ONLY A FRACTION OF THE HULK'S STRENGTH!
ALONE YOU DON'T STAND A CHANCE!
IRON MAN IS ABSOLUTELY CORRECT! WE ARE BEST SUITED TO DEAL WITH THIS MENACE!
ARE YOU, FISH-MAN?
ARE YOU?
17

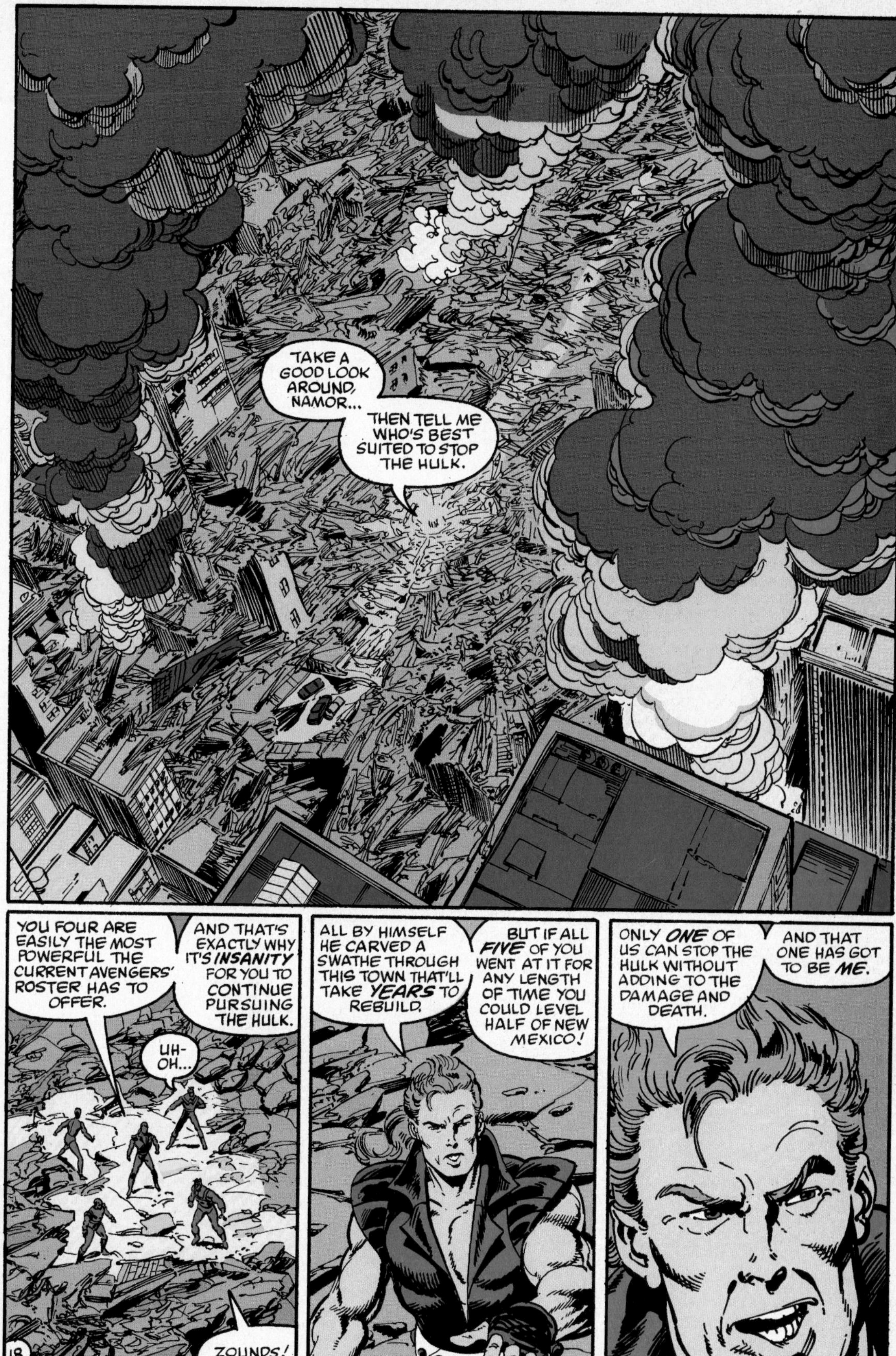
TAKE A GOOD LOOK AROUND, NAMOR...
THEN TELL ME WHO'S BEST SUITED TO STOP THE HULK.
YOU FOUR ARE EASILY THE MOST POWERFUL THE CURRENT AVENGERS' ROSTER HAS TO OFFER.
AND THAT'S EXACTLY WHY IT'S INSANITY FOR YOU TO CONTINUE PURSUING THE HULK.
UH-OH...
18
ZOUNDS!
ALL BY HIMSELF HE CARVED A SWATHE THROUGH THIS TOWN THAT'LL TAKE YEARS TO REBUILD.
BUT IF ALL FIVE OF YOU WENT AT IT FOR ANY LENGTH OF TIME YOU COULD LEVEL HALF OF NEW MEXICO!
ONLY ONE OF US CAN STOP THE HULK WITHOUT ADDING TO THE DAMAGE AND DEATH.
AND THAT ONE HAS GOT TO BE ME.

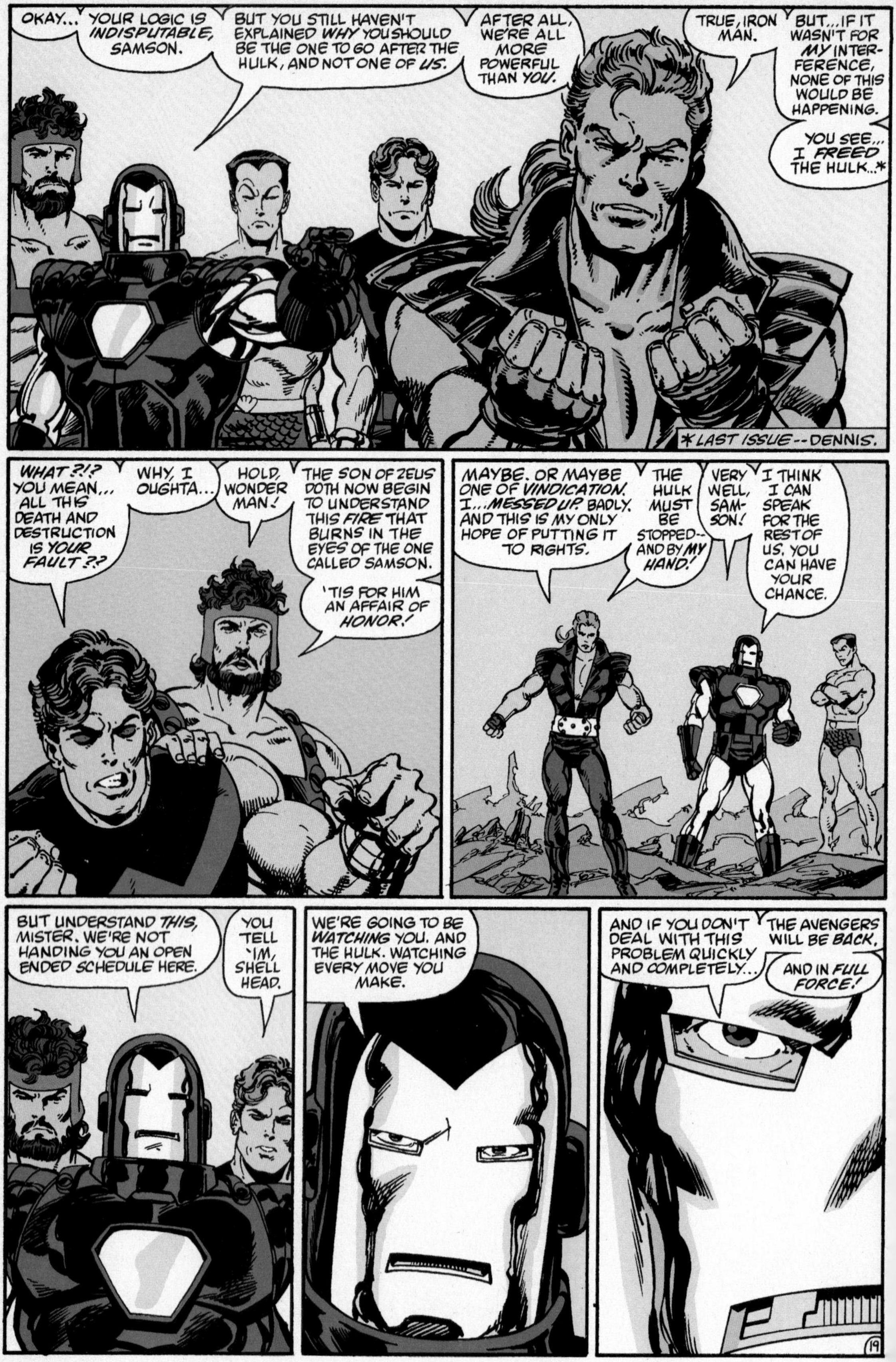
OKAY...
YOUR LOGIC IS INDISPUTABLE, SAMSON.
BUT YOU STILL HAVEN'T EXPLAINED WHY YOU SHOULD BE THE ONE TO GO AFTER THE HULK, AND NOT ONE OF US.
AFTER ALL, WE'RE ALL MORE POWERFUL THAN YOU.
TRUE, IRON MAN.
BUT... IF IT WASN'T FOR MY INTERFERENCE, NONE OF THIS WOULD BE HAPPENING.
YOU SEE... I FREED THE HULK...*
*LAST ISSUE--DENNIS.
WHAT?!? YOU MEAN... ALL THIS DEATH AND DESTRUCTION IS YOUR FAULT??
WHY, I OUGHTA...
HOLD, WONDER MAN!
THE SON OF ZEUS DOTH NOW BEGIN TO UNDERSTAND THIS FIRE THAT BURNS IN THE EYES OF THE ONE CALLED SAMSON.
'TIS FOR HIM AN AFFAIR OF HONOR!
MAYBE. OR MAYBE ONE OF VINDICATION. I... MESSED UP. BADLY. AND THIS IS MY ONLY HOPE OF PUTTING IT TO RIGHTS.
THE HULK MUST BE STOPPED-- AND BY MY HAND!
VERY WELL, SAMSON!
I THINK I CAN SPEAK FOR THE REST OF US. YOU CAN HAVE YOUR CHANCE.
BUT UNDERSTAND THIS, MISTER. WE'RE NOT HANDING YOU AN OPEN ENDED SCHEDULE HERE.
YOU TELL 'IM, SHELL HEAD.
WE'RE GOING TO BE WATCHING YOU. AND THE HULK. WATCHING EVERY MOVE YOU MAKE.
AND IF YOU DON'T DEAL WITH THIS PROBLEM QUICKLY AND COMPLETELY...
THE AVENGERS WILL BE BACK.
AND IN FULL FORCE!
19

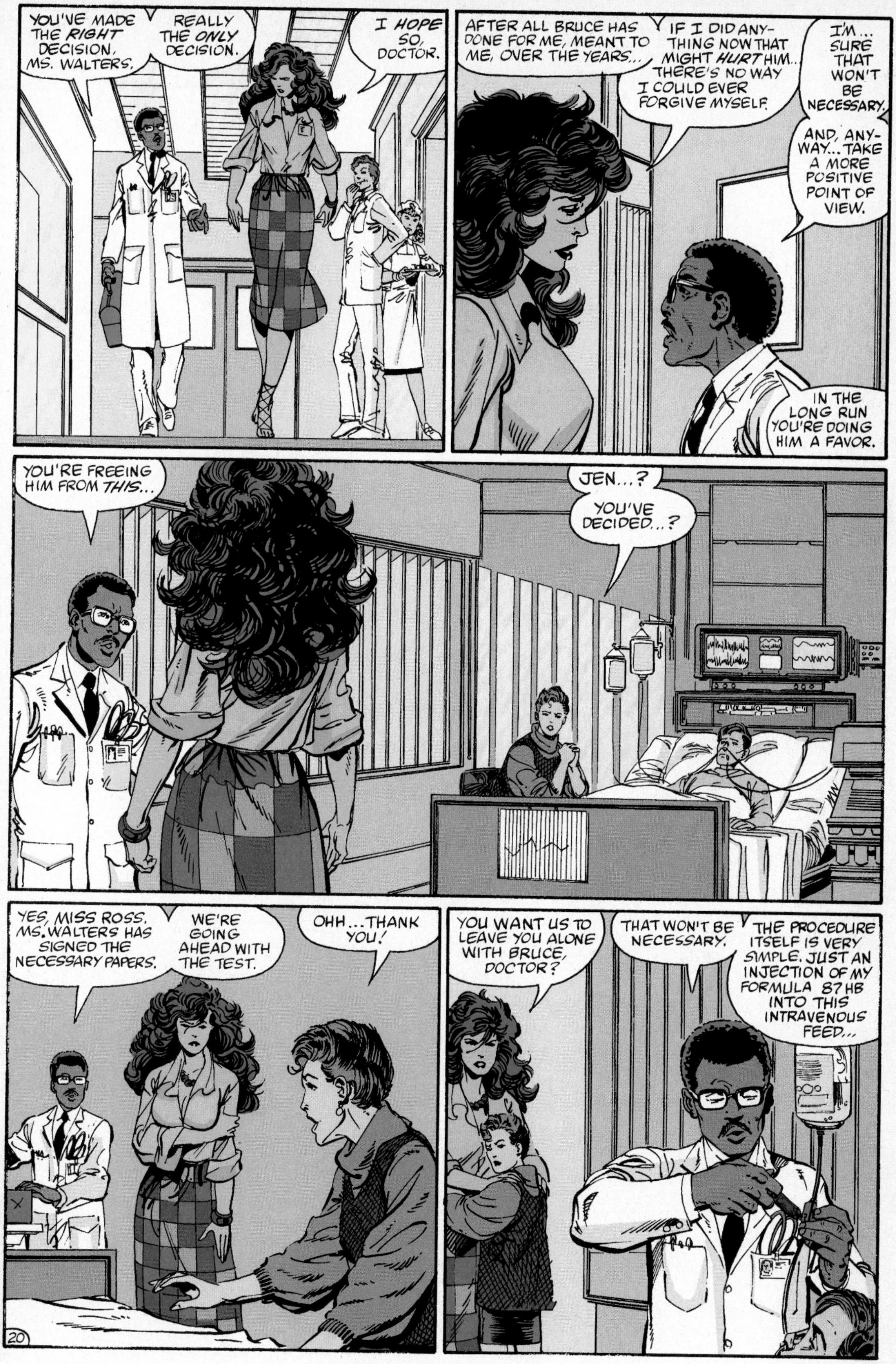

YOU'VE MADE THE RIGHT DECISION, MS. WALTERS,
REALLY THE ONLY DECISION.
I HOPE SO, DOCTOR.
AFTER ALL BRUCE HAS DONE FOR ME, MEANT TO ME, OVER THE YEARS...
IF I DID ANYTHING NOW THAT MIGHT HURT HIM... THERE'S NO WAY I COULD EVER FORGIVE MYSELF.
I'M... SURE THAT WON'T BE NECESSARY.
AND, ANYWAY... TAKE A MORE POSITIVE POINT OF VIEW.
IN THE LONG RUN YOU'RE DOING HIM A FAVOR.
YOU'RE FREEING HIM FROM THIS...
JEN...?
YOU'VE DECIDED...?
YES, MISS ROSS. MS. WALTERS HAS SIGNED THE NECESSARY PAPERS.
WE'RE GOING AHEAD WITH THE TEST.
OHH... THANK YOU!
YOU WANT US TO LEAVE YOU ALONE WITH BRUCE, DOCTOR?
THAT WON'T BE NECESSARY.
THE PROCEDURE ITSELF IS VERY SIMPLE. JUST AN INJECTION OF MY FORMULA 87HB INTO THIS INTRAVENOUS FEED...
20

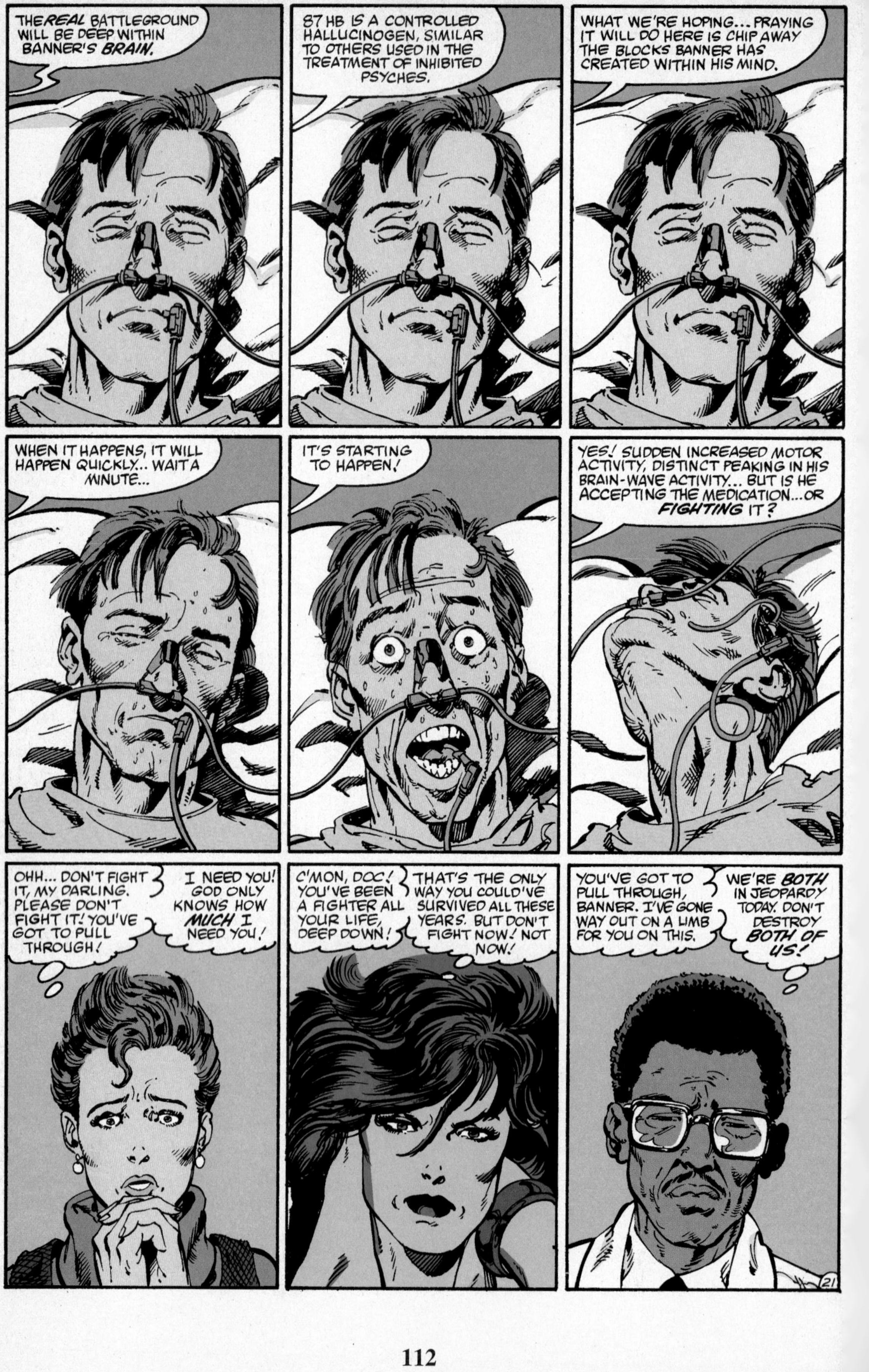
THE REAL BATTLEGROUND WILL BE DEEP WITHIN BANNER'S BRAIN.
87 HB IS A CONTROLLED HALLUCINOGEN, SIMILAR TO OTHERS USED IN THE TREATMENT OF INHIBITED PSYCHES.
WHAT WE'RE HOPING... PRAYING IT WILL DO HERE IS CHIP AWAY THE BLOCKS BANNER HAS CREATED WITHIN HIS MIND.
WHEN IT HAPPENS, IT WILL HAPPEN QUICKLY... WAIT A MINUTE...
IT'S STARTING TO HAPPEN!
YES! SUDDEN INCREASED MOTOR ACTIVITY, DISTINCT PEAKING IN HIS BRAIN-WAVE ACTIVITY... BUT IS HE ACCEPTING THE MEDICATION... OR FIGHTING IT?
OHH... DON'T FIGHT IT, MY DARLING. PLEASE DON'T FIGHT IT! YOU'VE GOT TO PULL THROUGH!
I NEED YOU! GOD ONLY KNOWS HOW MUCH I NEED YOU!
C'MON, DOC! YOU'VE BEEN A FIGHTER ALL YOUR LIFE, DEEP DOWN!
THAT'S THE ONLY WAY YOU COULD'VE SURVIVED ALL THESE YEARS. BUT DON'T FIGHT NOW! NOT NOW!
YOU'VE GOT TO PULL THROUGH, BANNER. I'VE GONE WAY OUT ON A LIMB FOR YOU ON THIS.
WE'RE BOTH IN JEOPARDY TODAY. DON'T DESTROY BOTH OF US!
21

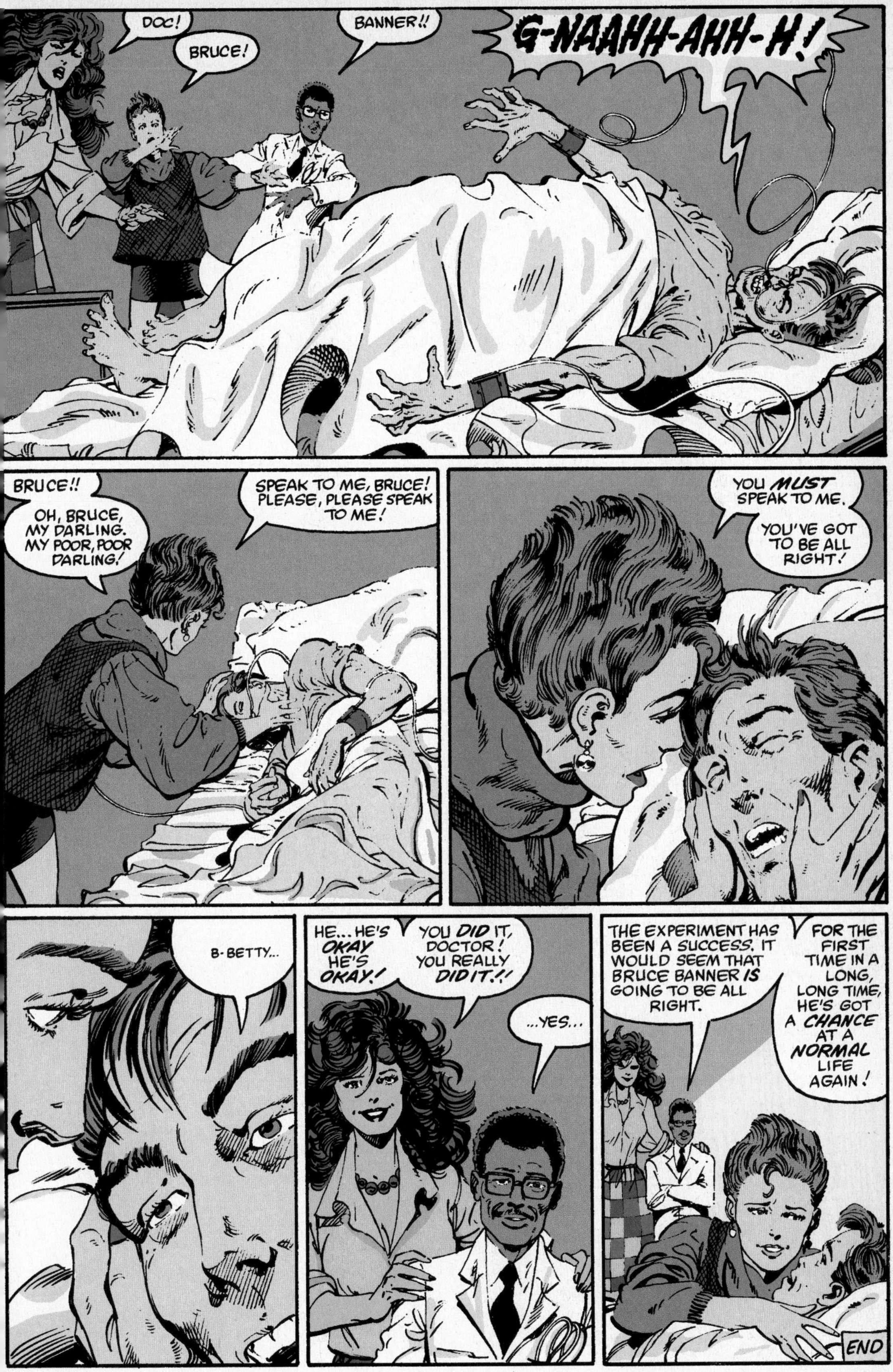
DOC!
BRUCE!
BANNER!!
G-NAAHH-AHH-H!
BRUCE!!
OH, BRUCE, MY DARLING. MY POOR, POOR DARLING!
SPEAK TO ME, BRUCE! PLEASE, PLEASE SPEAK TO ME!
YOU MUST SPEAK TO ME.
YOU'VE GOT TO BE ALL RIGHT!
B-BETTY...
HE... HE'S OKAY HE'S OKAY!
YOU DID IT, DOCTOR! YOU REALLY DID IT!!
...YES...
THE EXPERIMENT HAS BEEN A SUCCESS. IT WOULD SEEM THAT BRUCE BANNER IS GOING TO BE ALL RIGHT.
FOR THE FIRST TIME IN A LONG, LONG TIME, HE'S GOT A CHANCE AT A NORMAL LIFE AGAIN!
END

THE FIRST AND LAST HULK CONFERENCE!

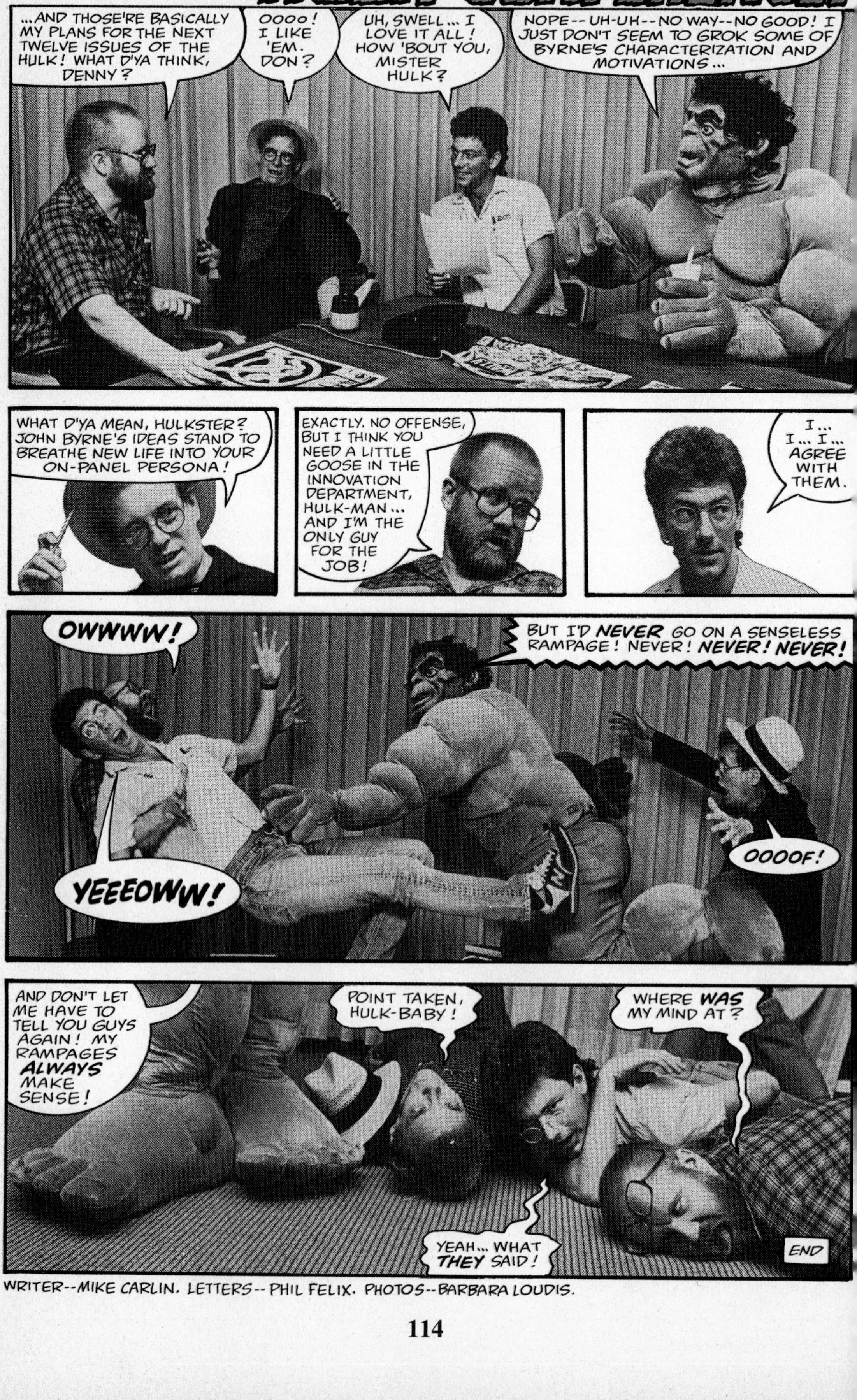

...AND THOSE'RE BASICALLY MY PLANS FOR THE NEXT TWELVE ISSUES OF THE HULK! WHAT D'YA THINK, DENNY?
OOOO! I LIKE 'EM. DON?
UH, SWELL... I LOVE IT ALL! HOW 'BOUT YOU, MISTER HULK?
NOPE--UH-UH--NO WAY--NO GOOD! I JUST DON'T SEEM TO GROK SOME OF BYRNE'S CHARACTERIZATION AND MOTIVATIONS...
WHAT D'YA MEAN, HULKSTER? JOHN BYRNE'S IDEAS STAND TO BREATHE NEW LIFE INTO YOUR ON-PANEL PERSONA!
EXACTLY. NO OFFENSE, BUT I THINK YOU NEED A LITTLE GOOSE IN THE INNOVATION DEPARTMENT, HULK-MAN... AND I'M THE ONLY GUY FOR THE JOB!
I... I... I... AGREE WITH THEM.
OWWWW!
BUT I'D NEVER GO ON A SENSELESS RAMPAGE! NEVER! NEVER! NEVER!
YEEEOWW!
OOOOF!
AND DON'T LET ME HAVE TO TELL YOU GUYS AGAIN! MY RAMPAGES ALWAYS MAKE SENSE!
POINT TAKEN, HULK-BABY!
WHERE WAS MY MIND AT?
YEAH... WHAT THEY SAID!
END

WRITER--MIKE CARLIN. LETTERS--PHIL FELIX. PHOTOS--BARBARA LOUDIS.

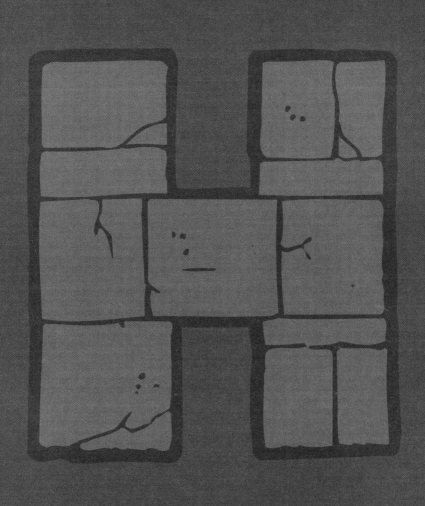

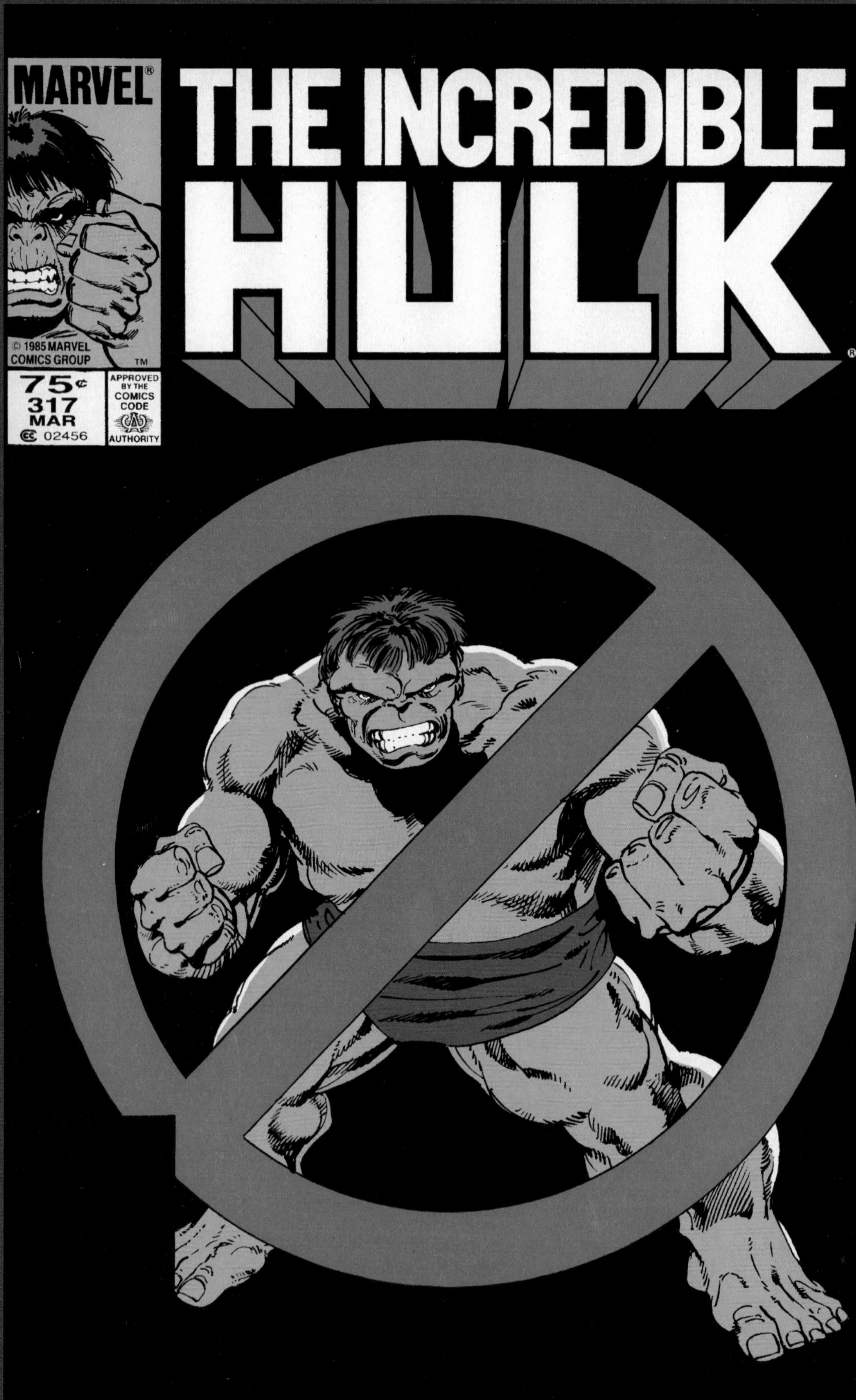

MARVEL®
THE INCREDIBLE
HULK®
© 1985 MARVEL COMICS GROUP
TM
75¢
317
MAR
02456
APPROVED BY THE COMICS CODE AUTHORITY

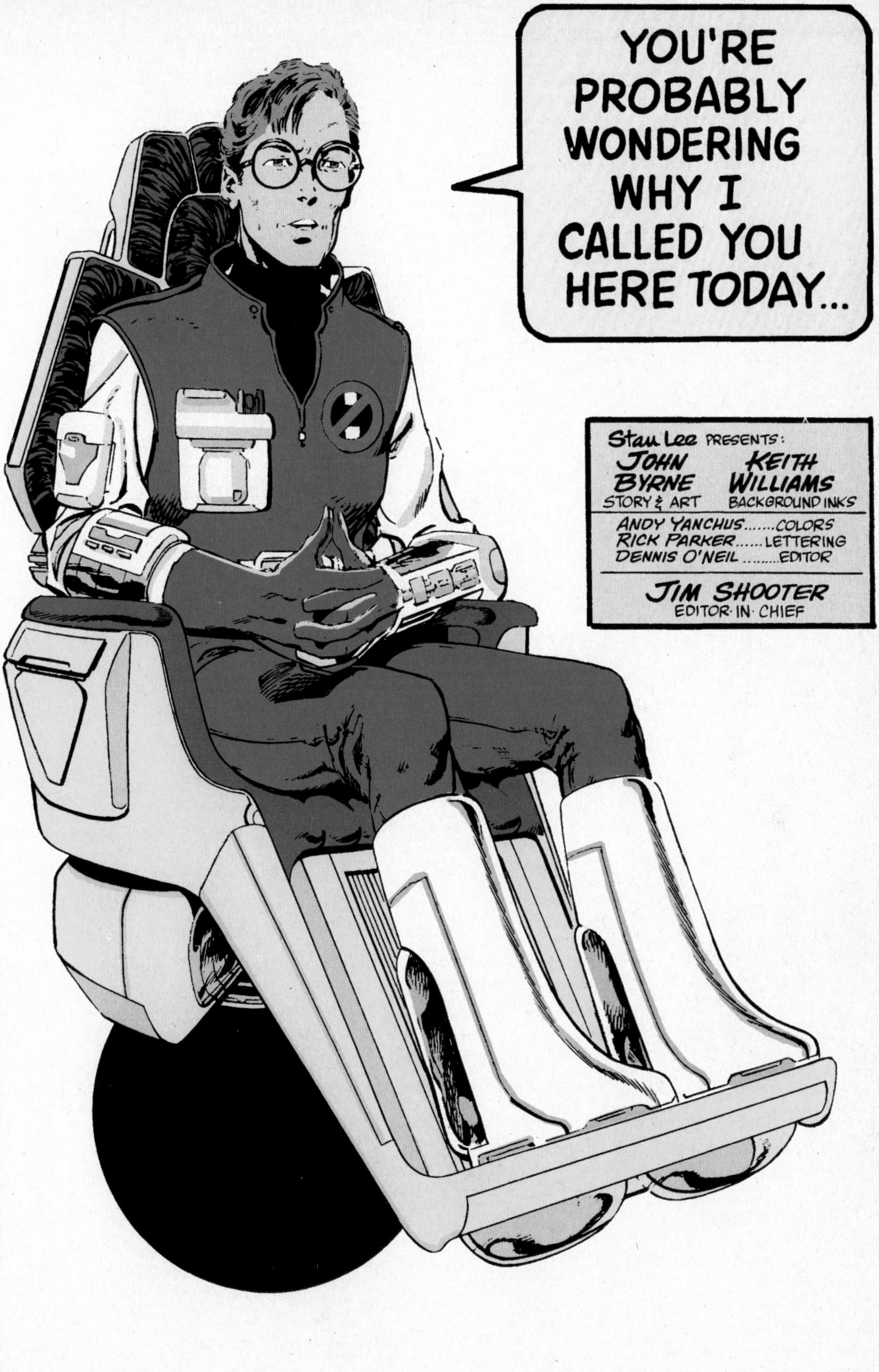
YOU'RE PROBABLY WONDERING WHY I CALLED YOU HERE TODAY...
Stan Lee PRESENTS:
JOHN BYRNE STORY & ART
KEITH WILLIAMS BACKGROUND INKS
ANDY YANCHUS.......COLORS
RICK PARKER......LETTERING
DENNIS O'NEIL ....EDITOR
JIM SHOOTER EDITOR-IN-CHIEF

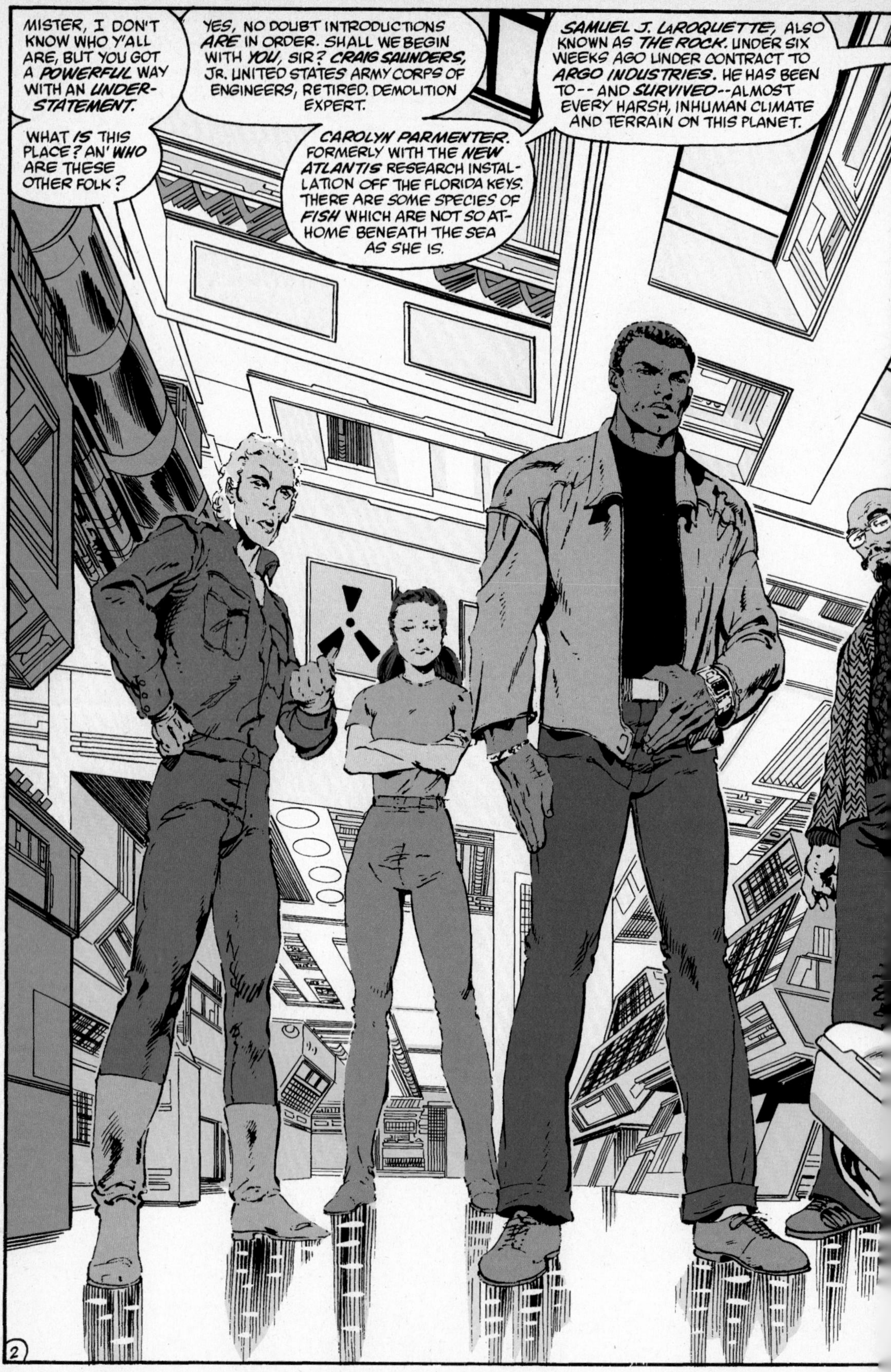
MISTER, I DON'T KNOW WHO Y'ALL ARE, BUT YOU GOT A POWERFUL WAY WITH AN UNDER-STATEMENT.
WHAT IS THIS PLACE? AN' WHO ARE THESE OTHER FOLK?
YES, NO DOUBT INTRODUCTIONS ARE IN ORDER. SHALL WE BEGIN WITH YOU, SIR? CRAIG SAUNDERS, JR. UNITED STATES ARMY CORPS OF ENGINEERS, RETIRED. DEMOLITION EXPERT.
CAROLYN PARMENTER. FORMERLY WITH THE NEW ATLANTIS RESEARCH INSTAL-LATION OFF THE FLORIDA KEYS. THERE ARE SOME SPECIES OF FISH WHICH ARE NOT SO AT-HOME BENEATH THE SEA AS SHE IS.
SAMUEL J. LAROQUETTE, ALSO KNOWN AS THE ROCK. UNDER SIX WEEKS AGO UNDER CONTRACT TO ARGO INDUSTRIES. HE HAS BEEN TO-- AND SURVIVED--ALMOST EVERY HARSH, INHUMAN CLIMATE AND TERRAIN ON THIS PLANET.
2

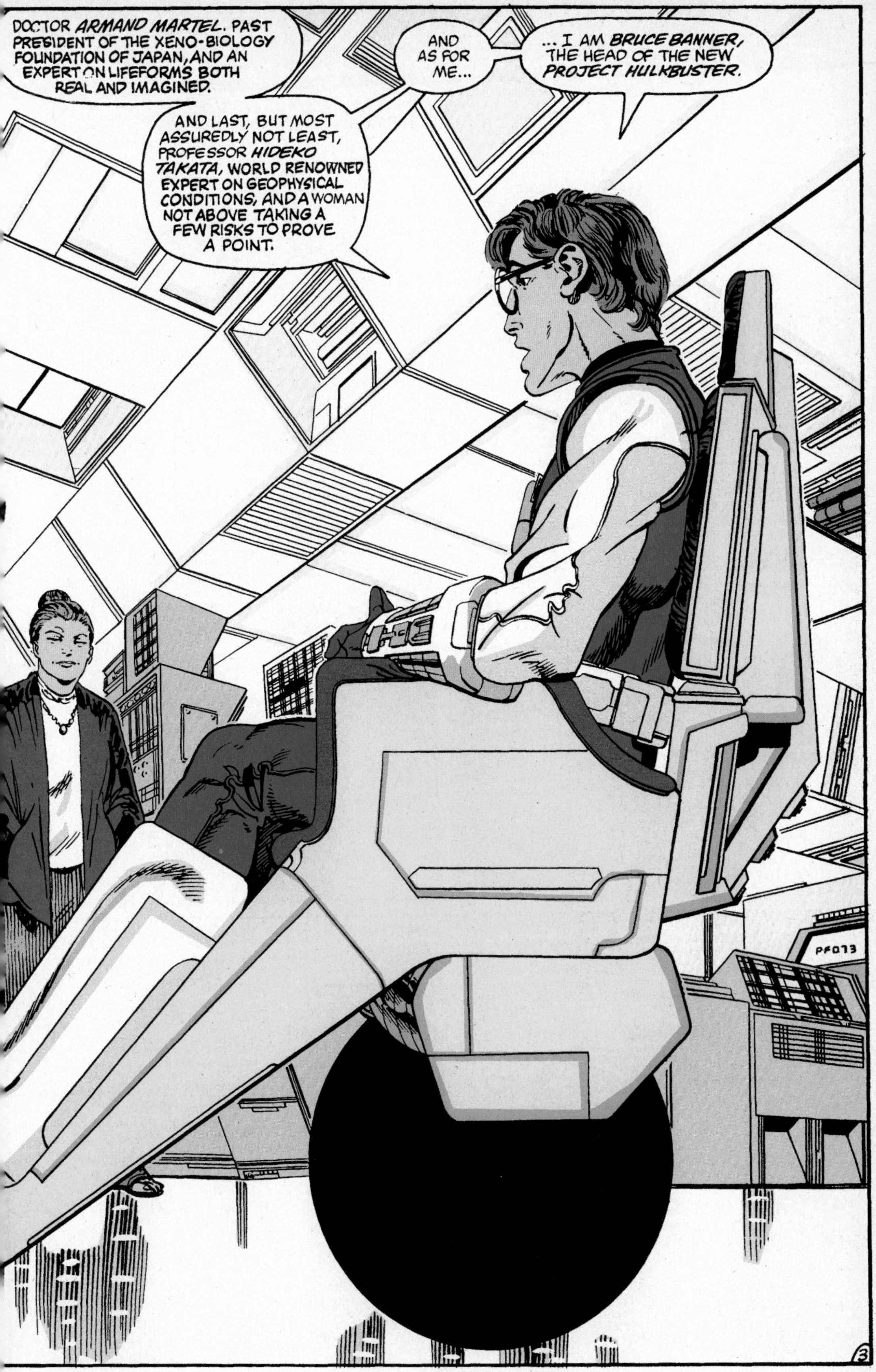
DOCTOR ARMAND MARTEL. PAST PRESIDENT OF THE XENO-BIOLOGY FOUNDATION OF JAPAN, AND AN EXPERT ON LIFEFORMS BOTH REAL AND IMAGINED.
AND LAST, BUT MOST ASSUREDLY NOT LEAST, PROFESSOR HIDEKO TAKATA, WORLD RENOWNED EXPERT ON GEOPHYSICAL CONDITIONS, AND A WOMAN NOT ABOVE TAKING A FEW RISKS TO PROVE A POINT.
AND AS FOR ME...
... I AM BRUCE BANNER, THE HEAD OF THE NEW PROJECT HULKBUSTER.
PF073
3

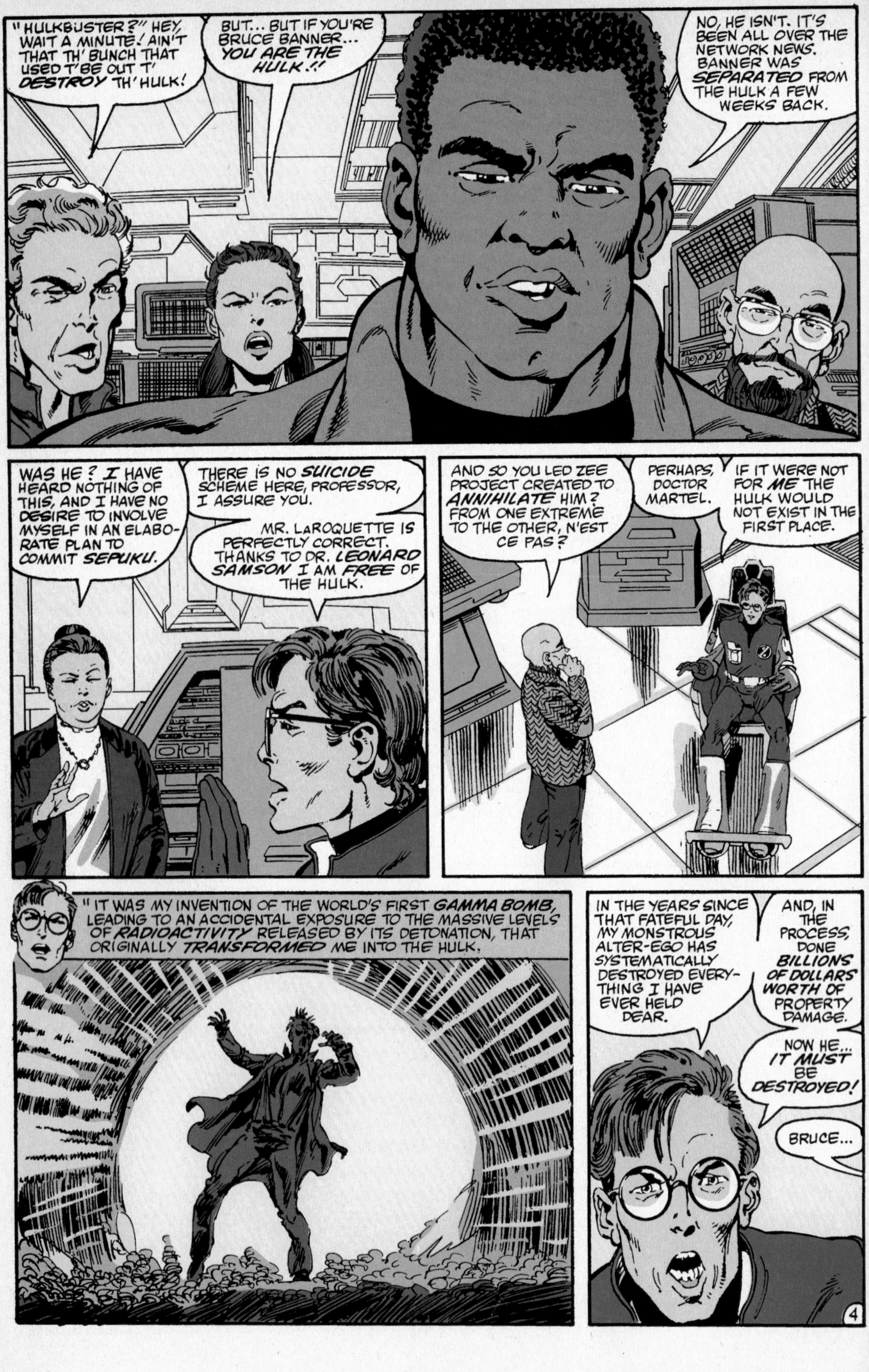
"HULKBUSTER?" HEY, WAIT A MINUTE! AIN'T THAT TH' BUNCH THAT USED T'BE OUT T' DESTROY TH' HULK!
BUT... BUT IF YOU'RE BRUCE BANNER... YOU ARE THE HULK!!
NO, HE ISN'T. IT'S BEEN ALL OVER THE NETWORK NEWS. BANNER WAS SEPARATED FROM THE HULK A FEW WEEKS BACK.
WAS HE? I HAVE HEARD NOTHING OF THIS, AND I HAVE NO DESIRE TO INVOLVE MYSELF IN AN ELABORATE PLAN TO COMMIT SEPUKU.
THERE IS NO SUICIDE SCHEME HERE, PROFESSOR, I ASSURE YOU.
MR. LaROQUETTE IS PERFECTLY CORRECT. THANKS TO DR. LEONARD SAMSON I AM FREE OF THE HULK.
AND SO YOU LED ZEE PROJECT CREATED TO ANNIHILATE HIM? FROM ONE EXTREME TO THE OTHER, N'EST CE PAS?
PERHAPS, DOCTOR MARTEL.
IF IT WERE NOT FOR ME THE HULK WOULD NOT EXIST IN THE FIRST PLACE.
"IT WAS MY INVENTION OF THE WORLD'S FIRST GAMMA BOMB, LEADING TO AN ACCIDENTAL EXPOSURE TO THE MASSIVE LEVELS OF RADIOACTIVITY RELEASED BY ITS DETONATION, THAT ORIGINALLY TRANSFORMED ME INTO THE HULK.
IN THE YEARS SINCE THAT FATEFUL DAY, MY MONSTROUS ALTER-EGO HAS SYSTEMATICALLY DESTROYED EVERYTHING I HAVE EVER HELD DEAR.
AND, IN THE PROCESS, DONE BILLIONS OF DOLLARS WORTH OF PROPERTY DAMAGE.
NOW HE... IT MUST BE DESTROYED!
BRUCE...
4

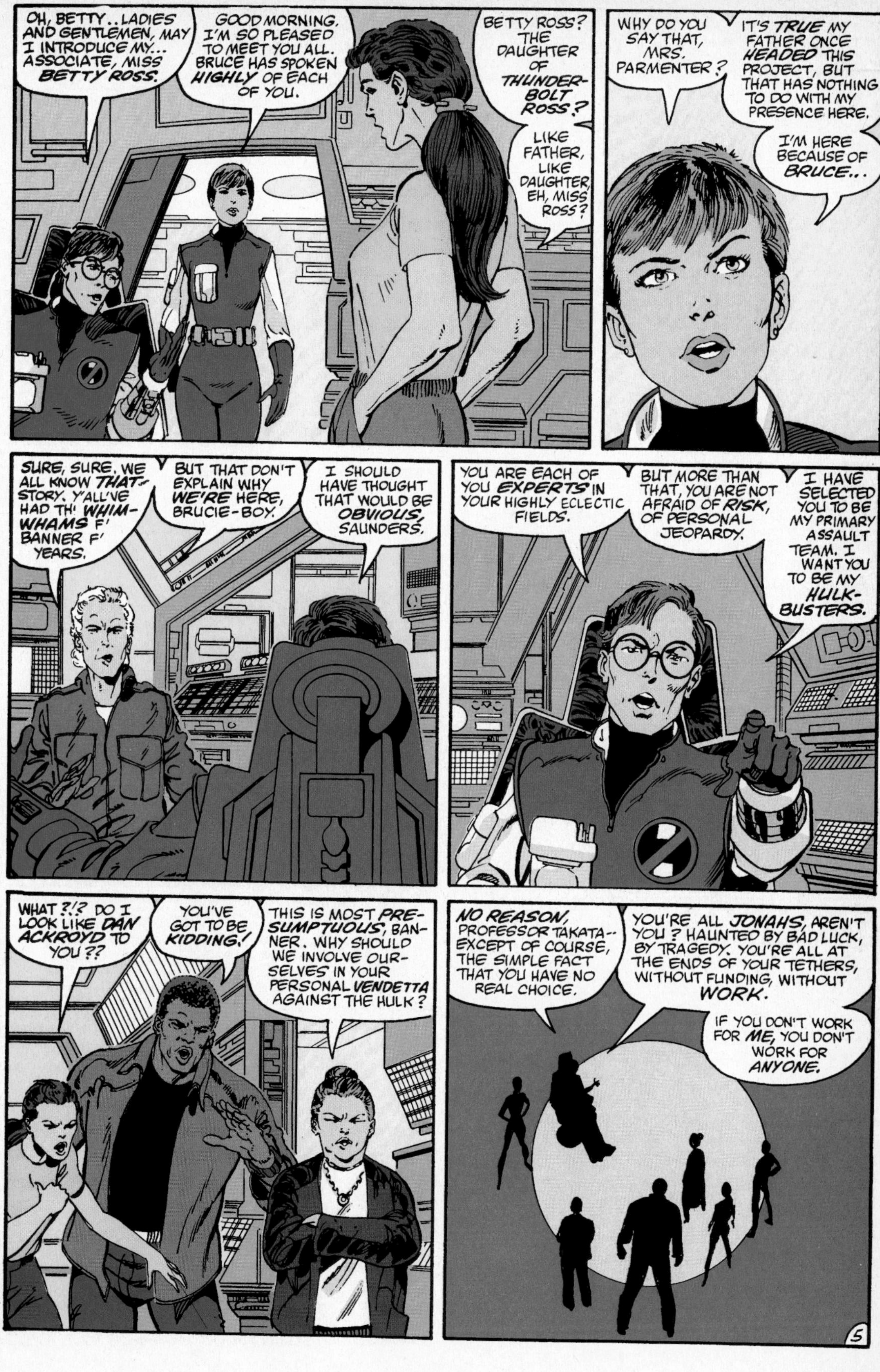
OH, BETTY.. LADIES AND GENTLEMEN, MAY I INTRODUCE MY... ASSOCIATE, MISS BETTY ROSS.
GOOD MORNING. I'M SO PLEASED TO MEET YOU ALL. BRUCE HAS SPOKEN HIGHLY OF EACH OF YOU.
BETTY ROSS? THE DAUGHTER OF THUNDER-BOLT ROSS?
LIKE FATHER, LIKE DAUGHTER, EH, MISS ROSS?
WHY DO YOU SAY THAT, MRS. PARMENTER?
IT'S TRUE MY FATHER ONCE HEADED THIS PROJECT, BUT THAT HAS NOTHING TO DO WITH MY PRESENCE HERE.
I'M HERE BECAUSE OF BRUCE...
SURE, SURE, WE ALL KNOW THAT-- STORY. Y'ALL'VE HAD TH' WHIM-WHAMS F' BANNER F' YEARS.
BUT THAT DON'T EXPLAIN WHY WE'RE HERE, BRUCIE-BOY.
I SHOULD HAVE THOUGHT THAT WOULD BE OBVIOUS, SAUNDERS.
YOU ARE EACH OF YOU EXPERTS IN YOUR HIGHLY ECLECTIC FIELDS.
BUT MORE THAN THAT, YOU ARE NOT AFRAID OF RISK, OF PERSONAL JEOPARDY.
I HAVE SELECTED YOU TO BE MY PRIMARY ASSAULT TEAM. I WANT YOU TO BE MY HULK-BUSTERS.
WHAT?!? DO I LOOK LIKE DAN ACKROYD TO YOU??
YOU'VE GOT TO BE KIDDING!
THIS IS MOST PRE-SUMPTUOUS, BAN-NER. WHY SHOULD WE INVOLVE OUR-SELVES IN YOUR PERSONAL VENDETTA AGAINST THE HULK?
NO REASON, PROFESSOR TAKATA-- EXCEPT OF COURSE, THE SIMPLE FACT THAT YOU HAVE NO REAL CHOICE.
YOU'RE ALL JONAHS, AREN'T YOU? HAUNTED BY BAD LUCK, BY TRAGEDY. YOU'RE ALL AT THE ENDS OF YOUR TETHERS, WITHOUT FUNDING, WITHOUT WORK.
IF YOU DON'T WORK FOR ME, YOU DON'T WORK FOR ANYONE.
5

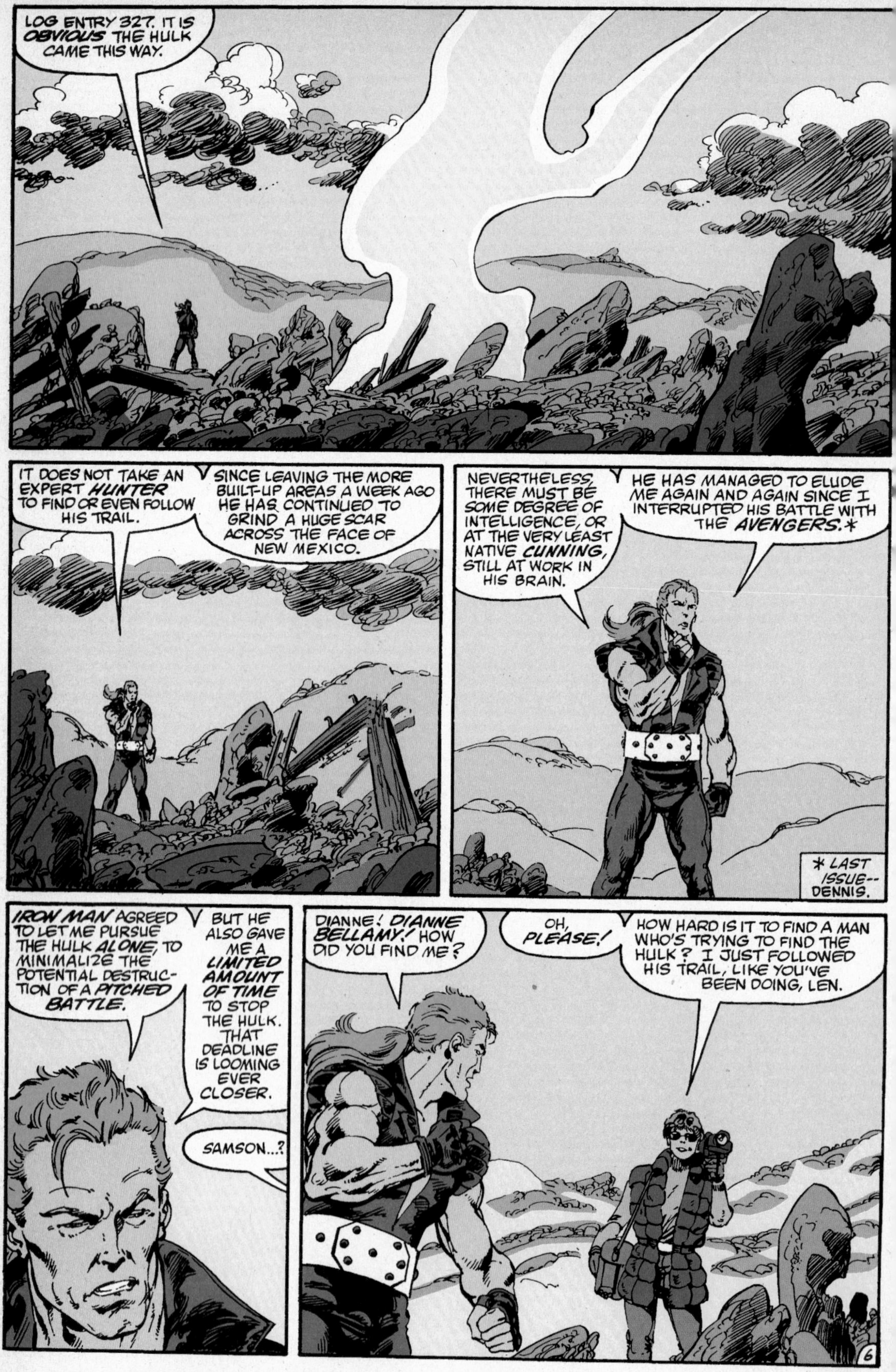
LOG ENTRY 327. IT IS OBVIOUS THE HULK CAME THIS WAY.
IT DOES NOT TAKE AN EXPERT HUNTER TO FIND OR EVEN FOLLOW HIS TRAIL.
SINCE LEAVING THE MORE BUILT-UP AREAS A WEEK AGO HE HAS CONTINUED TO GRIND A HUGE SCAR ACROSS THE FACE OF NEW MEXICO.
NEVERTHELESS, THERE MUST BE SOME DEGREE OF INTELLIGENCE, OR AT THE VERY LEAST NATIVE CUNNING, STILL AT WORK IN HIS BRAIN.
HE HAS MANAGED TO ELUDE ME AGAIN AND AGAIN SINCE I INTERRUPTED HIS BATTLE WITH THE AVENGERS.*
*LAST ISSUE--DENNIS.
IRON MAN AGREED TO LET ME PURSUE THE HULK ALONE, TO MINIMALIZE THE POTENTIAL DESTRUCTION OF A PITCHED BATTLE.
BUT HE ALSO GAVE ME A LIMITED AMOUNT OF TIME TO STOP THE HULK. THAT DEADLINE IS LOOMING EVER CLOSER.
SAMSON...?
DIANNE! DIANNE BELLAMY! HOW DID YOU FIND ME?
OH, PLEASE!
HOW HARD IS IT TO FIND A MAN WHO'S TRYING TO FIND THE HULK? I JUST FOLLOWED HIS TRAIL, LIKE YOU'VE BEEN DOING, LEN.
6

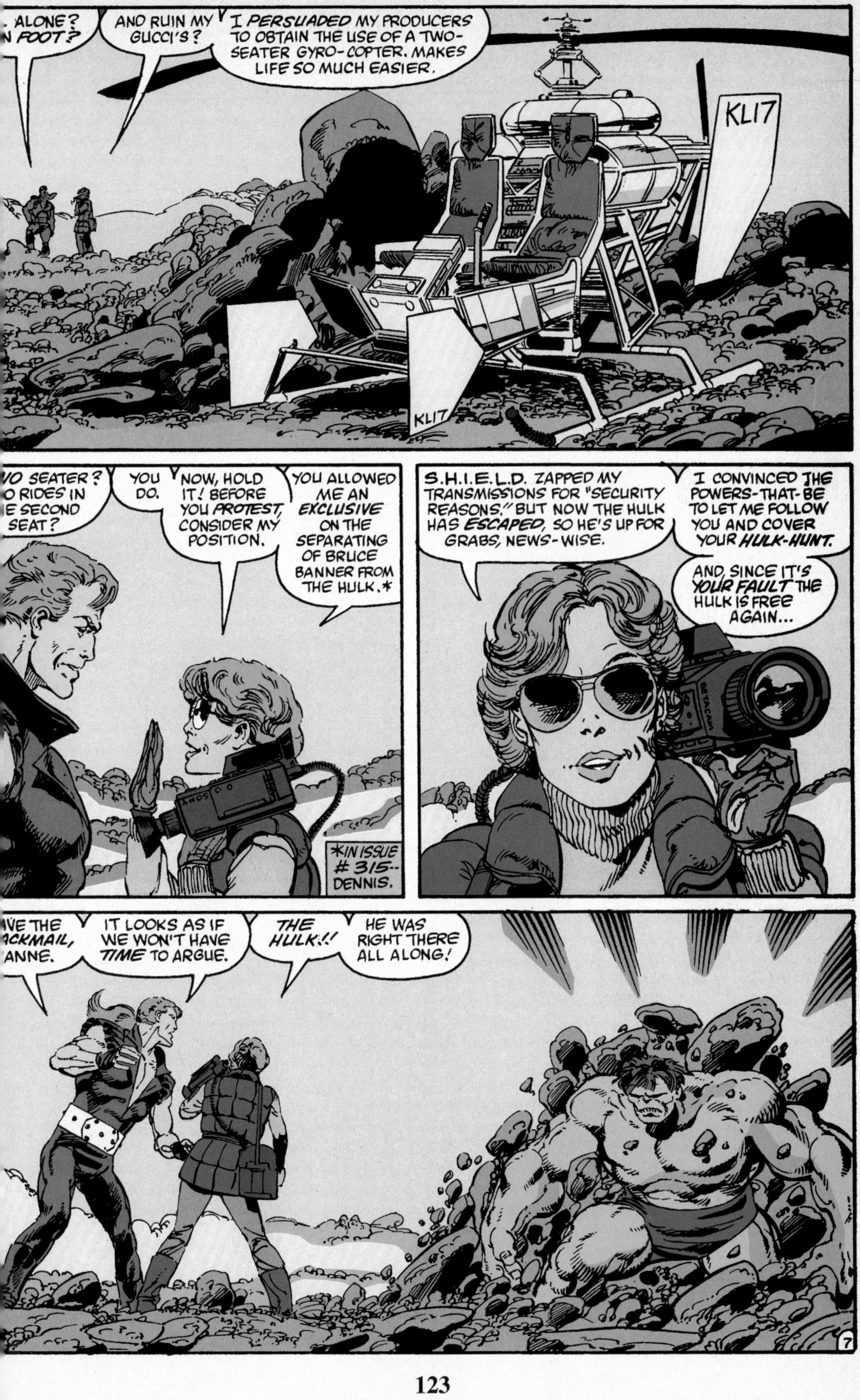

. ALONE?
N FOOT?
AND RUIN MY GUCCI'S?
I PERSUADED MY PRODUCERS TO OBTAIN THE USE OF A TWO-SEATER GYRO-COPTER. MAKES LIFE SO MUCH EASIER.
KL17
KL17
VO SEATER?
O RIDES IN
E SECOND
SEAT?
YOU DO.
NOW, HOLD IT! BEFORE YOU PROTEST, CONSIDER MY POSITION.
YOU ALLOWED ME AN EXCLUSIVE ON THE SEPARATING OF BRUCE BANNER FROM THE HULK.*
*IN ISSUE #315-- DENNIS.
S.H.I.E.L.D. ZAPPED MY TRANSMISSIONS FOR "SECURITY REASONS." BUT NOW THE HULK HAS ESCAPED, SO HE'S UP FOR GRABS, NEWS-WISE.
I CONVINCED THE POWERS-THAT-BE TO LET ME FOLLOW YOU AND COVER YOUR HULK-HUNT.
AND, SINCE IT'S YOUR FAULT THE HULK IS FREE AGAIN...
AVE THE
ACKMAIL,
ANNE.
IT LOOKS AS IF WE WON'T HAVE TIME TO ARGUE.
THE HULK!!
HE WAS RIGHT THERE ALL ALONG!
7

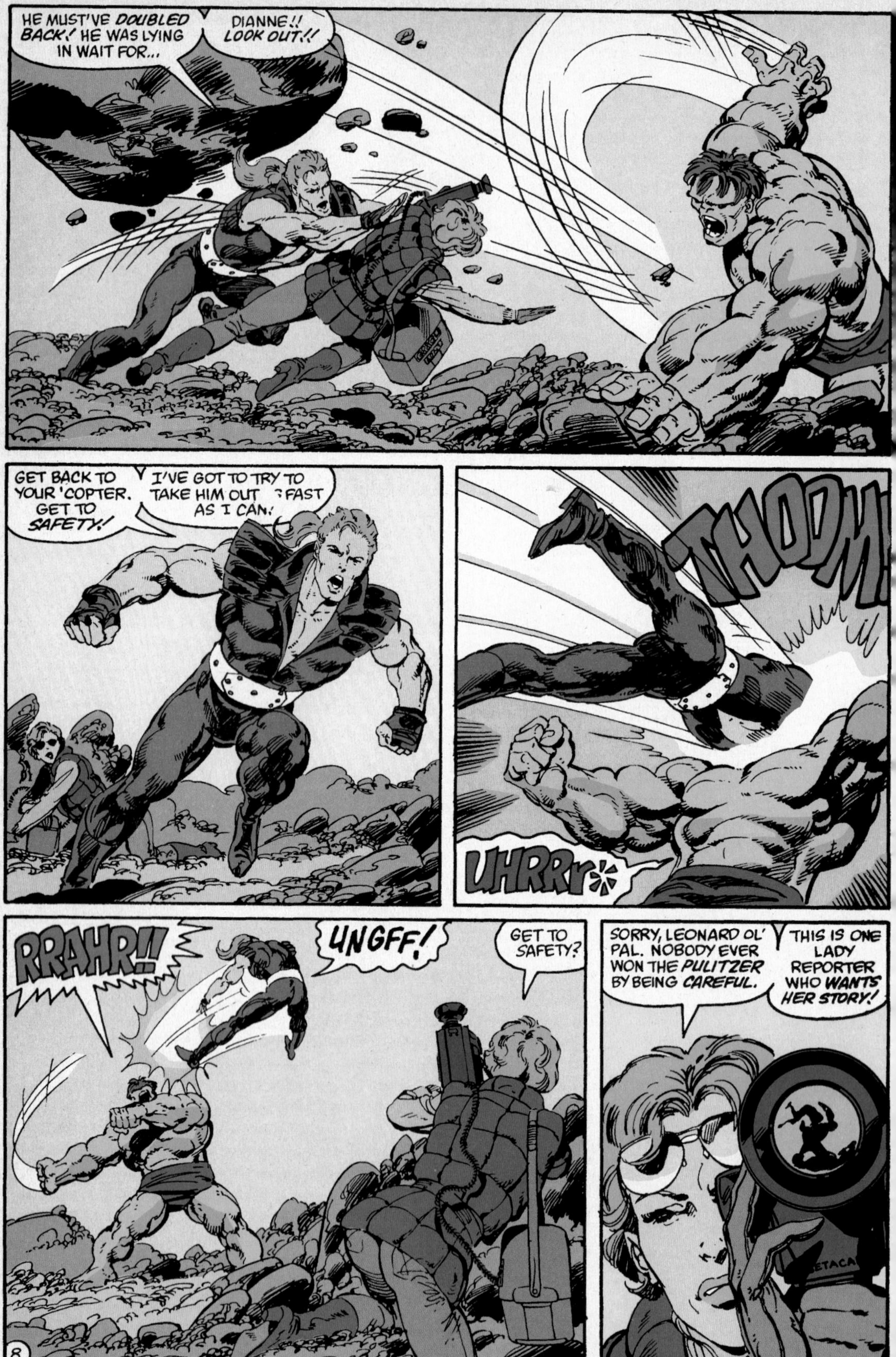

HE MUST'VE DOUBLED BACK! HE WAS LYING IN WAIT FOR...
DIANNE!! LOOK OUT!!
GET BACK TO YOUR 'COPTER. GET TO SAFETY!
I'VE GOT TO TRY TO TAKE HIM OUT AS FAST AS I CAN!
THOOM!
UHRRr!
RRAHR!!
UNGFF!
GET TO SAFETY?
SORRY, LEONARD OL' PAL. NOBODY EVER WON THE PULITZER BY BEING CAREFUL.
THIS IS ONE LADY REPORTER WHO WANTS HER STORY!
8

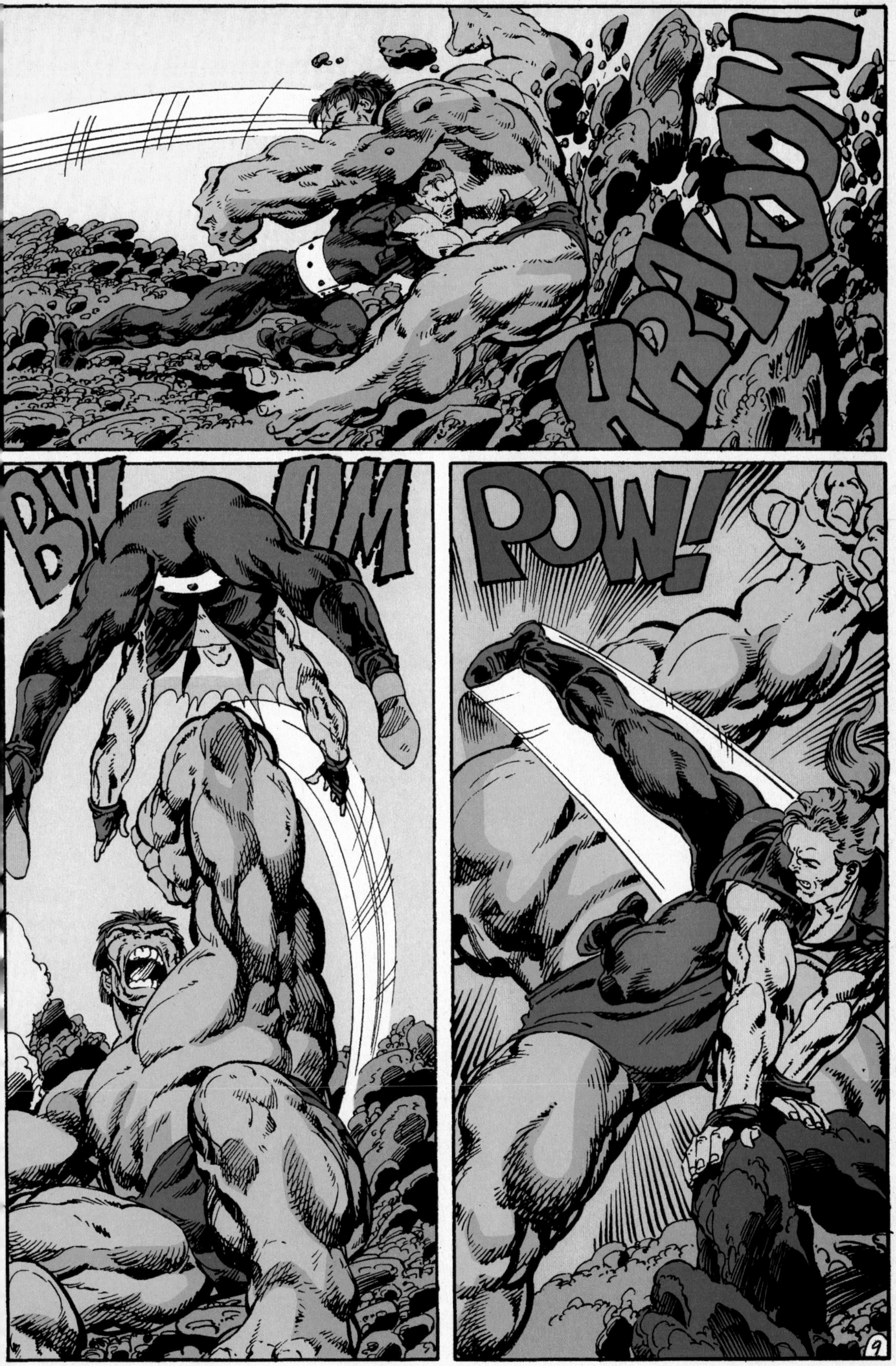
KRAKOOM
B OM
POW!
9

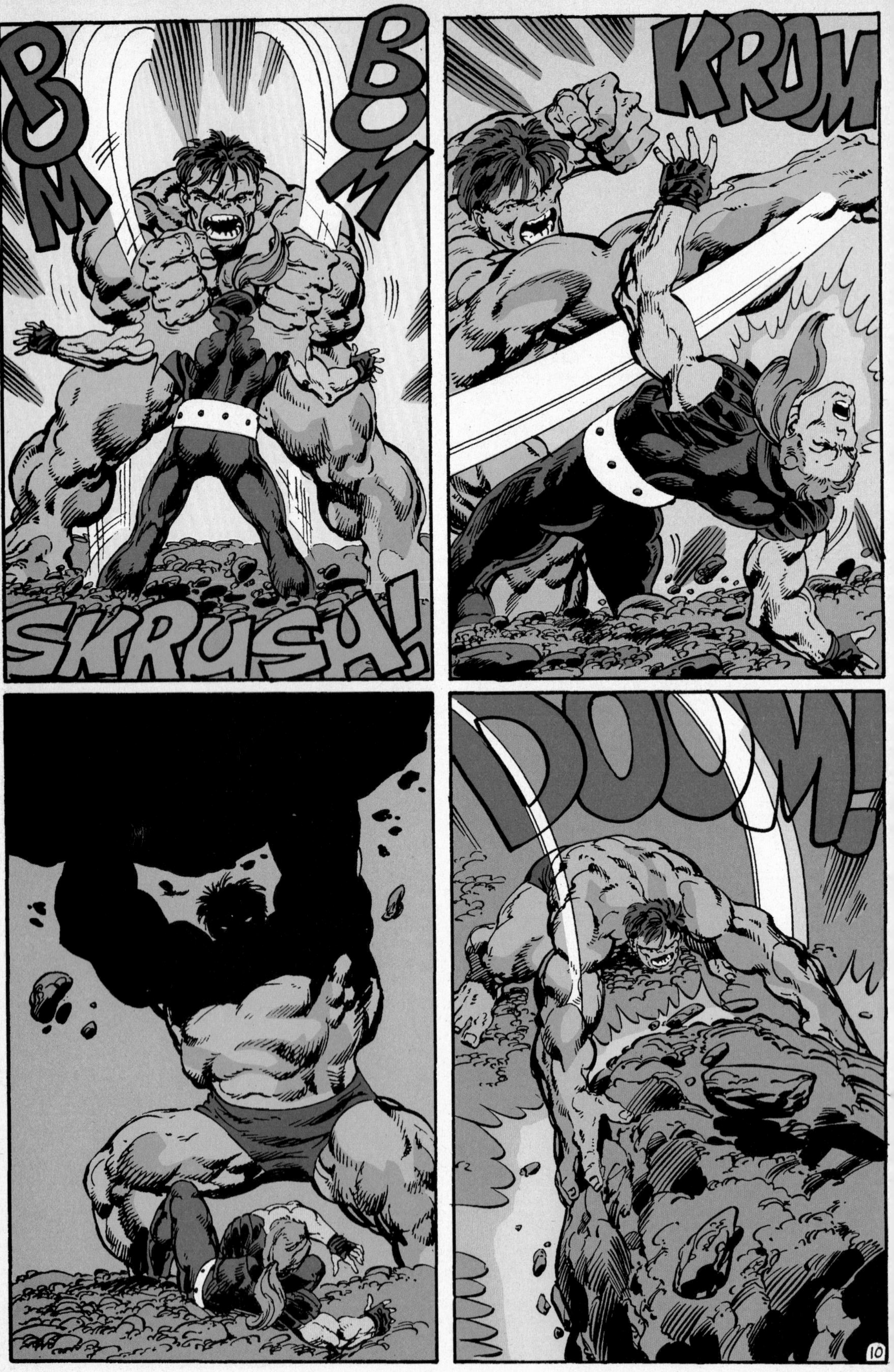
BOOM
BOOM
SKRUSH!
KROM
DOOM!
10

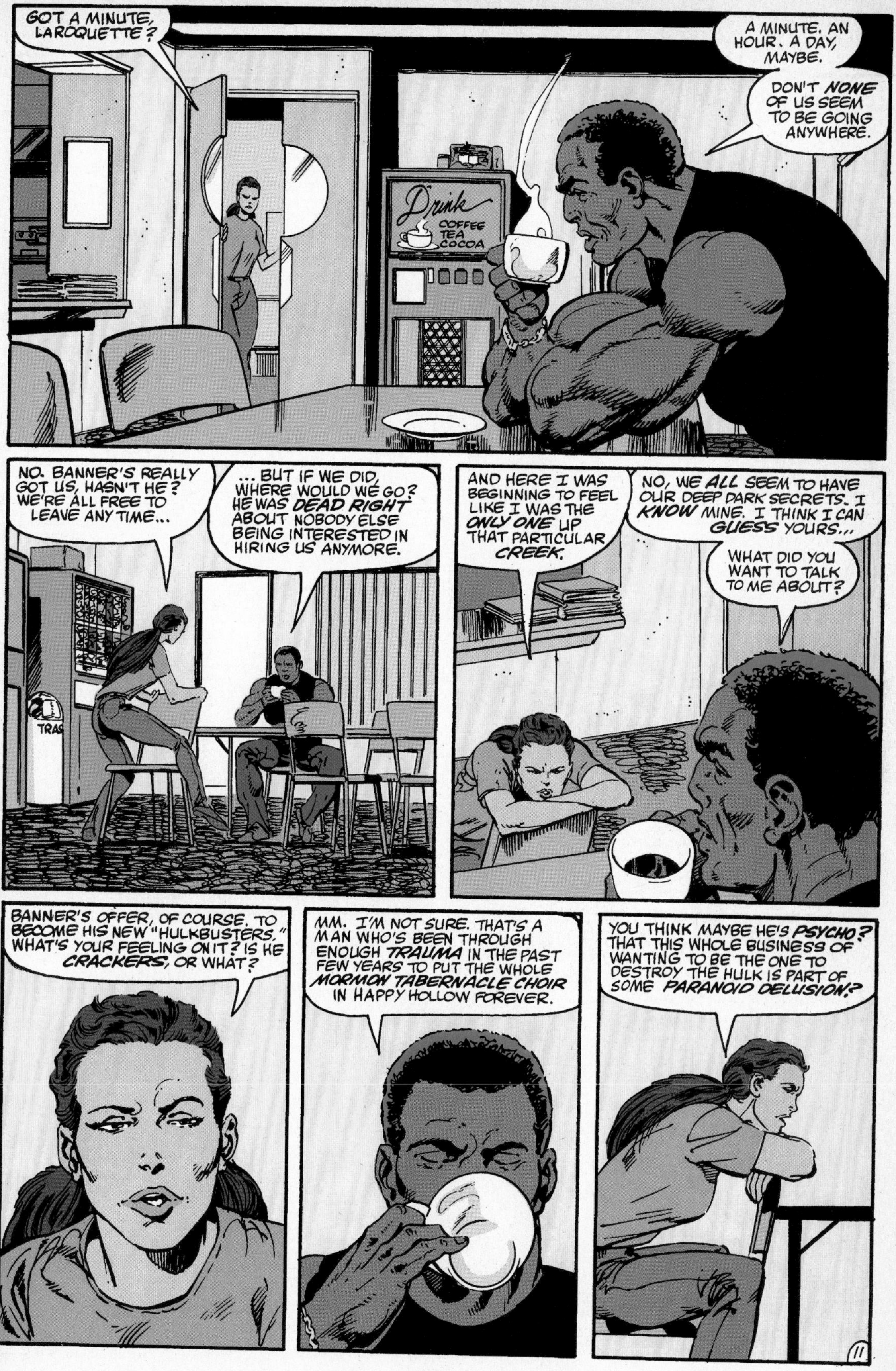
GOT A MINUTE, LAROQUETTE?
A MINUTE. AN HOUR. A DAY, MAYBE.
DON'T NONE OF US SEEM TO BE GOING ANYWHERE.
Drink COFFEE TEA COCOA
NO. BANNER'S REALLY GOT US, HASN'T HE? WE'RE ALL FREE TO LEAVE ANY TIME...
...BUT IF WE DID, WHERE WOULD WE GO? HE WAS DEAD RIGHT ABOUT NOBODY ELSE BEING INTERESTED IN HIRING US ANYMORE.
AND HERE I WAS BEGINNING TO FEEL LIKE I WAS THE ONLY ONE UP THAT PARTICULAR CREEK.
NO, WE ALL SEEM TO HAVE OUR DEEP DARK SECRETS. I KNOW MINE. I THINK I CAN GUESS YOURS...
WHAT DID YOU WANT TO TALK TO ME ABOUT?
BANNER'S OFFER, OF COURSE. TO BECOME HIS NEW "HULKBUSTERS." WHAT'S YOUR FEELING ON IT? IS HE CRACKERS, OR WHAT?
MM. I'M NOT SURE. THAT'S A MAN WHO'S BEEN THROUGH ENOUGH TRAUMA IN THE PAST FEW YEARS TO PUT THE WHOLE MORMON TABERNACLE CHOIR IN HAPPY HOLLOW FOREVER.
YOU THINK MAYBE HE'S PSYCHO? THAT THIS WHOLE BUSINESS OF WANTING TO BE THE ONE TO DESTROY THE HULK IS PART OF SOME PARANOID DELUSION?
11

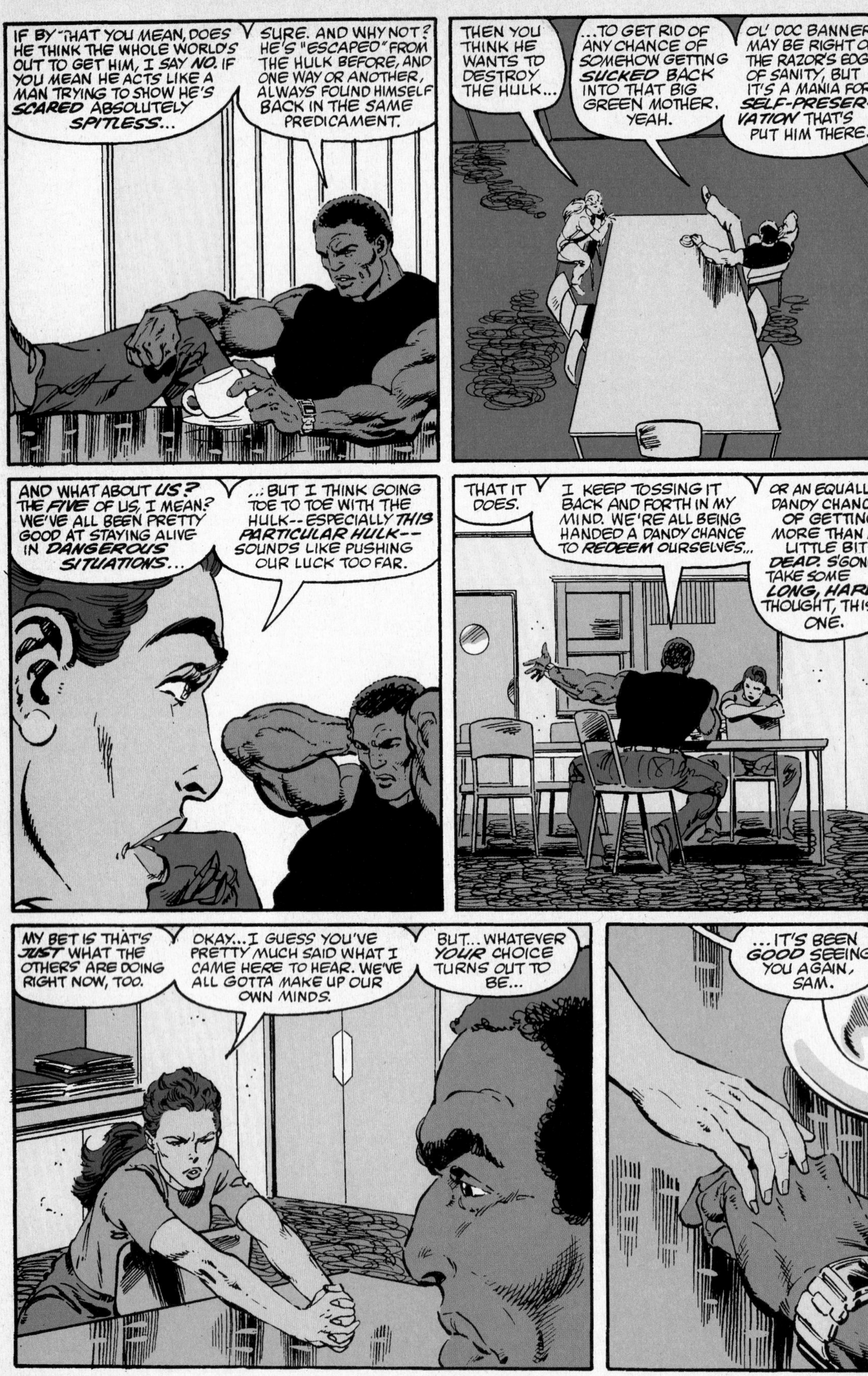
IF BY THAT YOU MEAN, DOES HE THINK THE WHOLE WORLD'S OUT TO GET HIM, I SAY NO. IF YOU MEAN HE ACTS LIKE A MAN TRYING TO SHOW HE'S SCARED ABSOLUTELY SPITLESS...
SURE. AND WHY NOT? HE'S "ESCAPED" FROM THE HULK BEFORE, AND ONE WAY OR ANOTHER, ALWAYS FOUND HIMSELF BACK IN THE SAME PREDICAMENT.
THEN YOU THINK HE WANTS TO DESTROY THE HULK...
...TO GET RID OF ANY CHANCE OF SOMEHOW GETTING SUCKED BACK INTO THAT BIG GREEN MOTHER. YEAH.
OL' DOC BANNER MAY BE RIGHT ON THE RAZOR'S EDGE OF SANITY, BUT IT'S A MANIA FOR SELF-PRESERVATION THAT'S PUT HIM THERE.
AND WHAT ABOUT US? THE FIVE OF US, I MEAN? WE'VE ALL BEEN PRETTY GOOD AT STAYING ALIVE IN DANGEROUS SITUATIONS...
...BUT I THINK GOING TOE TO TOE WITH THE HULK--ESPECIALLY THIS PARTICULAR HULK--SOUNDS LIKE PUSHING OUR LUCK TOO FAR.
THAT IT DOES.
I KEEP TOSSING IT BACK AND FORTH IN MY MIND. WE'RE ALL BEING HANDED A DANDY CHANCE TO REDEEM OURSELVES...
OR AN EQUALLY DANDY CHANCE OF GETTING MORE THAN A LITTLE BIT-- DEAD. S'GONNA TAKE SOME LONG, HARD THOUGHT, THIS ONE.
MY BET IS THAT'S JUST WHAT THE OTHERS ARE DOING RIGHT NOW, TOO.
OKAY... I GUESS YOU'VE PRETTY MUCH SAID WHAT I CAME HERE TO HEAR. WE'VE ALL GOTTA MAKE UP OUR OWN MINDS.
BUT... WHATEVER YOUR CHOICE TURNS OUT TO BE...
...IT'S BEEN GOOD SEEING YOU AGAIN, SAM.
12

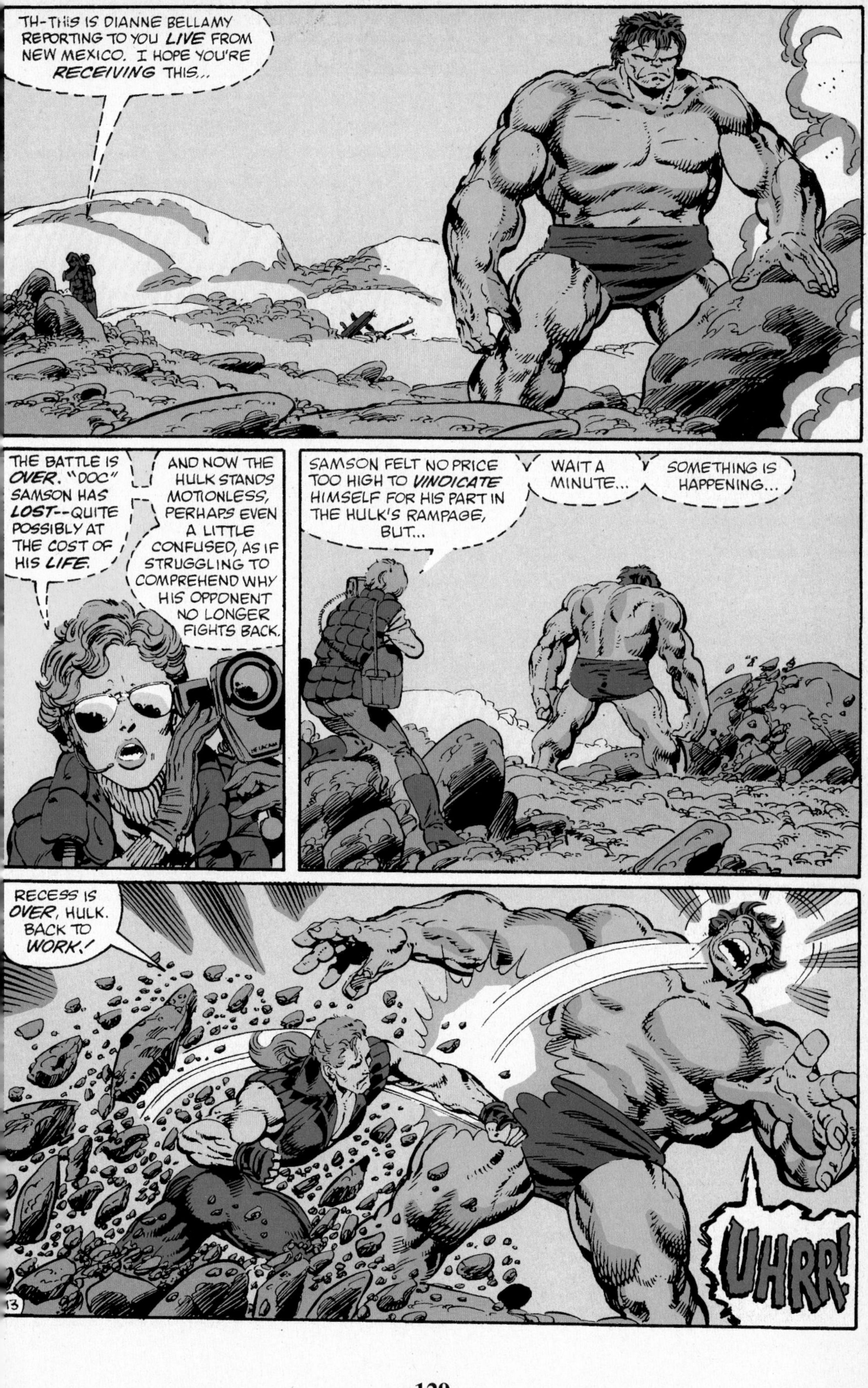
TH-THIS IS DIANNE BELLAMY REPORTING TO YOU LIVE FROM NEW MEXICO. I HOPE YOU'RE RECEIVING THIS...
THE BATTLE IS OVER. "DOC" SAMSON HAS LOST--QUITE POSSIBLY AT THE COST OF HIS LIFE.
AND NOW THE HULK STANDS MOTIONLESS, PERHAPS EVEN A LITTLE CONFUSED, AS IF STRUGGLING TO COMPREHEND WHY HIS OPPONENT NO LONGER FIGHTS BACK.
SAMSON FELT NO PRICE TOO HIGH TO VINDICATE HIMSELF FOR HIS PART IN THE HULK'S RAMPAGE, BUT...
WAIT A MINUTE...
SOMETHING IS HAPPENING...
RECESS IS OVER, HULK. BACK TO WORK!
UHRR!
13

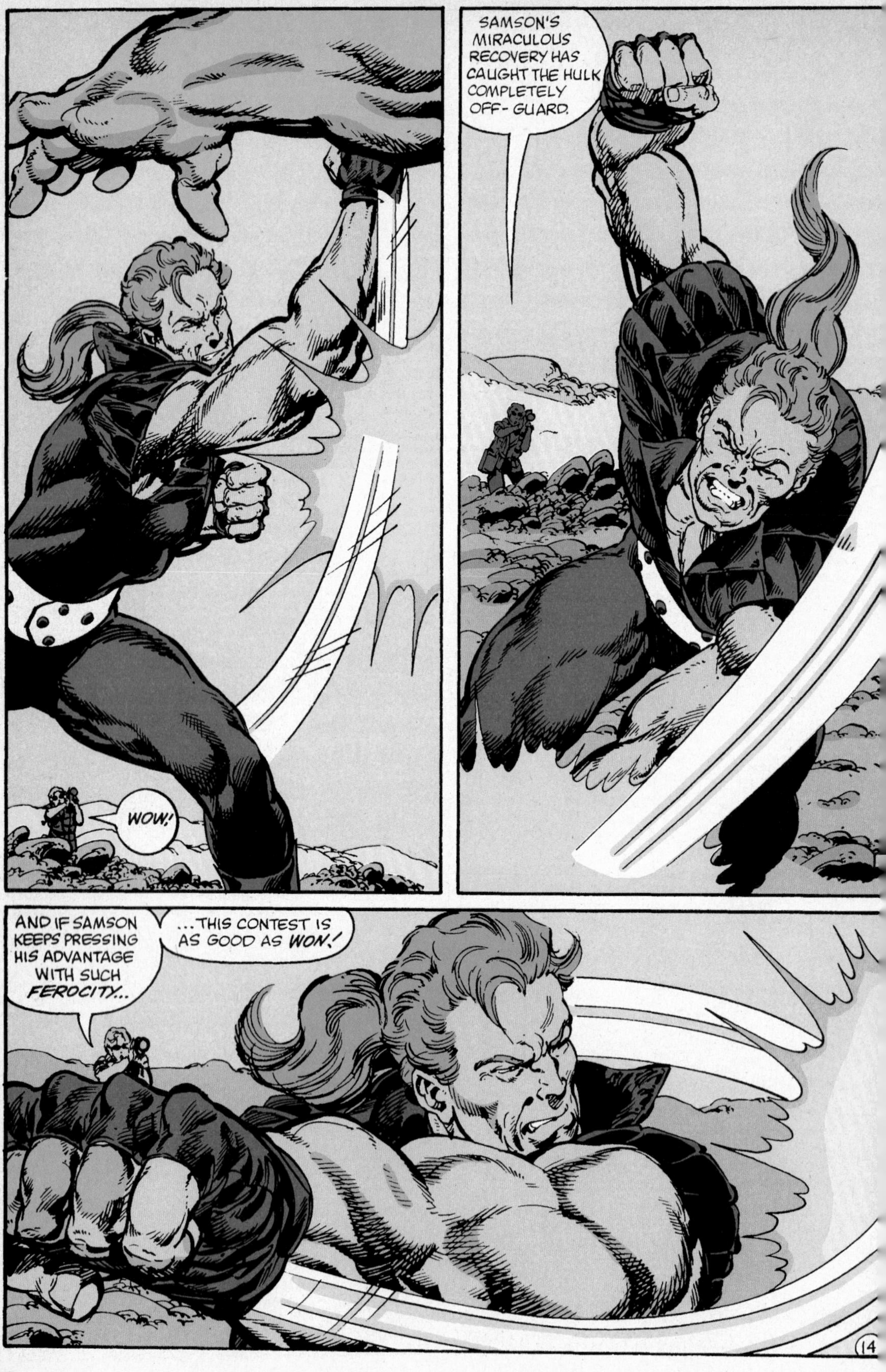
WOW!
SAMSON'S MIRACULOUS RECOVERY HAS CAUGHT THE HULK COMPLETELY OFF-GUARD.
AND IF SAMSON KEEPS PRESSING HIS ADVANTAGE WITH SUCH FEROCITY...
...THIS CONTEST IS AS GOOD AS WON!
14

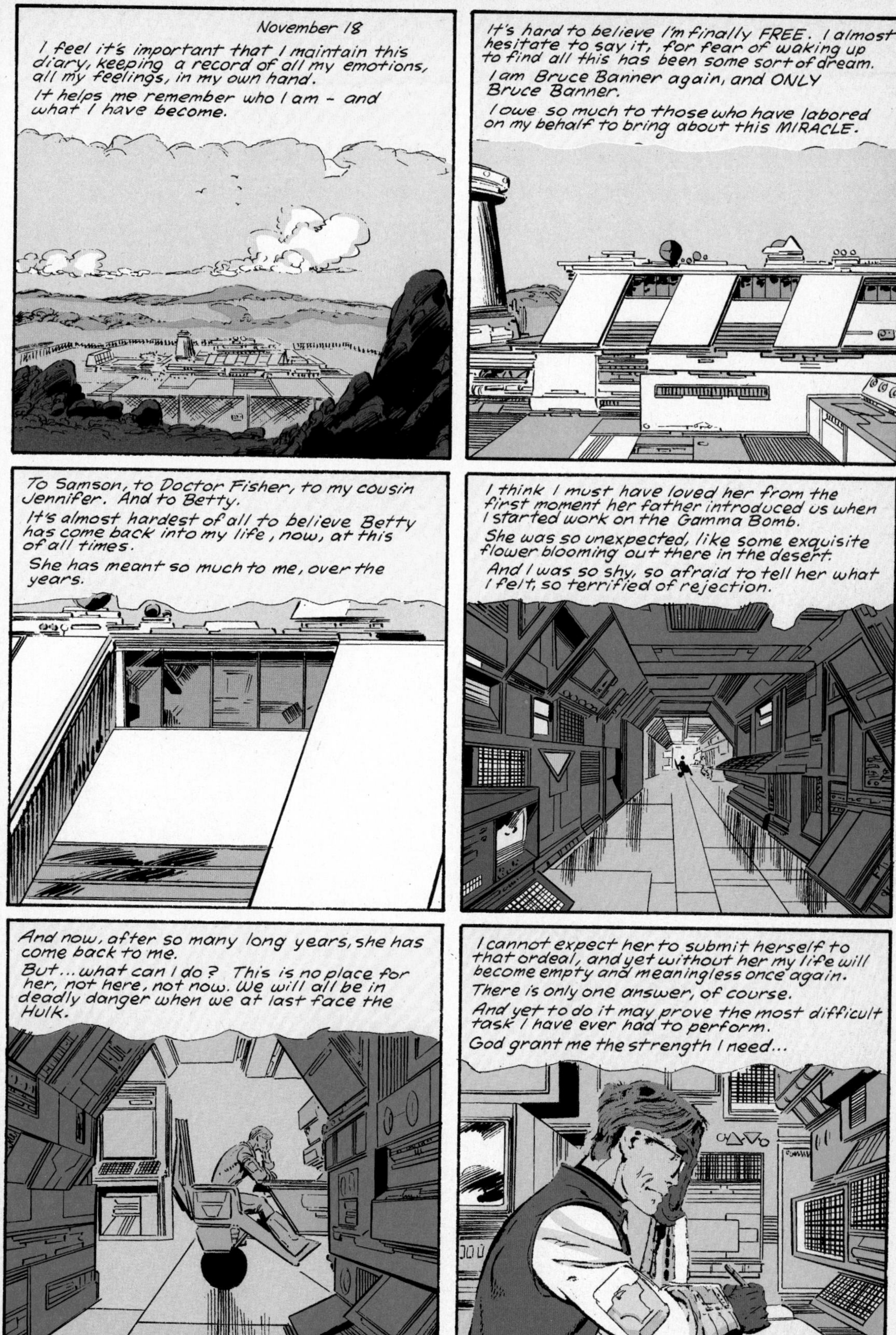
November 18
I feel it's important that I maintain this diary, keeping a record of all my emotions, all my feelings, in my own hand.
It helps me remember who I am - and what I have become.
It's hard to believe I'm finally FREE. I almost hesitate to say it, for fear of waking up to find all this has been some sort of dream.
I am Bruce Banner again, and ONLY Bruce Banner.
I owe so much to those who have labored on my behalf to bring about this MIRACLE.
To Samson, to Doctor Fisher, to my cousin Jennifer. And to Betty.
It's almost hardest of all to believe Betty has come back into my life, now, at this of all times.
She has meant so much to me, over the years.
I think I must have loved her from the first moment her father introduced us when I started work on the Gamma Bomb.
She was so unexpected, like some exquisite flower blooming out there in the desert.
And I was so shy, so afraid to tell her what I felt, so terrified of rejection.
And now, after so many long years, she has come back to me.
But... what can I do? This is no place for her, not here, not now. We will all be in deadly danger when we at last face the Hulk.
I cannot expect her to submit herself to that ordeal, and yet without her my life will become empty and meaningless once again.
There is only one answer, of course.
And yet to do it may prove the most difficult task I have ever had to perform.
God grant me the strength I need...
15

...A BATTLE WHICH HAS RAGED NOW FOR ALMOST *SIX FULL HOURS*, WITHOUT EITHER SIDE SHOWING ANY SIGN OF *TIRING*.

IT CAN ONLY BE THIS INCREDIBLE *STAMINA* WHICH KEEPS SAMSON GOING NOW, FOR ALTHOUGH HE IS *STRONGER* THAN ALMOST ANY OTHER *HUMAN*...

...HIS GREAT POWER IS EQUAL ONLY TO THAT OF THE HULK IN A *CALM* STATE. AND AS YOU PROBABLY KNOW, THE *MADDER THE HULK GETS, THE STRONGER HE GETS!*

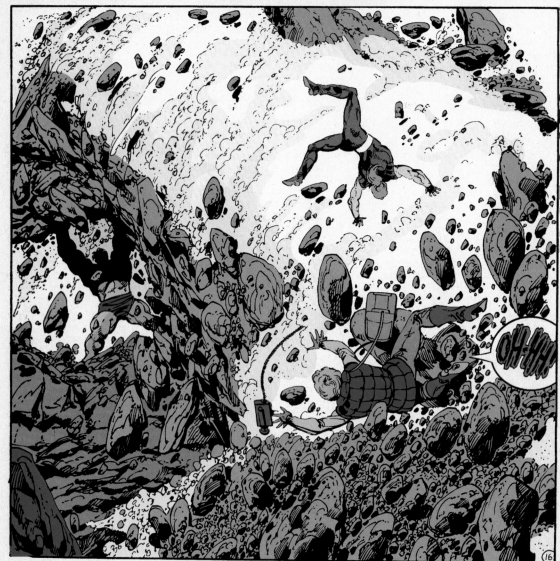

OH-HH!

132

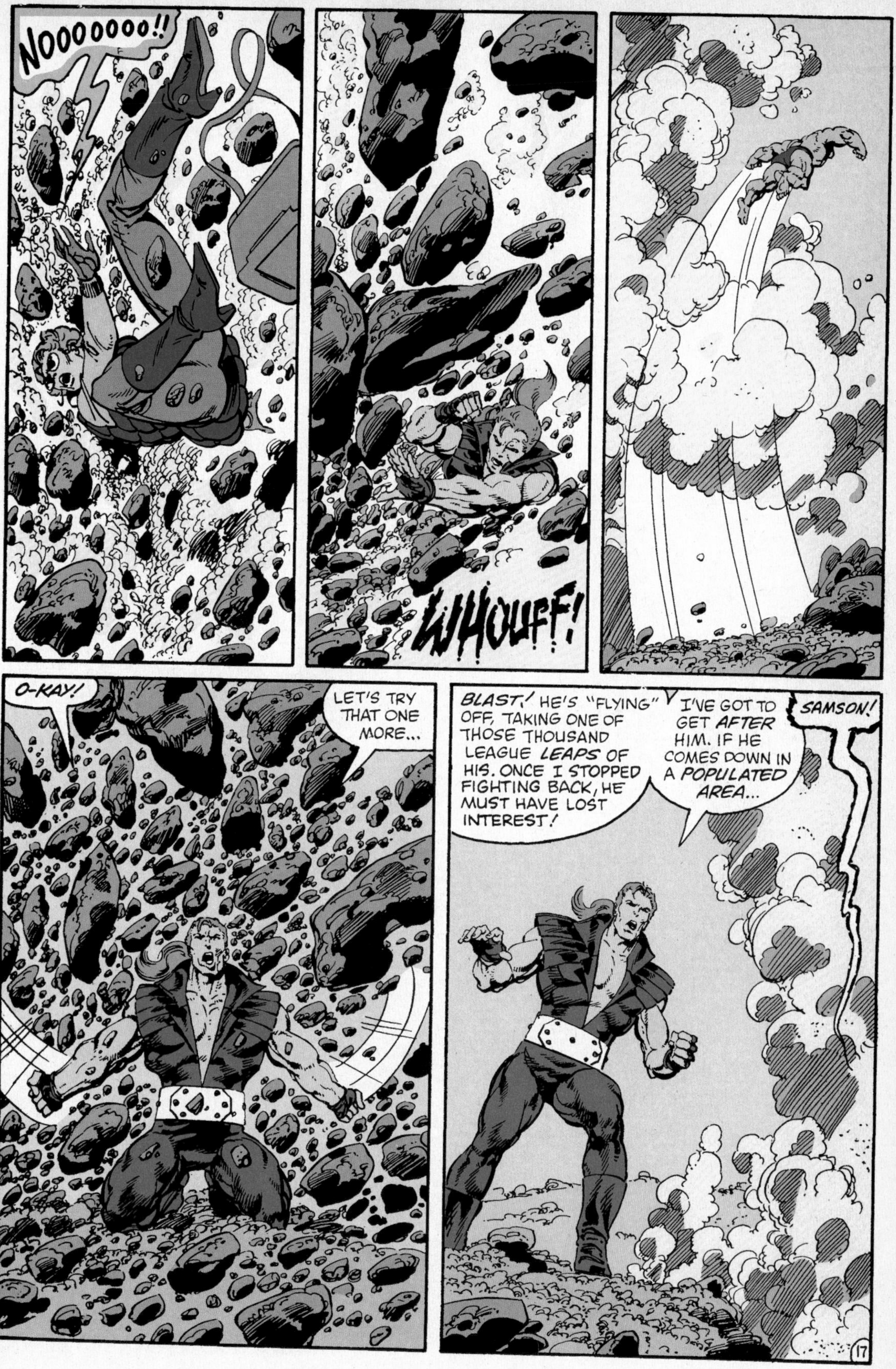

NOOOOOOO!!
WHOUFF!
O-KAY!
LET'S TRY THAT ONE MORE...
BLAST! HE'S "FLYING" OFF, TAKING ONE OF THOSE THOUSAND LEAGUE LEAPS OF HIS. ONCE I STOPPED FIGHTING BACK, HE MUST HAVE LOST INTEREST!
I'VE GOT TO GET AFTER HIM. IF HE COMES DOWN IN A POPULATED AREA...
SAMSON!
17

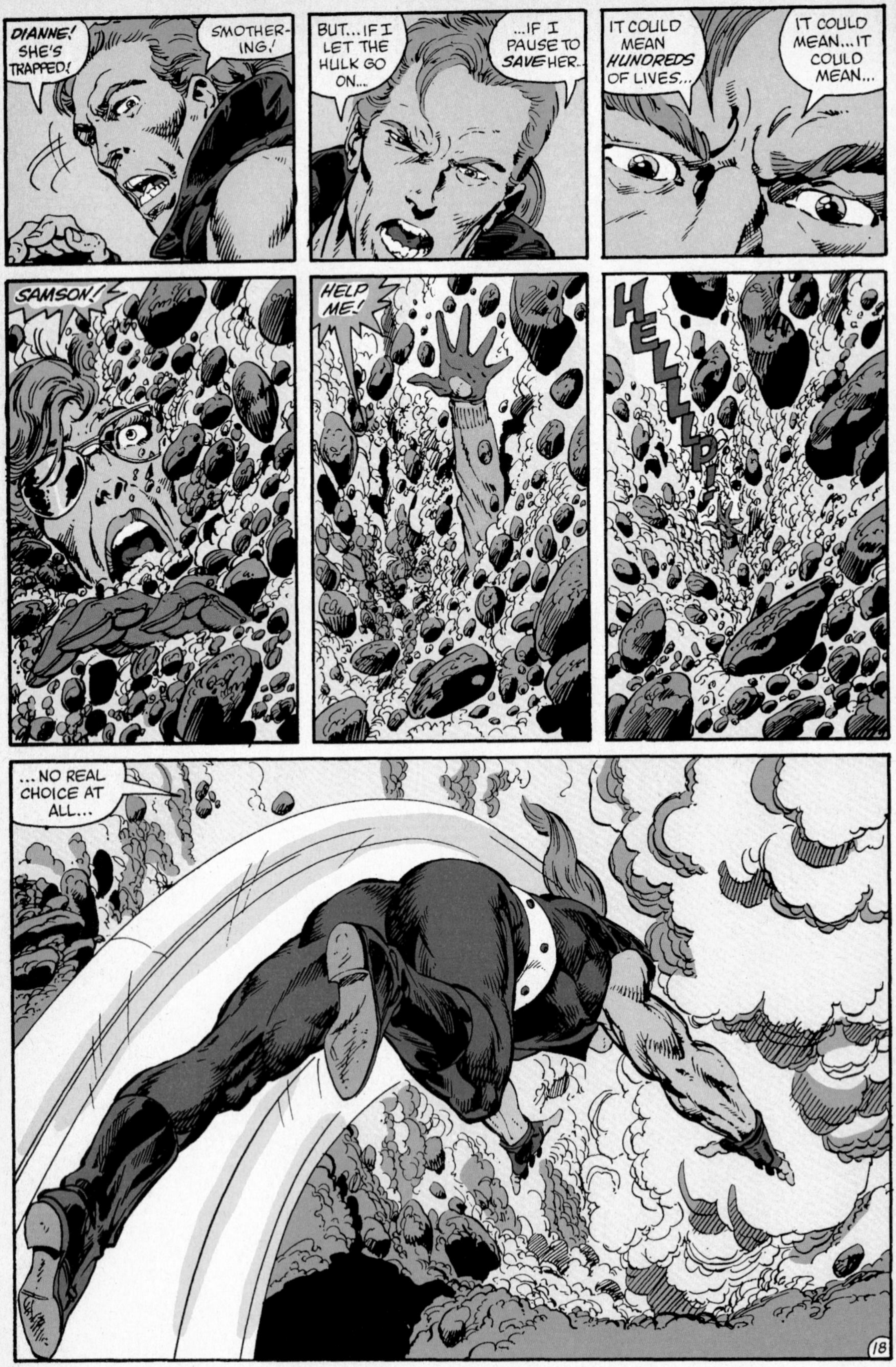
DIANNE! SHE'S TRAPPED!
SMOTHERING!
BUT...IF I LET THE HULK GO ON...
...IF I PAUSE TO SAVE HER...
IT COULD MEAN HUNDREDS OF LIVES...
IT COULD MEAN...IT COULD MEAN...
SAMSON!
HELP ME!
HELLLP!
...NO REAL CHOICE AT ALL...
18

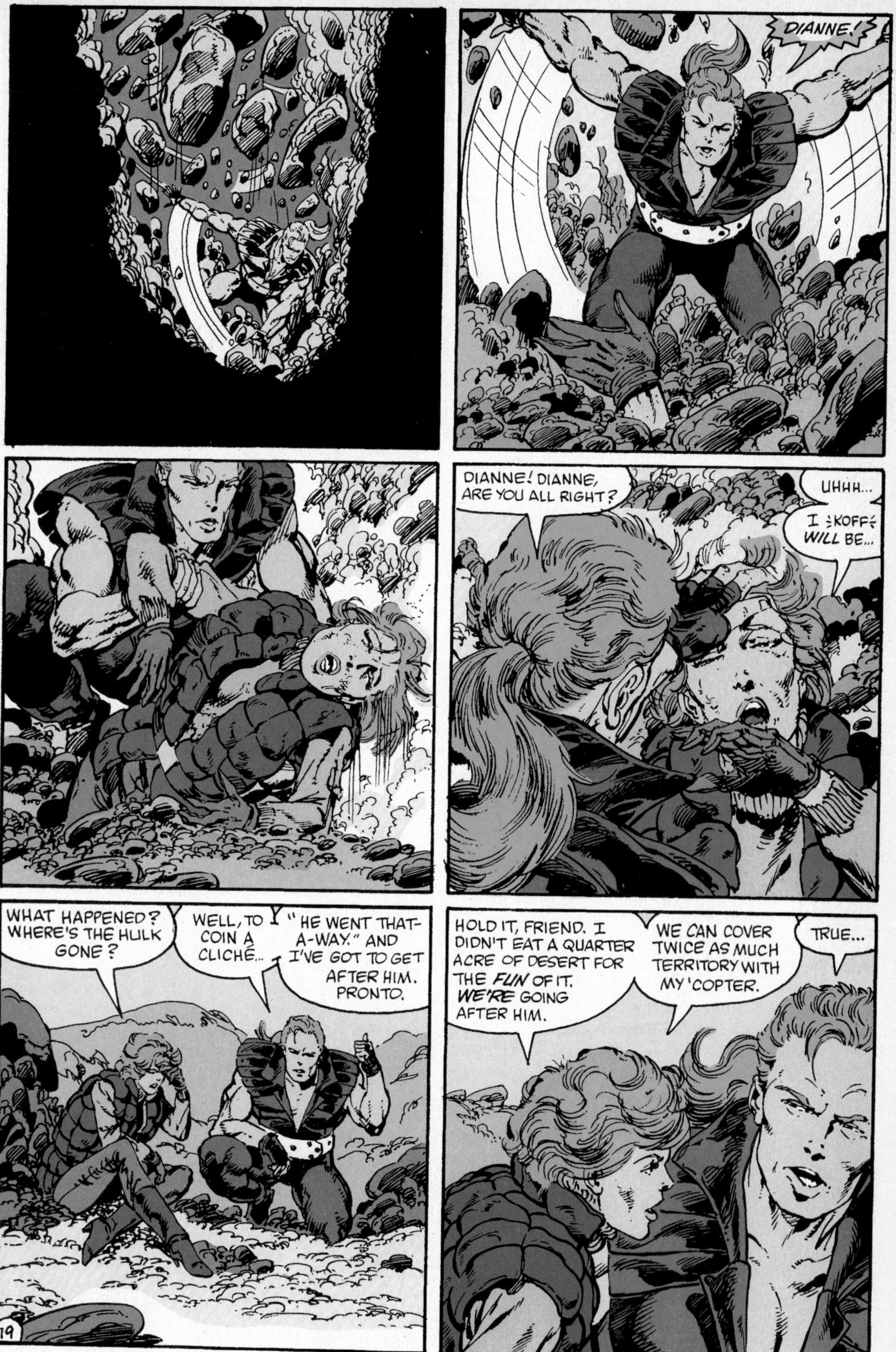
DIANNE!
DIANNE! DIANNE, ARE YOU ALL RIGHT?
UHHH...
I ≑KOFF≑ WILL BE...
WHAT HAPPENED? WHERE'S THE HULK GONE?
WELL, TO COIN A CLICHÉ...
"HE WENT THAT-A-WAY." AND I'VE GOT TO GET AFTER HIM. PRONTO.
19
HOLD IT, FRIEND. I DIDN'T EAT A QUARTER ACRE OF DESERT FOR THE FUN OF IT. WE'RE GOING AFTER HIM.
WE CAN COVER TWICE AS MUCH TERRITORY WITH MY 'COPTER.
TRUE...

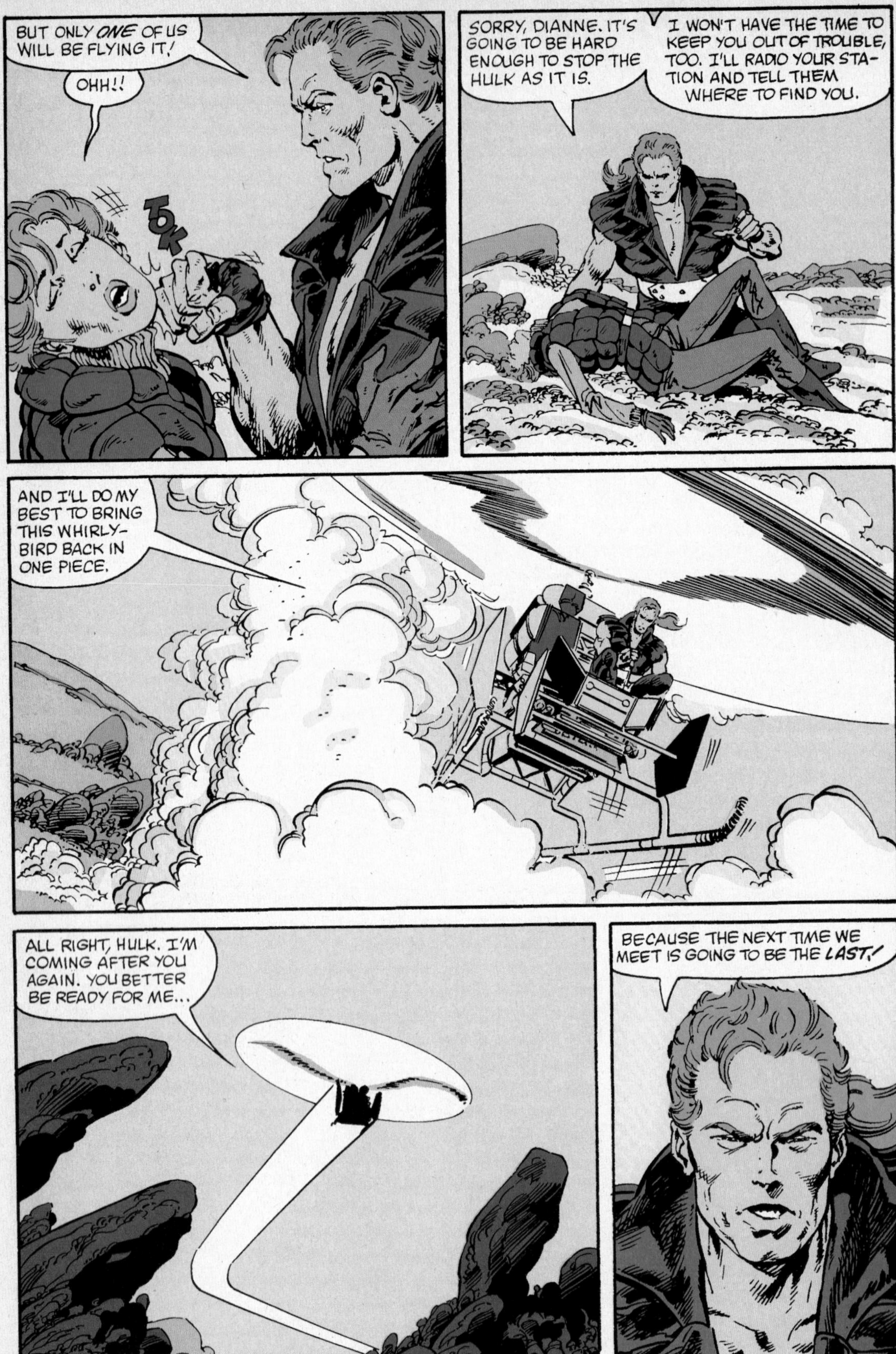
BUT ONLY ONE OF US WILL BE FLYING IT!
OHH!!
TOK
SORRY, DIANNE. IT'S GOING TO BE HARD ENOUGH TO STOP THE HULK AS IT IS.
I WON'T HAVE THE TIME TO KEEP YOU OUT OF TROUBLE, TOO. I'LL RADIO YOUR STATION AND TELL THEM WHERE TO FIND YOU.
AND I'LL DO MY BEST TO BRING THIS WHIRLYBIRD BACK IN ONE PIECE.
ALL RIGHT, HULK. I'M COMING AFTER YOU AGAIN. YOU BETTER BE READY FOR ME...
BECAUSE THE NEXT TIME WE MEET IS GOING TO BE THE LAST!
20

... AND SINCE THE AMERICAN GOVERNMENT HAS SEEN FIT TO PROVIDE DOCTOR BANNER WITH THIS BRAND NEW FACILITY...

...THE OPPORTUNITY FOR EACH OF US TO PURSUE OUR RESPECTIVE DISCIPLINES WOULD SEEM TO OUTWEIGH-- OR AT LEAST BALANCE-- THE DANGERS.

D'ACCORD, PROFESSOR TAKATA.

I COULD NOT AGREE MORE. I 'AVE STROLLED AROUND ZIZ FACILITY SEVERAL TIME IN ZEE PAST FEW DAYS, AND IT IS SUPERIOR, PER'APS, EVEN TO ZEE ORIGINAL GAMMA BASE.

WHICH GOT BUSTED UP BY THEM THAR U-FOES. A WHILE BACK. IF WE DO BECOME BANNER'S NEW HULKBUSTERS...

THAR'S SOME FOLKS AROUND WHO MIGHT THINK WE'RE CROWDIN' IN ON THEIR PRIVATE TERRAIN. THE HULK HAS A LOT OF ENEMIES OUT THERE.

NEVERTHELESS, I THINK THE REST OF US ARE IN AGREEMENT, AM I RIGHT?

I BELIEVE SO, M'SIEUR LAROQUETTE. LET ME BE ZEE FIRST TO JOIN HANDS IN COMMITMENT!

AND ME. IF THIS IS GONNA HAPPEN, I'M IN FOR THE RIDE.

AND SO AM I.

M'SIEUR SAUNDERS? YOUR DECISION?

WALLLLL... S'BOUT THE MOST CRACKERS THING AH'VE EVER GOT INTO, BUT WHAT TH' HEY!

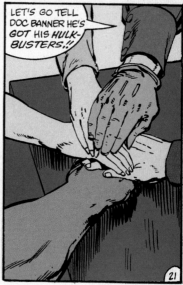

LET'S GO TELL DOC BANNER HE'S GOT HIS HULK-BUSTERS.!!

21

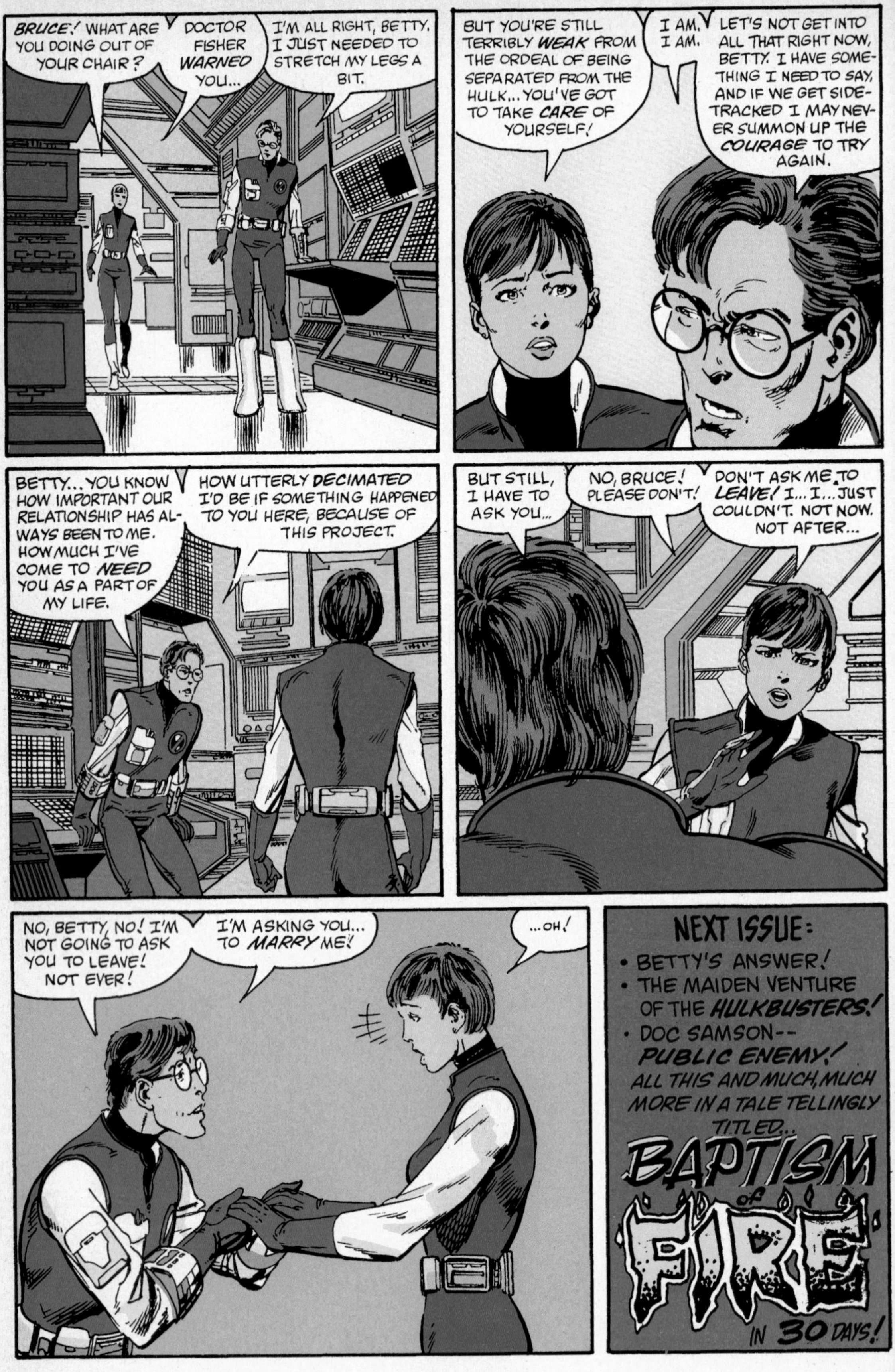
BRUCE! WHAT ARE YOU DOING OUT OF YOUR CHAIR?
DOCTOR FISHER WARNED YOU...
I'M ALL RIGHT, BETTY. I JUST NEEDED TO STRETCH MY LEGS A BIT.
BUT YOU'RE STILL TERRIBLY WEAK FROM THE ORDEAL OF BEING SEPARATED FROM THE HULK... YOU'VE GOT TO TAKE CARE OF YOURSELF!
I AM. I AM.
LET'S NOT GET INTO ALL THAT RIGHT NOW, BETTY. I HAVE SOMETHING I NEED TO SAY, AND IF WE GET SIDETRACKED I MAY NEVER SUMMON UP THE COURAGE TO TRY AGAIN.
BETTY... YOU KNOW HOW IMPORTANT OUR RELATIONSHIP HAS ALWAYS BEEN TO ME. HOW MUCH I'VE COME TO NEED YOU AS A PART OF MY LIFE.
HOW UTTERLY DECIMATED I'D BE IF SOMETHING HAPPENED TO YOU HERE, BECAUSE OF THIS PROJECT.
BUT STILL, I HAVE TO ASK YOU...
NO, BRUCE! PLEASE DON'T!
DON'T ASK ME TO LEAVE! I... I... JUST COULDN'T. NOT NOW. NOT AFTER...
NO, BETTY, NO! I'M NOT GOING TO ASK YOU TO LEAVE! NOT EVER!
I'M ASKING YOU... TO MARRY ME!
...OH!
NEXT ISSUE:
• BETTY'S ANSWER!
• THE MAIDEN VENTURE OF THE HULKBUSTERS!
• DOC SAMSON-- PUBLIC ENEMY!
ALL THIS AND MUCH, MUCH MORE IN A TALE TELLINGLY TITLED...
BAPTISM of FIRE
IN 30 DAYS!

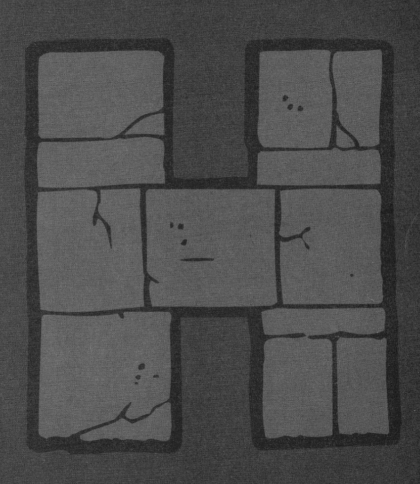

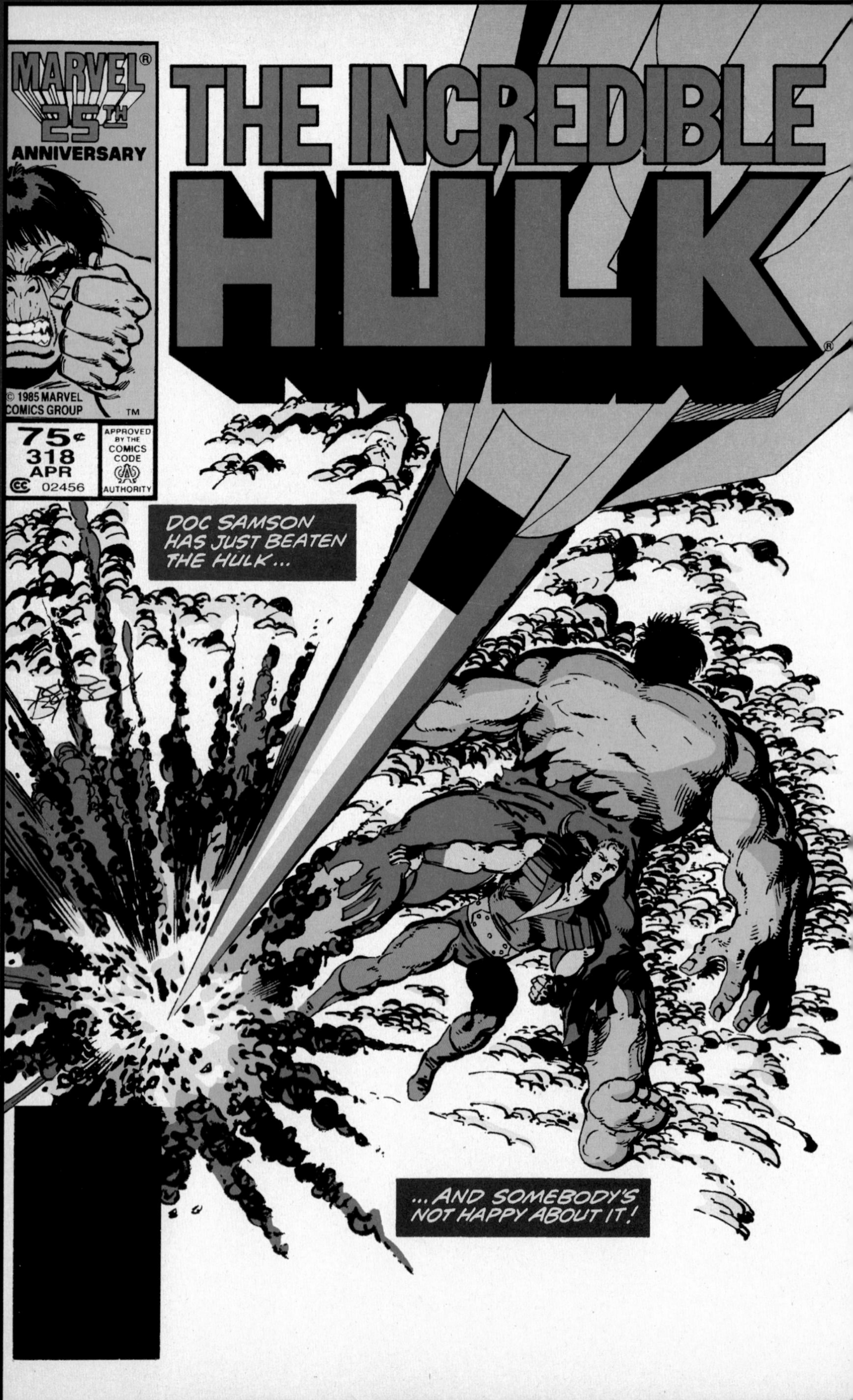

MARVEL® 25TH ANNIVERSARY
THE INCREDIBLE
HULK®
© 1985 MARVEL COMICS GROUP TM
75¢ 318 APR
02456
APPROVED BY THE COMICS CODE AUTHORITY
DOC SAMSON HAS JUST BEATEN THE HULK...
...AND SOMEBODY'S NOT HAPPY ABOUT IT!

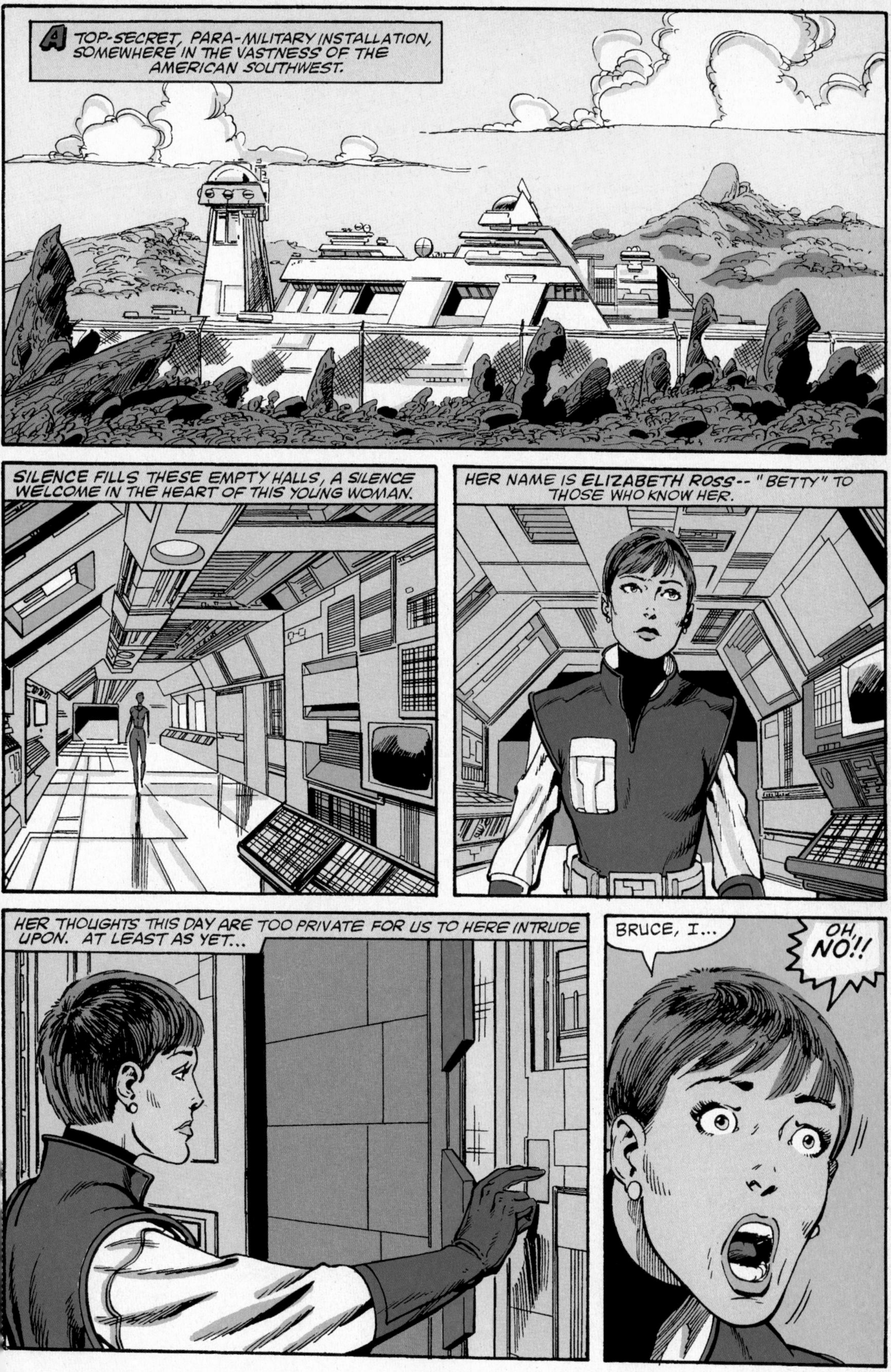
A TOP-SECRET, PARA-MILITARY INSTALLATION, SOMEWHERE IN THE VASTNESS OF THE AMERICAN SOUTHWEST.
SILENCE FILLS THESE EMPTY HALLS, A SILENCE WELCOME IN THE HEART OF THIS YOUNG WOMAN.
HER NAME IS ELIZABETH ROSS-- "BETTY" TO THOSE WHO KNOW HER.
HER THOUGHTS THIS DAY ARE TOO PRIVATE FOR US TO HERE INTRUDE UPON. AT LEAST AS YET...
BRUCE, I...
OH, NO!!

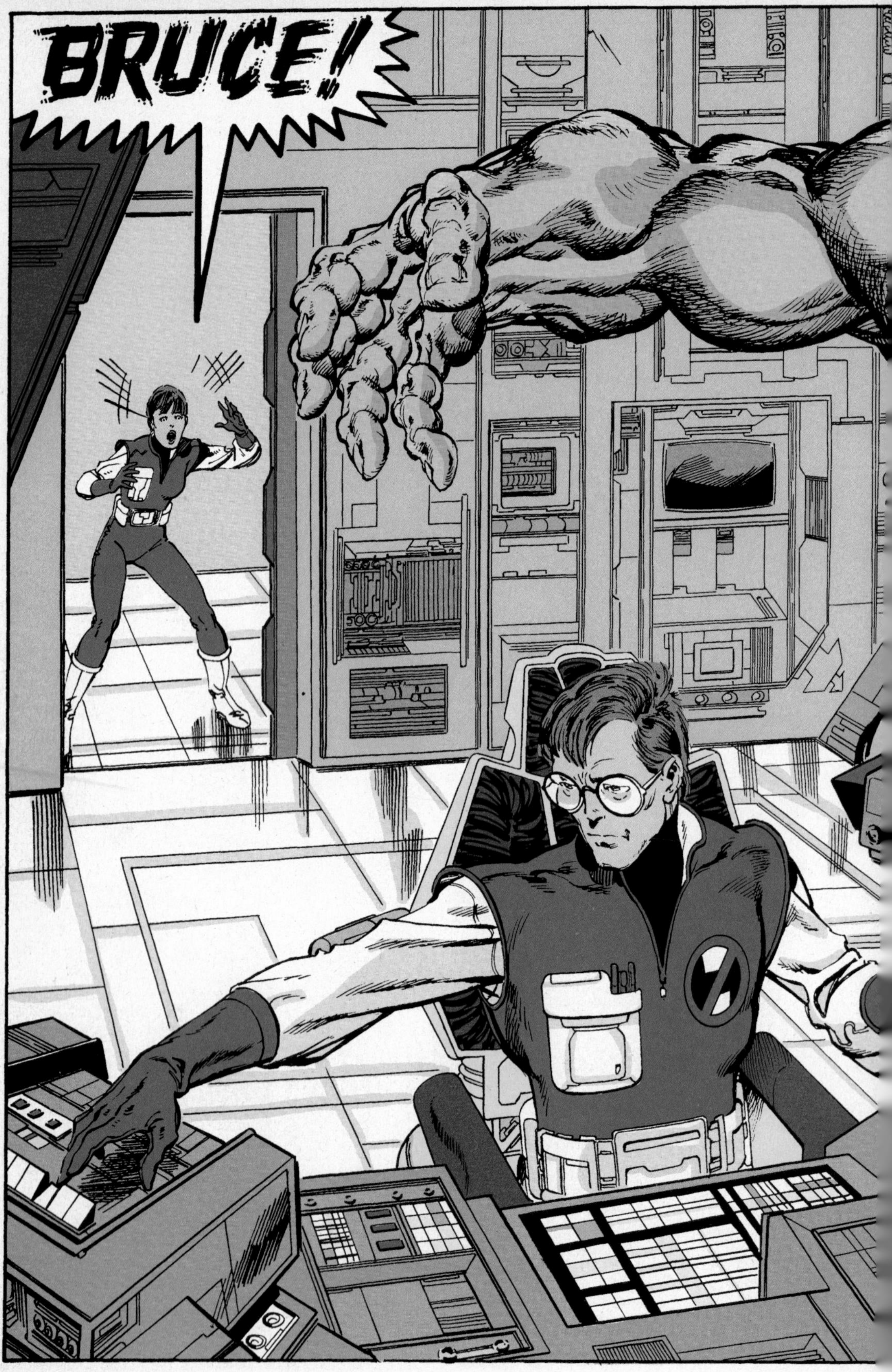
BRUCE!

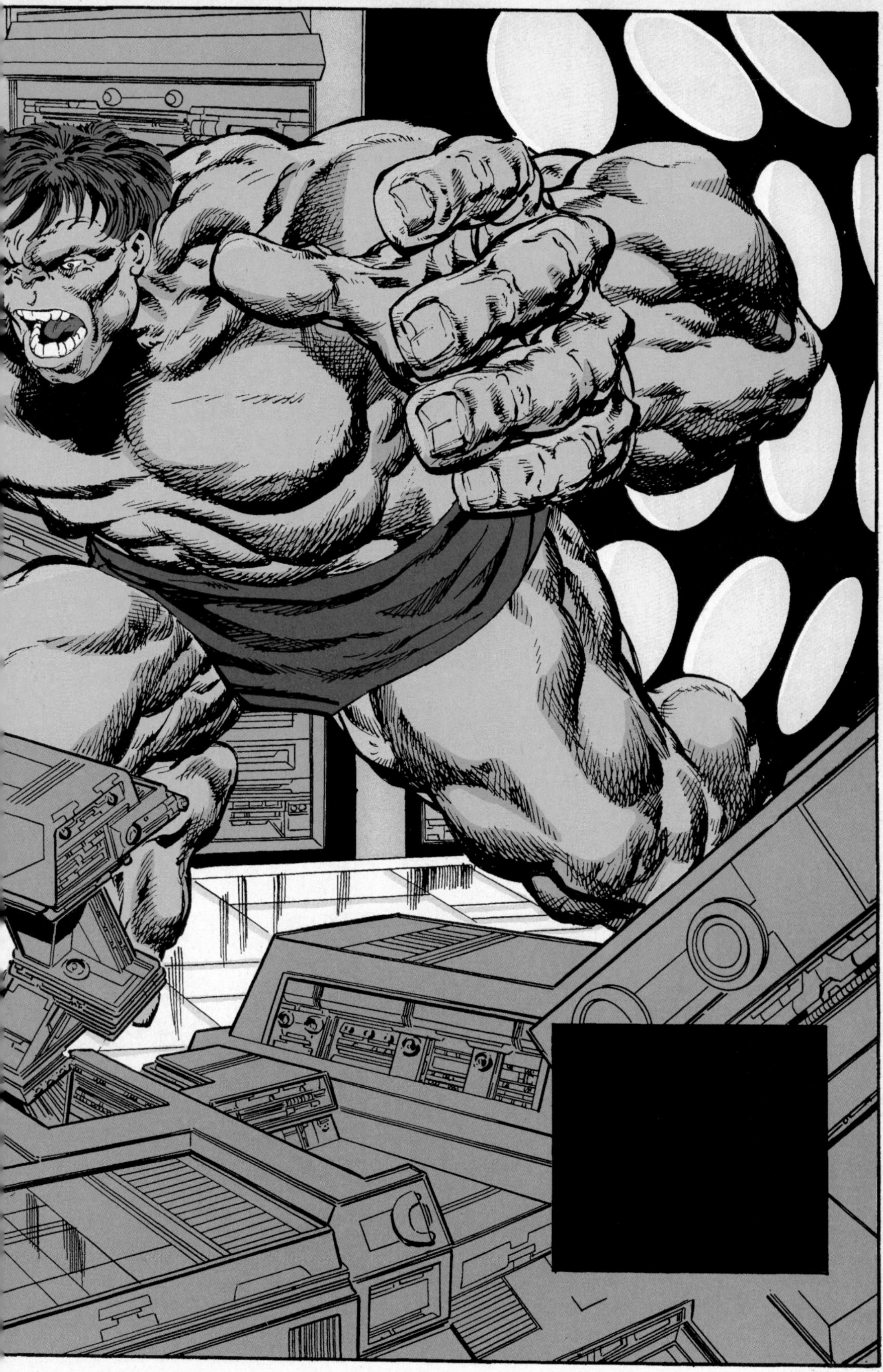
[redacted]

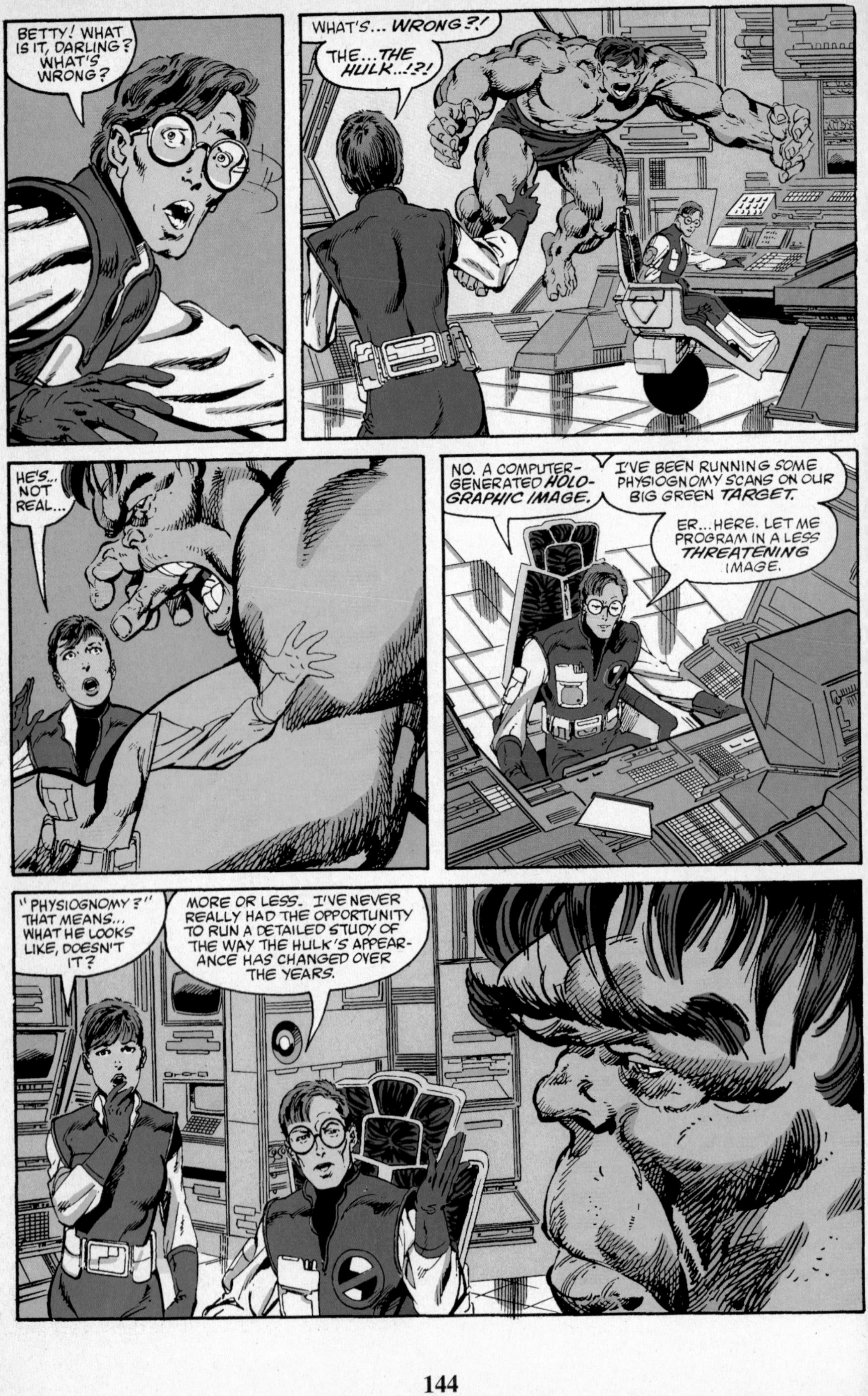

BETTY! WHAT IS IT, DARLING? WHAT'S WRONG?
WHAT'S... WRONG?!
THE... THE HULK..!?!
HE'S... NOT REAL...
NO. A COMPUTER-GENERATED HOLOGRAPHIC IMAGE.
I'VE BEEN RUNNING SOME PHYSIOGNOMY SCANS ON OUR BIG GREEN TARGET.
ER... HERE. LET ME PROGRAM IN A LESS THREATENING IMAGE.
"PHYSIOGNOMY?" THAT MEANS... WHAT HE LOOKS LIKE, DOESN'T IT?
MORE OR LESS. I'VE NEVER REALLY HAD THE OPPORTUNITY TO RUN A DETAILED STUDY OF THE WAY THE HULK'S APPEARANCE HAS CHANGED OVER THE YEARS.

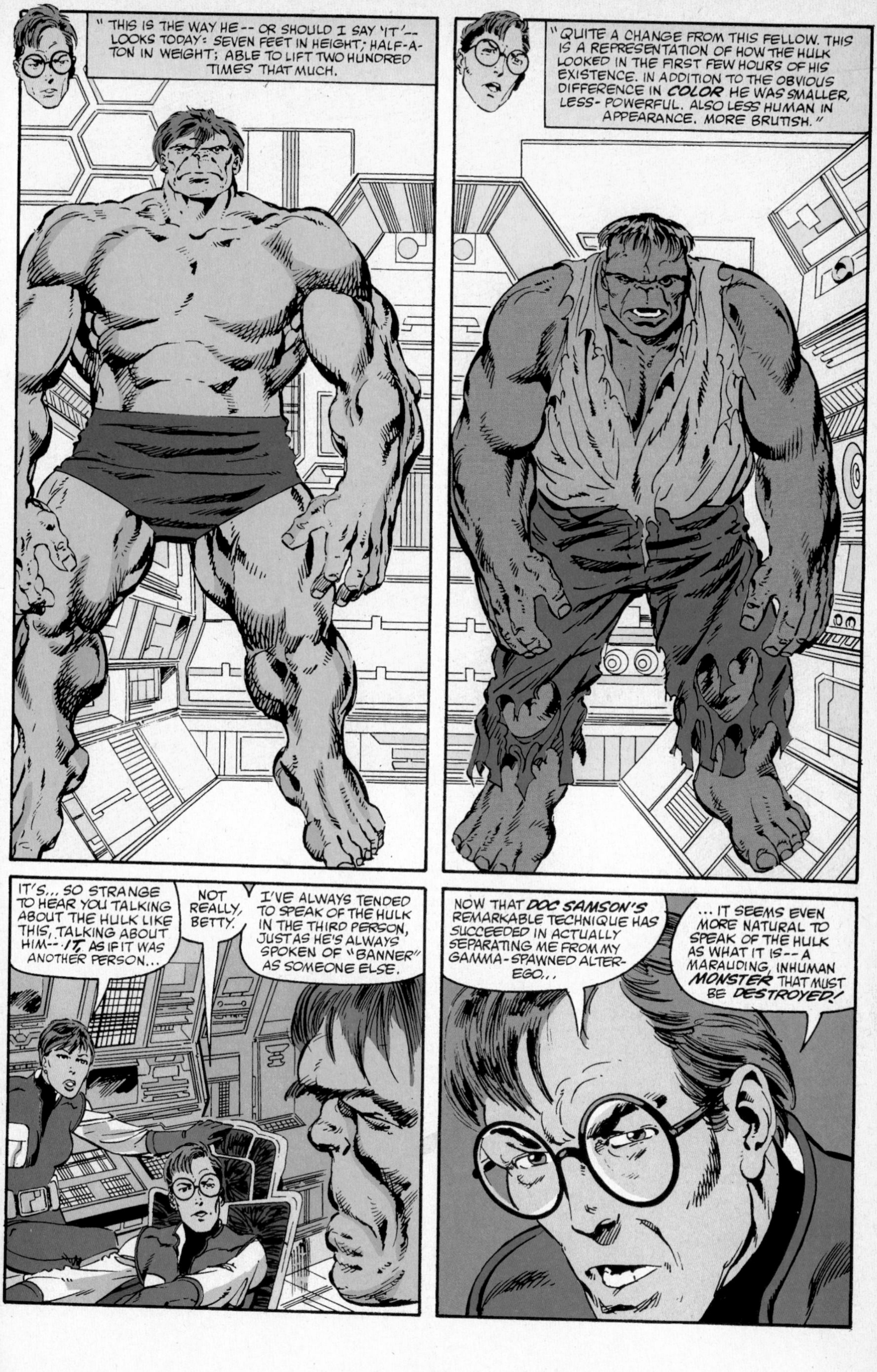
"THIS IS THE WAY HE -- OR SHOULD I SAY 'IT'-- LOOKS TODAY: SEVEN FEET IN HEIGHT; HALF-A-TON IN WEIGHT; ABLE TO LIFT TWO HUNDRED TIMES THAT MUCH.
"QUITE A CHANGE FROM THIS FELLOW. THIS IS A REPRESENTATION OF HOW THE HULK LOOKED IN THE FIRST FEW HOURS OF HIS EXISTENCE. IN ADDITION TO THE OBVIOUS DIFFERENCE IN COLOR HE WAS SMALLER, LESS-POWERFUL. ALSO LESS HUMAN IN APPEARANCE. MORE BRUTISH."
IT'S... SO STRANGE TO HEAR YOU TALKING ABOUT THE HULK LIKE THIS, TALKING ABOUT HIM-- IT, AS IF IT WAS ANOTHER PERSON...
NOT REALLY, BETTY.
I'VE ALWAYS TENDED TO SPEAK OF THE HULK IN THE THIRD PERSON, JUST AS HE'S ALWAYS SPOKEN OF "BANNER" AS SOMEONE ELSE.
NOW THAT DOC SAMSON'S REMARKABLE TECHNIQUE HAS SUCCEEDED IN ACTUALLY SEPARATING ME FROM MY GAMMA-SPAWNED ALTER-EGO...
... IT SEEMS EVEN MORE NATURAL TO SPEAK OF THE HULK AS WHAT IT IS-- A MARAUDING, INHUMAN MONSTER THAT MUST BE DESTROYED!

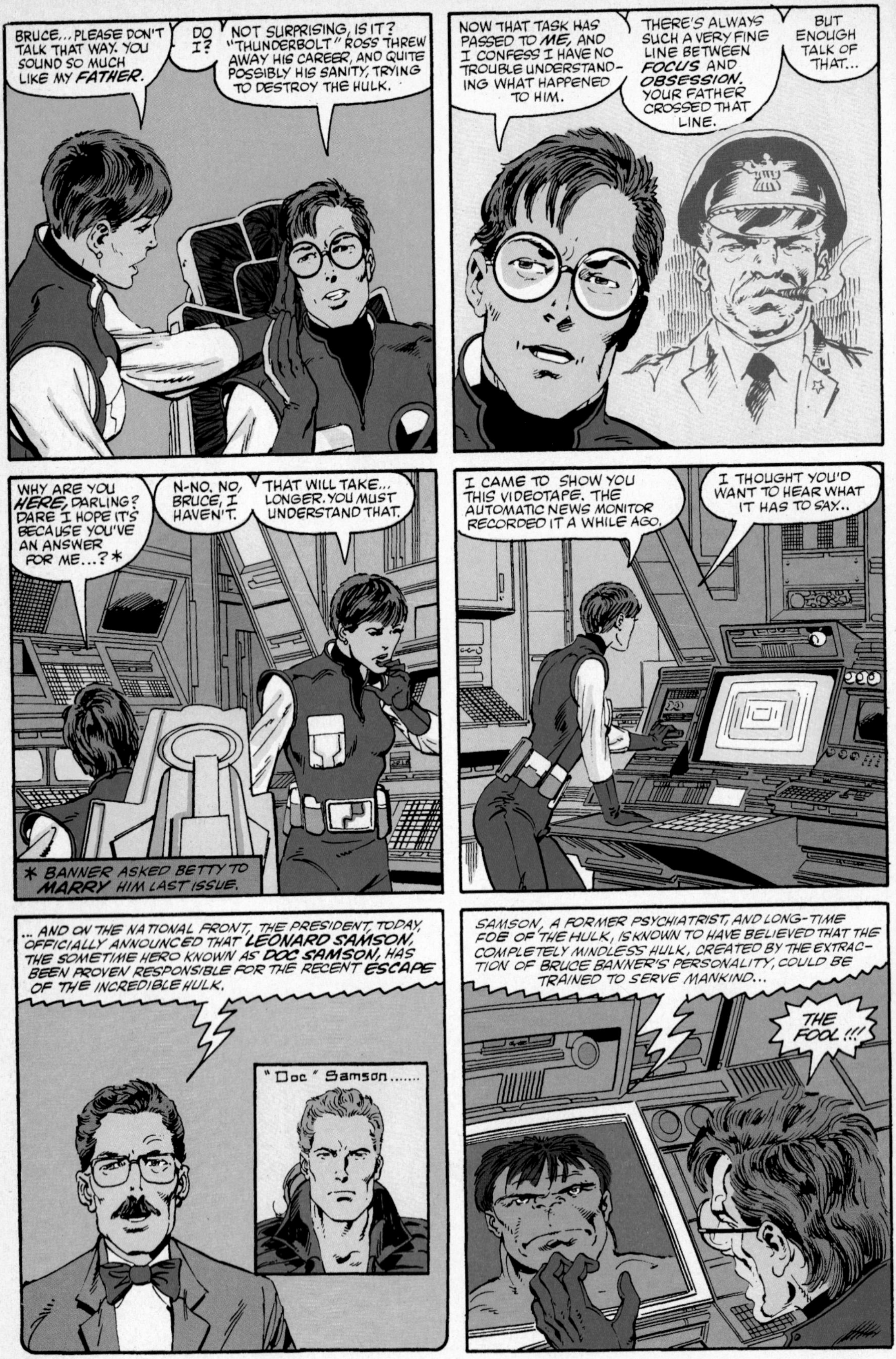

BRUCE... PLEASE DON'T TALK THAT WAY. YOU SOUND SO MUCH LIKE MY FATHER.
DO I?
NOT SURPRISING, IS IT? "THUNDERBOLT" ROSS THREW AWAY HIS CAREER, AND QUITE POSSIBLY HIS SANITY, TRYING TO DESTROY THE HULK.
NOW THAT TASK HAS PASSED TO ME, AND I CONFESS I HAVE NO TROUBLE UNDERSTANDING WHAT HAPPENED TO HIM.
THERE'S ALWAYS SUCH A VERY FINE LINE BETWEEN FOCUS AND OBSESSION. YOUR FATHER CROSSED THAT LINE.
BUT ENOUGH TALK OF THAT...
WHY ARE YOU HERE, DARLING? DARE I HOPE IT'S BECAUSE YOU'VE AN ANSWER FOR ME...?*
N-NO. NO, BRUCE, I HAVEN'T.
THAT WILL TAKE... LONGER. YOU MUST UNDERSTAND THAT.
* BANNER ASKED BETTY TO MARRY HIM LAST ISSUE.
I CAME TO SHOW YOU THIS VIDEOTAPE. THE AUTOMATIC NEWS MONITOR RECORDED IT A WHILE AGO.
I THOUGHT YOU'D WANT TO HEAR WHAT IT HAS TO SAY...
...AND ON THE NATIONAL FRONT, THE PRESIDENT, TODAY, OFFICIALLY ANNOUNCED THAT LEONARD SAMSON, THE SOMETIME HERO KNOWN AS DOC SAMSON, HAS BEEN PROVEN RESPONSIBLE FOR THE RECENT ESCAPE OF THE INCREDIBLE HULK.
"Doc" Samson.......
SAMSON, A FORMER PSYCHIATRIST, AND LONG-TIME FOE OF THE HULK, IS KNOWN TO HAVE BELIEVED THAT THE COMPLETELY MINDLESS HULK, CREATED BY THE EXTRACTION OF BRUCE BANNER'S PERSONALITY, COULD BE TRAINED TO SERVE MANKIND...
THE FOOL!!!

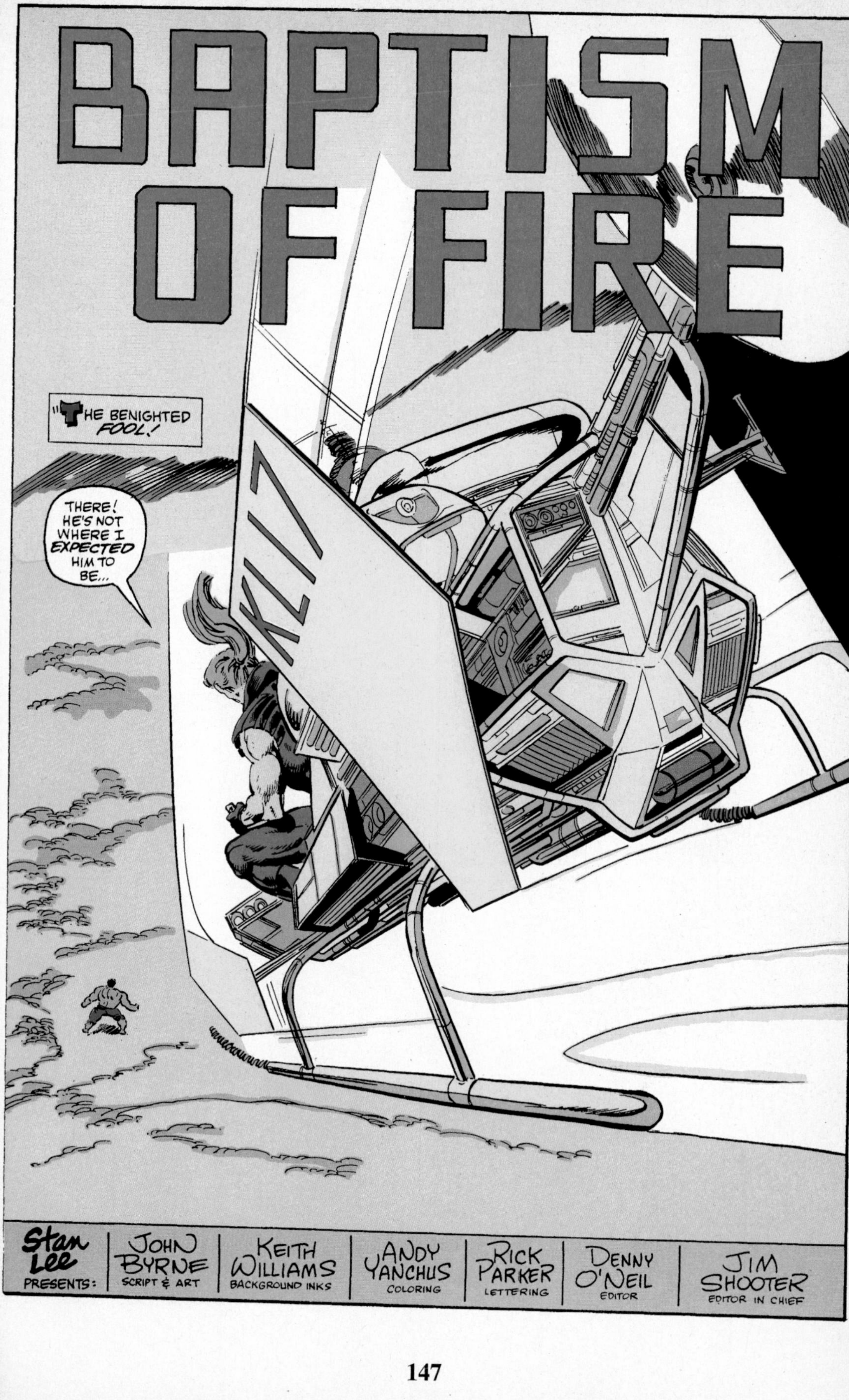
BAPTISM OF FIRE
"THE BENIGHTED FOOL!
THERE! HE'S NOT WHERE I EXPECTED HIM TO BE...
KL17
STAN LEE PRESENTS: JOHN BYRNE SCRIPT & ART KEITH WILLIAMS BACKGROUND INKS ANDY YANCHUS COLORING RICK PARKER LETTERING DENNY O'NEIL EDITOR JIM SHOOTER EDITOR IN CHIEF

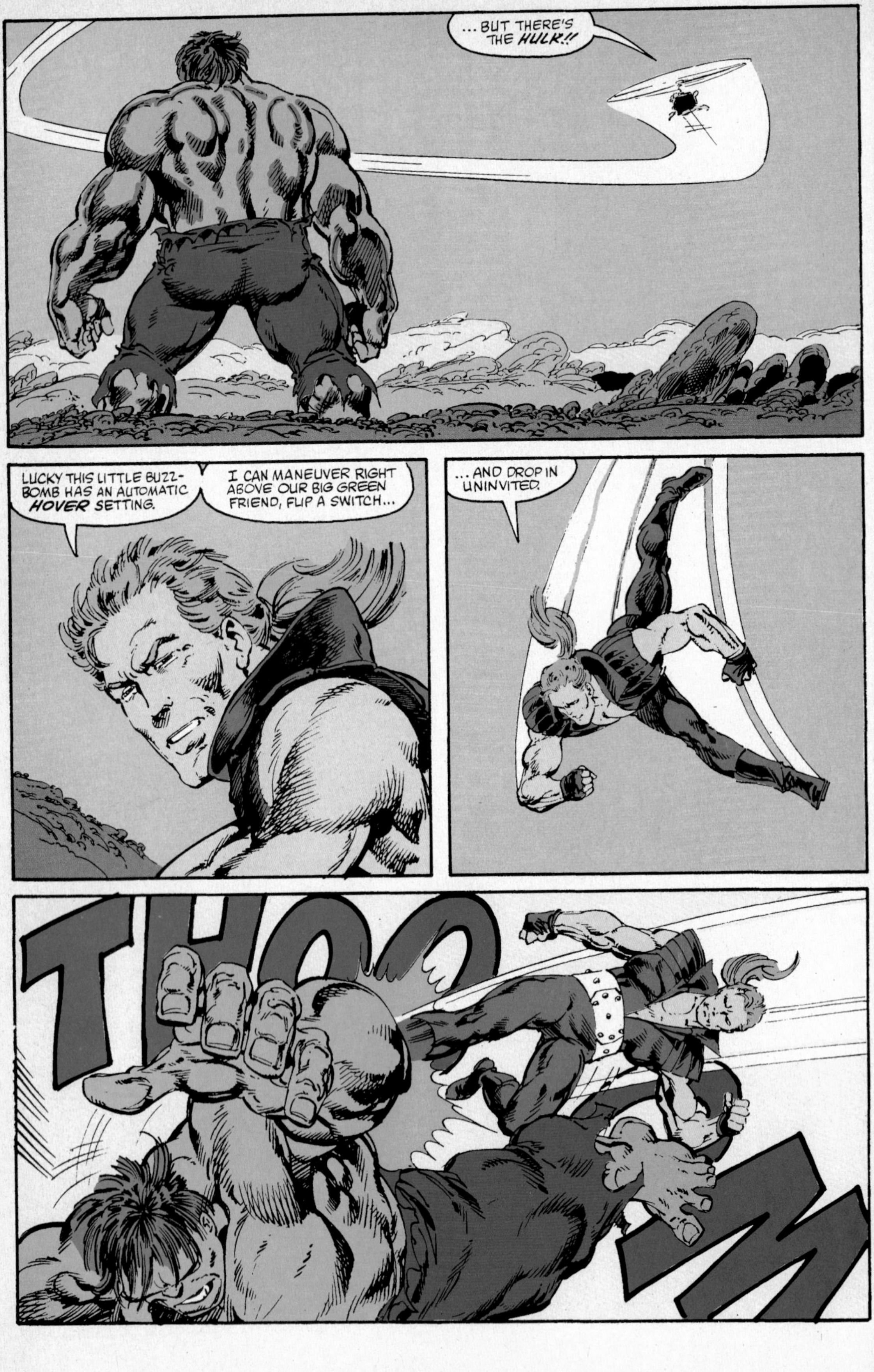
... BUT THERE'S THE HULK!!
LUCKY THIS LITTLE BUZZ-BOMB HAS AN AUTOMATIC HOVER SETTING.
I CAN MANEUVER RIGHT ABOVE OUR BIG GREEN FRIEND, FLIP A SWITCH...
... AND DROP IN UNINVITED.
THOOM

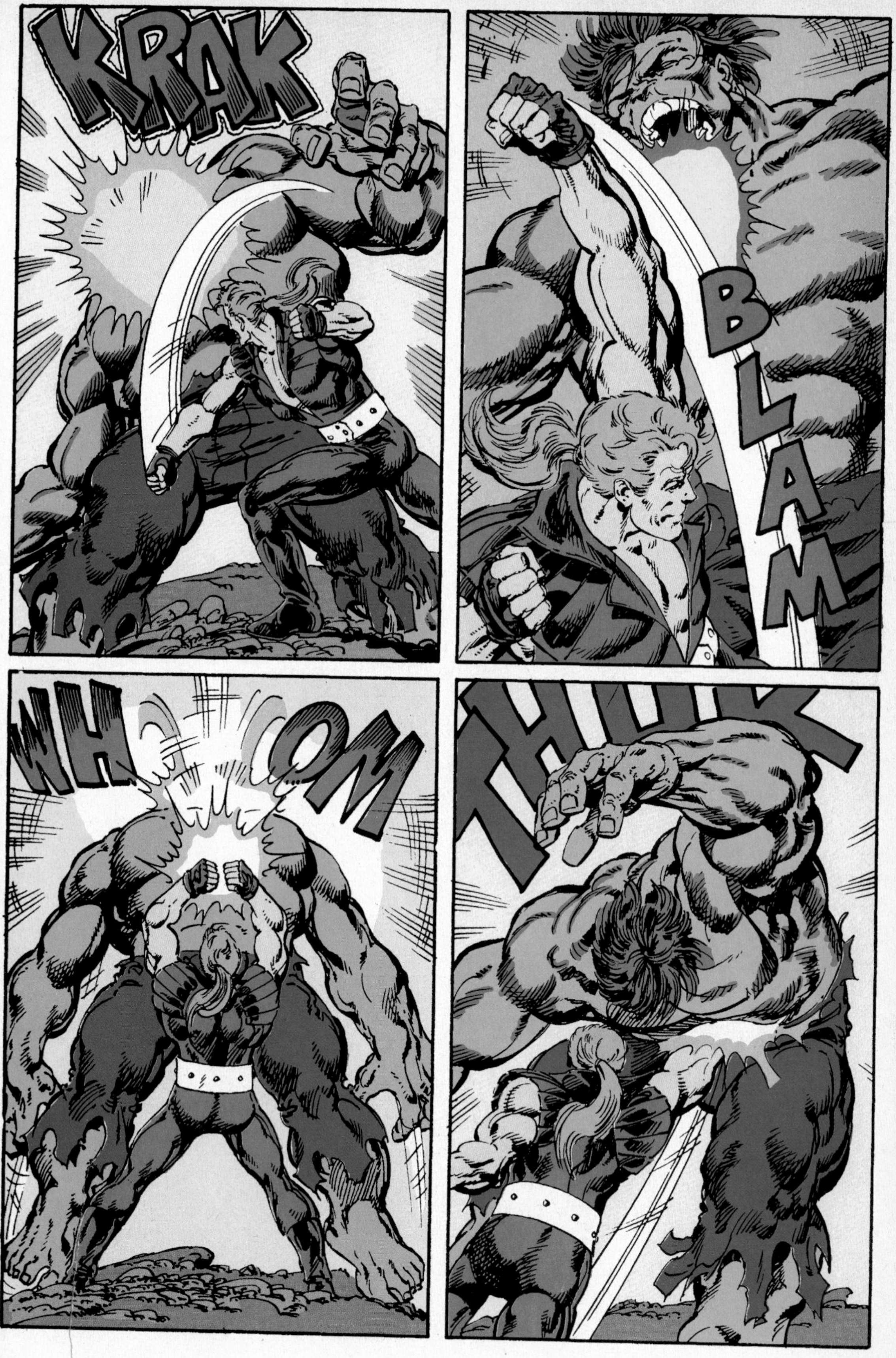
KRAK
BLAM
WH OM

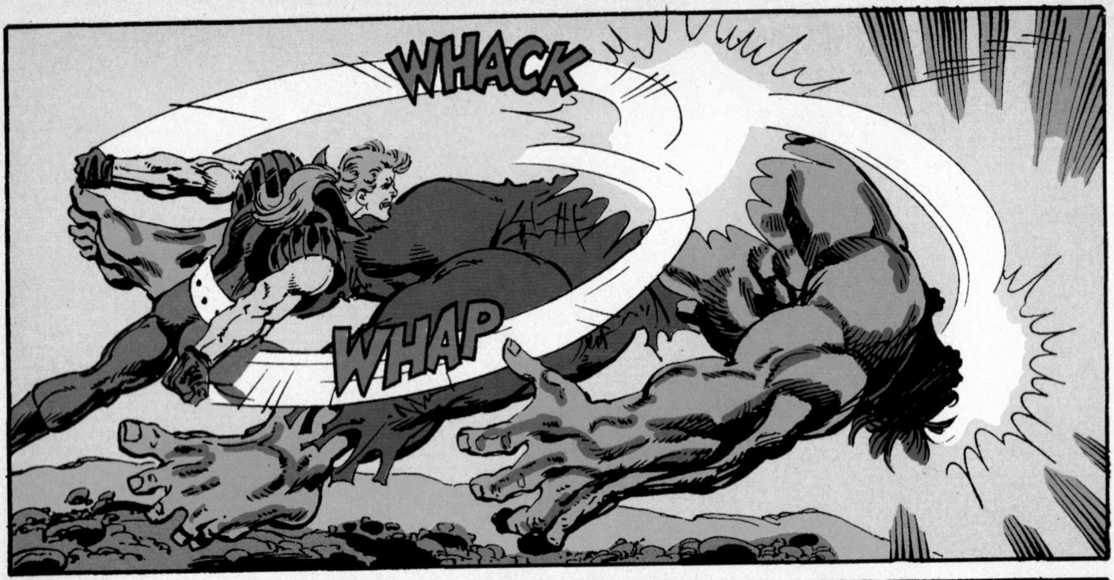
WHACK
WHAP

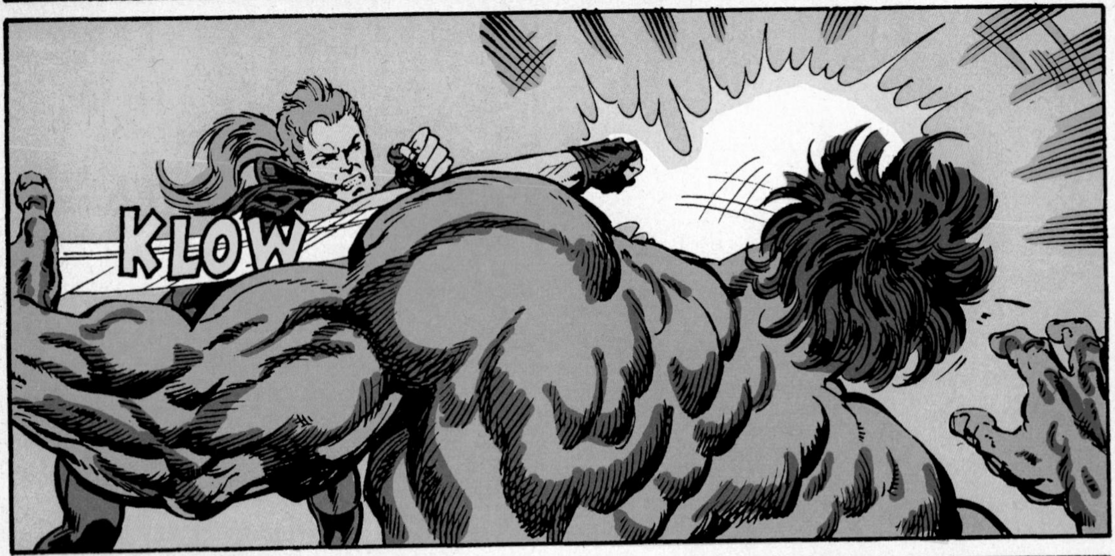
KLOW

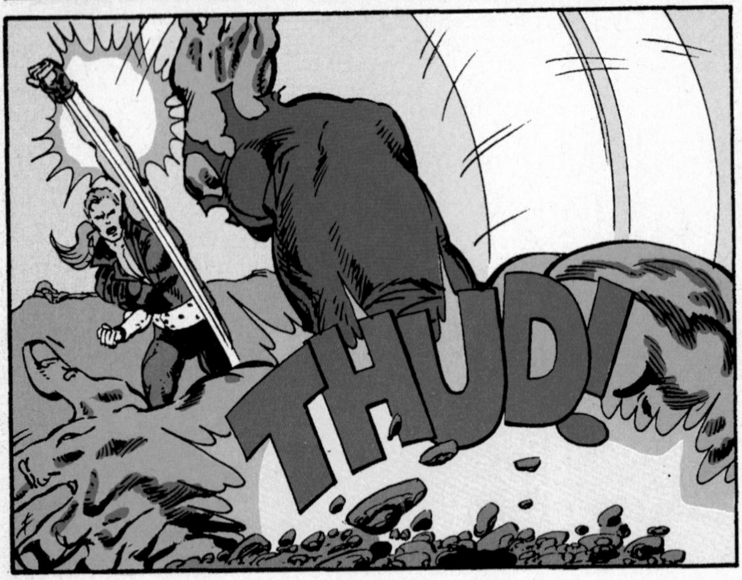
THUD!

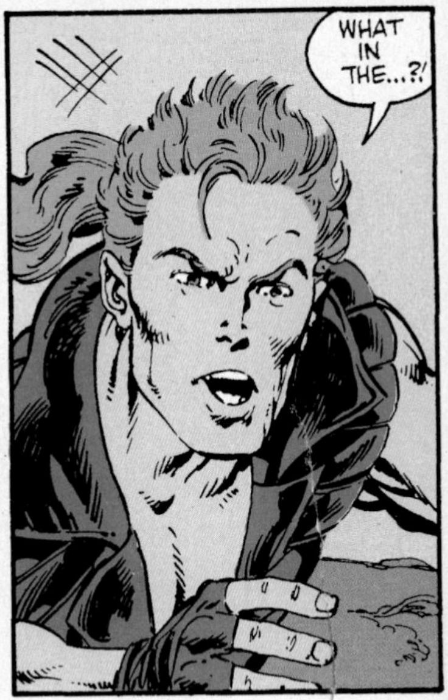
WHAT IN THE...?!

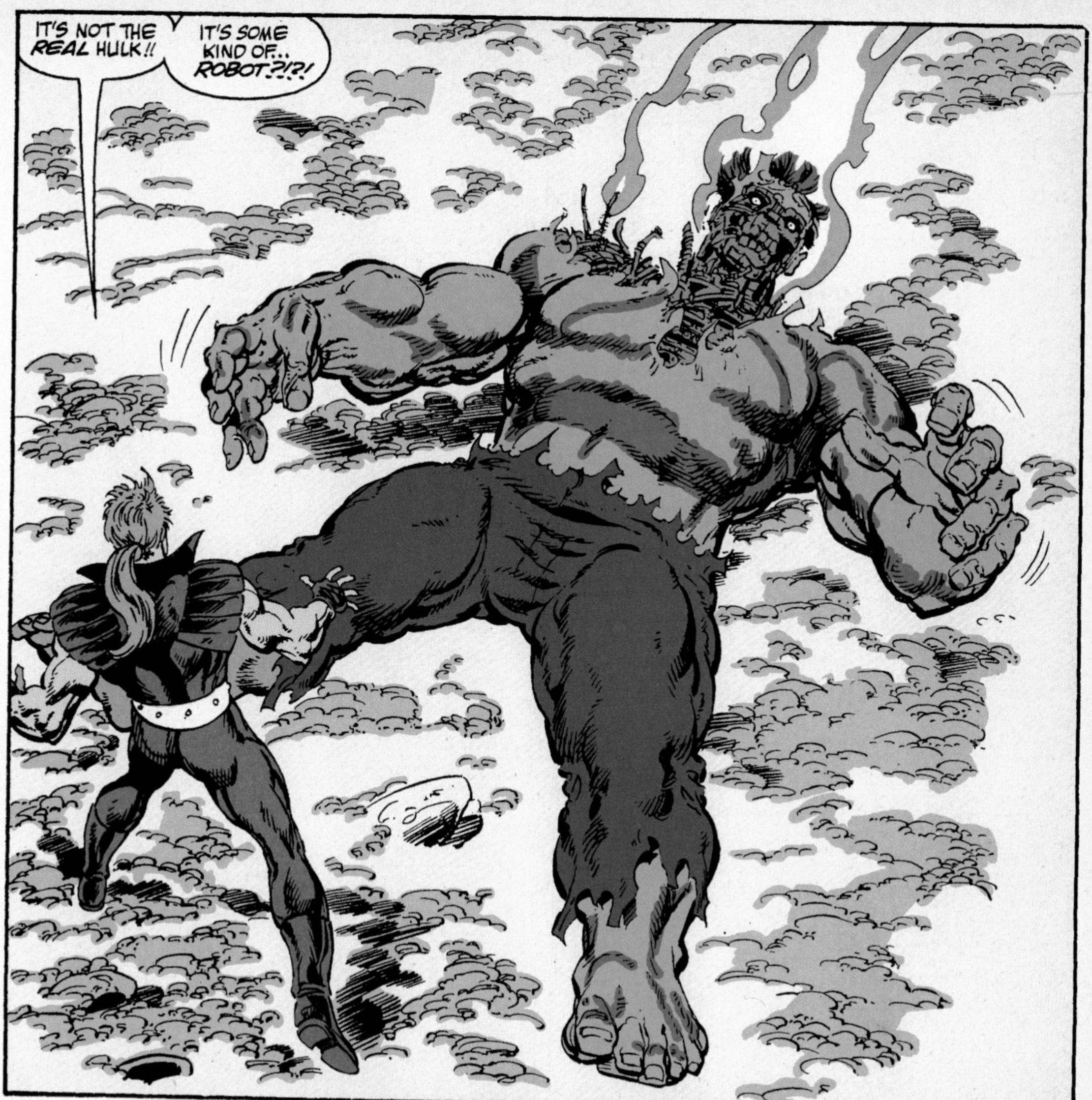
IT'S NOT THE *REAL* HULK!!
IT'S SOME KIND OF... *ROBOT?!?!*

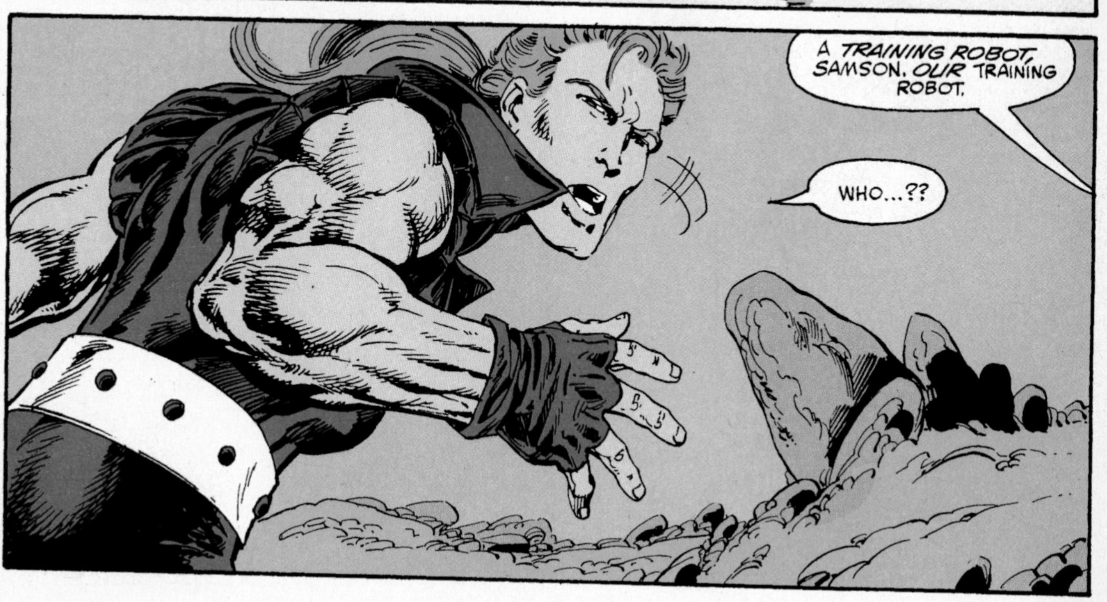
A *TRAINING ROBOT,* SAMSON. *OUR* TRAINING ROBOT.
WHO...??

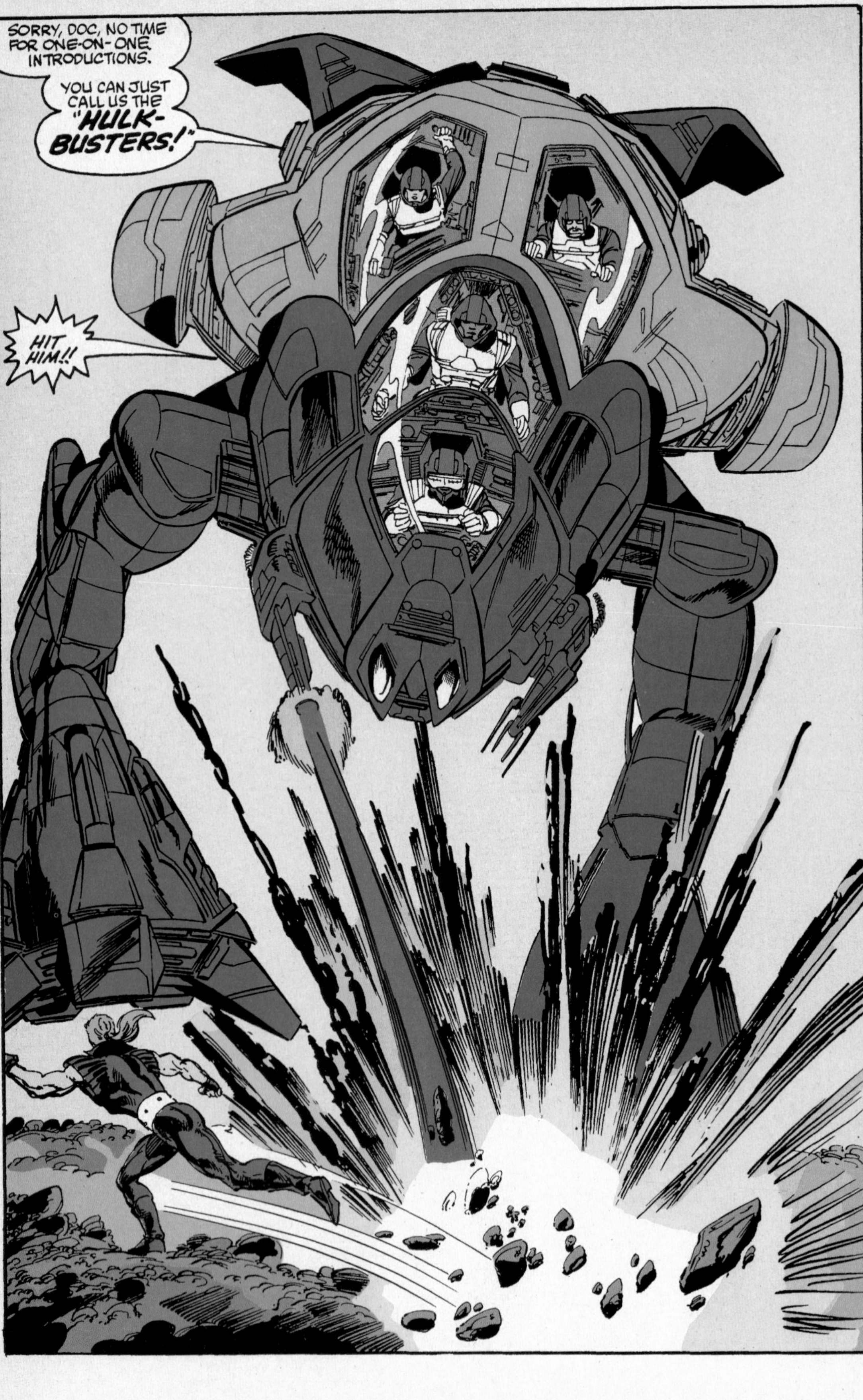
SORRY, DOC, NO TIME FOR ONE-ON-ONE INTRODUCTIONS.
YOU CAN JUST CALL US THE "HULK-BUSTERS!"
HIT HIM!!

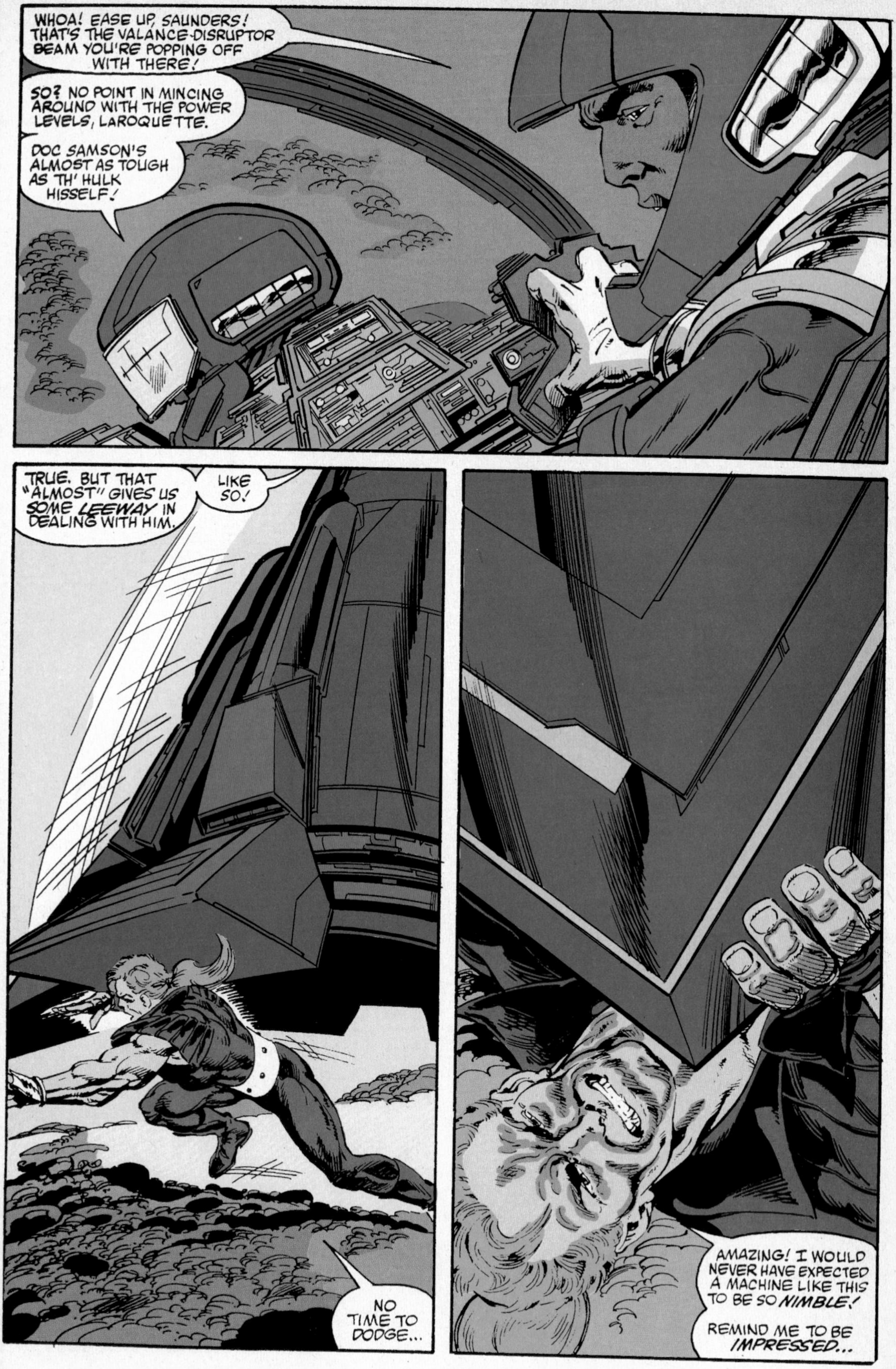
WHOA! EASE UP, SAUNDERS! THAT'S THE VALANCE-DISRUPTOR BEAM YOU'RE POPPING OFF WITH THERE!
SO? NO POINT IN MINCING AROUND WITH THE POWER LEVELS, LAROQUETTE.
DOC SAMSON'S ALMOST AS TOUGH AS 'TH' HULK HISSELF!
TRUE. BUT THAT "ALMOST" GIVES US SOME LEEWAY IN DEALING WITH HIM.
LIKE SO!
NO TIME TO DODGE...
AMAZING! I WOULD NEVER HAVE EXPECTED A MACHINE LIKE THIS TO BE SO NIMBLE!
REMIND ME TO BE IMPRESSED...

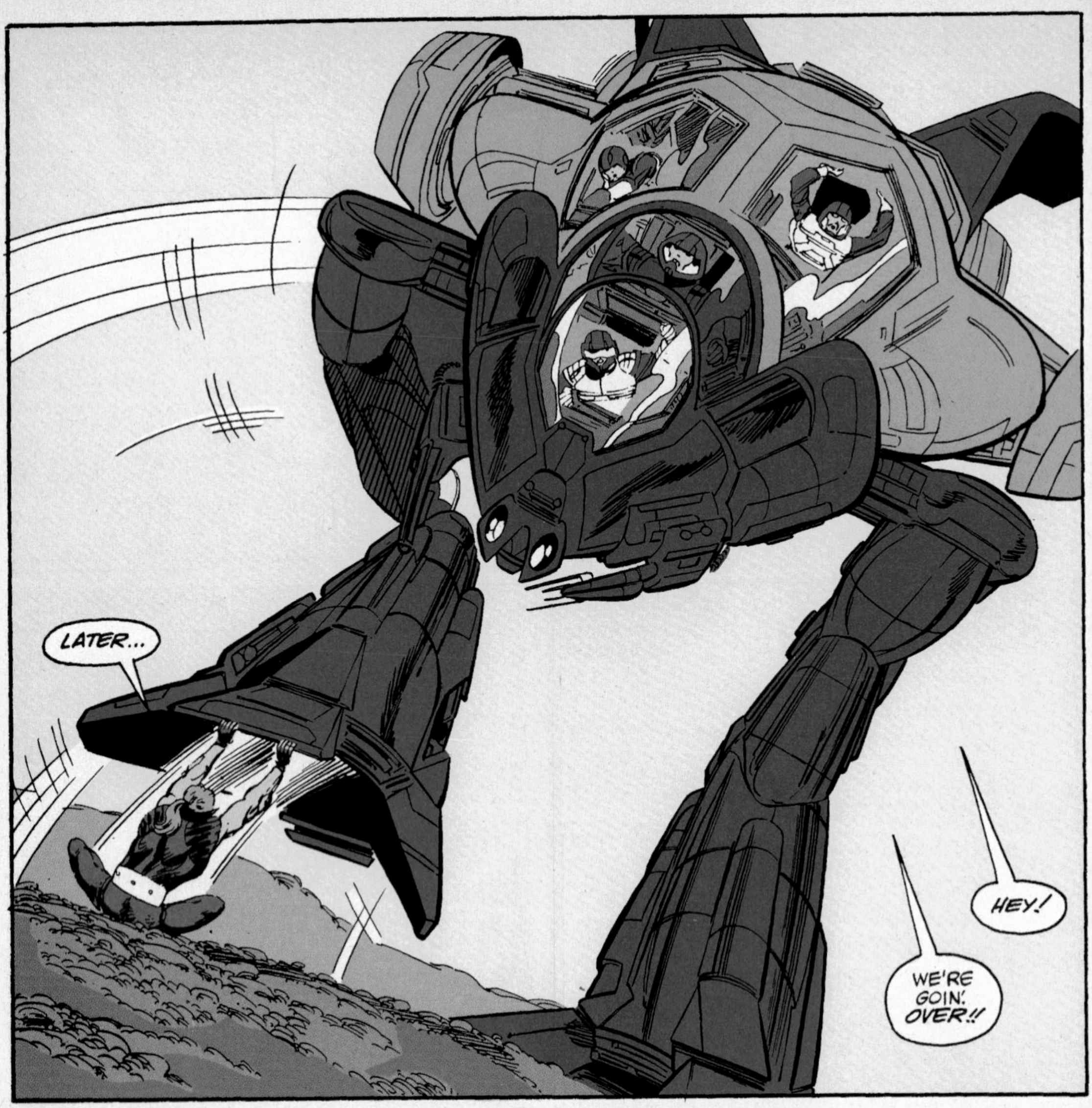
LATER...
HEY!
WE'RE GOIN'. OVER!!

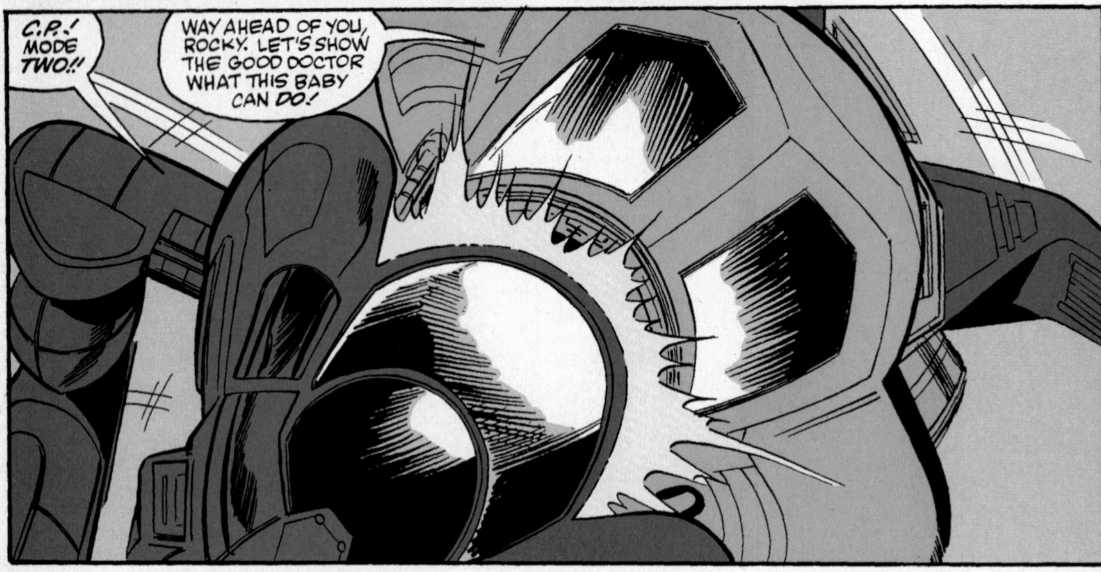
C.P.! MODE TWO!!
WAY AHEAD OF YOU, ROCKY. LET'S SHOW THE GOOD DOCTOR WHAT THIS BABY CAN DO!

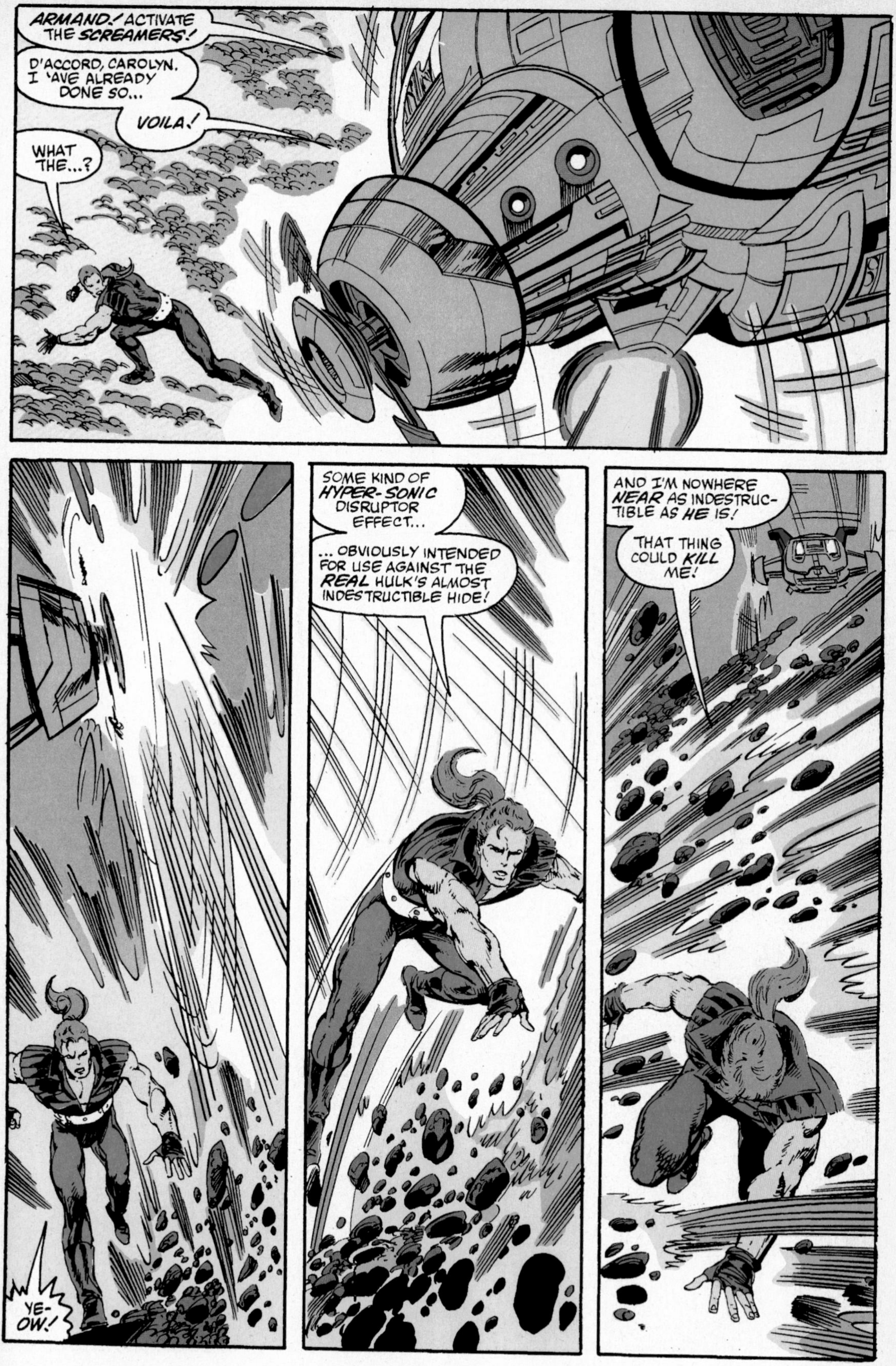

ARMAND! ACTIVATE THE SCREAMERS!
D'ACCORD, CAROLYN. I 'AVE ALREADY DONE SO...
VOILA!
WHAT THE...?
YE-OW!
SOME KIND OF HYPER-SONIC DISRUPTOR EFFECT...
... OBVIOUSLY INTENDED FOR USE AGAINST THE REAL HULK'S ALMOST INDESTRUCTIBLE HIDE!
AND I'M NOWHERE NEAR AS INDESTRUCTIBLE AS HE IS!
THAT THING COULD KILL ME!

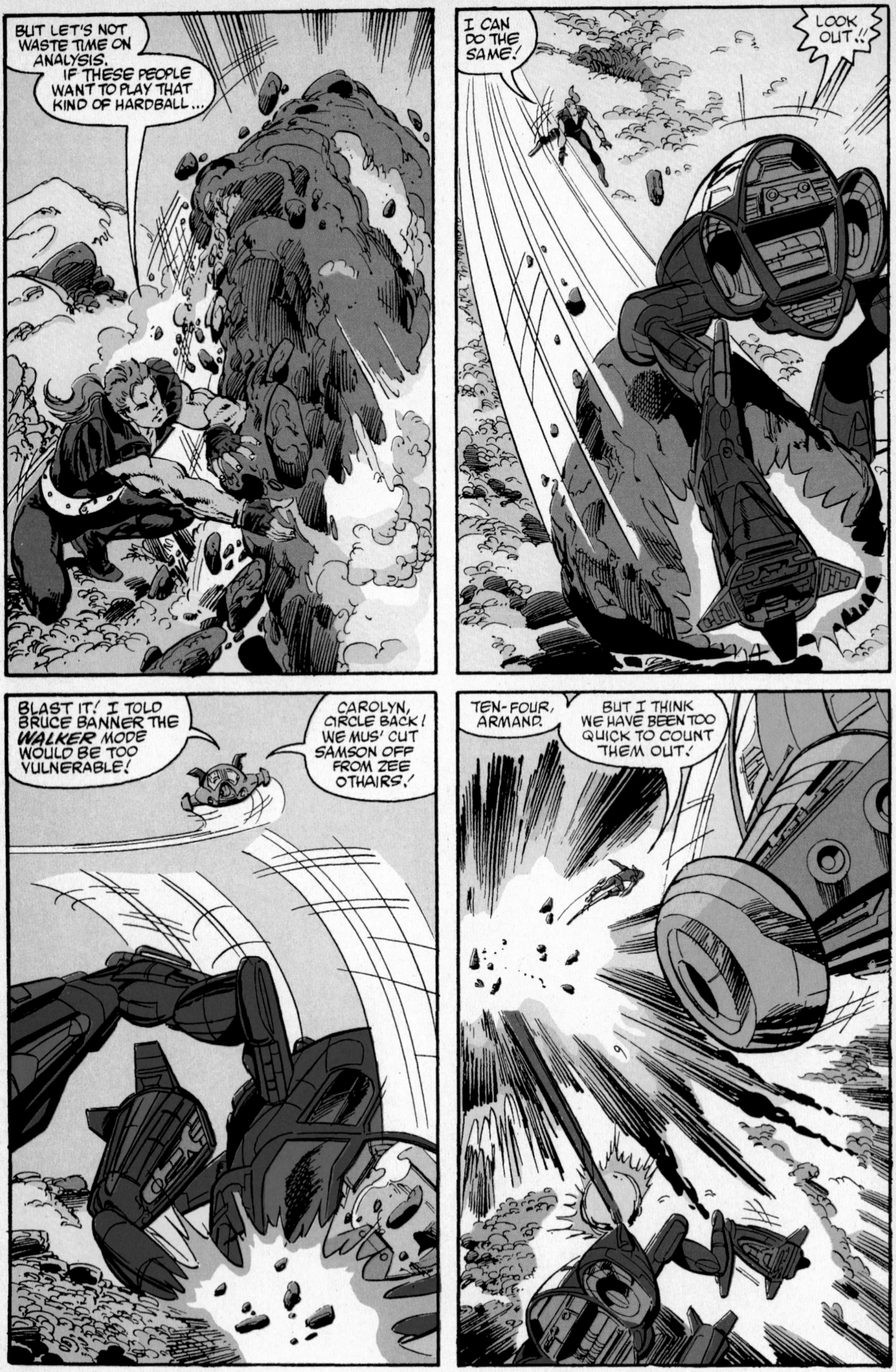
BUT LET'S NOT WASTE TIME ON ANALYSIS. IF THESE PEOPLE WANT TO PLAY THAT KIND OF HARDBALL...
I CAN DO THE SAME!
LOOK OUT!!
BLAST IT! I TOLD BRUCE BANNER THE WALKER MODE WOULD BE TOO VULNERABLE!
CAROLYN, CIRCLE BACK! WE MUS' CUT SAMSON OFF FROM ZEE OTHAIRS!
TEN-FOUR, ARMAND.
BUT I THINK WE HAVE BEEN TOO QUICK TO COUNT THEM OUT!

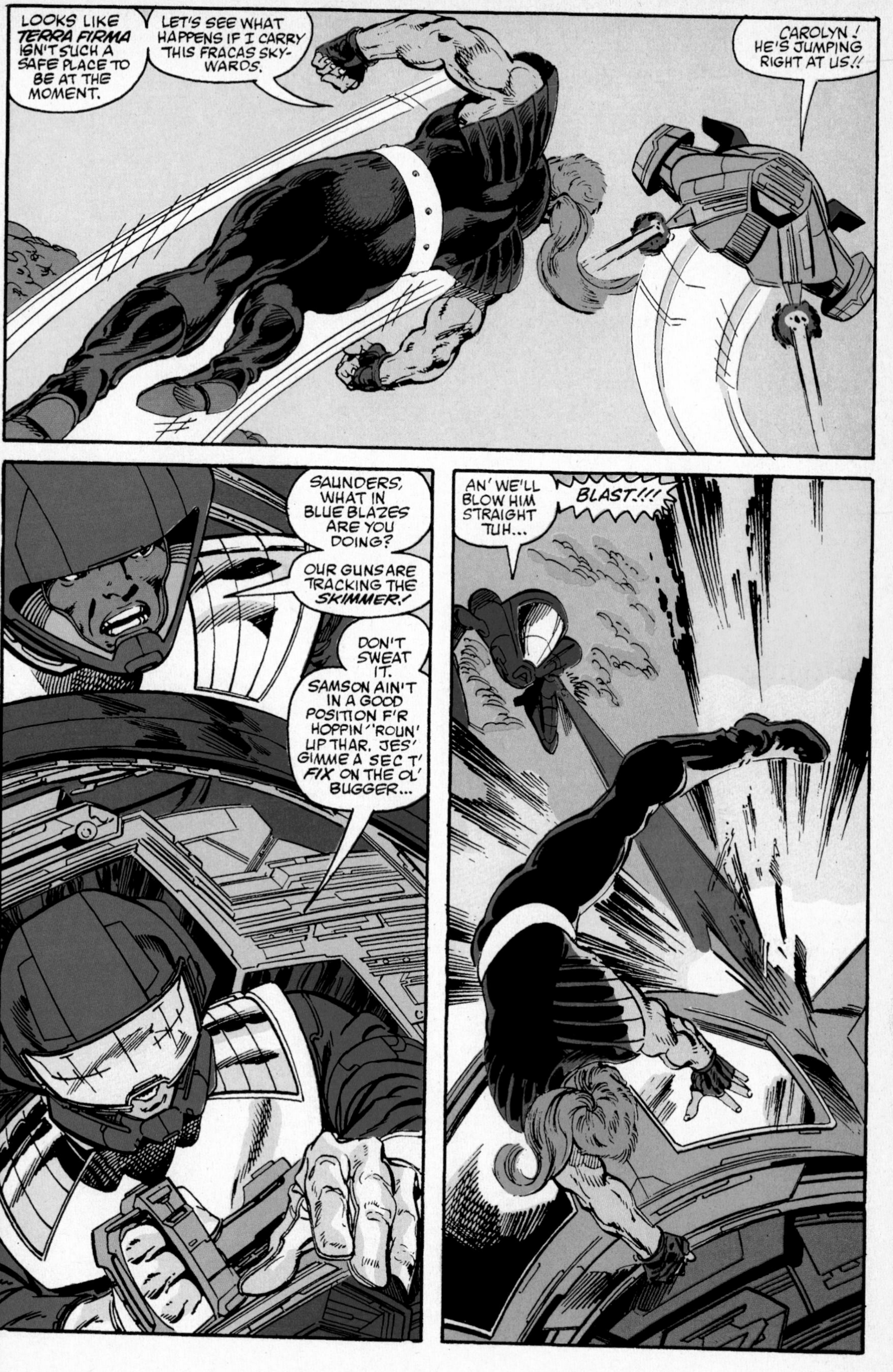
LOOKS LIKE TERRA FIRMA ISN'T SUCH A SAFE PLACE TO BE AT THE MOMENT.
LET'S SEE WHAT HAPPENS IF I CARRY THIS FRACAS SKY-WARDS.
CAROLYN! HE'S JUMPING RIGHT AT US!!
SAUNDERS, WHAT IN BLUE BLAZES ARE YOU DOING?
OUR GUNS ARE TRACKING THE SKIMMER!
DON'T SWEAT IT. SAMSON AIN'T IN A GOOD POSITION F'R HOPPIN' 'ROUN' UP THAR. JES' GIMME A SEC T' FIX ON THE OL' BUGGER...
AN' WE'LL BLOW HIM STRAIGHT TUH...
BLAST!!!

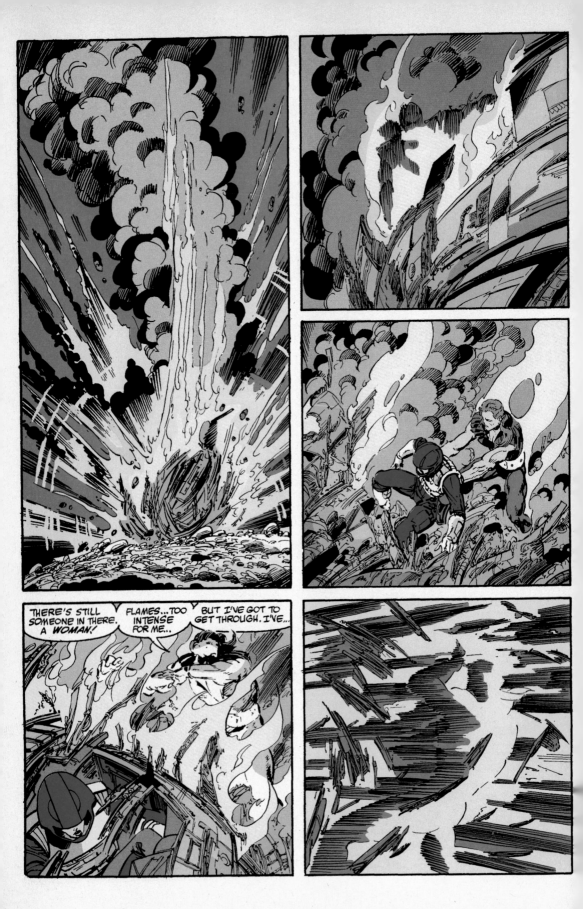

THERE'S STILL SOMEONE IN THERE. A *WOMAN!*

FLAMES...TOO INTENSE FOR ME...

BUT I'VE GOT TO GET THROUGH. I'VE...

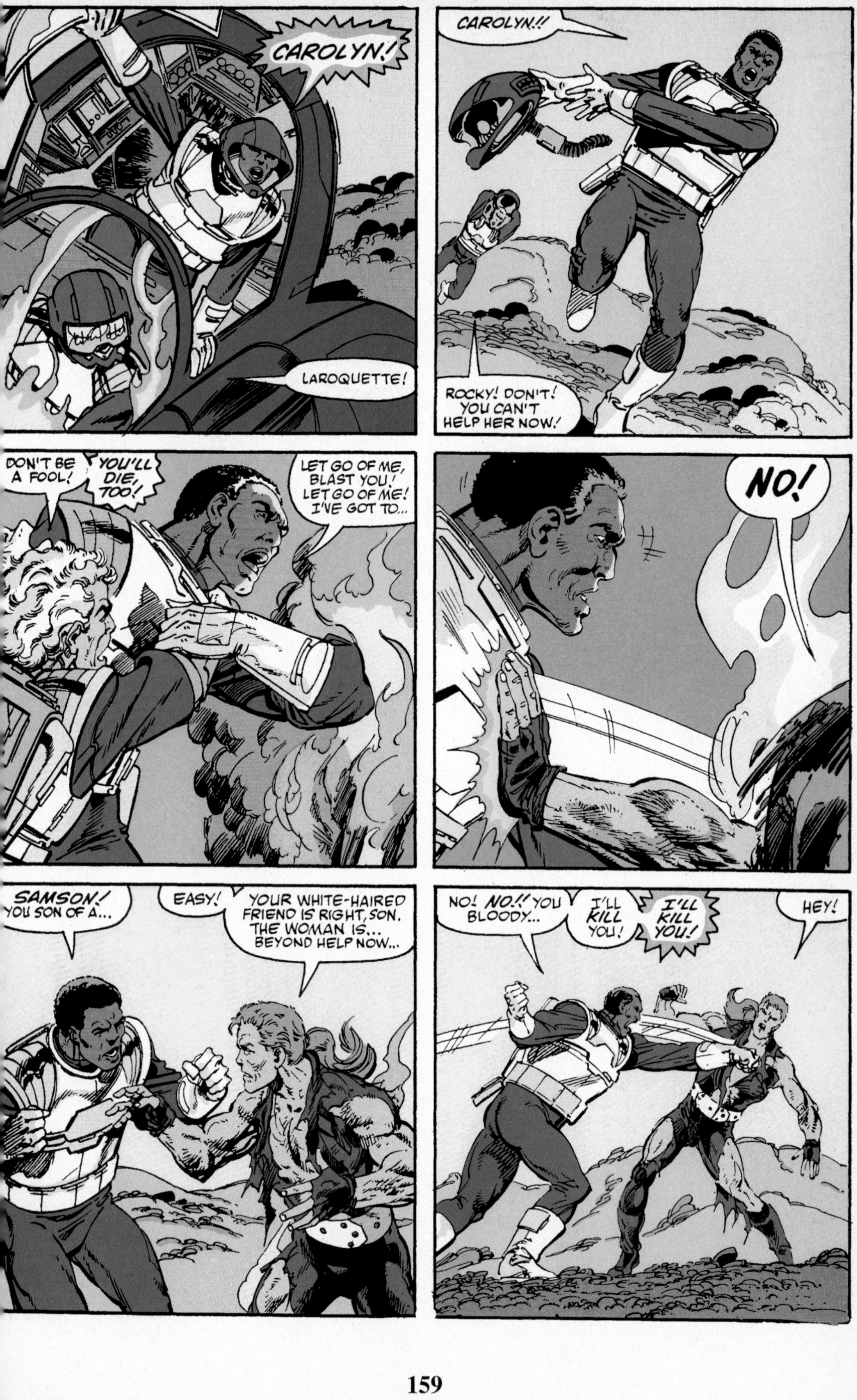
CAROLYN!
LAROQUETTE!
CAROLYN!!
ROCKY! DON'T! YOU CAN'T HELP HER NOW!
DON'T BE A FOOL!
YOU'LL DIE, TOO!
LET GO OF ME, BLAST YOU! LET GO OF ME! I'VE GOT TO...
NO!
SAMSON! YOU SON OF A...
EASY!
YOUR WHITE-HAIRED FRIEND IS RIGHT, SON. THE WOMAN IS... BEYOND HELP NOW...
NO! NO!! YOU BLOODY...
I'LL KILL YOU!
I'LL KILL YOU!
HEY!

DON'T GET *TOUGH*, BIG MAN. YOU'RE JUST NOT IN MY LEAGUE!

LAROQUETTE!

OOUFF!

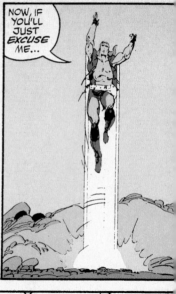

NOW, IF YOU'LL JUST *EXCUSE* ME...

...I HAVE MORE IMPORTANT FISH TO FRY.

THE *REAL* HULK!!

HE... HE'S JES' FLYIN' OFF.' LIKE NOTHIN' EVEN HAPPENED HERE!

MAN, O MAN, THAT BOY IS *OBSESSED!*

OBSESSED?

SAUNDERS, YOU HAVEN'T EVEN *SEEN* OBSESSION YET.

THAT MAN WAS JUST RESPONSIBLE FOR THE DEATH OF A WOMAN I... CARED FOR. VERY MUCH.

ARMAND!

OKAY... SO NOW HE'S GONE AFTER THE HULK AGAIN.

WELL, WE'RE AFTER THE HULK, TOO!

THAT MEANS OUR *PATHS* WILL *CROSS* AGAIN.

AND WHEN THEY DO, I PROMISE YOU LEONARD SAMSON IS GONNA *PAY*..

...IN *FULL!*

AH... GOOD AFTERNOON, MISS ROSS. I DID NOT REALIZE THERE WAS ANYONE ELSE IN HERE.

I'M SORRY TO HAVE DISTURBED YOU.

OH, YOU'RE NOT DISTURBING ME, PROFESSOR TAKATA. I WAS JUST... THINKING.

IT IS A *GOOD DAY* FOR THOUGHT. OUT THERE, SOMEWHERE IN THE GREAT DESERT, MY FELLOW "HULKBUSTERS" BATTLE TOGETHER FOR THE FIRST TIME.

ONLY PLAY ACTING, AGAINST A ROBOT OF OUR TRUE ADVERSARY, YET STILL A SHADOW OF THE VERY REAL DANGERS THAT LIE AHEAD WHEN AT LAST WE FACE THE *HULK!*

MM.

THAT'S NOT REALLY WHAT I WAS THINKING ABOUT. I *AM* WORRIED ABOUT WHAT MIGHT HAPPEN TO THE HULKBUSTERS, YES...

... BUT WHAT'S REALLY BEEN ON MY MIND IS... WELL, TWO WEEKS AGO BRUCE ASKED ME TO *MARRY* HIM...

WONDERFUL! MY CONGRATULATIONS. THIS IS SOMETHING YOU HAVE DESIRED FOR MANY YEARS, *HAI?*

YES.

BUT... BUT I DON'T KNOW HOW TO RESPOND, HIDEKO. BRUCE AND I NEARLY GOT MARRIED ONCE BEFORE. THE HULK DESTROYED OUR PLANS.

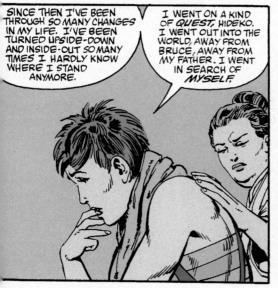

SINCE THEN I'VE BEEN THROUGH SO MANY CHANGES IN MY LIFE. I'VE BEEN TURNED UPSIDE-DOWN AND INSIDE-OUT SO MANY TIMES I HARDLY KNOW WHERE I STAND ANYMORE.

I WENT ON A KIND OF *QUEST*, HIDEKO. I WENT OUT INTO THE WORLD, AWAY FROM BRUCE, AWAY FROM MY FATHER. I WENT IN SEARCH OF *MYSELF.*

AND WHAT I *FOUND*, I DIDN'T LIKE VERY MUCH.

BUT I MUST MAKE A DECISION. THE MOST IMPORTANT DECISION OF MY LIFE. AND IT HAS TO BE THE RIGHT ONE!

IT *HAS* TO BE!

TRUST YOUR *HEART*, BETTY, AND I'M SURE IT *WILL* BE.

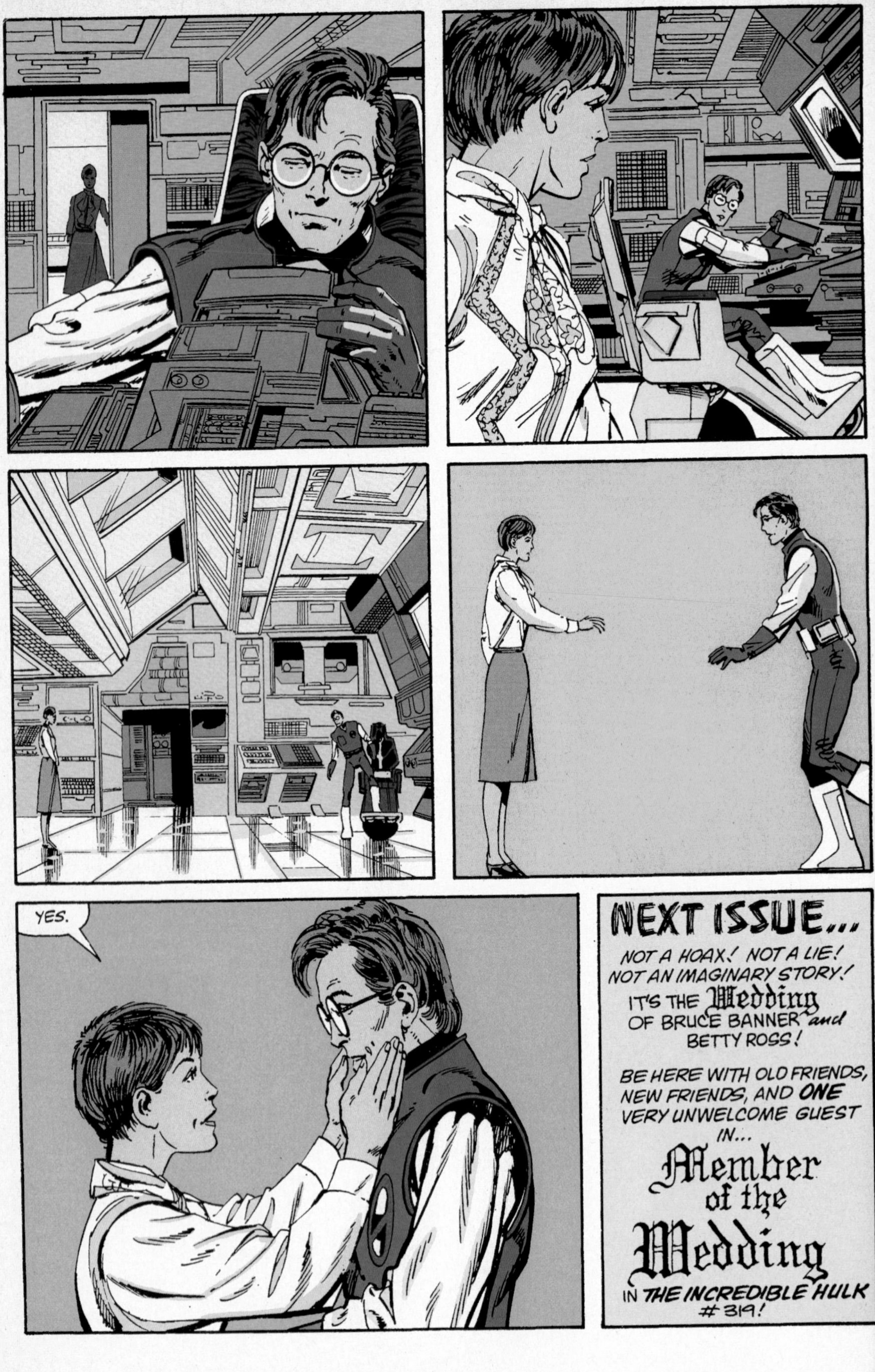
YES.
NEXT ISSUE...
NOT A HOAX! NOT A LIE! NOT AN IMAGINARY STORY!
IT'S THE Wedding OF BRUCE BANNER and BETTY ROSS!
BE HERE WITH OLD FRIENDS, NEW FRIENDS, AND ONE VERY UNWELCOME GUEST IN...
Member of the Wedding
IN THE INCREDIBLE HULK #319!

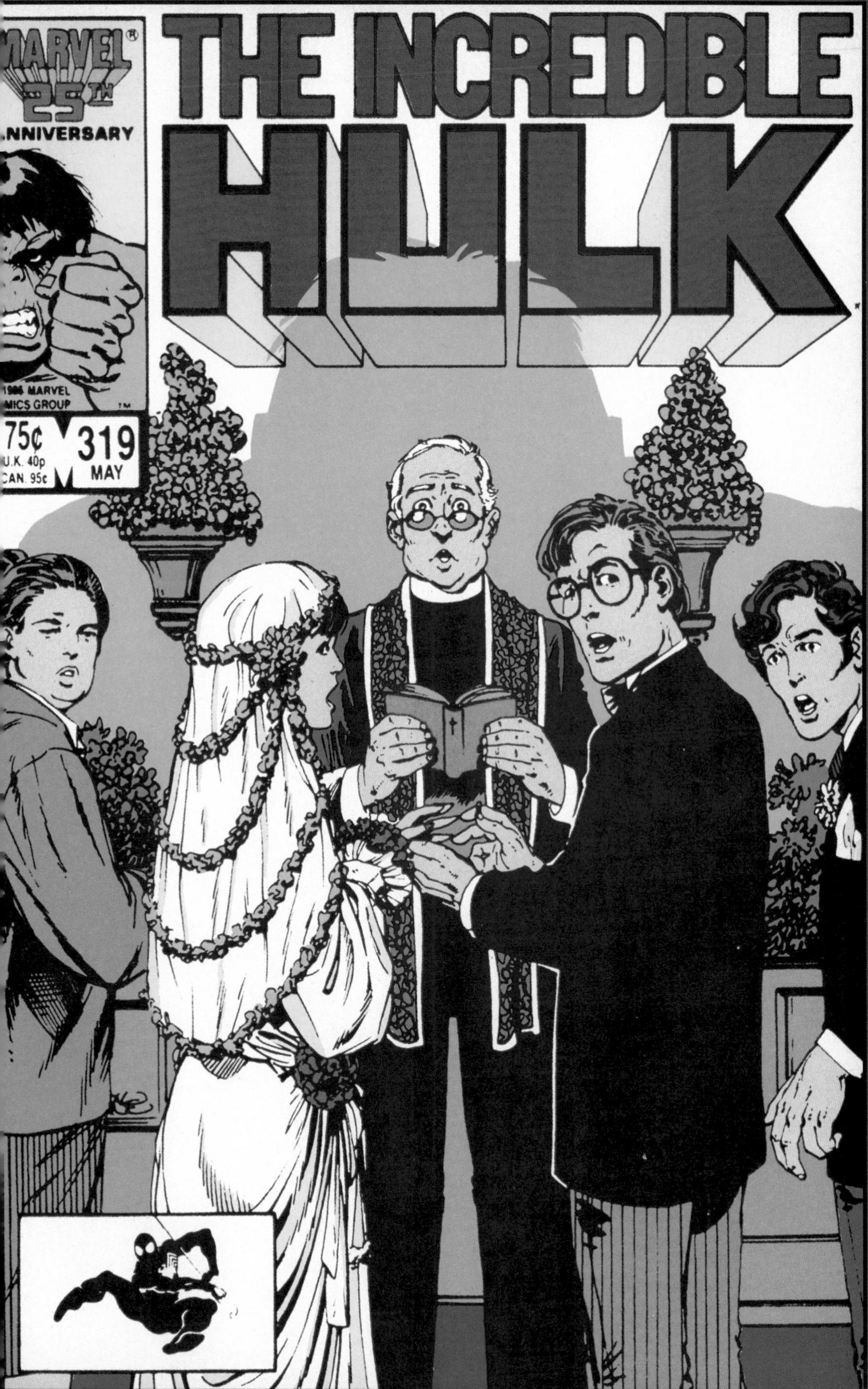

MARVEL
25TH ANNIVERSARY
THE INCREDIBLE HULK
©1986 MARVEL COMICS GROUP
75¢
U.K. 40p
CAN. 95¢
319
MAY

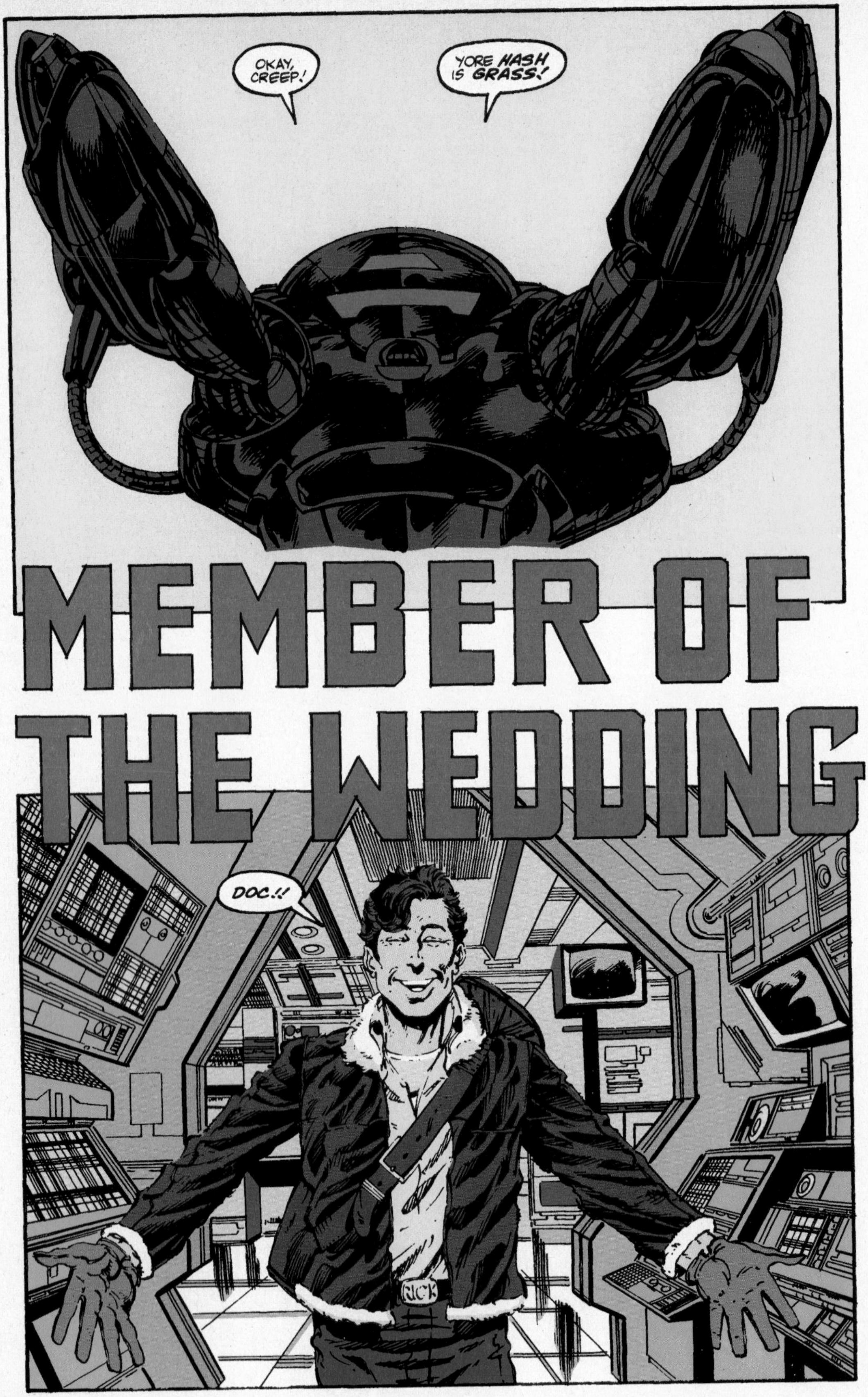
OKAY, CREEP!
YORE HASH IS GRASS!
MEMBER OF THE WEDDING
DOC.!!
NICK

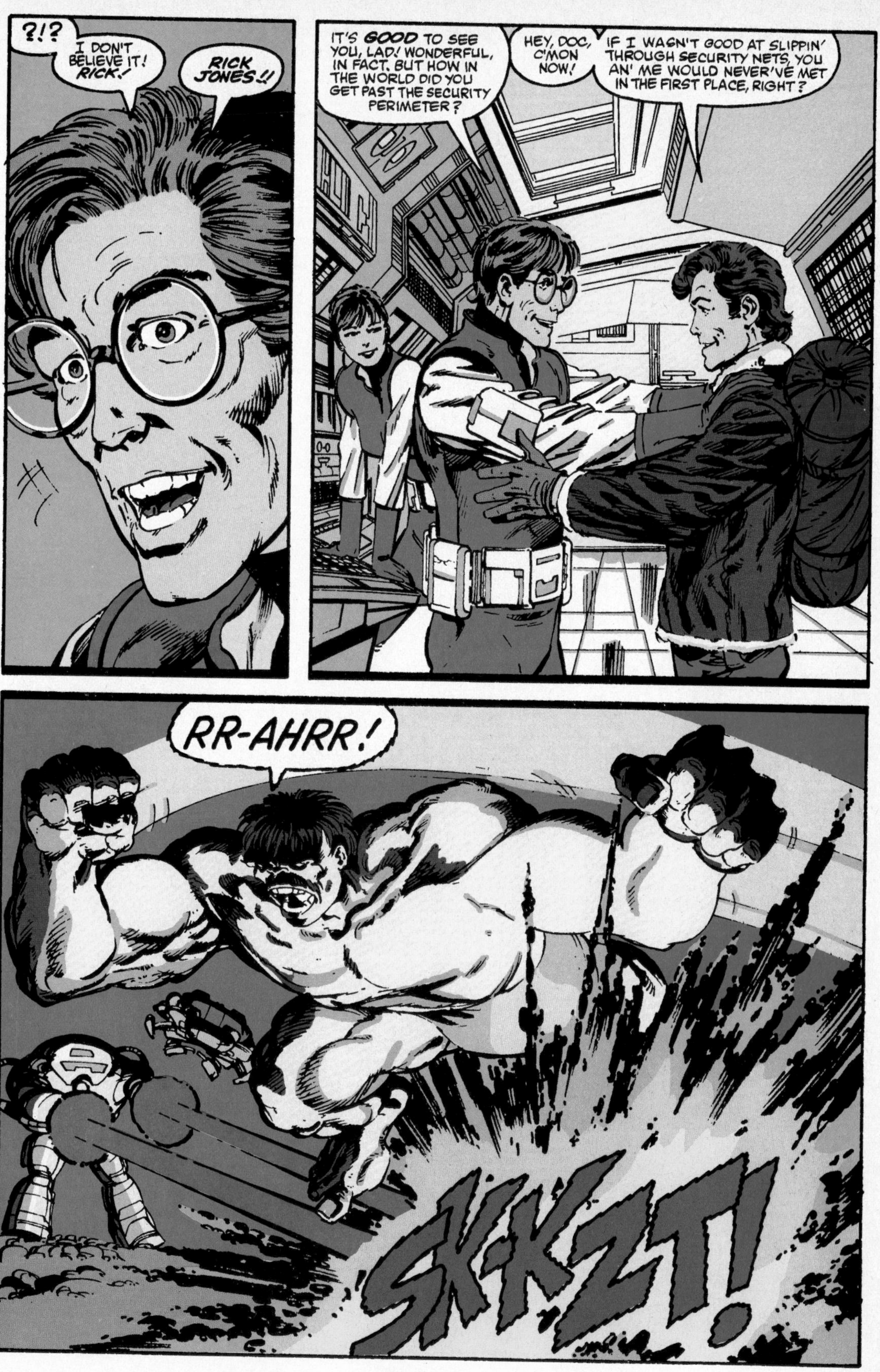
?!?
I DON'T BELIEVE IT! RICK!
RICK JONES!!
IT'S GOOD TO SEE YOU, LAD! WONDERFUL, IN FACT. BUT HOW IN THE WORLD DID YOU GET PAST THE SECURITY PERIMETER?
HEY, DOC, C'MON NOW!
IF I WASN'T GOOD AT SLIPPIN' THROUGH SECURITY NETS, YOU AN' ME WOULD NEVER'VE MET IN THE FIRST PLACE, RIGHT?
RR-AHRR!
SK-KZT!

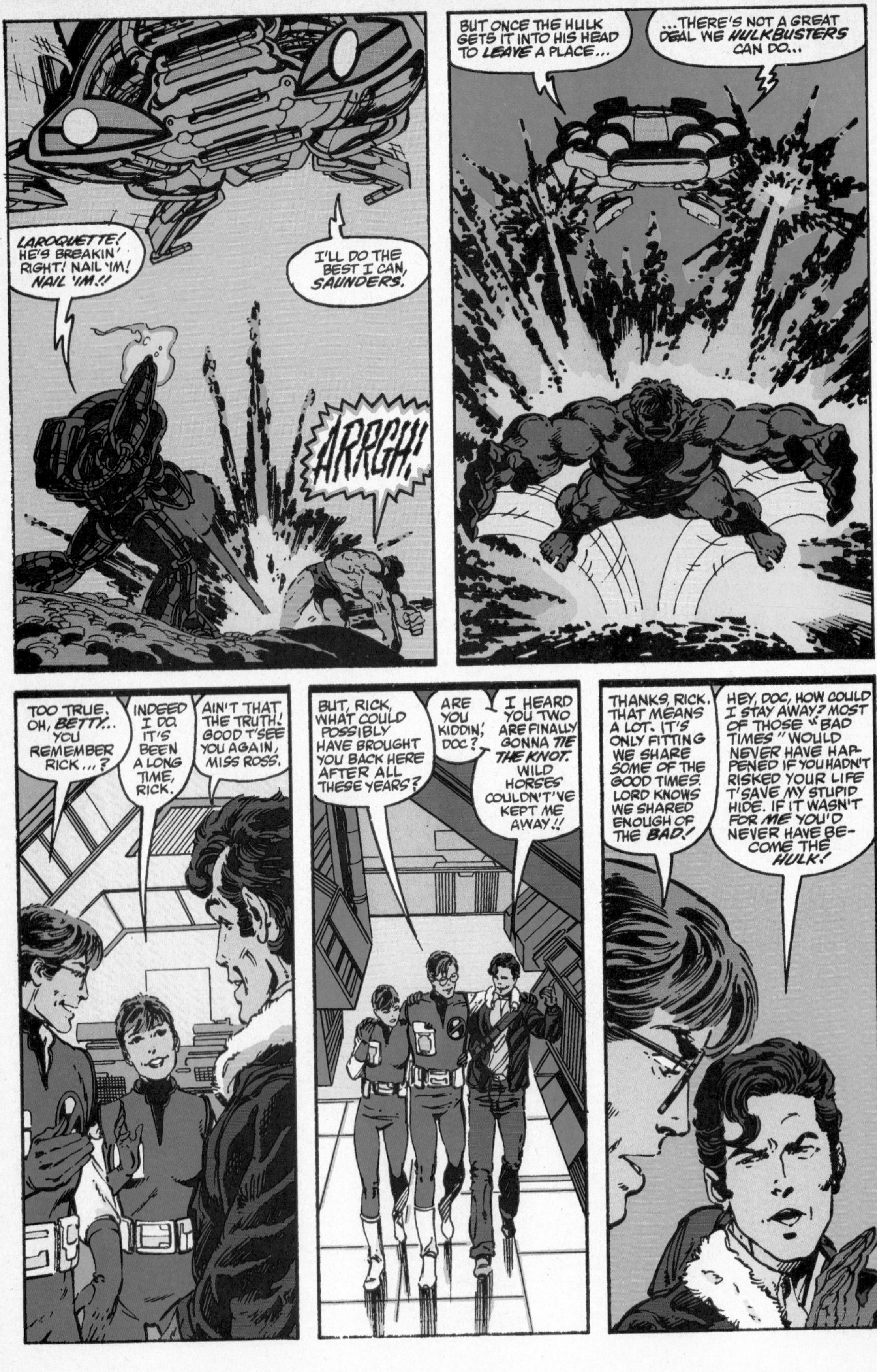
LAROQUETTE! HE'S BREAKIN' RIGHT! NAIL 'IM! NAIL 'IM!!
I'LL DO THE BEST I CAN, SAUNDERS.
ARRGH!
BUT ONCE THE HULK GETS IT INTO HIS HEAD TO LEAVE A PLACE...
...THERE'S NOT A GREAT DEAL WE HULKBUSTERS CAN DO...
TOO TRUE. OH, BETTY... YOU REMEMBER RICK...?
INDEED I DO. IT'S BEEN A LONG TIME, RICK.
AIN'T THAT THE TRUTH! GOOD T'SEE YOU AGAIN, MISS ROSS.
BUT, RICK, WHAT COULD POSSIBLY HAVE BROUGHT YOU BACK HERE AFTER ALL THESE YEARS?
ARE YOU KIDDIN', DOC?
I HEARD YOU TWO ARE FINALLY GONNA TIE THE KNOT. WILD HORSES COULDN'T'VE KEPT ME AWAY!!
THANKS, RICK. THAT MEANS A LOT. IT'S ONLY FITTING WE SHARE SOME OF THE GOOD TIMES. LORD KNOWS WE SHARED ENOUGH OF THE BAD!
HEY, DOC, HOW COULD I STAY AWAY? MOST OF THOSE "BAD TIMES" WOULD NEVER HAVE HAPPENED IF YOU HADN'T RISKED YOUR LIFE T'SAVE MY STUPID HIDE. IF IT WASN'T FOR ME YOU'D NEVER HAVE BECOME THE HULK!

DON'T SAY THAT, RICK. WHAT HAPPENED, HAPPENED. YOU'RE NOT TO BLAME. IF FAULT LIES WITH ANYONE, IT'S *ME*, FOR BUILDING THE *GAMMA BOMB* IN THE FIRST PLACE!

MAYBE... BUT IF *I* HADN'T GOT INVOLVED, YOU'D ONLY BE THE INVENTOR OF A VERY NASTY WEAPON -- NOT A MAN WHO TURNS INTO A *MONSTER!*

"THAT WOULD NEVER HAVE HAPPENED IF I HADN'T TAKEN A STUPID *DARE* AND SNUCK PAST THE TEST-SITE SECURITY.

" IF I HADN'T BEEN SITTIN' ALMOST *ON TOP* OF THAT BOMB, YOU'D NEVER'VE COME RUNNIN' OUT TO *SAVE* ME.

" AND YOU'D NEVER'VE GOT *ZAPPED* BY THE *GAMMA RAYS* WHEN TH' THING WENT OFF. "

...EXCEPT, PERHAPS, BLOWING A LARGE *HOLE* THROUGH HIS NASTY GREEN HIDE!

ROCKY! PULL BACK! HE'S FLEXING HIS LEG MUSCLES!

HE'S GONNA...

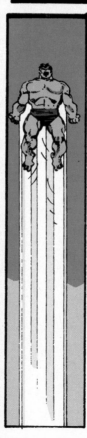

H-HRARRHHR!

YE-OW!!

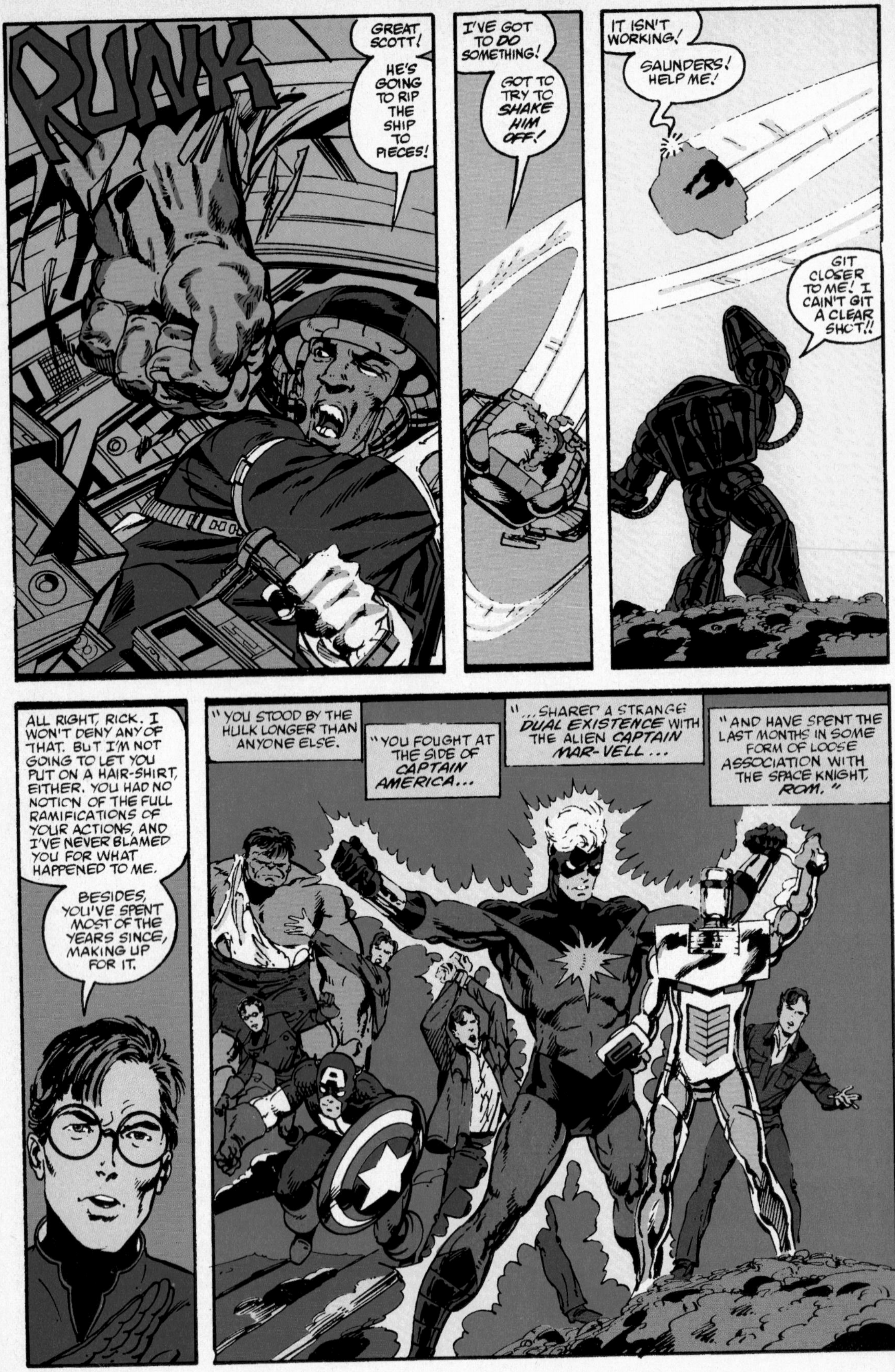
RUNK
GREAT SCOTT!
HE'S GOING TO RIP THE SHIP TO PIECES!
I'VE GOT TO DO SOMETHING!
GOT TO TRY TO SHAKE HIM OFF!
IT ISN'T WORKING!
SAUNDERS! HELP ME!
GIT CLOSER TO ME! I CAIN'T GIT A CLEAR SHOT!!
ALL RIGHT, RICK. I WON'T DENY ANY OF THAT. BUT I'M NOT GOING TO LET YOU PUT ON A HAIR-SHIRT, EITHER. YOU HAD NO NOTION OF THE FULL RAMIFICATIONS OF YOUR ACTIONS, AND I'VE NEVER BLAMED YOU FOR WHAT HAPPENED TO ME.
BESIDES, YOU'VE SPENT MOST OF THE YEARS SINCE, MAKING UP FOR IT.
"YOU STOOD BY THE HULK LONGER THAN ANYONE ELSE.
"YOU FOUGHT AT THE SIDE OF CAPTAIN AMERICA...
"...SHARED A STRANGE DUAL EXISTENCE WITH THE ALIEN CAPTAIN MAR-VELL...
"AND HAVE SPENT THE LAST MONTHS IN SOME FORM OF LOOSE ASSOCIATION WITH THE SPACE KNIGHT, ROM."

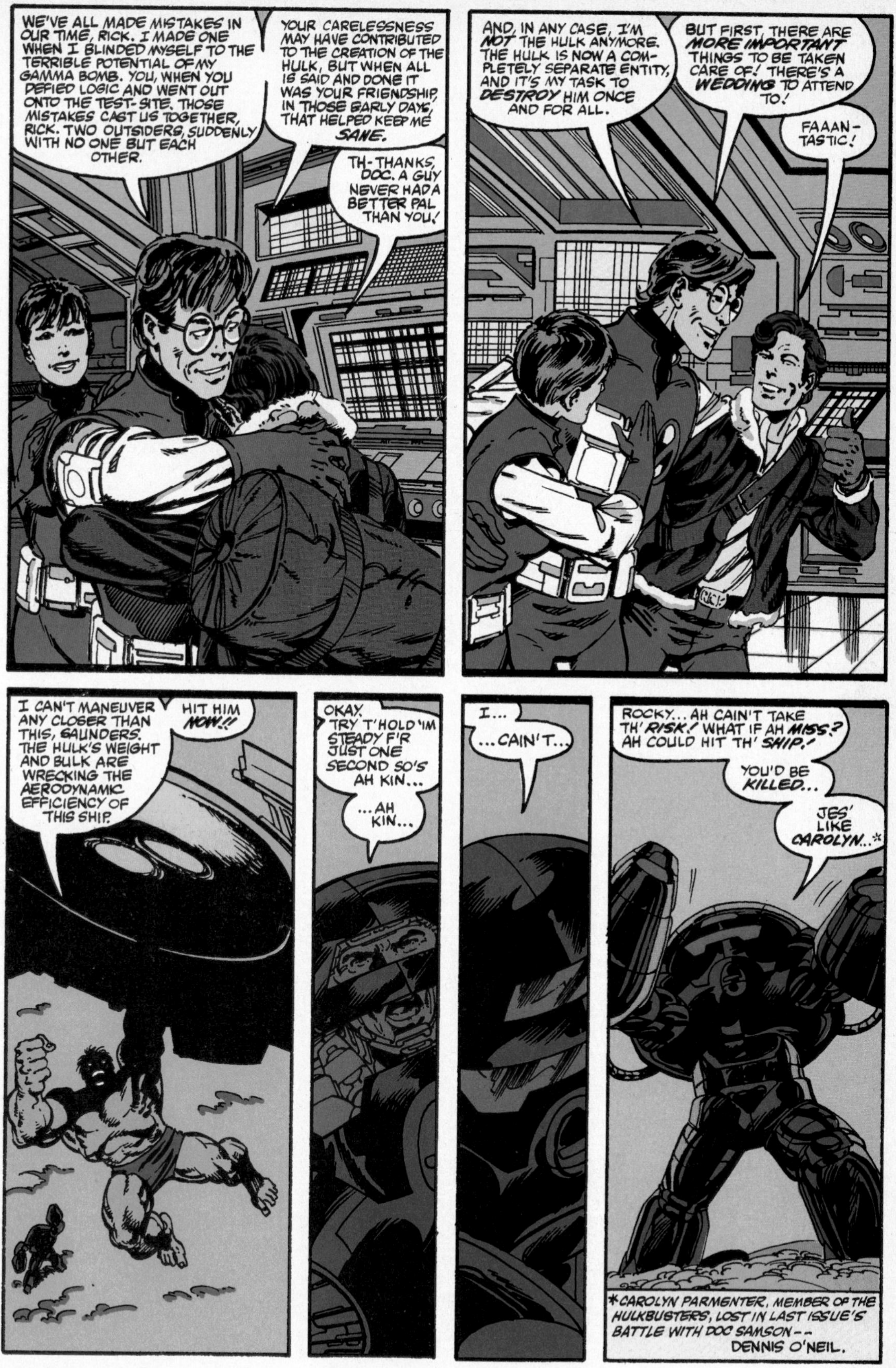
WE'VE ALL MADE MISTAKES IN OUR TIME, RICK. I MADE ONE WHEN I BLINDED MYSELF TO THE TERRIBLE POTENTIAL OF MY GAMMA BOMB. YOU, WHEN YOU DEFIED LOGIC AND WENT OUT ONTO THE TEST-SITE. THOSE MISTAKES CAST US TOGETHER, RICK. TWO OUTSIDERS, SUDDENLY WITH NO ONE BUT EACH OTHER.
YOUR CARELESSNESS MAY HAVE CONTRIBUTED TO THE CREATION OF THE HULK, BUT WHEN ALL IS SAID AND DONE IT WAS YOUR FRIENDSHIP, IN THOSE EARLY DAYS, THAT HELPED KEEP ME SANE.
TH-THANKS, DOC. A GUY NEVER HAD A BETTER PAL THAN YOU!
AND, IN ANY CASE, I'M NOT THE HULK ANYMORE. THE HULK IS NOW A COMPLETELY SEPARATE ENTITY, AND IT'S MY TASK TO DESTROY HIM ONCE AND FOR ALL.
BUT FIRST, THERE ARE MORE IMPORTANT THINGS TO BE TAKEN CARE OF! THERE'S A WEDDING TO ATTEND TO!
FAAAN-TASTIC!
I CAN'T MANEUVER ANY CLOSER THAN THIS, SAUNDERS. THE HULK'S WEIGHT AND BULK ARE WRECKING THE AERODYNAMIC EFFICIENCY OF THIS SHIP.
HIT HIM NOW!!
OKAY. TRY T'HOLD 'IM STEADY F'R JUST ONE SECOND SO'S AH KIN...
...AH KIN...
I...
...CAIN'T...
ROCKY... AH CAIN'T TAKE TH' RISK! WHAT IF AH MISS? AH COULD HIT TH' SHIP!
YOU'D BE KILLED...
JES' LIKE CAROLYN...*
*CAROLYN PARMENTER, MEMBER OF THE HULKBUSTERS, LOST IN LAST ISSUE'S BATTLE WITH DOC SAMSON-- DENNIS O'NEIL.

CAROLYN...?

YOU CAN'T BLAME YOURSELF FOR *THAT,* MAN!

IT WAS *SAMSON!* NOW, *DO SOMETHING!!*

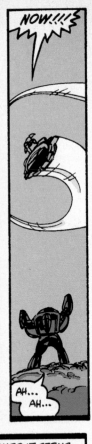

NOW!!!!

AH... AH...

WELL, IF YOU'RE JUST GOING TO STAND THERE LIKE AN ARMOR-PLATED *LUMP,* SAUNDERS...

I GUESS YOU WON'T *MIND* IF I DO SOMETHING.

SAMSON!!

BOY, DOC, I REALLY NEVER THOUGHT I'D LIVE TO SEE THIS DAY. IT'S BEEN A *LOOOONG* TIME COMIN'!

SOMETIMES IT SEEMS LIKE *CENTURIES,* RICK. THE HULK HASN'T *REALLY* BEEN AROUND A TERRIBLY LONG TIME, BUT HE'S DONE ENOUGH DAMAGE-- PHYSICAL AND EMOTIONAL --FOR A HUNDRED LIFE-TIMES.

BUT NOW I'M *FREE.* HIS SHADOW NO LONGER HANGS OVER MY SOUL AND I CAN AT LAST DO THE THINGS THAT FOR SO MANY YEARS HAVE BEEN NO MORE THAN *DREAMS.*

I'VE LONGED TO MAKE BETTY MY OWN SINCE THE FIRST MOMENTS I SET EYES ON HER. SHE SEEMED SO DELICATE, SO BEAUTIFUL...

SHE EMBODIED EVERYTHING I'D EVER DREAMED OF IN A WOMAN, BUT SHE WAS A *GENERAL'S* DAUGHTER...

...AND YOU WERE ALWAYS SO PAINFULLY *SHY.*

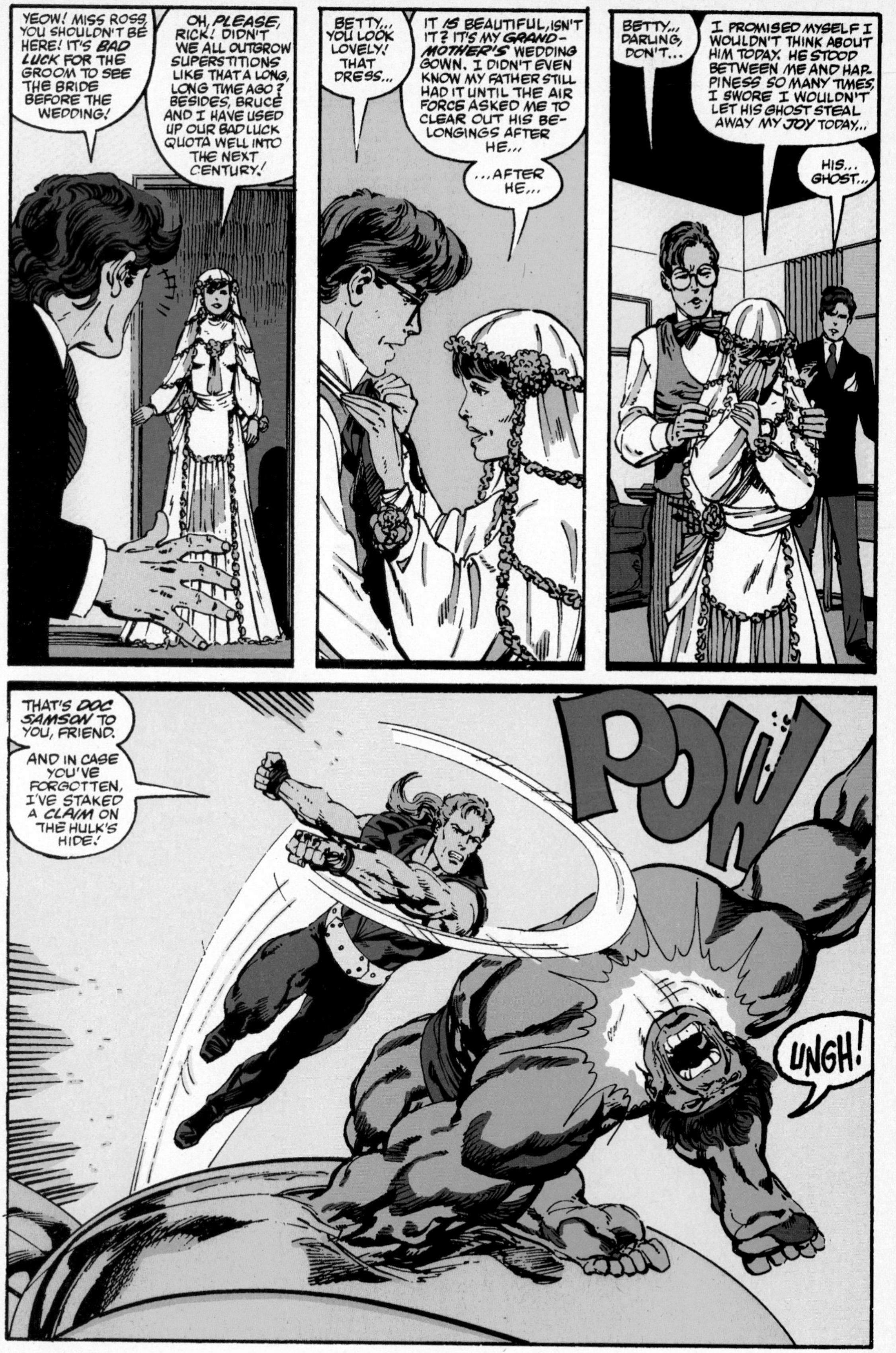

YEOW! MISS ROSS, YOU SHOULDN'T BE HERE! IT'S BAD LUCK FOR THE GROOM TO SEE THE BRIDE BEFORE THE WEDDING!
OH, PLEASE, RICK! DIDN'T WE ALL OUTGROW SUPERSTITIONS LIKE THAT A LONG, LONG TIME AGO? BESIDES, BRUCE AND I HAVE USED UP OUR BAD LUCK QUOTA WELL INTO THE NEXT CENTURY!
BETTY... YOU LOOK LOVELY! THAT DRESS...
IT IS BEAUTIFUL, ISN'T IT? IT'S MY GRAND-MOTHER'S WEDDING GOWN. I DIDN'T EVEN KNOW MY FATHER STILL HAD IT UNTIL THE AIR FORCE ASKED ME TO CLEAR OUT HIS BE-LONGINGS AFTER HE...
...AFTER HE...
BETTY... DARLING, DON'T...
I PROMISED MYSELF I WOULDN'T THINK ABOUT HIM TODAY. HE STOOD BETWEEN ME AND HAP-PINESS SO MANY TIMES, I SWORE I WOULDN'T LET HIS GHOST STEAL AWAY MY JOY TODAY...
HIS... GHOST...
THAT'S DOC SAMSON TO YOU, FRIEND.
AND IN CASE YOU'VE FORGOTTEN, I'VE STAKED A CLAIM ON THE HULK'S HIDE!
POW
UNGH!

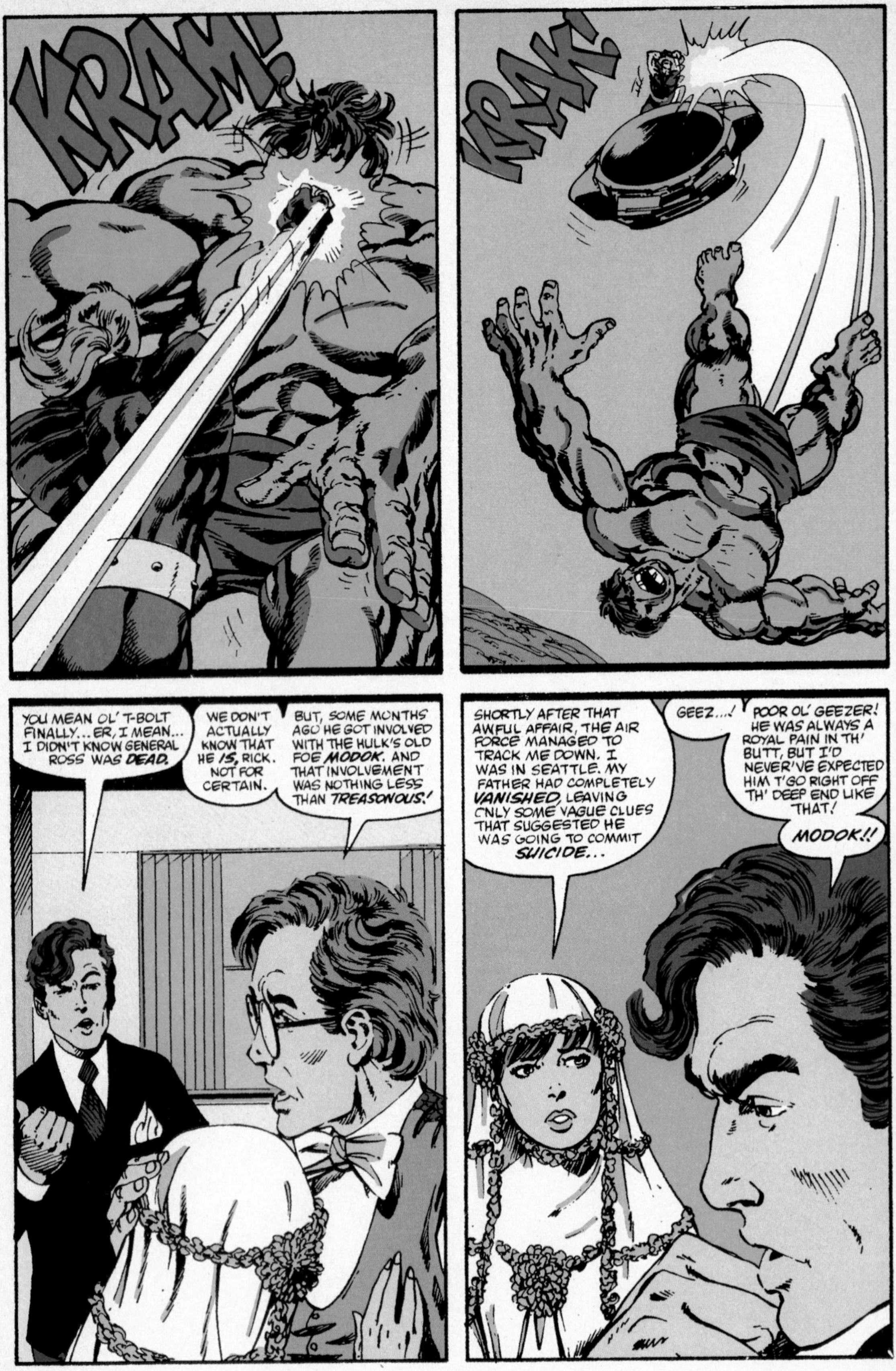
KRAM!
KRAK!
YOU MEAN OL' T-BOLT FINALLY... ER, I MEAN... I DIDN'T KNOW GENERAL ROSS WAS DEAD.
WE DON'T ACTUALLY KNOW THAT HE IS, RICK. NOT FOR CERTAIN.
BUT, SOME MONTHS AGO HE GOT INVOLVED WITH THE HULK'S OLD FOE MODOK. AND THAT INVOLVEMENT WAS NOTHING LESS THAN TREASONOUS!
SHORTLY AFTER THAT AWFUL AFFAIR, THE AIR FORCE MANAGED TO TRACK ME DOWN. I WAS IN SEATTLE. MY FATHER HAD COMPLETELY VANISHED, LEAVING ONLY SOME VAGUE CLUES THAT SUGGESTED HE WAS GOING TO COMMIT SUICIDE...
GEEZ...!
POOR OL' GEEZER! HE WAS ALWAYS A ROYAL PAIN IN TH' BUTT, BUT I'D NEVER'VE EXPECTED HIM T'GO RIGHT OFF TH' DEEP END LIKE THAT!
MODOK!!

BETTY-- EXCUSE ME FOR INTERRUPTING, BUT REVEREND MORRIS WOULD LIKE A FEW WORDS WITH YOU BEFORE THE CEREMONY.

OH, YES. THANK YOU, HIDEKO.

ENOUGH SAD MEMORIES, BRUCE DARLING. I'LL SEE YOU IN A FEW MINUTES.

WELL, DOC, TH' CLOCK IS RUNNIN' FOR SURE NOW! THIS IS YOUR LAST CHANCE T' SNEAK OUT THE BACK DOOR!

IT'S NOT A JOKING MATTER, RICK. IN THE WEEKS SINCE I PROPOSED TO BETTY I'VE GONE BACK AND FORTH A HUNDRED TIMES ON WHETHER OR NOT THIS IS REALLY THE RIGHT THING TO DO.

HEY, DOC, WHAT COULD BE MORE RIGHT? YOU TWO LOVE EACH OTHER. YOU ALWAYS HAVE.

TRUE. BUT IS LOVE ENOUGH? WITH ALL THE OTHER FACTORS, IS THE ADDITION OF LOVE ENOUGH TO MAKE THE EQUATION POSITIVE?

WHERE IS THE GUARANTEE WE'RE NOT ABOUT TO MAKE A HORRIBLE MISTAKE?

SHOOM!

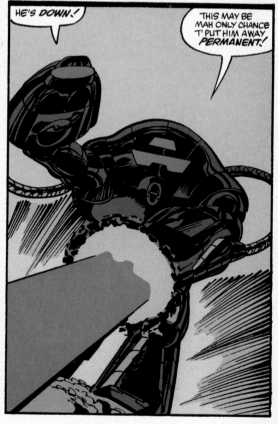

HE'S DOWN!

THIS MAY BE MAH ONLY CHANCE T' PUT HIM AWAY PERMANENT!

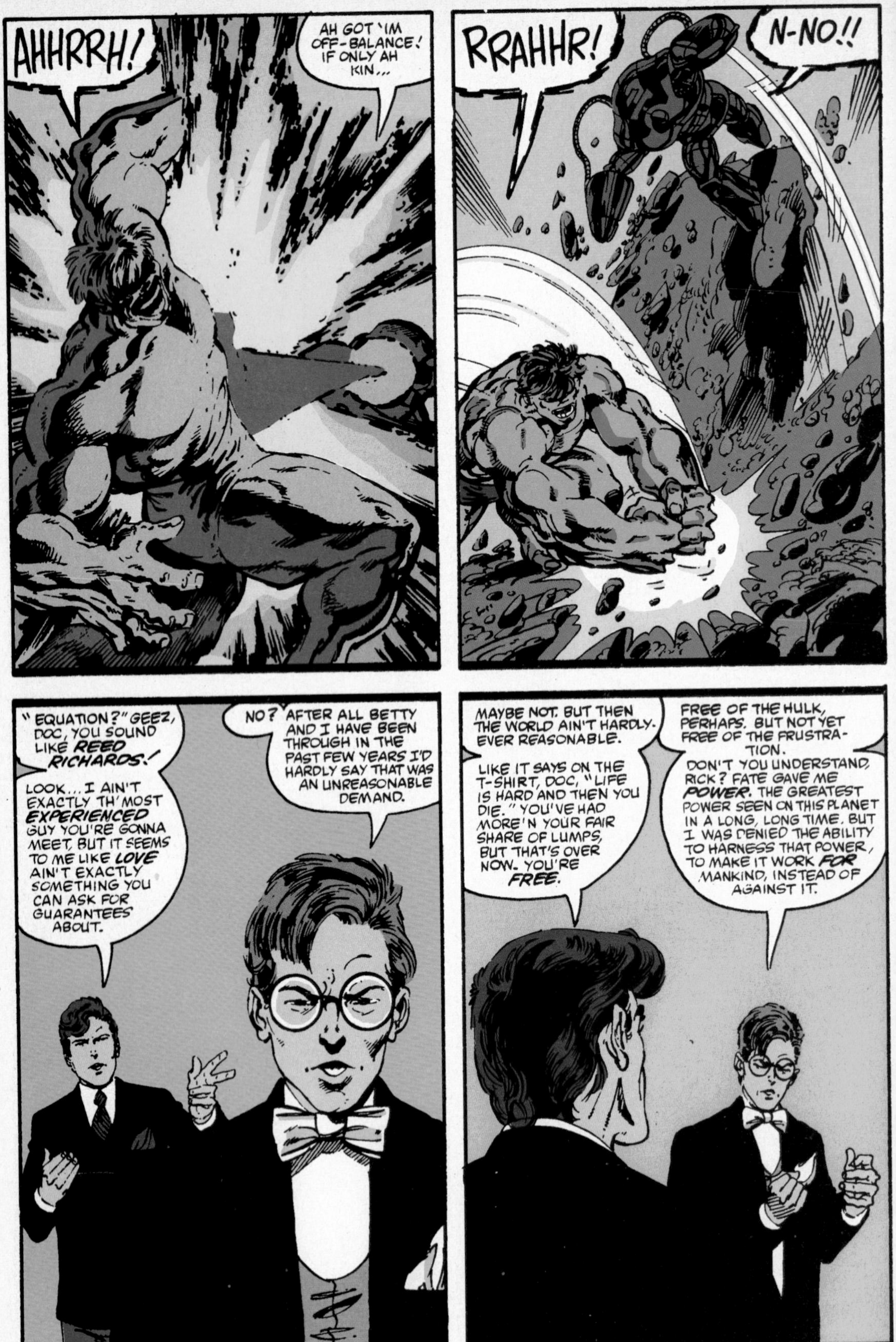
AHHRRH!
AH GOT 'IM OFF-BALANCE! IF ONLY AH KIN...
RRAHHR!
N-NO!!
"EQUATION?" GEEZ, DOC, YOU SOUND LIKE REED RICHARDS!
LOOK... I AIN'T EXACTLY TH' MOST EXPERIENCED GUY YOU'RE GONNA MEET, BUT IT SEEMS TO ME LIKE LOVE AIN'T EXACTLY SOMETHING YOU CAN ASK FOR GUARANTEES ABOUT.
NO? AFTER ALL BETTY AND I HAVE BEEN THROUGH IN THE PAST FEW YEARS I'D HARDLY SAY THAT WAS AN UNREASONABLE DEMAND.
MAYBE NOT. BUT THEN THE WORLD AIN'T HARDLY EVER REASONABLE.
LIKE IT SAYS ON THE T-SHIRT, DOC, "LIFE IS HARD AND THEN YOU DIE." YOU'VE HAD MORE'N YOUR FAIR SHARE OF LUMPS, BUT THAT'S OVER NOW. YOU'RE FREE.
FREE OF THE HULK, PERHAPS. BUT NOT YET FREE OF THE FRUSTRATION.
DON'T YOU UNDERSTAND, RICK? FATE GAVE ME POWER. THE GREATEST POWER SEEN ON THIS PLANET IN A LONG, LONG TIME. BUT I WAS DENIED THE ABILITY TO HARNESS THAT POWER, TO MAKE IT WORK FOR MANKIND, INSTEAD OF AGAINST IT.

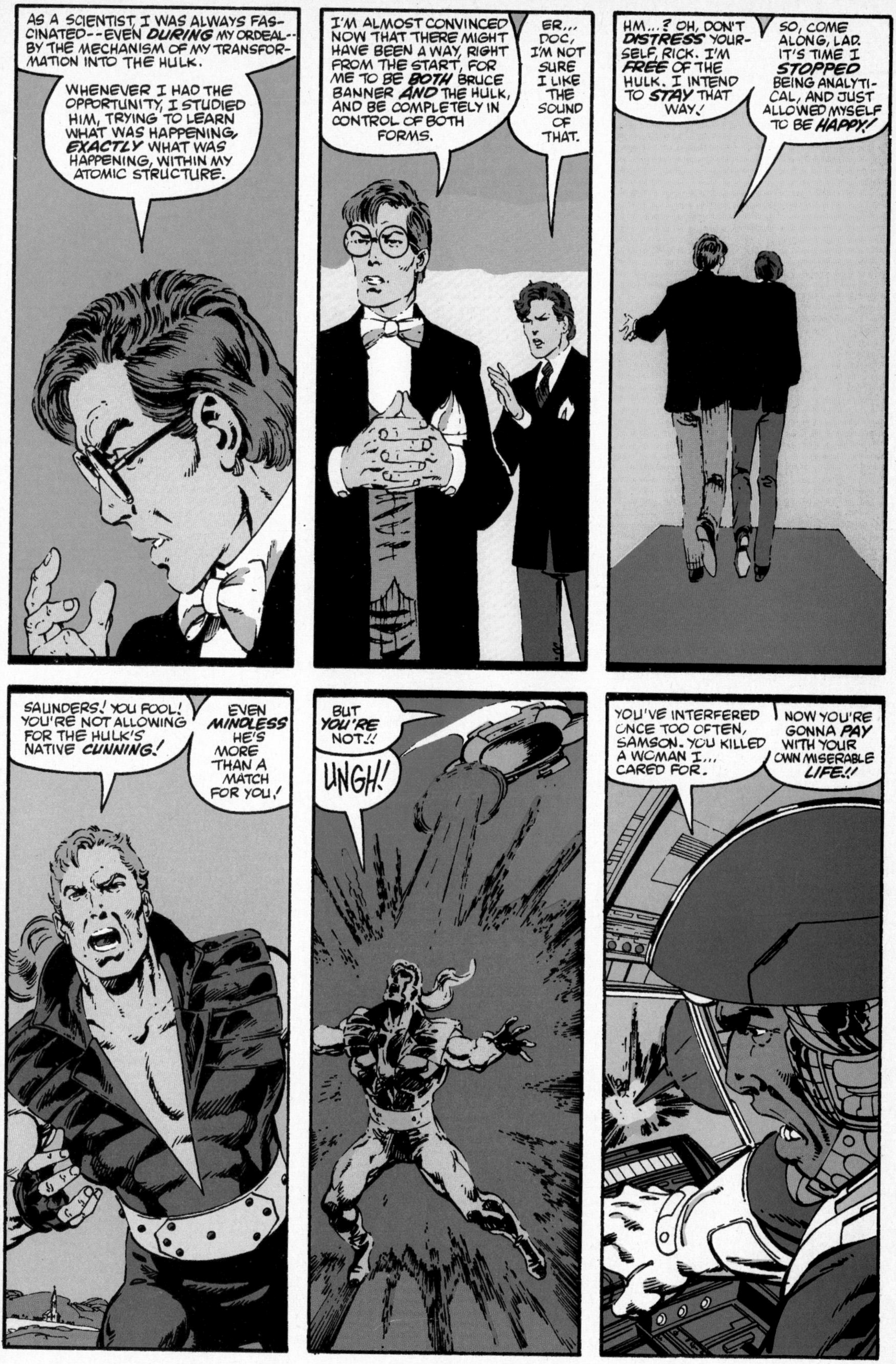
AS A SCIENTIST, I WAS ALWAYS FASCINATED--EVEN DURING MY ORDEAL--BY THE MECHANISM OF MY TRANSFORMATION INTO THE HULK.
WHENEVER I HAD THE OPPORTUNITY, I STUDIED HIM, TRYING TO LEARN WHAT WAS HAPPENING, EXACTLY WHAT WAS HAPPENING, WITHIN MY ATOMIC STRUCTURE.
I'M ALMOST CONVINCED NOW THAT THERE MIGHT HAVE BEEN A WAY, RIGHT FROM THE START, FOR ME TO BE BOTH BRUCE BANNER AND THE HULK, AND BE COMPLETELY IN CONTROL OF BOTH FORMS.
ER... DOC, I'M NOT SURE I LIKE THE SOUND OF THAT.
HM...? OH, DON'T DISTRESS YOURSELF, RICK. I'M FREE OF THE HULK. I INTEND TO STAY THAT WAY!
SO, COME ALONG, LAD. IT'S TIME I STOPPED BEING ANALYTICAL, AND JUST ALLOWED MYSELF TO BE HAPPY!
SAUNDERS! YOU FOOL! YOU'RE NOT ALLOWING FOR THE HULK'S NATIVE CUNNING!
EVEN MINDLESS HE'S MORE THAN A MATCH FOR YOU!
BUT YOU'RE NOT!!
UNGH!
YOU'VE INTERFERED ONCE TOO OFTEN, SAMSON. YOU KILLED A WOMAN I... CARED FOR.
NOW YOU'RE GONNA PAY WITH YOUR OWN MISERABLE LIFE!!

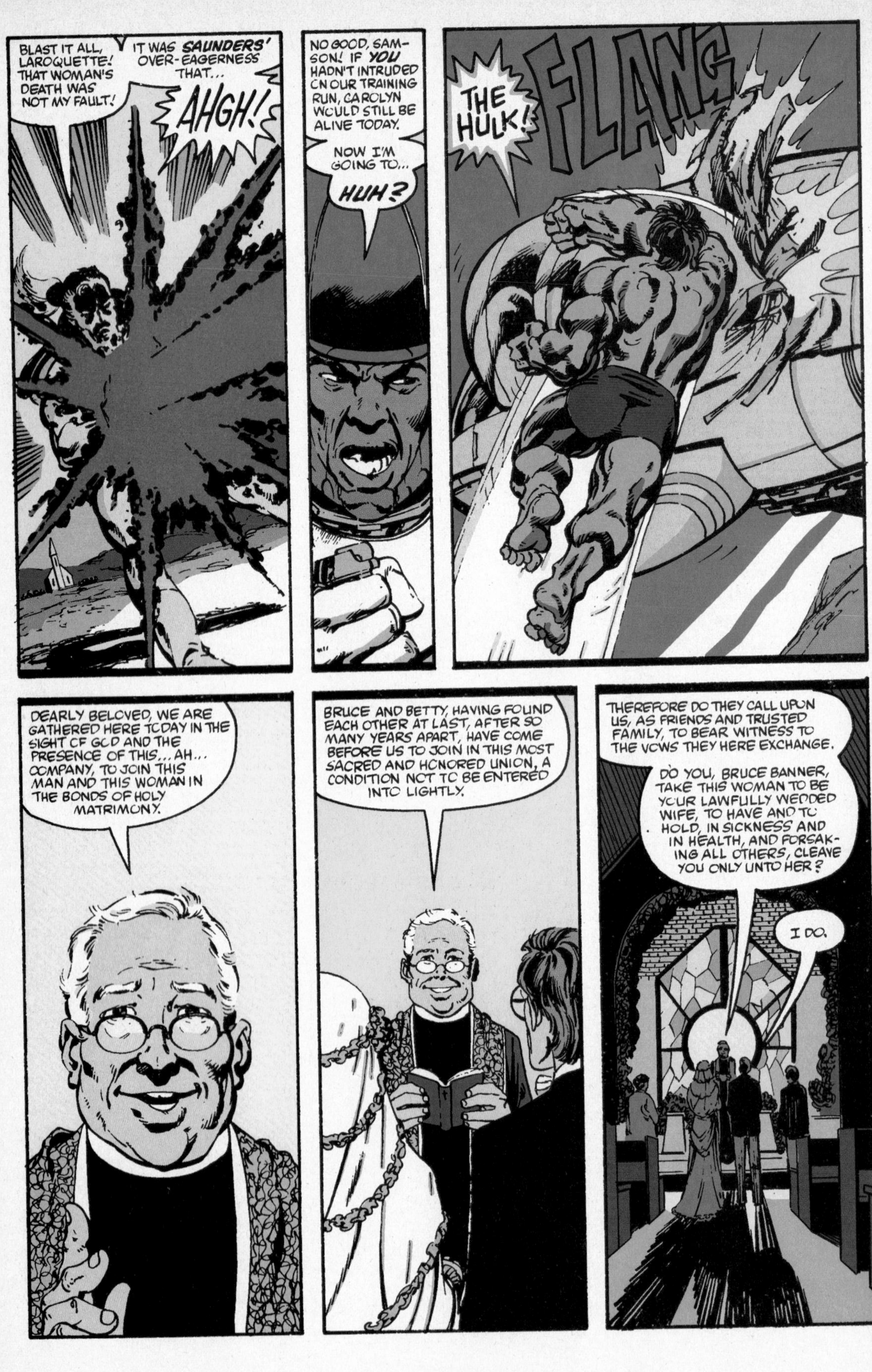
BLAST IT ALL, LAROQUETTE! THAT WOMAN'S DEATH WAS NOT MY FAULT!
IT WAS SAUNDERS' OVER-EAGERNESS THAT...
AHGH!
NO GOOD, SAMSON! IF YOU HADN'T INTRUDED ON OUR TRAINING RUN, CAROLYN WOULD STILL BE ALIVE TODAY.
NOW I'M GOING TO...
HUH?
THE HULK!
FLANG
DEARLY BELOVED, WE ARE GATHERED HERE TODAY IN THE SIGHT OF GOD AND THE PRESENCE OF THIS... AH... COMPANY, TO JOIN THIS MAN AND THIS WOMAN IN THE BONDS OF HOLY MATRIMONY.
BRUCE AND BETTY, HAVING FOUND EACH OTHER AT LAST, AFTER SO MANY YEARS APART, HAVE COME BEFORE US TO JOIN IN THIS MOST SACRED AND HONORED UNION, A CONDITION NOT TO BE ENTERED INTO LIGHTLY.
THEREFORE DO THEY CALL UPON US, AS FRIENDS AND TRUSTED FAMILY, TO BEAR WITNESS TO THE VOWS THEY HERE EXCHANGE.
DO YOU, BRUCE BANNER, TAKE THIS WOMAN TO BE YOUR LAWFULLY WEDDED WIFE, TO HAVE AND TO HOLD, IN SICKNESS AND IN HEALTH, AND FORSAKING ALL OTHERS, CLEAVE YOU ONLY UNTO HER?
I DO.

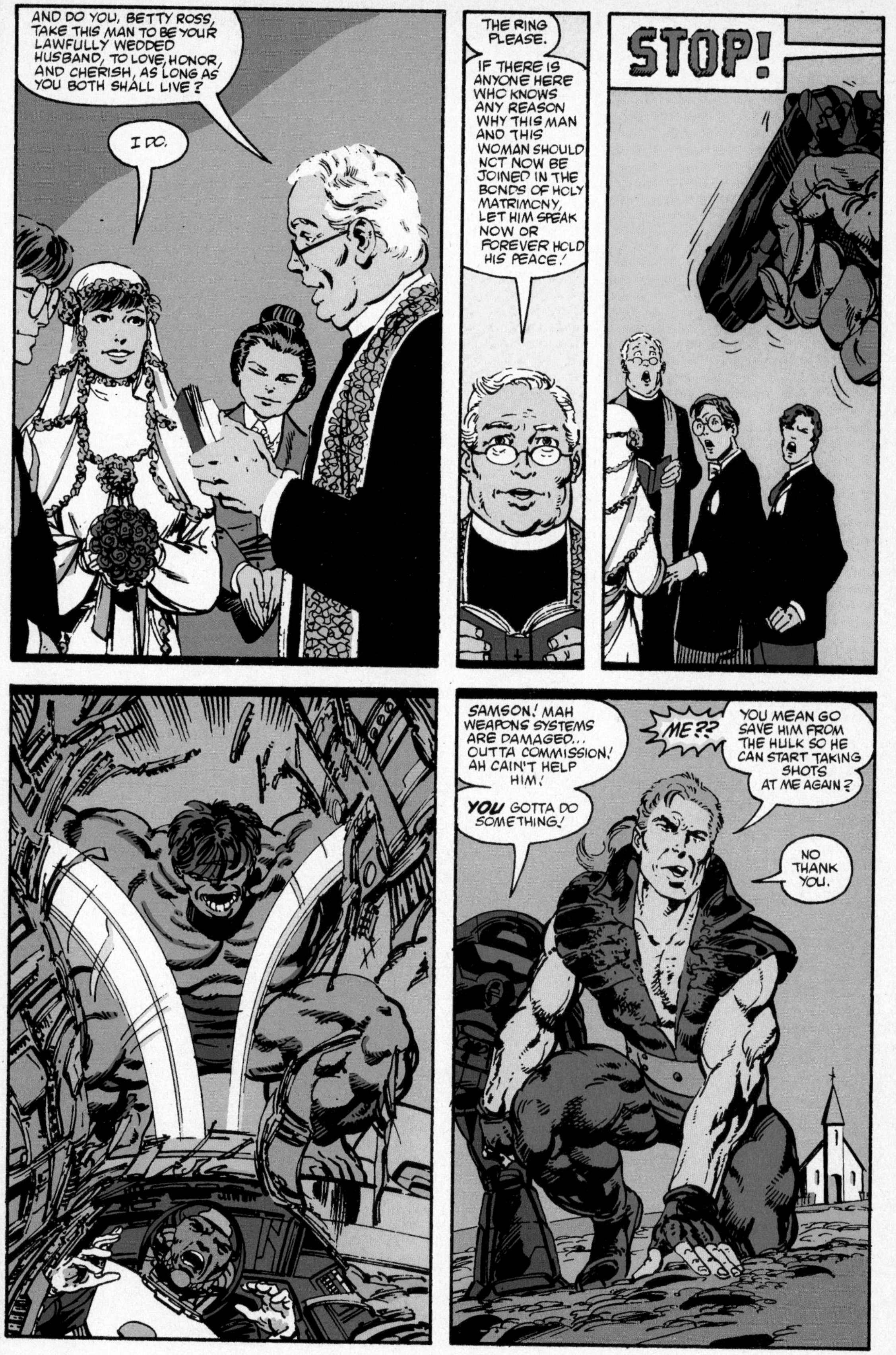
AND DO YOU, BETTY ROSS, TAKE THIS MAN TO BE YOUR LAWFULLY WEDDED HUSBAND, TO LOVE, HONOR, AND CHERISH, AS LONG AS YOU BOTH SHALL LIVE?
I DO.
THE RING PLEASE.
IF THERE IS ANYONE HERE WHO KNOWS ANY REASON WHY THIS MAN AND THIS WOMAN SHOULD NOT NOW BE JOINED IN THE BONDS OF HOLY MATRIMONY, LET HIM SPEAK NOW OR FOREVER HOLD HIS PEACE!
STOP!
SAMSON! MAH WEAPONS SYSTEMS ARE DAMAGED... OUTTA COMMISSION! AH CAIN'T HELP HIM!
YOU GOTTA DO SOMETHING!
ME??
YOU MEAN GO SAVE HIM FROM THE HULK SO HE CAN START TAKING SHOTS AT ME AGAIN?
NO THANK YOU.

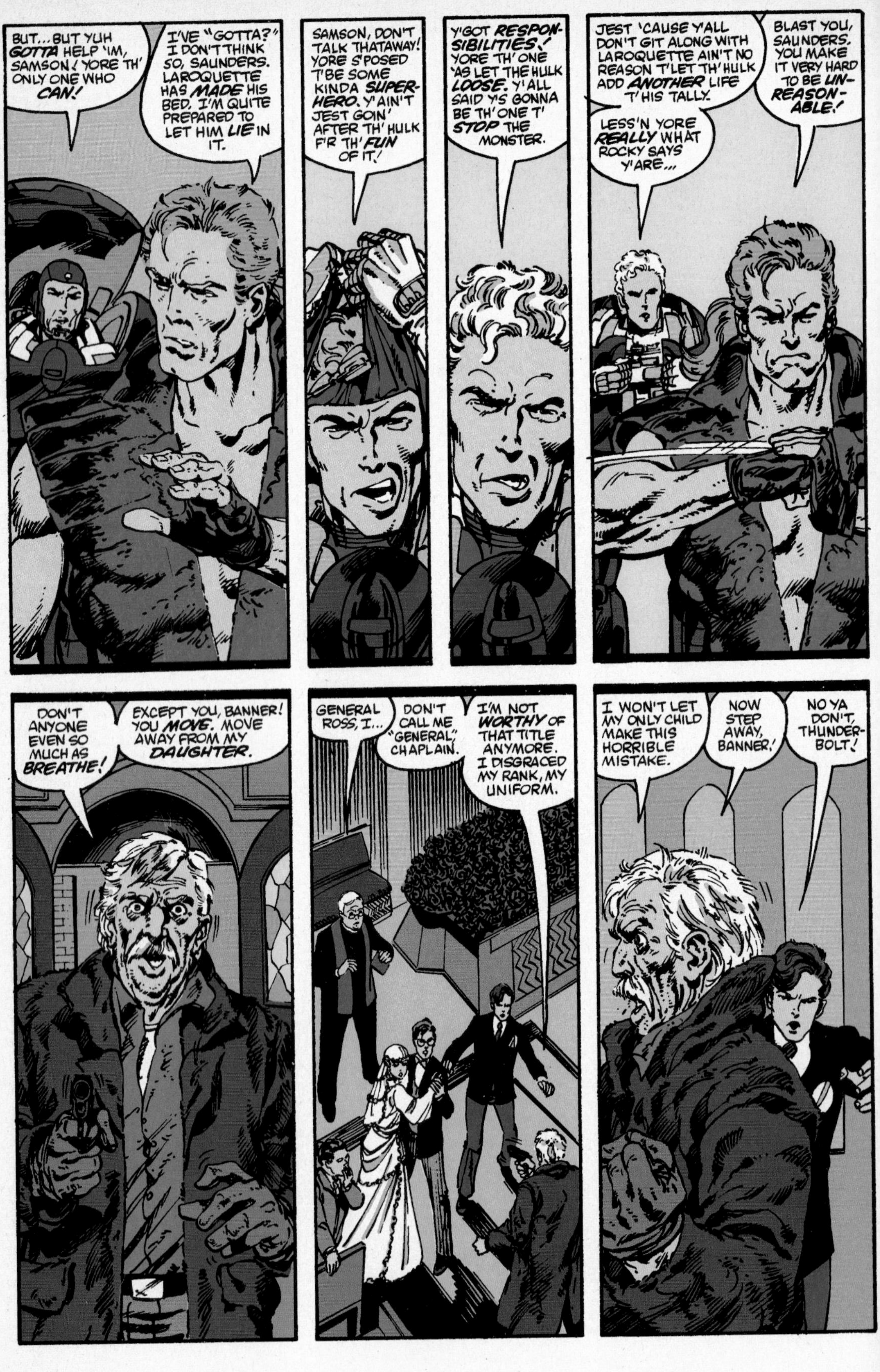

BUT... BUT YUH GOTTA HELP 'IM, SAMSON! YORE TH' ONLY ONE WHO CAN!
I'VE "GOTTA?" I DON'T THINK SO, SAUNDERS. LAROQUETTE HAS MADE HIS BED. I'M QUITE PREPARED TO LET HIM LIE IN IT.
SAMSON, DON'T TALK THATAWAY! YORE S'POSED T'BE SOME KINDA SUPER-HERO. Y'AIN'T JEST GOIN' AFTER TH' HULK F'R TH' FUN OF IT!
Y'GOT RESPON-SIBILITIES! YORE TH' ONE 'AS LET THE HULK LOOSE. Y'ALL SAID Y'S GONNA BE TH' ONE T' STOP THE MONSTER.
JEST 'CAUSE Y'ALL DON'T GIT ALONG WITH LAROQUETTE AIN'T NO REASON T'LET TH' HULK ADD ANOTHER LIFE T'HIS TALLY.
LESS'N YORE REALLY WHAT ROCKY SAYS Y'ARE...
BLAST YOU, SAUNDERS. YOU MAKE IT VERY HARD TO BE UN-REASON-ABLE!
DON'T ANYONE EVEN SO MUCH AS BREATHE!
EXCEPT YOU, BANNER! YOU MOVE. MOVE AWAY FROM MY DAUGHTER.
GENERAL ROSS, I...
DON'T CALL ME "GENERAL," CHAPLAIN.
I'M NOT WORTHY OF THAT TITLE ANYMORE. I DISGRACED MY RANK, MY UNIFORM.
I WON'T LET MY ONLY CHILD MAKE THIS HORRIBLE MISTAKE.
NOW STEP AWAY, BANNER!
NO YA DON'T, THUNDER-BOLT!

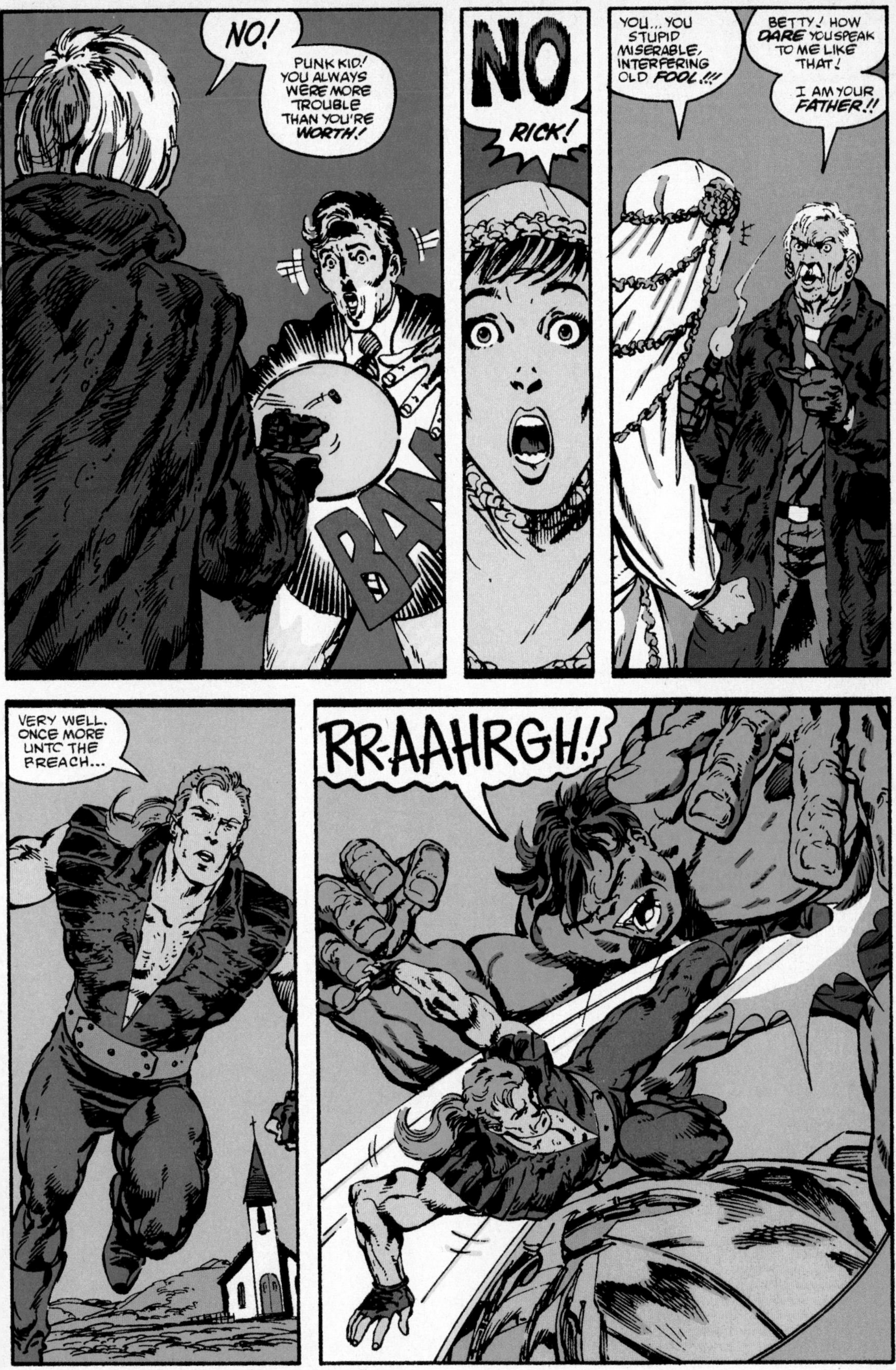

NO!
PUNK KID! YOU ALWAYS WERE MORE TROUBLE THAN YOU'RE WORTH!
BA
NO
RICK!
YOU... YOU STUPID MISERABLE, INTERFERING OLD FOOL!!!
BETTY! HOW DARE YOU SPEAK TO ME LIKE THAT!
I AM YOUR FATHER!!
VERY WELL. ONCE MORE UNTO THE BREACH...
RR-AAHRGH!

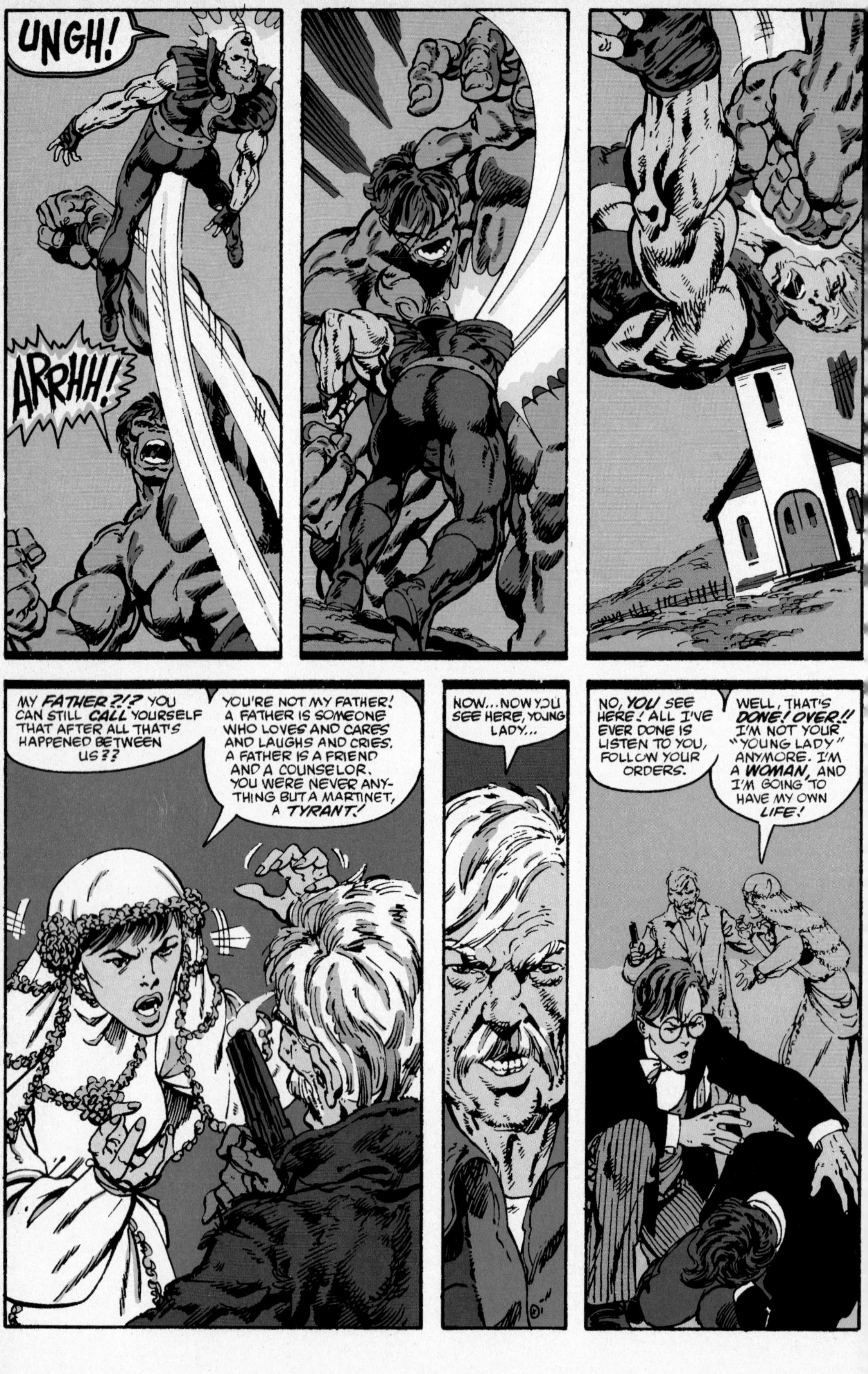

UNGH!
ARRHH!
MY FATHER?!? YOU CAN STILL CALL YOURSELF THAT AFTER ALL THAT'S HAPPENED BETWEEN US??
YOU'RE NOT MY FATHER! A FATHER IS SOMEONE WHO LOVES AND CARES AND LAUGHS AND CRIES. A FATHER IS A FRIEND AND A COUNSELOR. YOU WERE NEVER ANYTHING BUT A MARTINET, A TYRANT!
NOW... NOW YOU SEE HERE, YOUNG LADY...
NO, YOU SEE HERE! ALL I'VE EVER DONE IS LISTEN TO YOU, FOLLOW YOUR ORDERS.
WELL, THAT'S DONE! OVER!! I'M NOT YOUR "YOUNG LADY" ANYMORE. I'M A WOMAN, AND I'M GOING TO HAVE MY OWN LIFE!

BETTY...
I'M NOT FINISHED!

YOU'VE LOOMED OVER ME ALL MY LIFE, DOMINATED ME, TOLD ME HOW TO THINK. HOW TO FEEL. YOU NEVER LET ME HAVE A MOMENT I COULD CALL MY OWN.

AND THEN I MET *BRUCE*. HE SHOWED ME MEN WEREN'T ALL LIKE YOU. HE SHOWED ME MEN COULD HAVE A TENDER SIDE, A SWEET, SHY, LOVING SIDE.

BUT YOU *MOCKED* HIM FOR THAT. YOU CALLED HIM A *MILKSOP*. YOU *RAGED* AT MY GROWING LOVE FOR HIM.

YOU DID EVERYTHING IN YOUR POWER TO STAND IN OUR WAY, TO *KILL* OUR LOVE. AND NOW YOU'RE DOING IT AGAIN.

WELL, THERE'S ONLY *ONE WAY* YOU'LL SUCCEED THIS TIME. YOU'LL HAVE TO KILL *ME!*

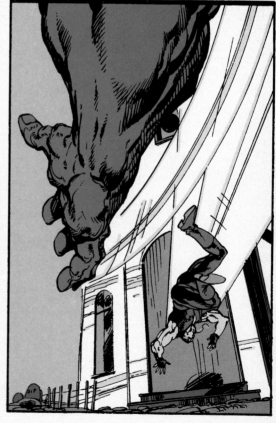

181

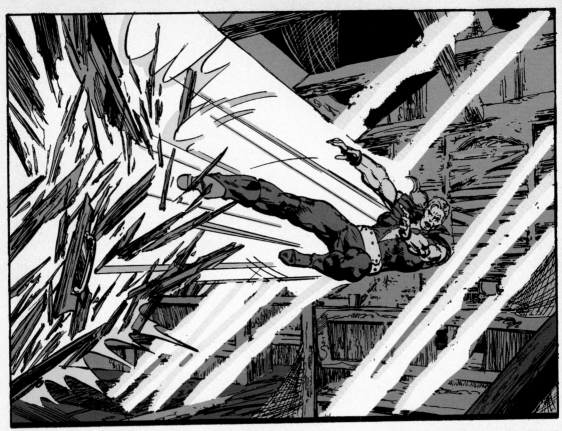

WELL? MISTER *WAR HERO!* MISTER TAKE *COMMAND!* WHAT ARE YOU GOING TO *DO?*

WHAT ARE YOU GOING TO DO?!?!

BETTY...

...PLEASE...

...I NEVER *KNEW.* I NEVER *UNDERSTOOD...*

OF COURSE NOT. YOU NEVER *WANTED* TO.

I ONLY...

...WANTED TO...

...MAKE YOU...

...*HAPPY...*

BETTY! DARLING, THAT WAS *MAGNIFICENT!*

WAS IT?

A TIRED FOOLISH OLD MAN. AND I *CRUSHED* HIM, AS HE TRIED SO MANY TIMES TO CRUSH ME.

QUITE A *TRIUMPH.!!*

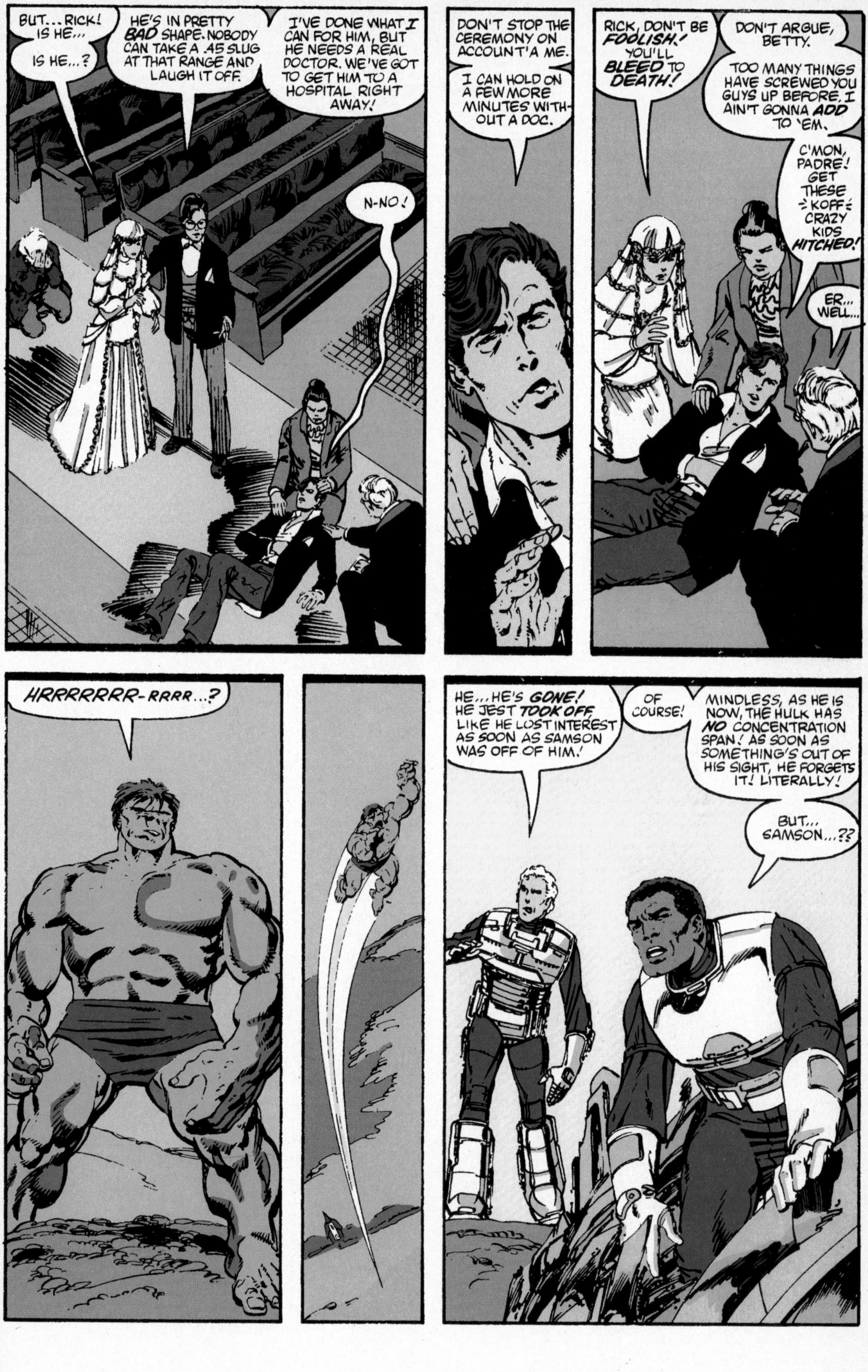

BUT... RICK! IS HE... IS HE...?
HE'S IN PRETTY BAD SHAPE. NOBODY CAN TAKE A .45 SLUG AT THAT RANGE AND LAUGH IT OFF.
I'VE DONE WHAT I CAN FOR HIM, BUT HE NEEDS A REAL DOCTOR. WE'VE GOT TO GET HIM TO A HOSPITAL RIGHT AWAY!
N-NO!
DON'T STOP THE CEREMONY ON ACCOUNT'A ME.
I CAN HOLD ON A FEW MORE MINUTES WITH-OUT A DOC.
RICK, DON'T BE FOOLISH! YOU'LL BLEED TO DEATH!
DON'T ARGUE, BETTY.
TOO MANY THINGS HAVE SCREWED YOU GUYS UP BEFORE. I AIN'T GONNA ADD TO 'EM.
C'MON, PADRE! GET THESE *KOFF* CRAZY KIDS HITCHED!
ER... WELL...
HRRRRRRR-RRRR...?
HE... HE'S GONE! HE JEST TOOK OFF LIKE HE LOST INTEREST AS SOON AS SAMSON WAS OFF OF HIM!
OF COURSE!
MINDLESS, AS HE IS NOW, THE HULK HAS NO CONCENTRATION SPAN! AS SOON AS SOMETHING'S OUT OF HIS SIGHT, HE FORGETS IT! LITERALLY!
BUT... SAMSON...??

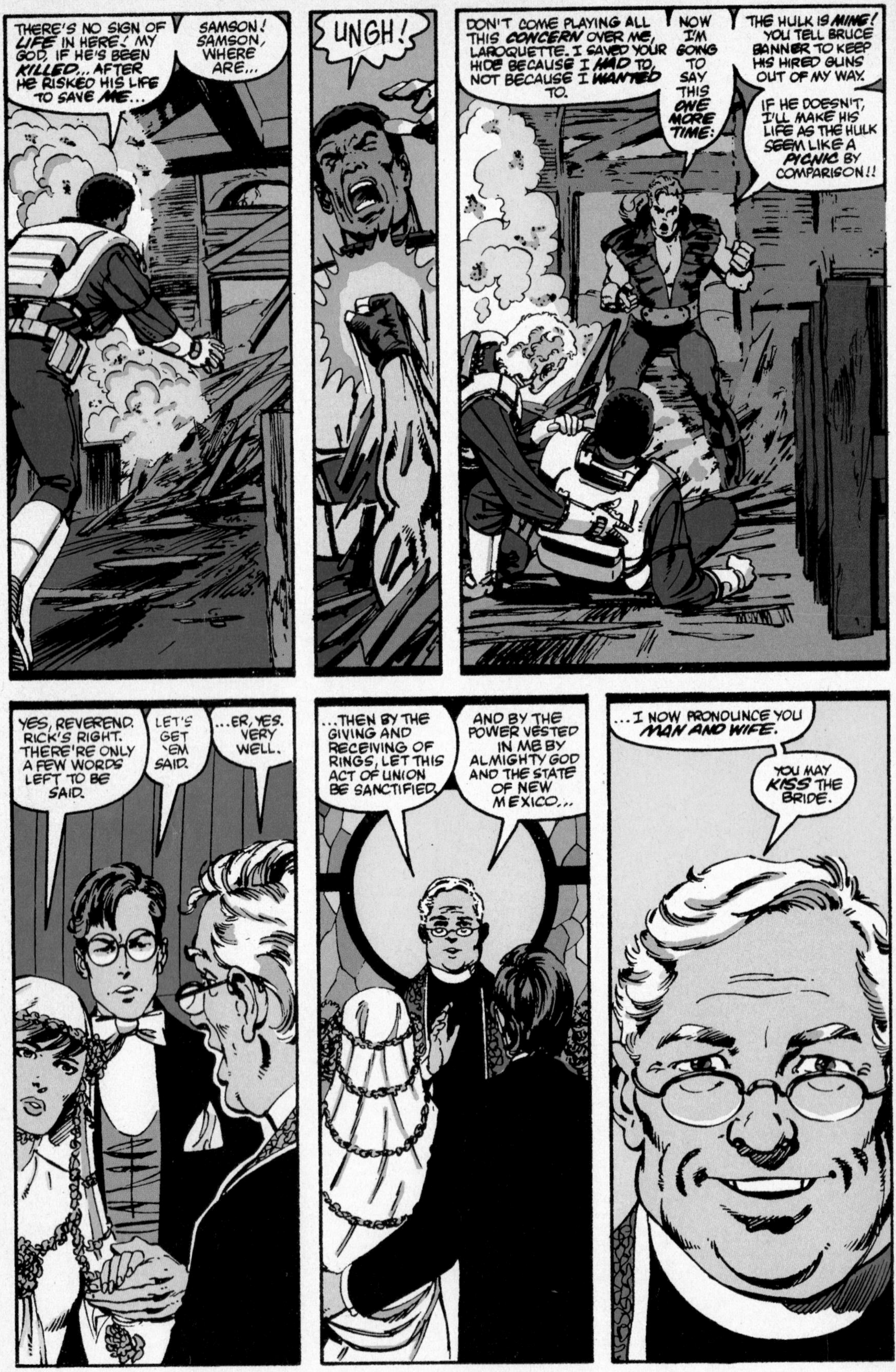
THERE'S NO SIGN OF LIFE IN HERE! MY GOD, IF HE'S BEEN KILLED... AFTER HE RISKED HIS LIFE TO SAVE ME...
SAMSON! SAMSON, WHERE ARE...
UNGH!
DON'T COME PLAYING ALL THIS CONCERN OVER ME, LAROQUETTE. I SAVED YOUR HIDE BECAUSE I HAD TO, NOT BECAUSE I WANTED TO.
NOW I'M GOING TO SAY THIS ONE MORE TIME:
THE HULK IS MINE! YOU TELL BRUCE BANNER TO KEEP HIS HIRED GUNS OUT OF MY WAY.
IF HE DOESN'T, I'LL MAKE HIS LIFE AS THE HULK SEEM LIKE A PICNIC BY COMPARISON!!
YES, REVEREND. RICK'S RIGHT. THERE'RE ONLY A FEW WORDS LEFT TO BE SAID.
LET'S GET 'EM SAID.
...ER, YES. VERY WELL.
...THEN BY THE GIVING AND RECEIVING OF RINGS, LET THIS ACT OF UNION BE SANCTIFIED.
AND BY THE POWER VESTED IN ME BY ALMIGHTY GOD AND THE STATE OF NEW MEXICO...
...I NOW PRONOUNCE YOU MAN AND WIFE.
YOU MAY KISS THE BRIDE.

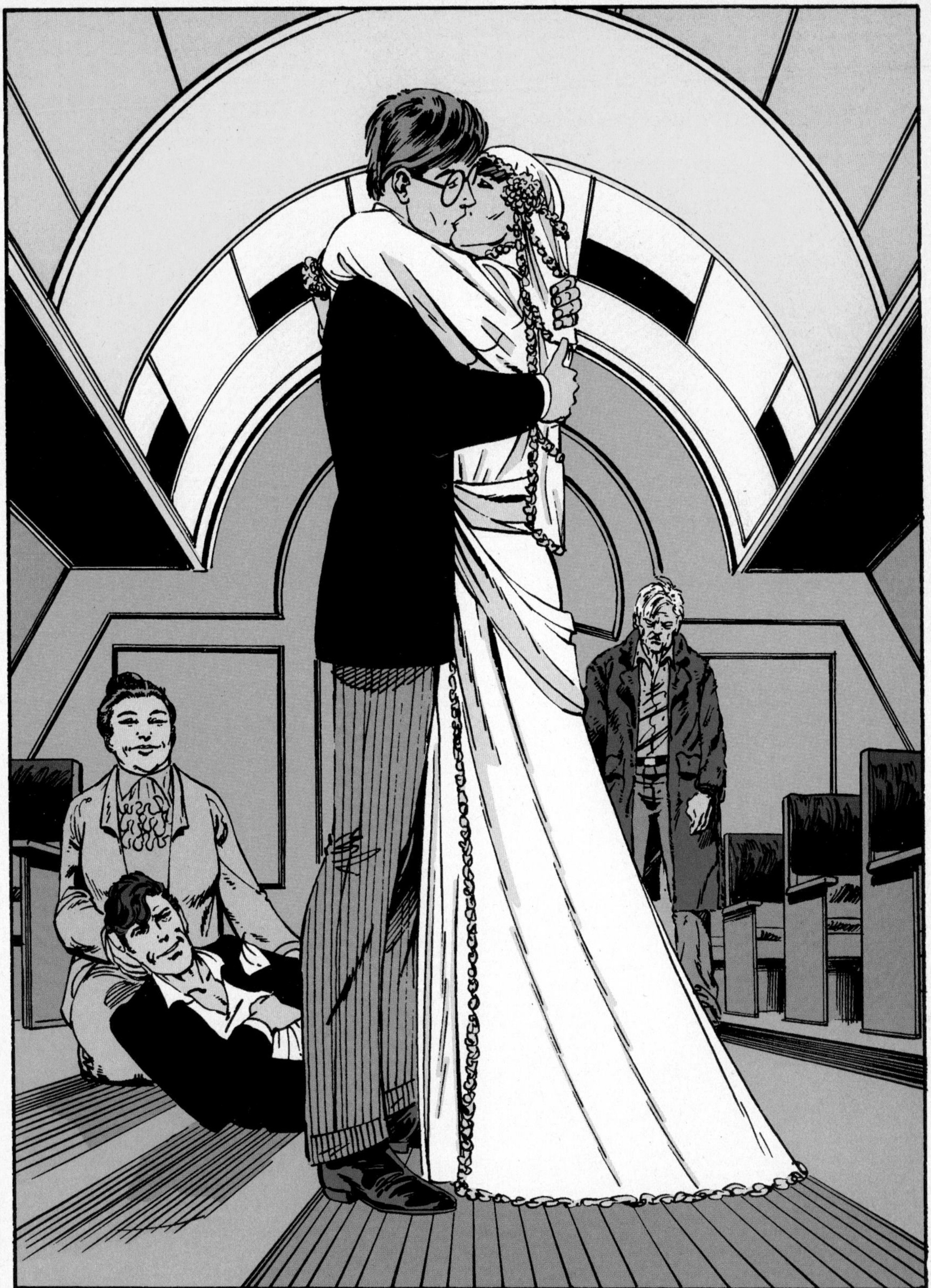

THIS ISSUE WAS A *Stan Lee* PRESENTATION. | JOHN BYRNE WRITER/ARTIST | KEITH WILLIAMS BACKGROUND INKS | ANDY YANCHUS COLORING | RICK PARKER LETTERING | DENNIS O'NEIL EDITOR & | JIM SHOOTER EDITOR IN CHIEF

NEXT ISSUE: THINK THINGS ARE MOVIN' FAST ***NOW***?!?! TUNE IN NEXT ISH FOR **"HONEYMOON'S OVER!!!"**

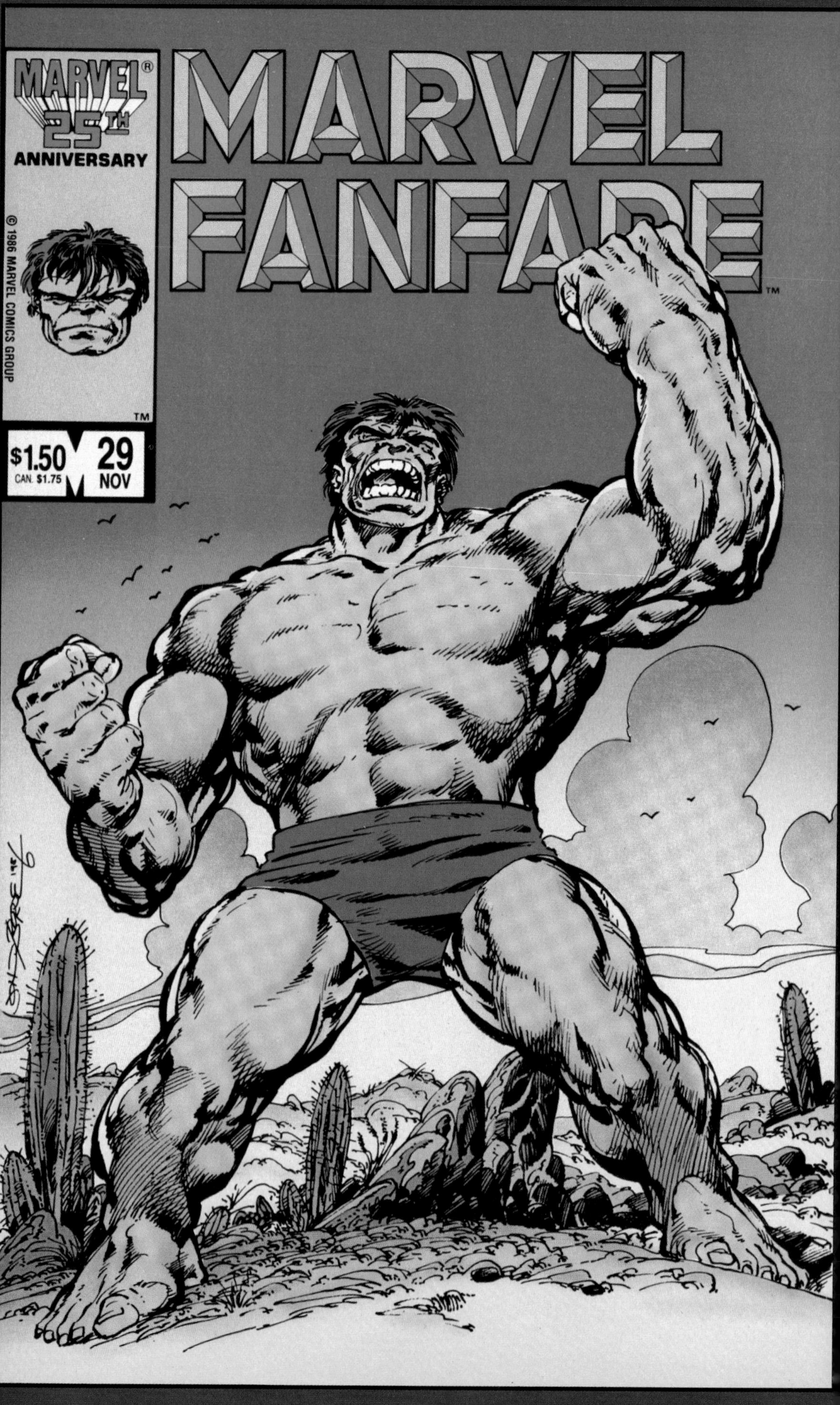
MARVEL®
25TH
ANNIVERSARY
© 1986 MARVEL COMICS GROUP
MARVEL FANFARE™
$1.50
CAN. $1.75
29
NOV

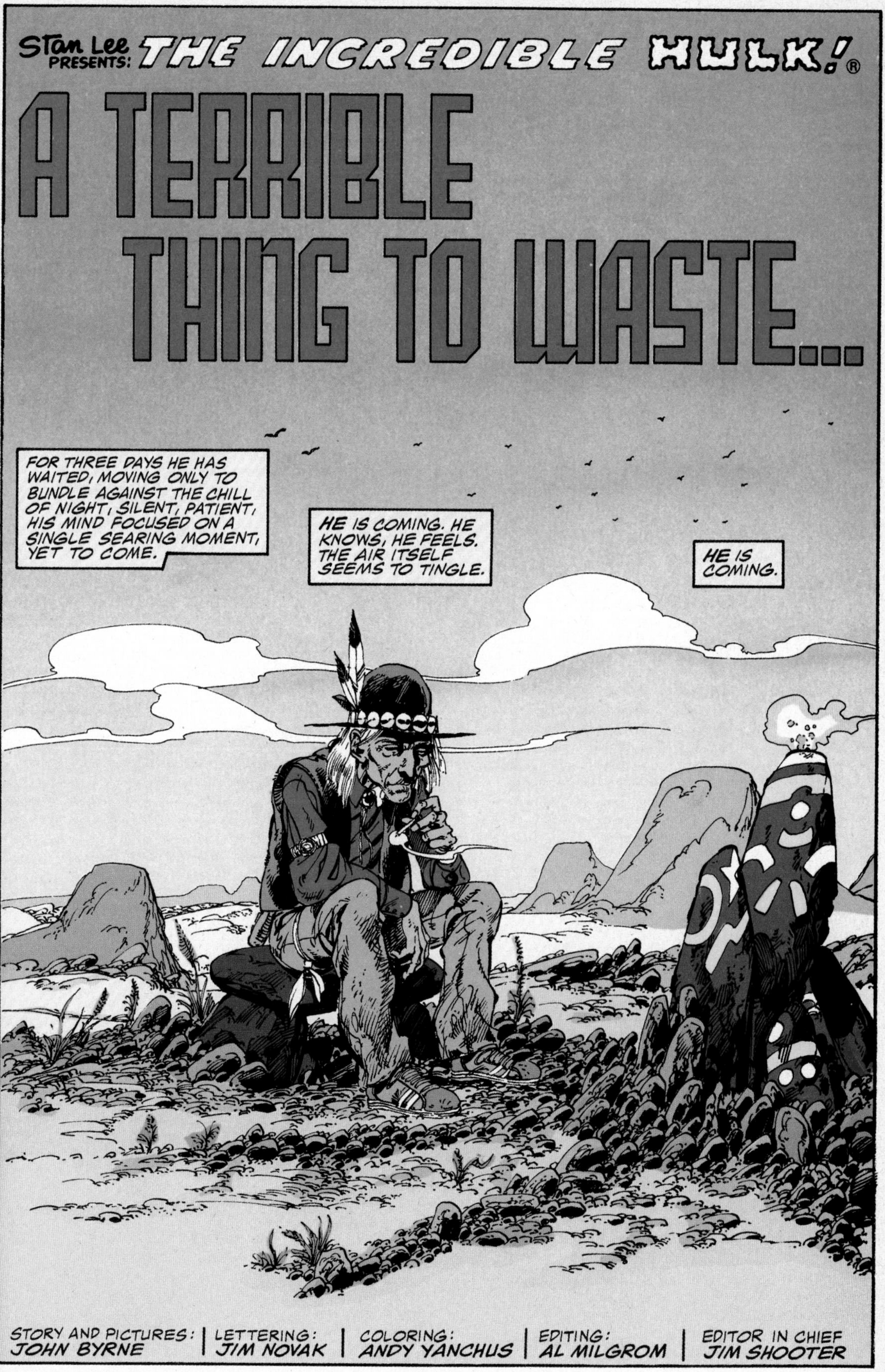
STAN LEE PRESENTS: THE INCREDIBLE HULK!®
A TERRIBLE THING TO WASTE...
FOR THREE DAYS HE HAS WAITED, MOVING ONLY TO BUNDLE AGAINST THE CHILL OF NIGHT, SILENT, PATIENT, HIS MIND FOCUSED ON A SINGLE SEARING MOMENT, YET TO COME.
HE IS COMING. HE KNOWS, HE FEELS. THE AIR ITSELF SEEMS TO TINGLE.
HE IS COMING.
STORY AND PICTURES: JOHN BYRNE | LETTERING: JIM NOVAK | COLORING: ANDY YANCHUS | EDITING: AL MILGROM | EDITOR IN CHIEF JIM SHOOTER

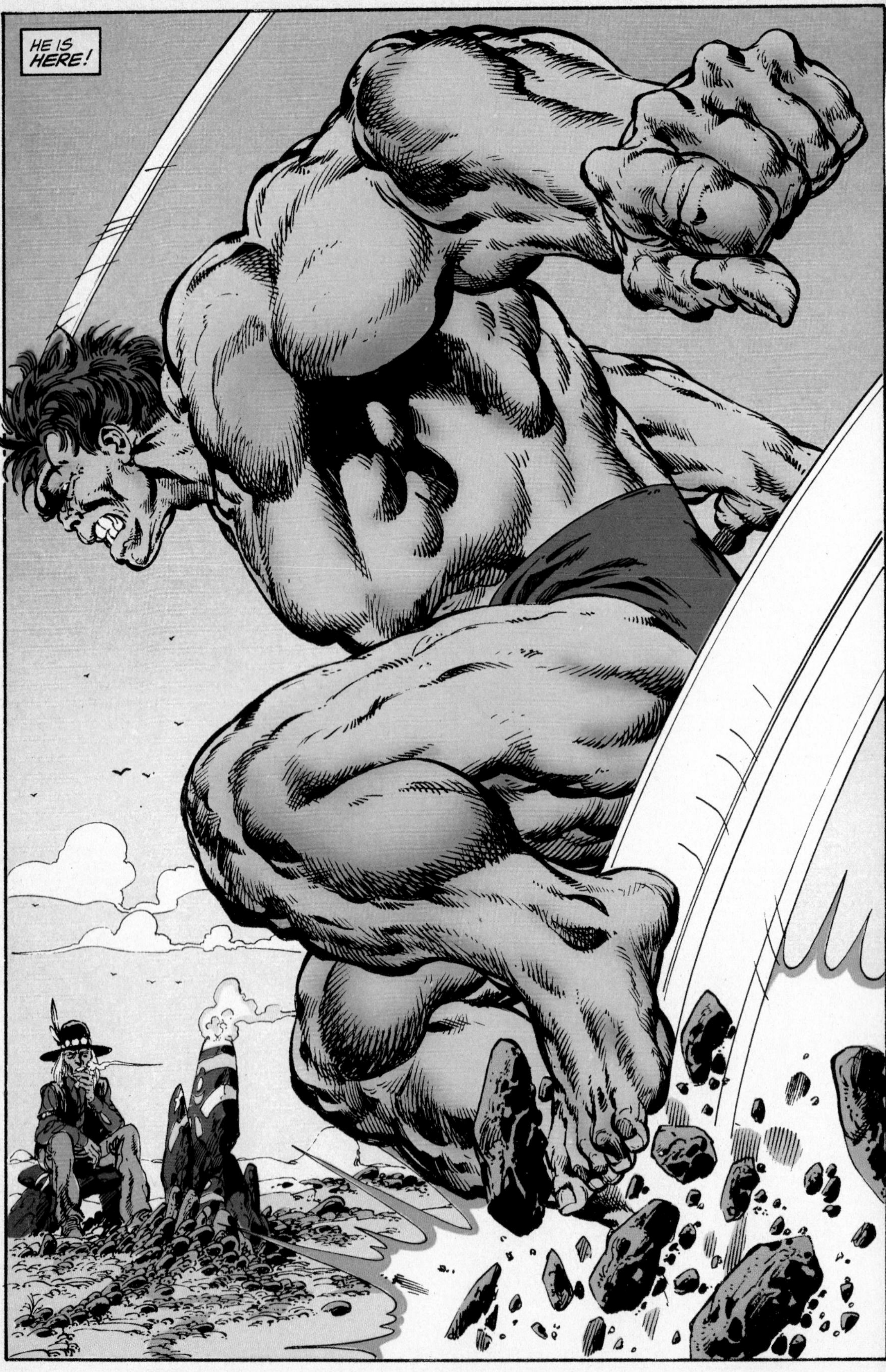
HE IS HERE!

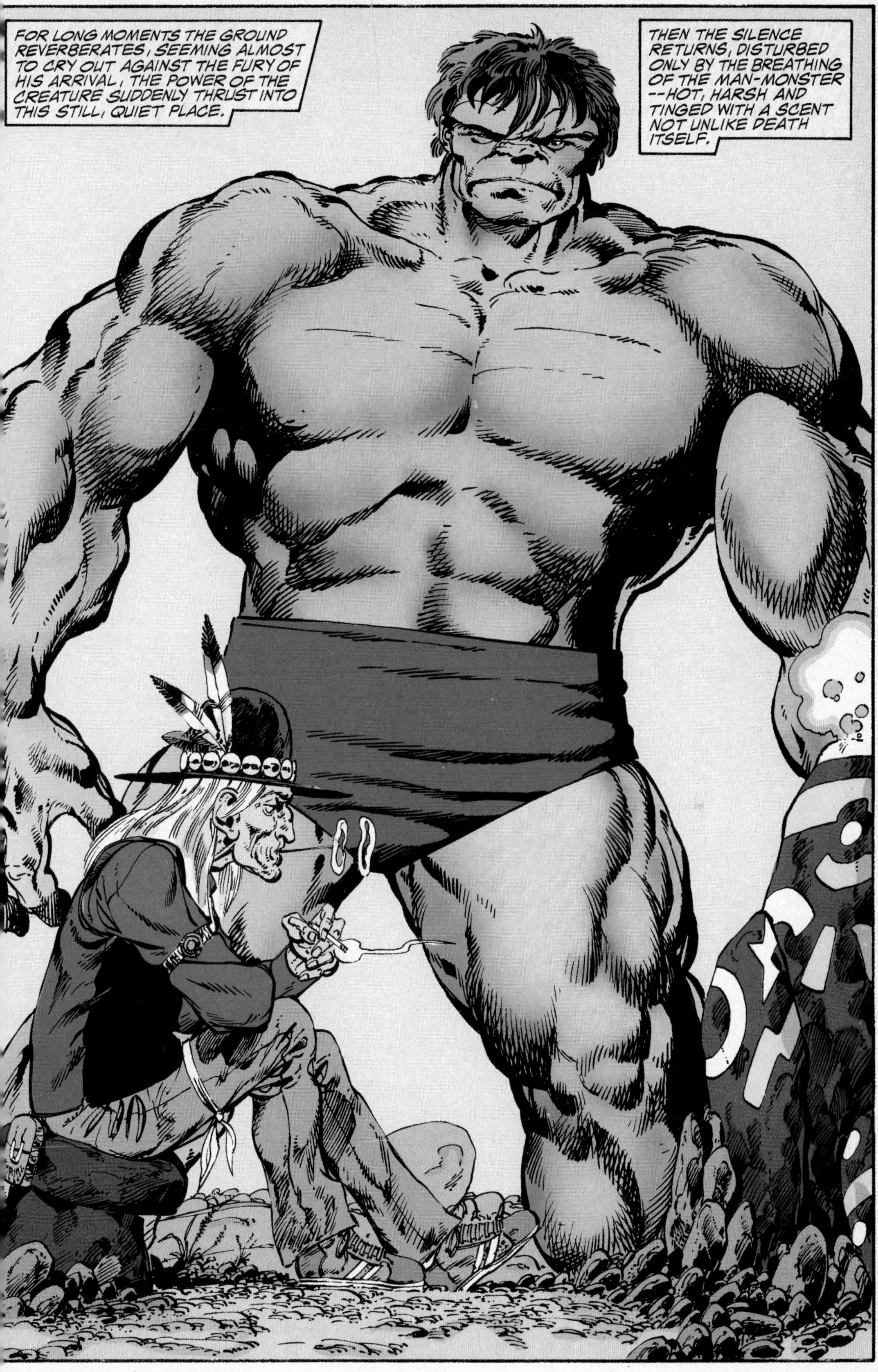
FOR LONG MOMENTS THE GROUND REVERBERATES, SEEMING ALMOST TO CRY OUT AGAINST THE FURY OF HIS ARRIVAL, THE POWER OF THE CREATURE SUDDENLY THRUST INTO THIS STILL, QUIET PLACE.
THEN THE SILENCE RETURNS, DISTURBED ONLY BY THE BREATHING OF THE MAN-MONSTER --HOT, HARSH AND TINGED WITH A SCENT NOT UNLIKE DEATH ITSELF.

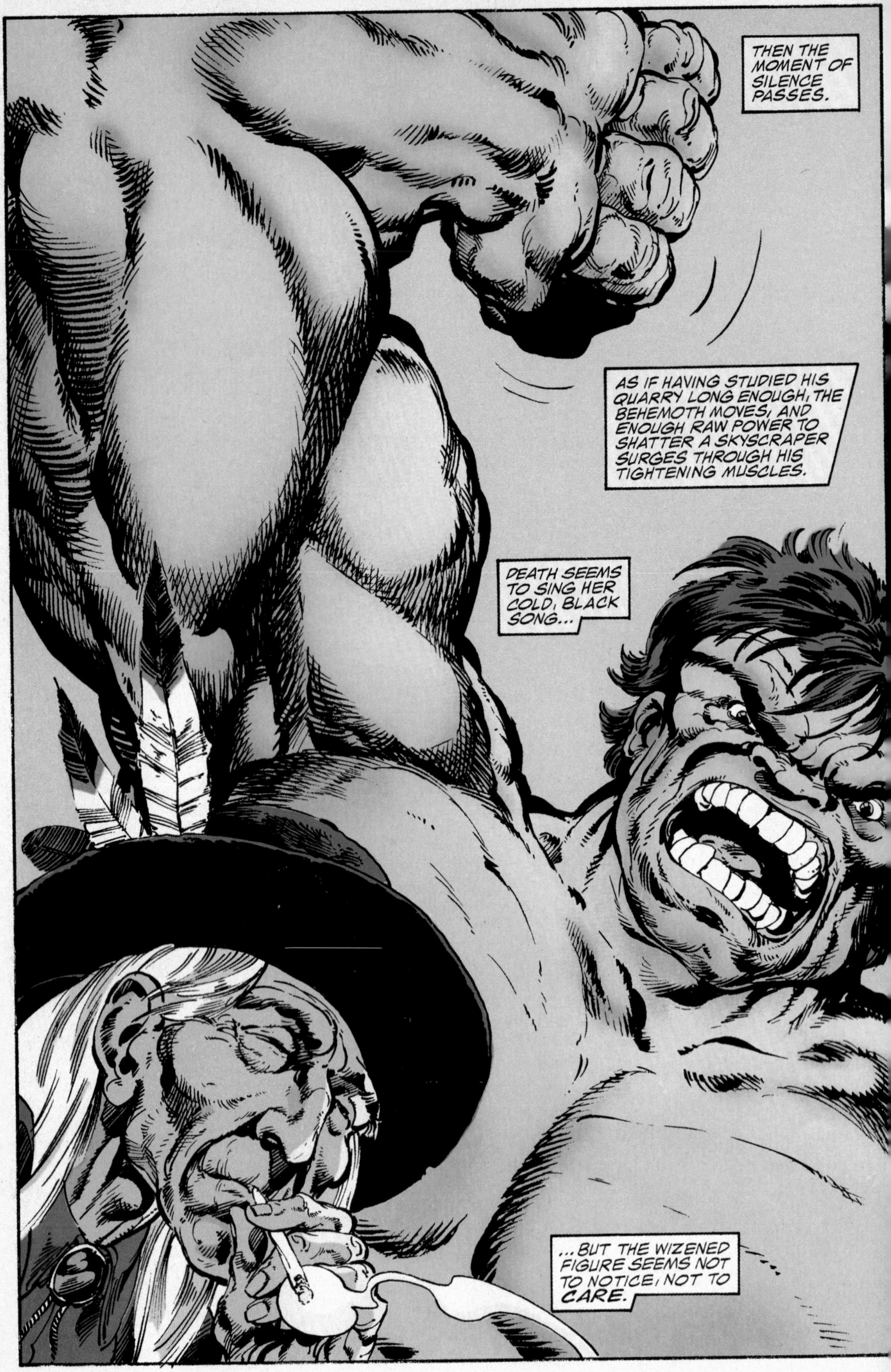
THEN THE MOMENT OF SILENCE PASSES.
AS IF HAVING STUDIED HIS QUARRY LONG ENOUGH, THE BEHEMOTH MOVES, AND ENOUGH RAW POWER TO SHATTER A SKYSCRAPER SURGES THROUGH HIS TIGHTENING MUSCLES.
DEATH SEEMS TO SING HER COLD, BLACK SONG...
...BUT THE WIZENED FIGURE SEEMS NOT TO NOTICE, NOT TO CARE.

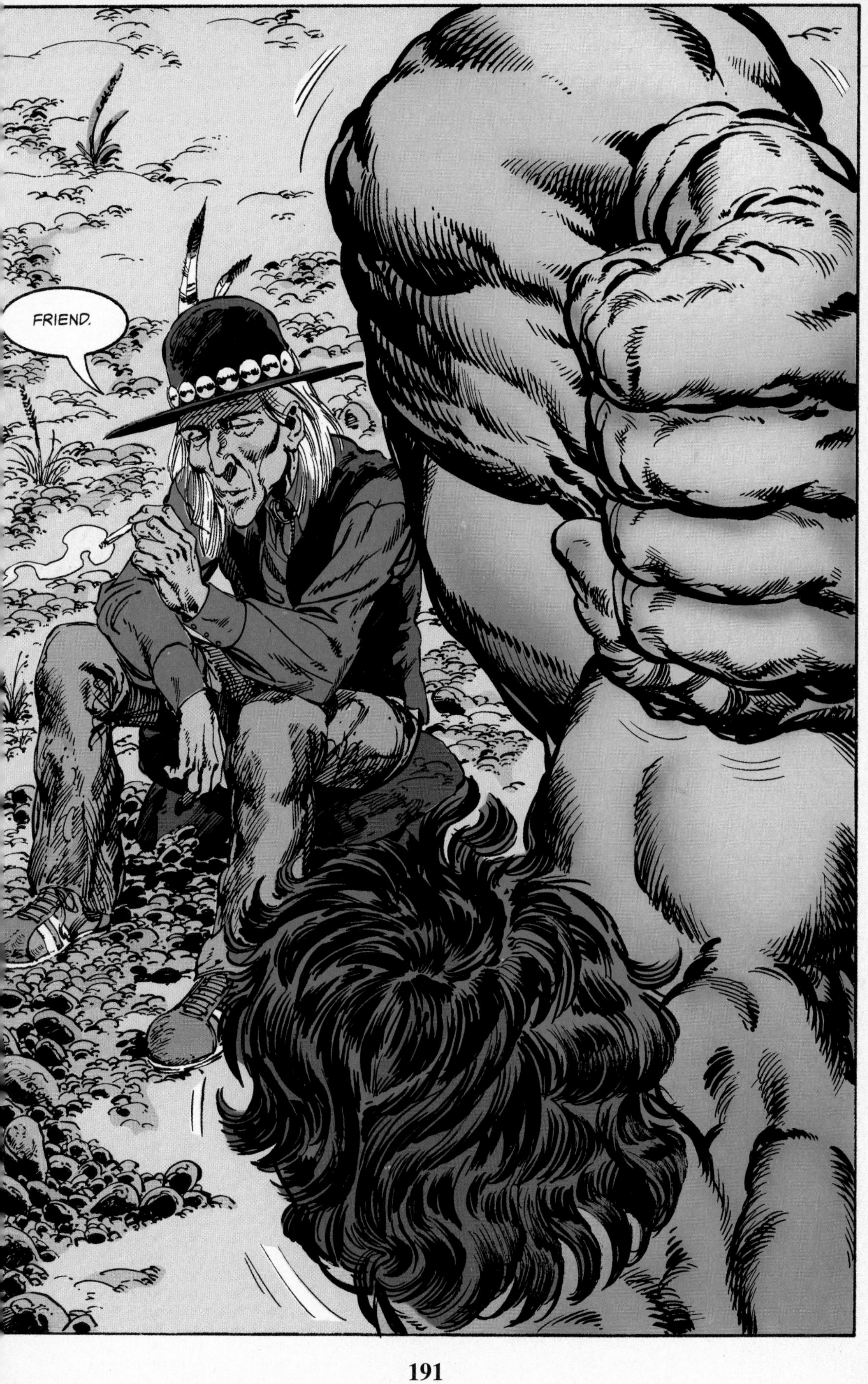
FRIEND.

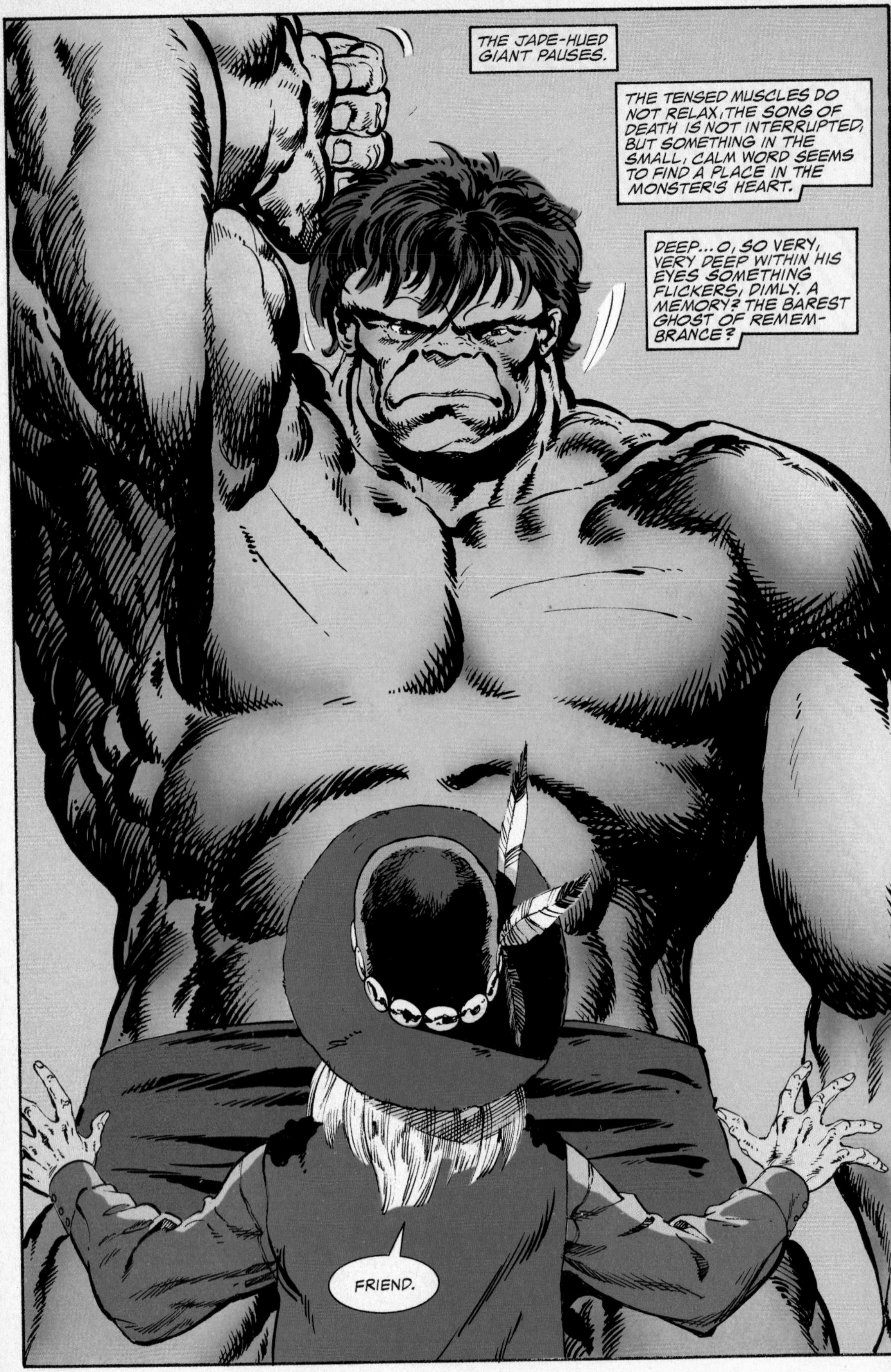
THE JADE-HUED GIANT PAUSES.
THE TENSED MUSCLES DO NOT RELAX, THE SONG OF DEATH IS NOT INTERRUPTED, BUT SOMETHING IN THE SMALL, CALM WORD SEEMS TO FIND A PLACE IN THE MONSTER'S HEART.
DEEP... O, SO VERY, VERY DEEP WITHIN HIS EYES SOMETHING FLICKERS, DIMLY. A MEMORY? THE BAREST GHOST OF REMEMBRANCE?
FRIEND.

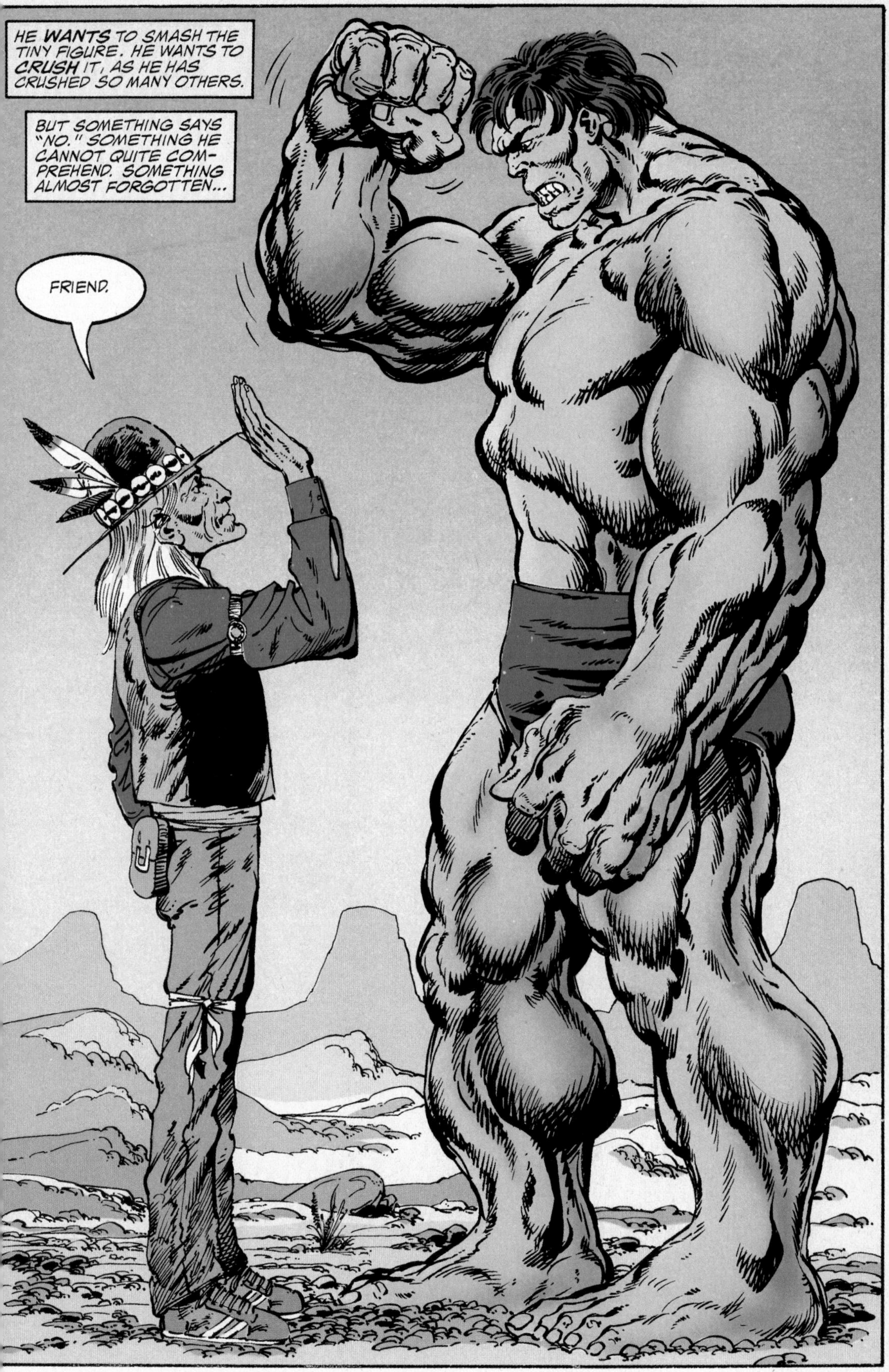
HE WANTS TO SMASH THE TINY FIGURE. HE WANTS TO CRUSH IT, AS HE HAS CRUSHED SO MANY OTHERS.
BUT SOMETHING SAYS "NO." SOMETHING HE CANNOT QUITE COMPREHEND. SOMETHING ALMOST FORGOTTEN...
FRIEND.

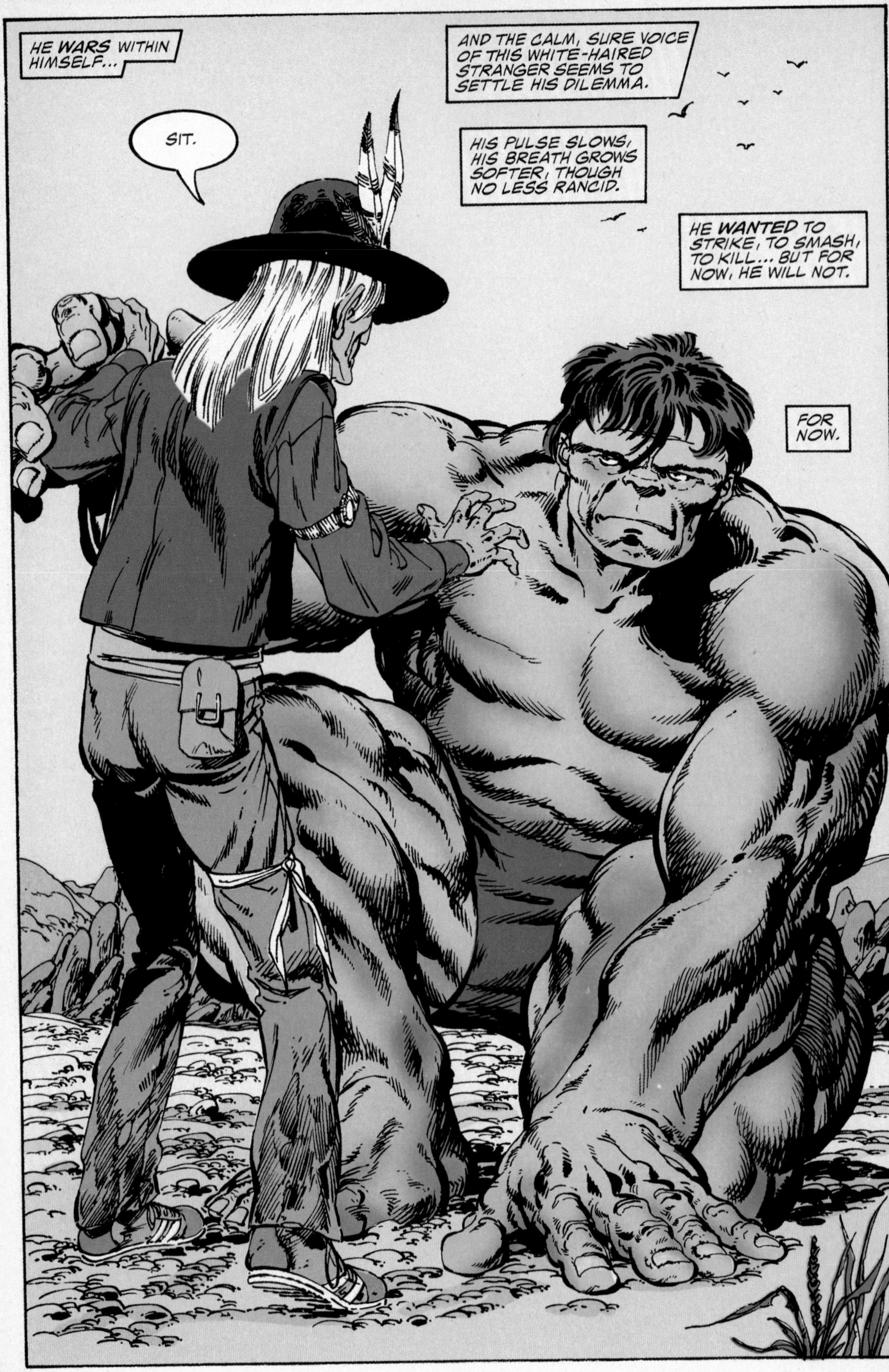
HE WARS WITHIN HIMSELF...
SIT.
AND THE CALM, SURE VOICE OF THIS WHITE-HAIRED STRANGER SEEMS TO SETTLE HIS DILEMMA.
HIS PULSE SLOWS, HIS BREATH GROWS SOFTER, THOUGH NO LESS RANCID.
HE WANTED TO STRIKE, TO SMASH, TO KILL... BUT FOR NOW, HE WILL NOT.
FOR NOW.

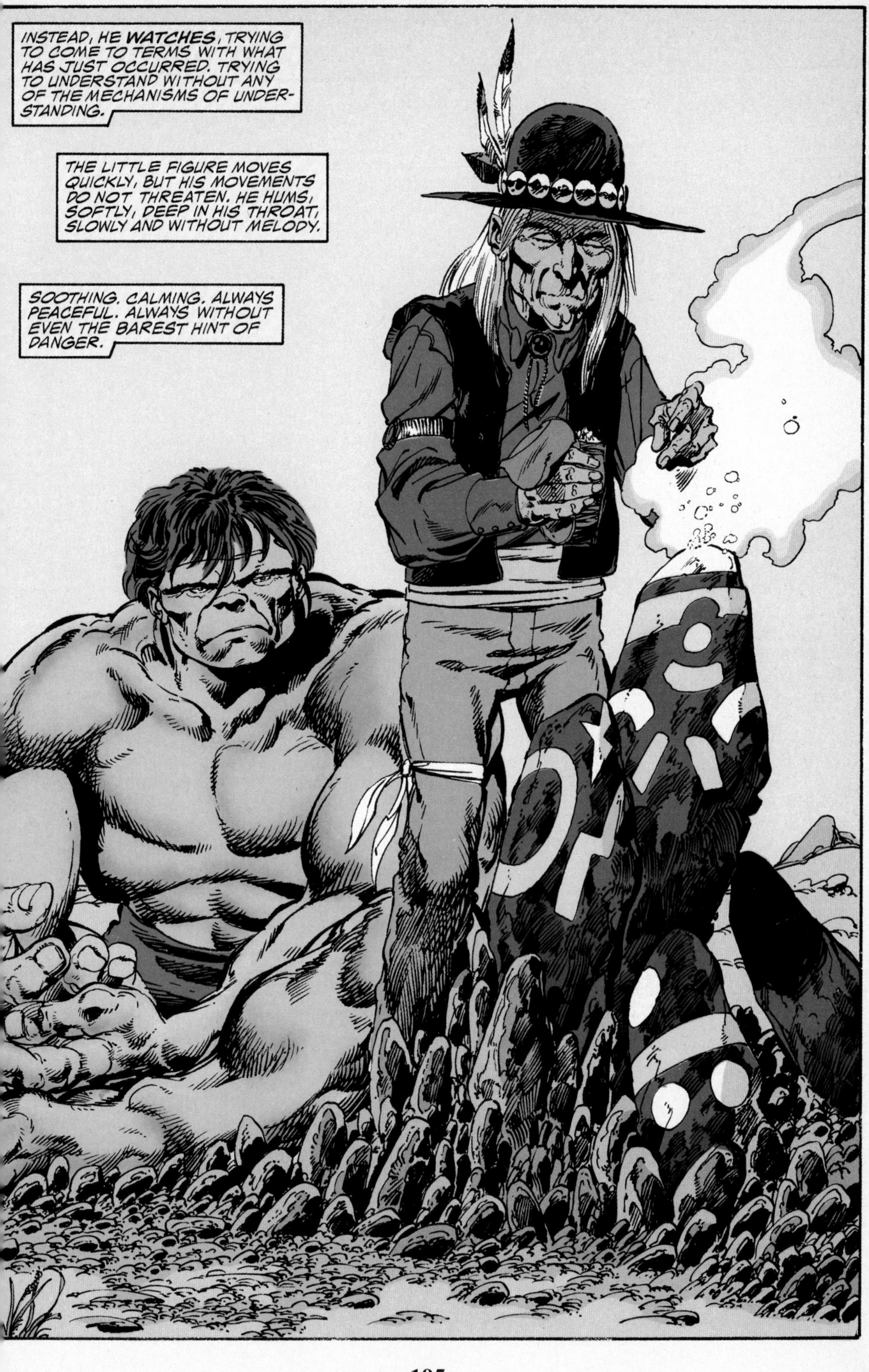
INSTEAD, HE WATCHES, TRYING TO COME TO TERMS WITH WHAT HAS JUST OCCURRED. TRYING TO UNDERSTAND WITHOUT ANY OF THE MECHANISMS OF UNDER-STANDING.
THE LITTLE FIGURE MOVES QUICKLY, BUT HIS MOVEMENTS DO NOT THREATEN. HE HUMS, SOFTLY, DEEP IN HIS THROAT, SLOWLY AND WITHOUT MELODY.
SOOTHING. CALMING. ALWAYS PEACEFUL. ALWAYS WITHOUT EVEN THE BAREST HINT OF DANGER.

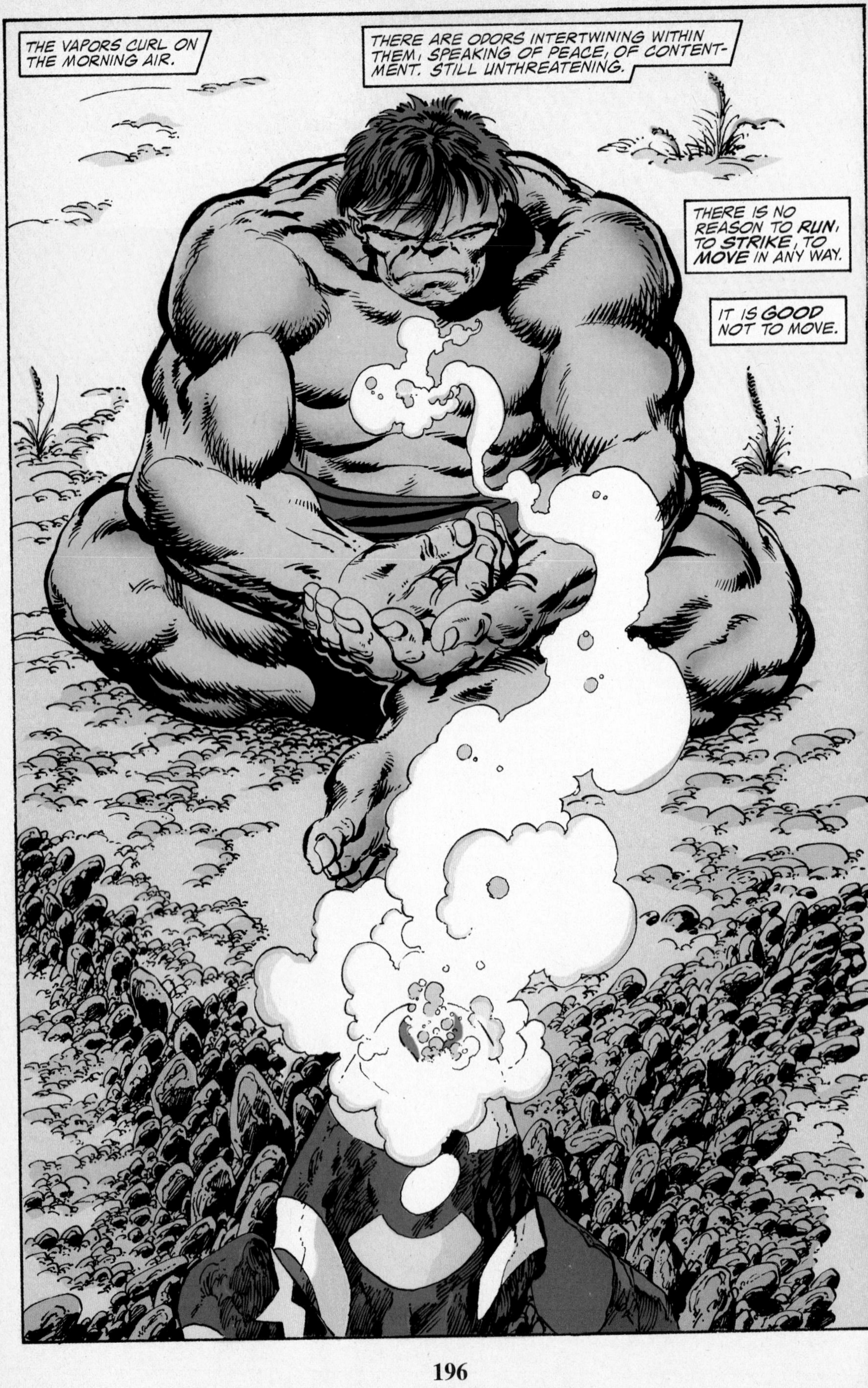
THE VAPORS CURL ON THE MORNING AIR.
THERE ARE ODORS INTERTWINING WITHIN THEM, SPEAKING OF PEACE, OF CONTENTMENT. STILL UNTHREATENING.
THERE IS NO REASON TO RUN, TO STRIKE, TO MOVE IN ANY WAY.
IT IS GOOD NOT TO MOVE.

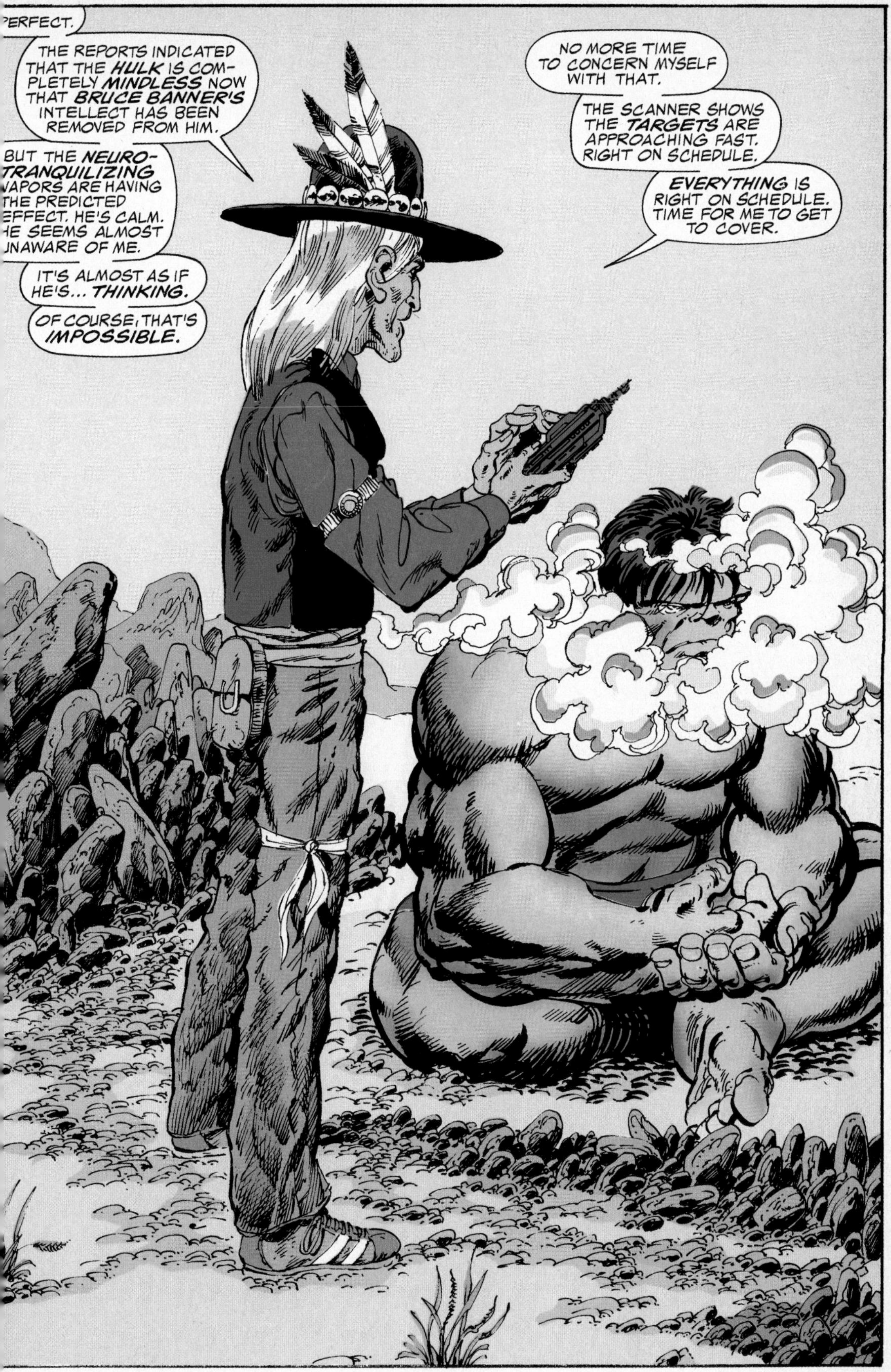
PERFECT.
THE REPORTS INDICATED THAT THE HULK IS COMPLETELY MINDLESS NOW THAT BRUCE BANNER'S INTELLECT HAS BEEN REMOVED FROM HIM.
BUT THE NEURO-TRANQUILIZING VAPORS ARE HAVING THE PREDICTED EFFECT. HE'S CALM. HE SEEMS ALMOST UNAWARE OF ME.
IT'S ALMOST AS IF HE'S... THINKING.
OF COURSE, THAT'S IMPOSSIBLE.
NO MORE TIME TO CONCERN MYSELF WITH THAT.
THE SCANNER SHOWS THE TARGETS ARE APPROACHING FAST. RIGHT ON SCHEDULE.
EVERYTHING IS RIGHT ON SCHEDULE. TIME FOR ME TO GET TO COVER.

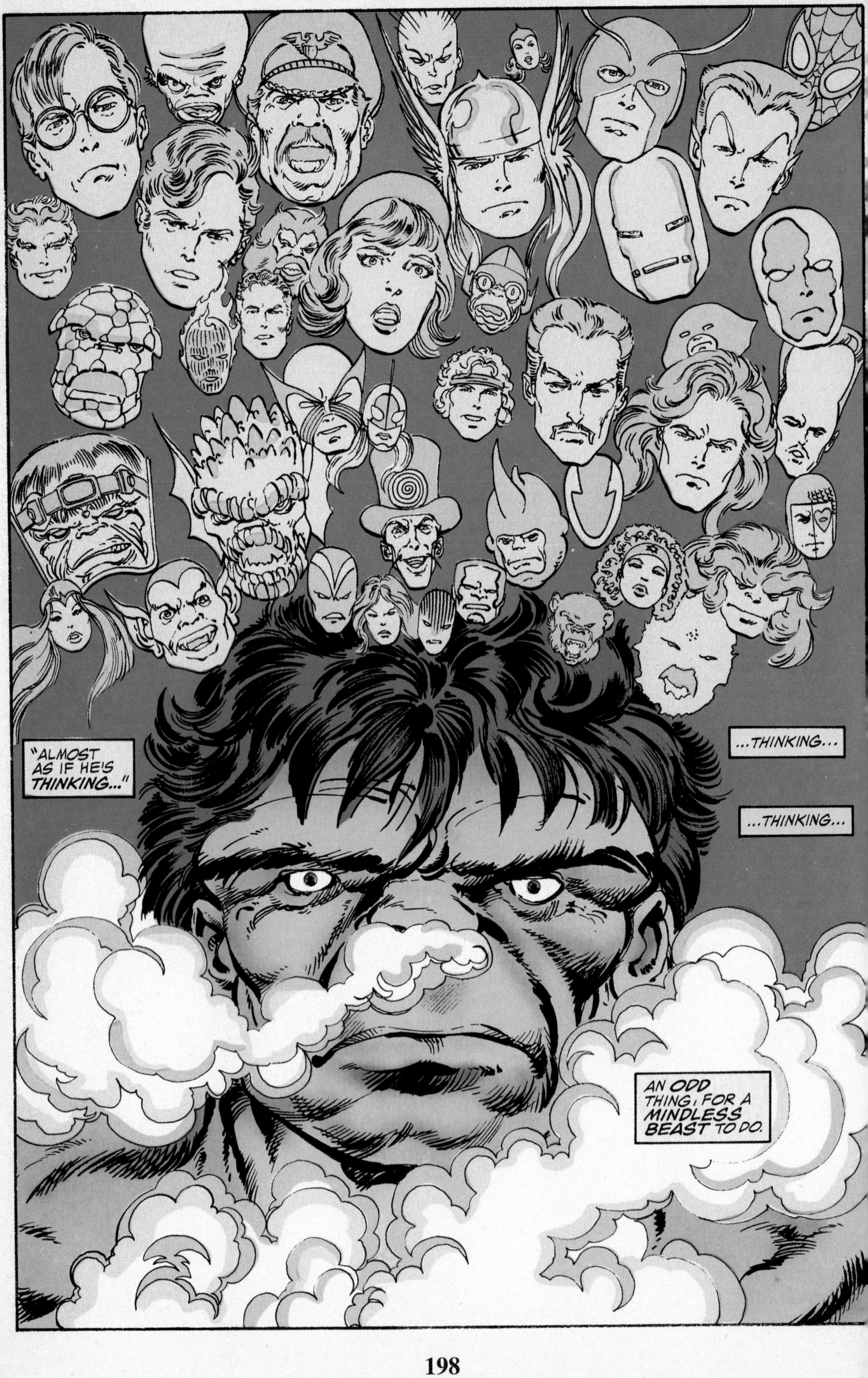
"ALMOST AS IF HE'S THINKING..."
...THINKING...
...THINKING...
AN ODD THING, FOR A MINDLESS BEAST TO DO.

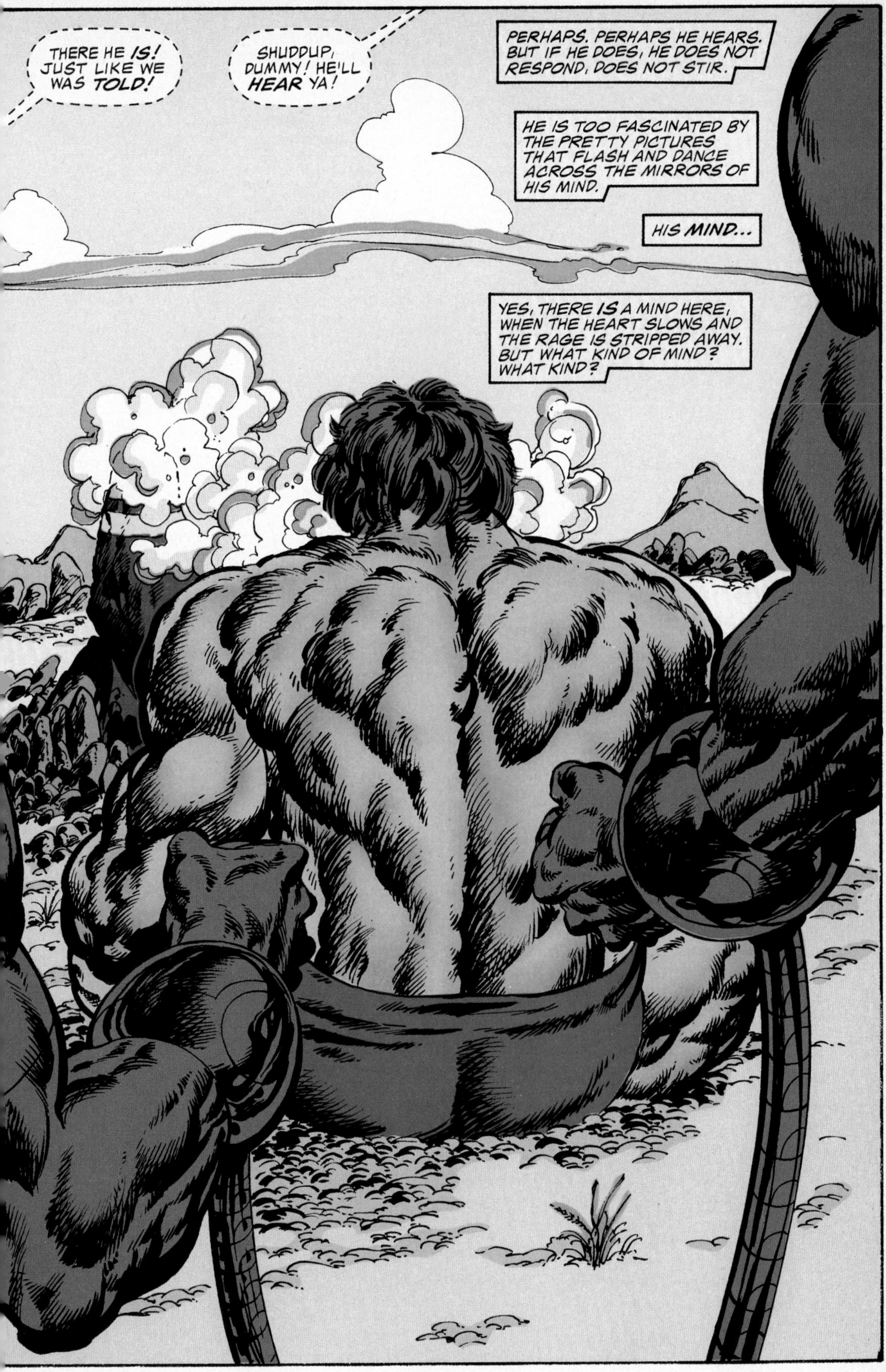
THERE HE IS! JUST LIKE WE WAS TOLD!
SHUDDUP, DUMMY! HE'LL HEAR YA!
PERHAPS. PERHAPS HE HEARS. BUT IF HE DOES, HE DOES NOT RESPOND, DOES NOT STIR.
HE IS TOO FASCINATED BY THE PRETTY PICTURES THAT FLASH AND DANCE ACROSS THE MIRRORS OF HIS MIND.
HIS MIND...
YES, THERE IS A MIND HERE, WHEN THE HEART SLOWS AND THE RAGE IS STRIPPED AWAY. BUT WHAT KIND OF MIND? WHAT KIND?

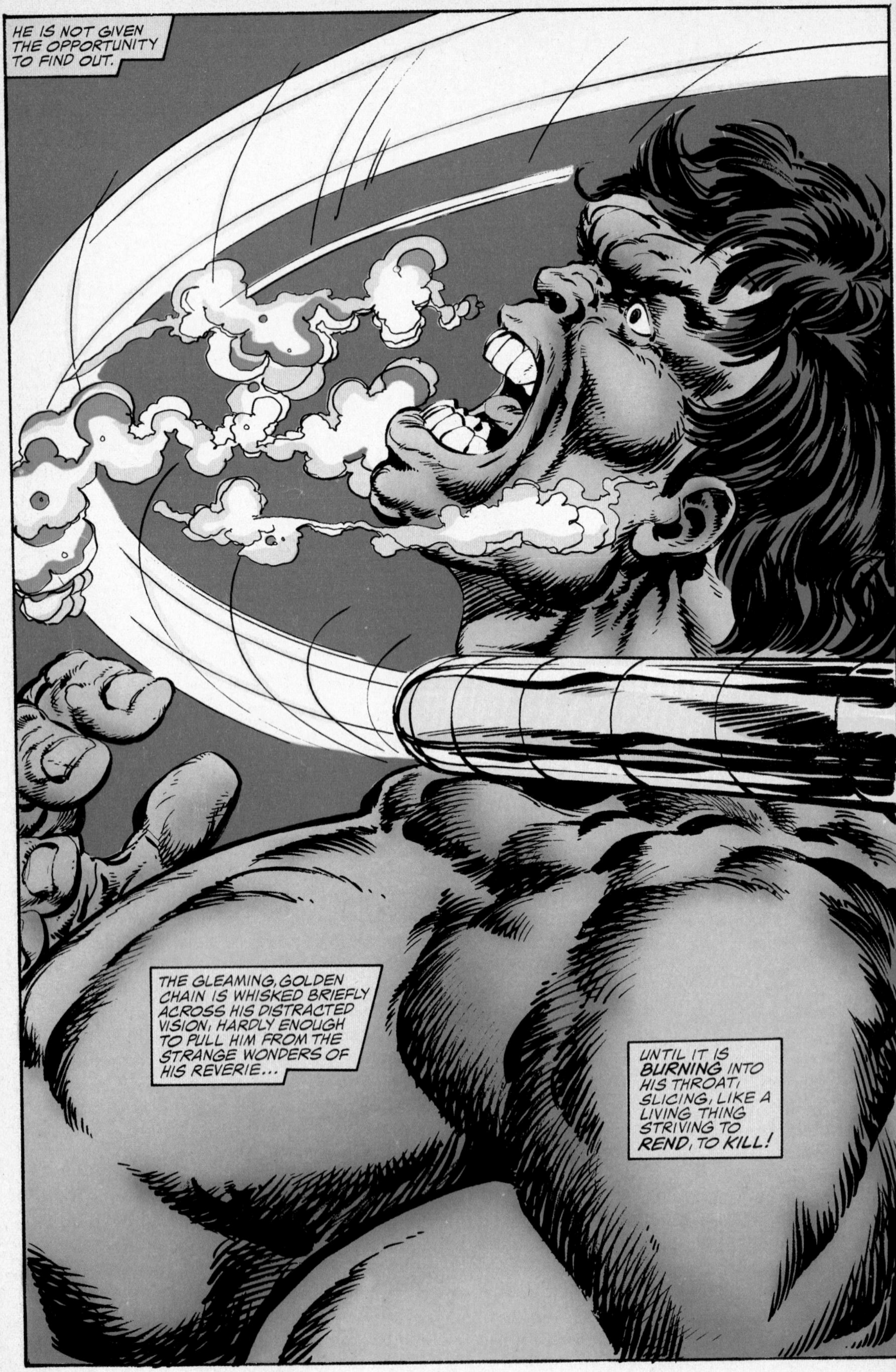
HE IS NOT GIVEN THE OPPORTUNITY TO FIND OUT.
THE GLEAMING, GOLDEN CHAIN IS WHISKED BRIEFLY ACROSS HIS DISTRACTED VISION, HARDLY ENOUGH TO PULL HIM FROM THE STRANGE WONDERS OF HIS REVERIE...
UNTIL IT IS BURNING INTO HIS THROAT, SLICING, LIKE A LIVING THING STRIVING TO REND, TO KILL!

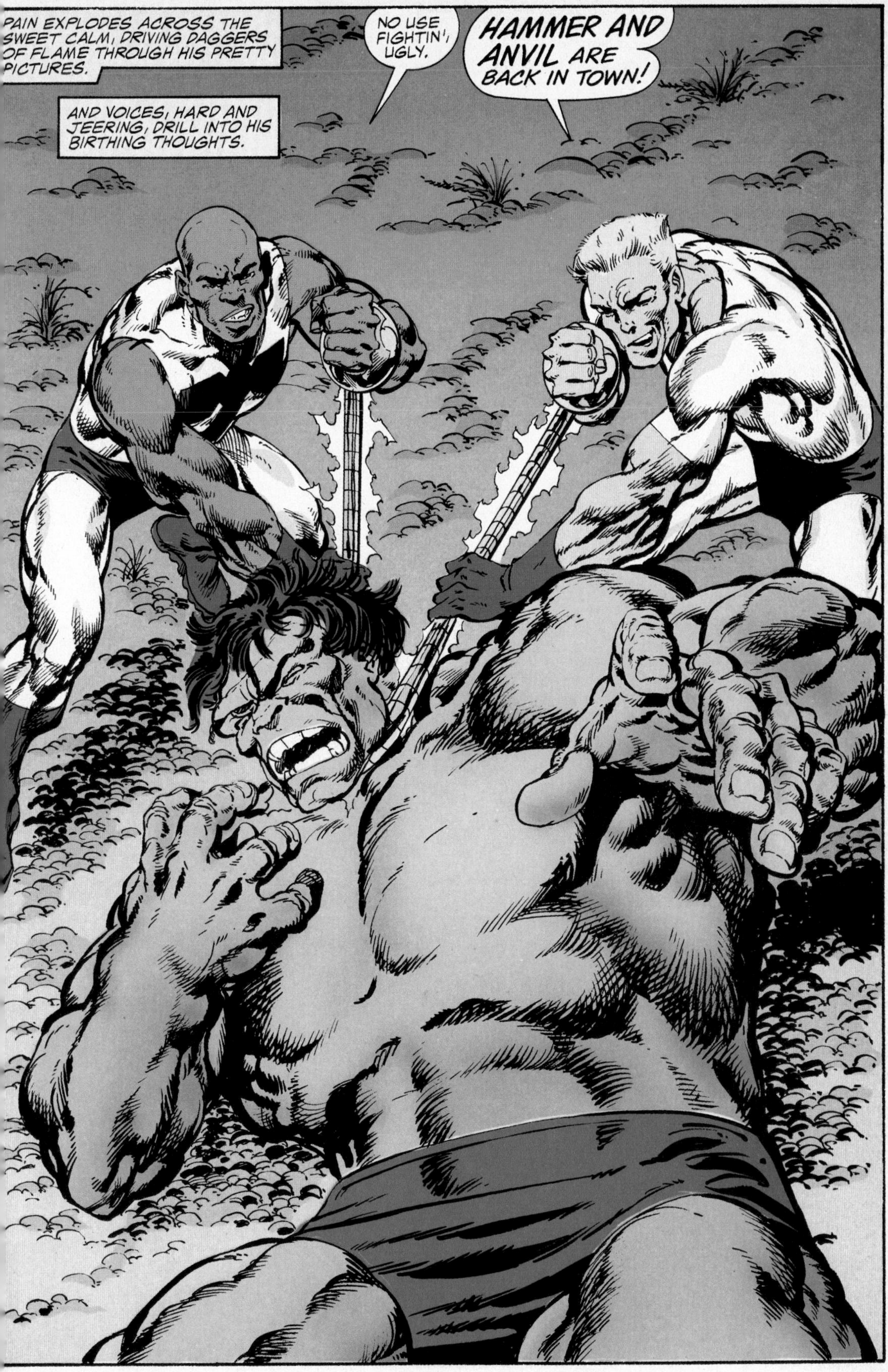
PAIN EXPLODES ACROSS THE SWEET CALM, DRIVING DAGGERS OF FLAME THROUGH HIS PRETTY PICTURES.
AND VOICES, HARD AND JEERING, DRILL INTO HIS BIRTHING THOUGHTS.
NO USE FIGHTIN', UGLY.
HAMMER AND ANVIL ARE BACK IN TOWN!

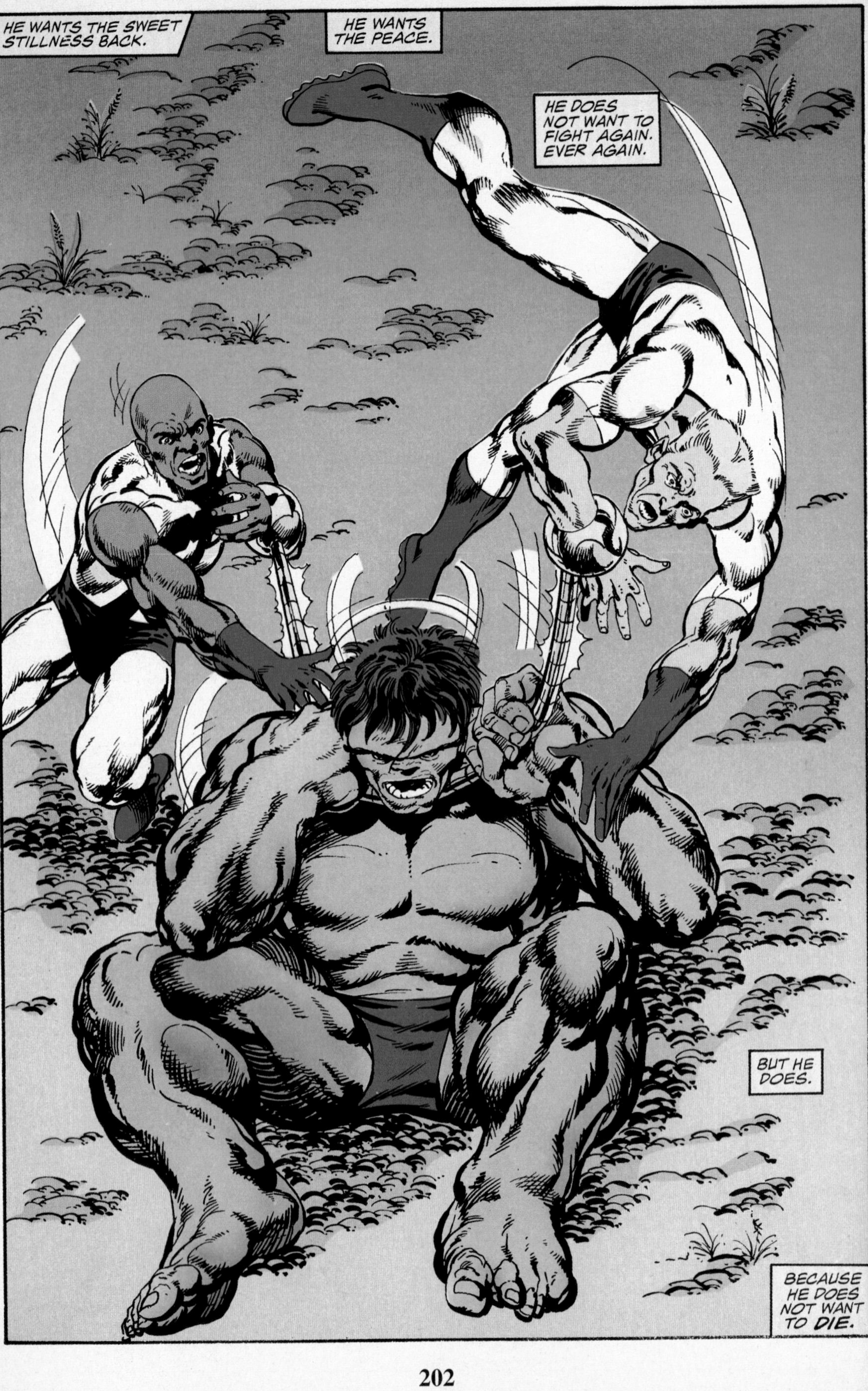
HE WANTS THE SWEET STILLNESS BACK.
HE WANTS THE PEACE.
HE DOES NOT WANT TO FIGHT AGAIN. EVER AGAIN.
BUT HE DOES.
BECAUSE HE DOES NOT WANT TO DIE.

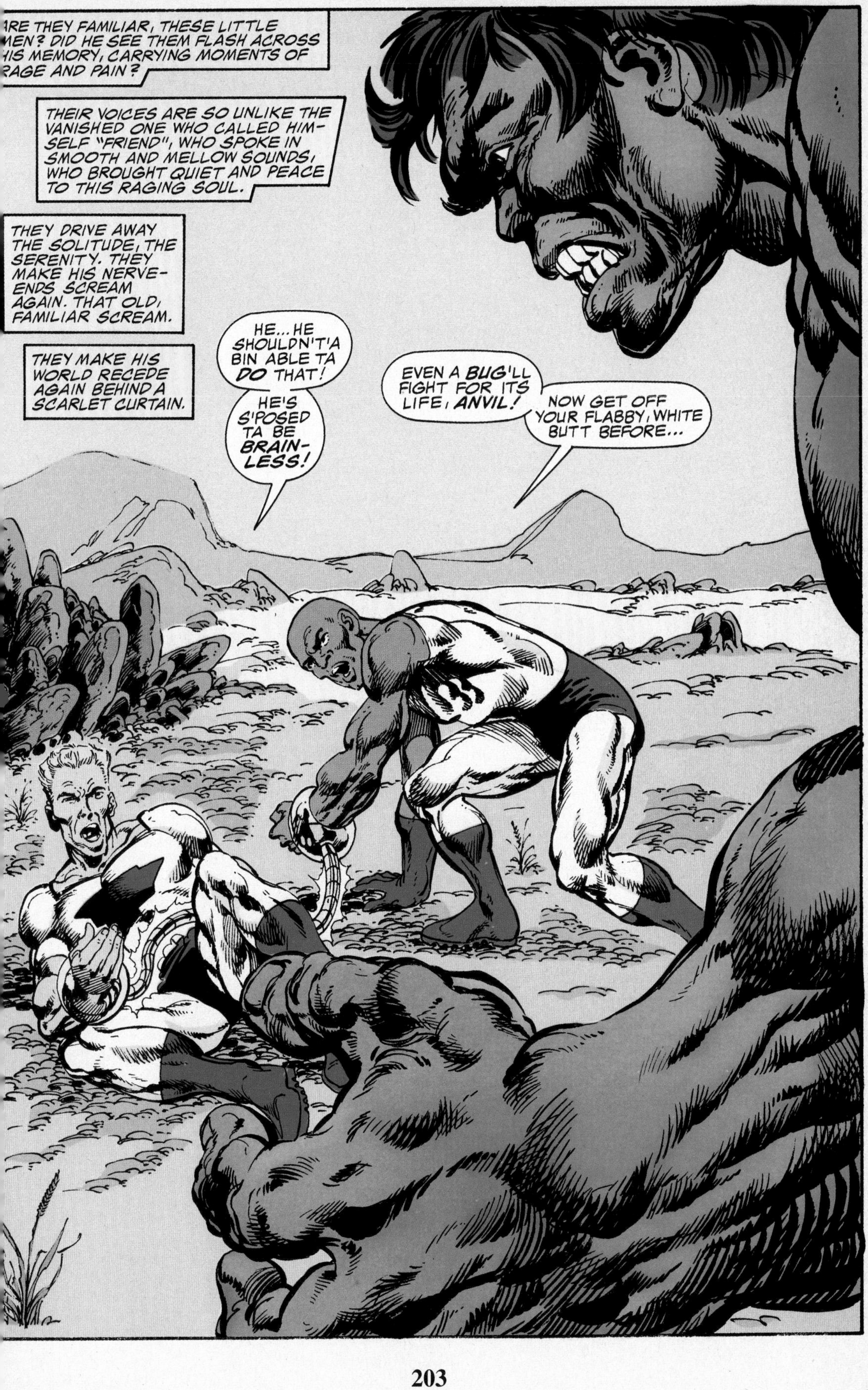
ARE THEY FAMILIAR, THESE LITTLE MEN? DID HE SEE THEM FLASH ACROSS HIS MEMORY, CARRYING MOMENTS OF RAGE AND PAIN?
THEIR VOICES ARE SO UNLIKE THE VANISHED ONE WHO CALLED HIM-SELF "FRIEND", WHO SPOKE IN SMOOTH AND MELLOW SOUNDS, WHO BROUGHT QUIET AND PEACE TO THIS RAGING SOUL.
THEY DRIVE AWAY THE SOLITUDE, THE SERENITY. THEY MAKE HIS NERVE-ENDS SCREAM AGAIN. THAT OLD, FAMILIAR SCREAM.
THEY MAKE HIS WORLD RECEDE AGAIN BEHIND A SCARLET CURTAIN.
HE... HE SHOULDN'T'A BIN ABLE TA DO THAT!
HE'S S'POSED TA BE BRAIN-LESS!
EVEN A BUG'LL FIGHT FOR ITS LIFE, ANVIL!
NOW GET OFF YOUR FLABBY, WHITE BUTT BEFORE...

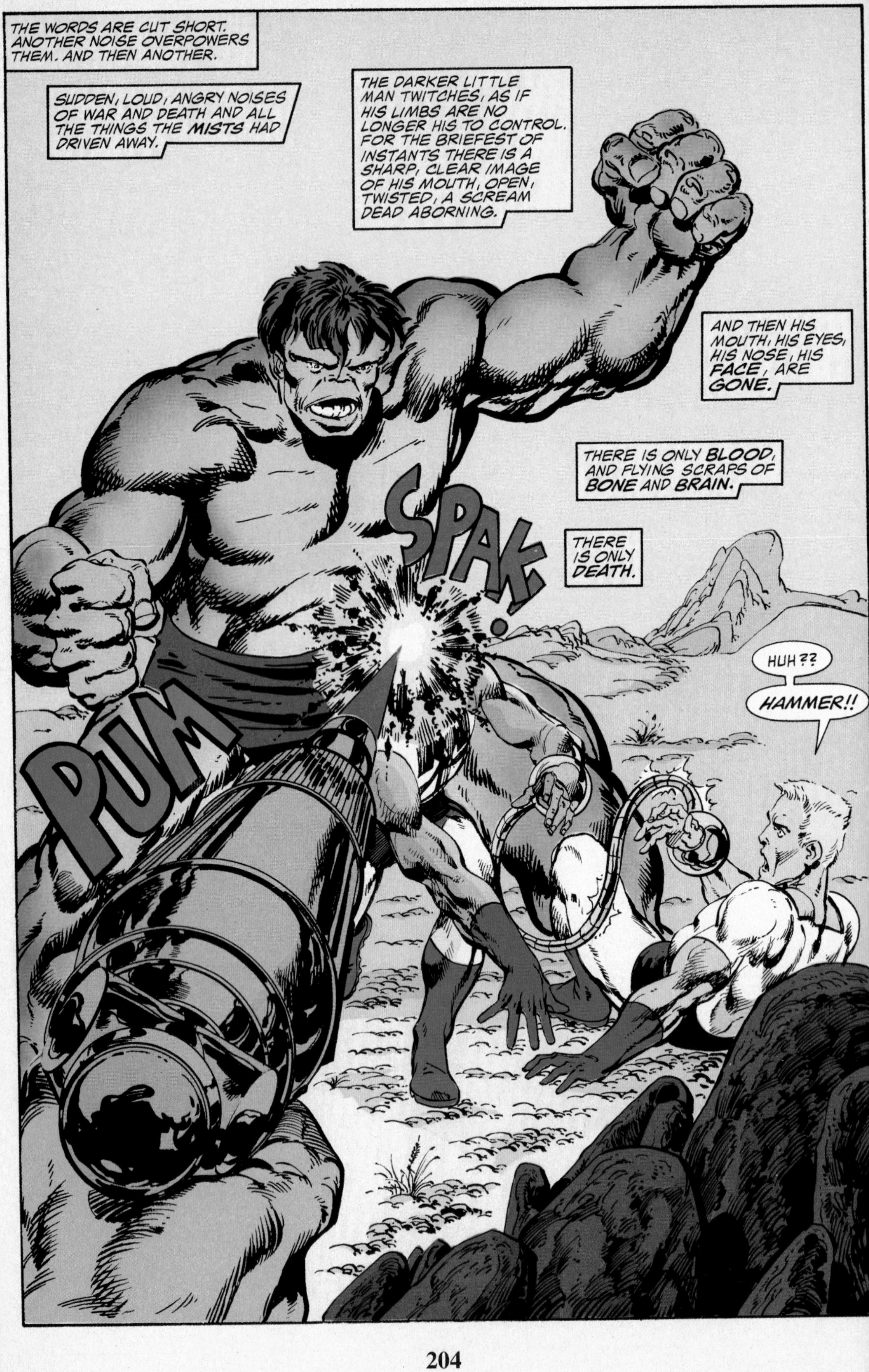

THE WORDS ARE CUT SHORT. ANOTHER NOISE OVERPOWERS THEM. AND THEN ANOTHER.
SUDDEN, LOUD, ANGRY NOISES OF WAR AND DEATH AND ALL THE THINGS THE MISTS HAD DRIVEN AWAY.
THE DARKER LITTLE MAN TWITCHES, AS IF HIS LIMBS ARE NO LONGER HIS TO CONTROL. FOR THE BRIEFEST OF INSTANTS THERE IS A SHARP, CLEAR IMAGE OF HIS MOUTH, OPEN, TWISTED, A SCREAM DEAD ABORNING.
AND THEN HIS MOUTH, HIS EYES, HIS NOSE, HIS FACE, ARE GONE.
THERE IS ONLY BLOOD, AND FLYING SCRAPS OF BONE AND BRAIN.
THERE IS ONLY DEATH.
PUM
SPAK!
HUH??
HAMMER!!

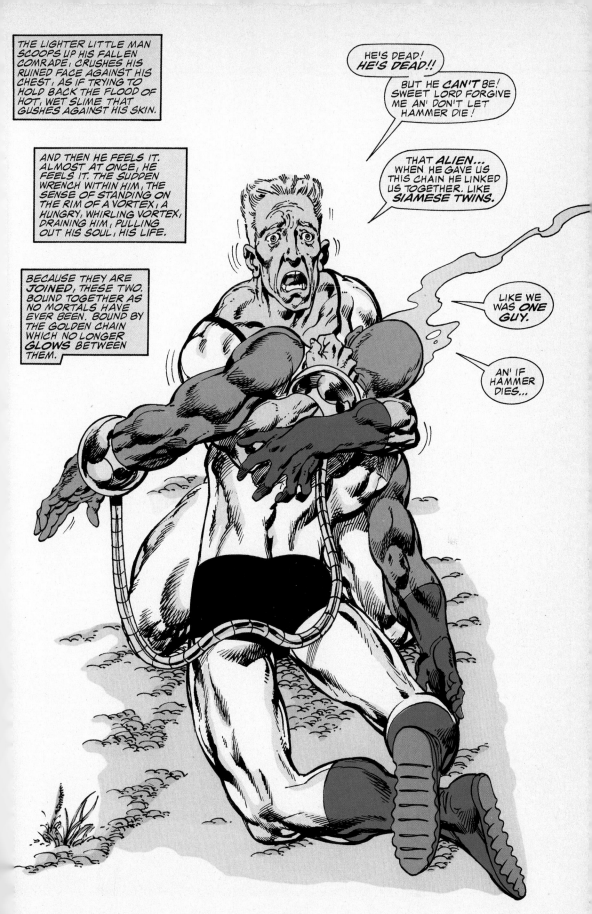

THE LIGHTER LITTLE MAN SCOOPS UP HIS FALLEN COMRADE, CRUSHES HIS RUINED FACE AGAINST HIS CHEST, AS IF TRYING TO HOLD BACK THE FLOOD OF HOT, WET SLIME THAT GUSHES AGAINST HIS SKIN.

AND THEN HE FEELS IT. ALMOST AT ONCE, HE FEELS IT. THE SUDDEN WRENCH WITHIN HIM, THE SENSE OF STANDING ON THE RIM OF A VORTEX, A HUNGRY, WHIRLING VORTEX, DRAINING HIM, PULLING OUT HIS SOUL, HIS LIFE.

BECAUSE THEY ARE *JOINED*, THESE TWO. BOUND TOGETHER AS NO MORTALS HAVE EVER BEEN. BOUND BY THE GOLDEN CHAIN WHICH NO LONGER *GLOWS* BETWEEN THEM.

HE'S DEAD! *HE'S DEAD!!*

BUT HE *CAN'T* BE! SWEET LORD FORGIVE ME AN' DON'T LET HAMMER DIE!

THAT *ALIEN*... WHEN HE GAVE US THIS CHAIN HE LINKED US TOGETHER. LIKE *SIAMESE TWINS.*

LIKE WE WAS *ONE GUY.*

AN' IF HAMMER DIES...

205

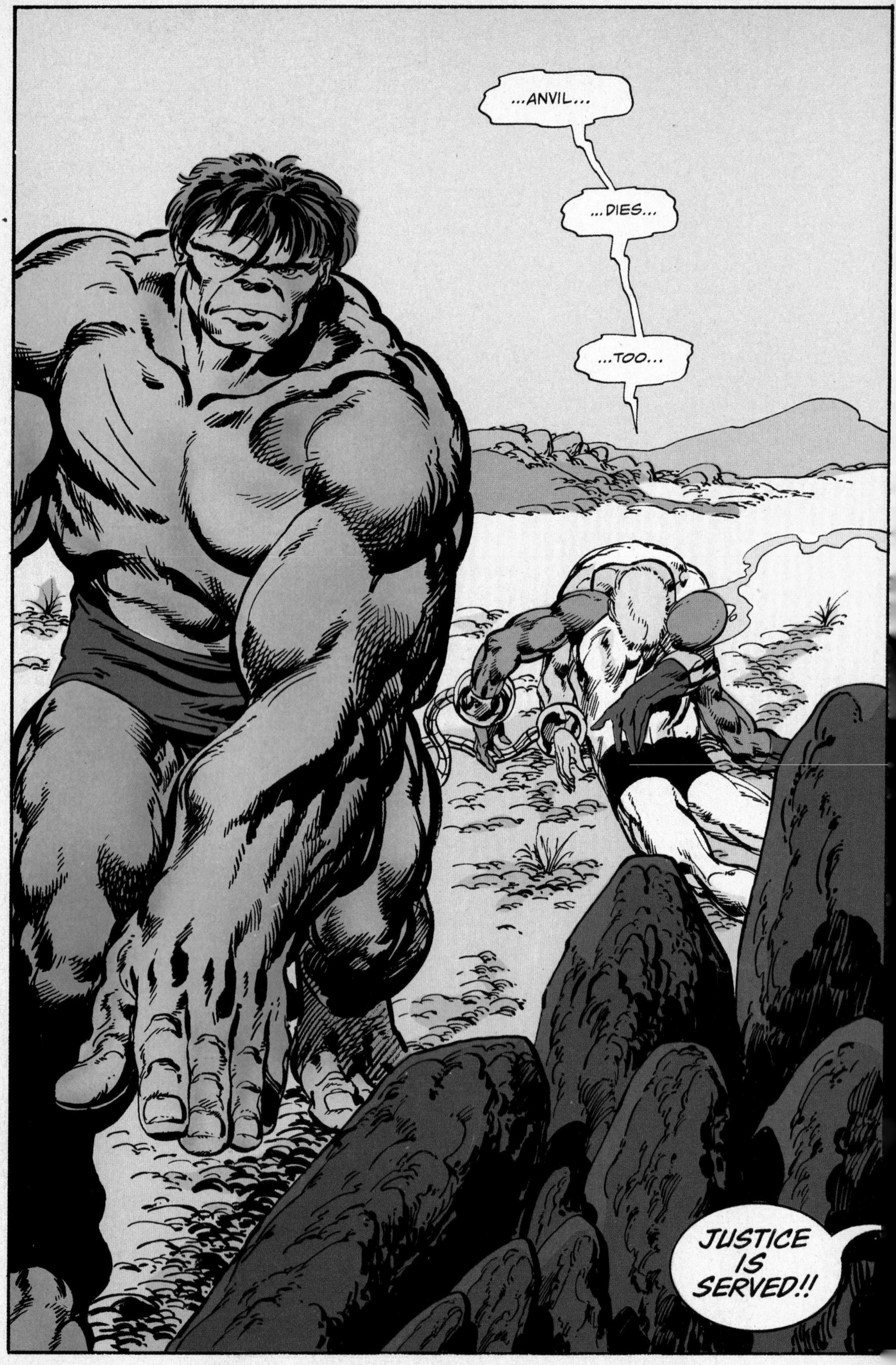
...ANVIL...
...DIES...
...TOO...
JUSTICE IS SERVED!!

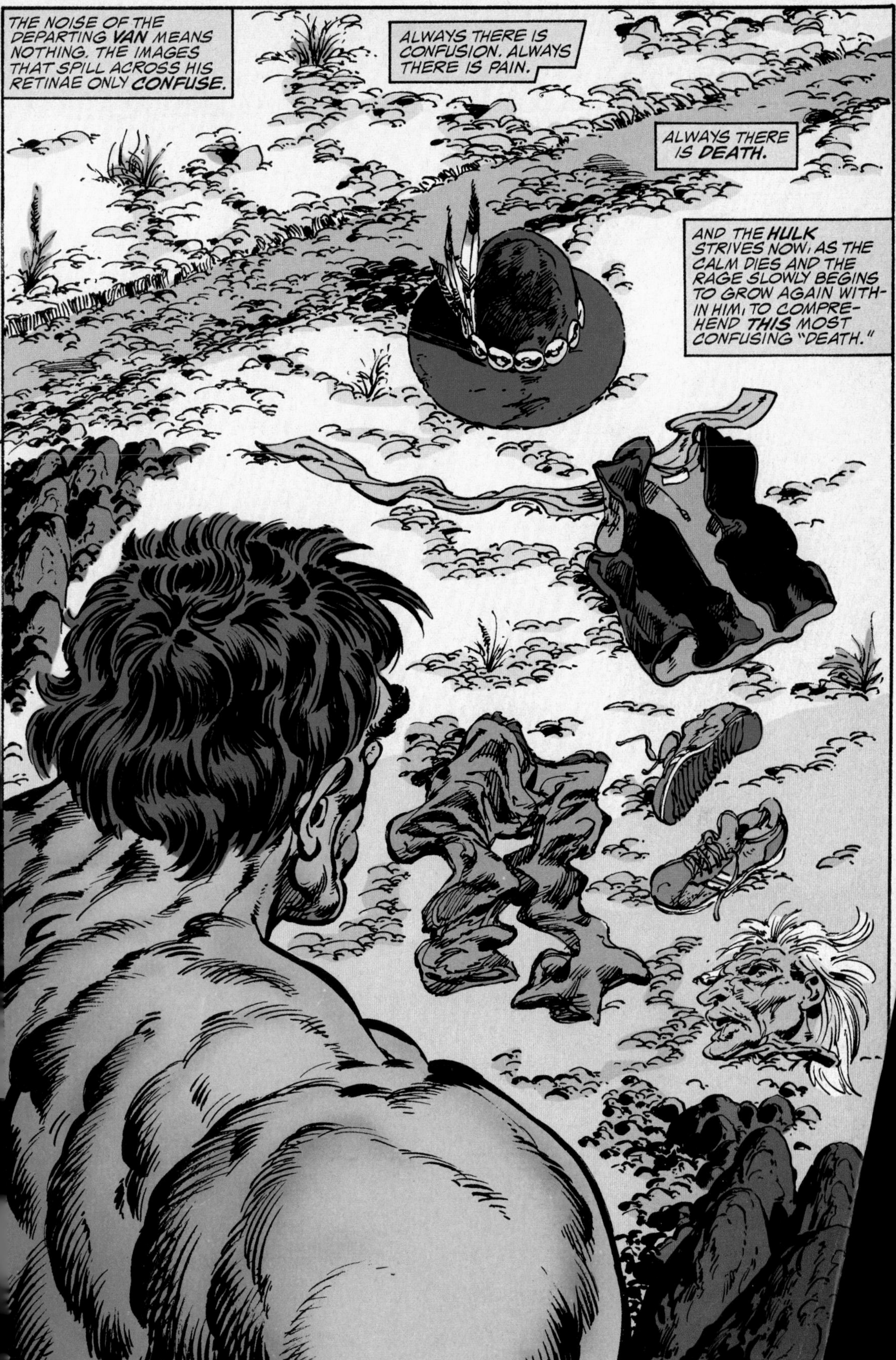
THE NOISE OF THE DEPARTING VAN MEANS NOTHING. THE IMAGES THAT SPILL ACROSS HIS RETINAE ONLY CONFUSE.
ALWAYS THERE IS CONFUSION. ALWAYS THERE IS PAIN.
ALWAYS THERE IS DEATH.
AND THE HULK STRIVES NOW, AS THE CALM DIES AND THE RAGE SLOWLY BEGINS TO GROW AGAIN WITH-IN HIM, TO COMPRE-HEND THIS MOST CONFUSING "DEATH."

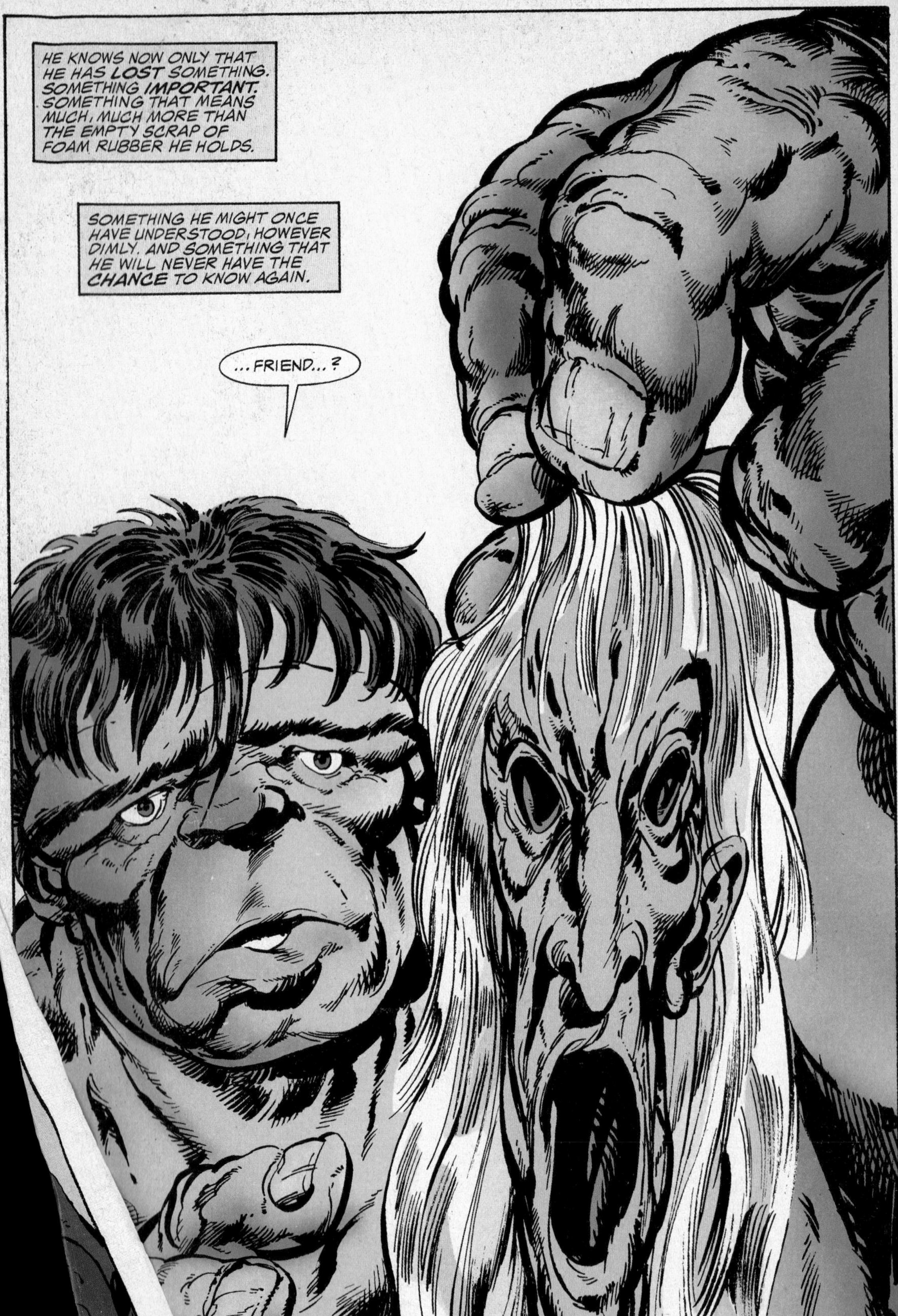
HE KNOWS NOW ONLY THAT HE HAS LOST SOMETHING. SOMETHING IMPORTANT. SOMETHING THAT MEANS MUCH, MUCH MORE THAN THE EMPTY SCRAP OF FOAM RUBBER HE HOLDS.
SOMETHING HE MIGHT ONCE HAVE UNDERSTOOD, HOWEVER DIMLY. AND SOMETHING THAT HE WILL NEVER HAVE THE CHANCE TO KNOW AGAIN.
...FRIEND...?